How does a country reconstitute itself as a functioning democracy after a period of dictatorship? The new community may execute, imprison, or temporarily disenfranchise some citizens, but it will be unable to exclude all who supported the fallen regime. Political reconciliation must lay the groundwork for political trust. Democracy offers the compromised—and many who were more than just compromised—a second chance.

In this new book, Anne Sa'adah explores twentieth-century Germany's second chances. Drawing on evidence from intellectual debates, trials, literary works, controversies about the actions of public figures, and partisan competition, Sa'adah analyzes German responses to the problem of reconciliation after 1945 and again after 1989. She depicts the frustrations, moral and political ambiguities, and disappointments inherent to even successful processes of democratization. She constantly underscores the difficult trade-off between achieving a modicum of justice and securing the legitimacy and stability of the new regime. A strategy of reconciliation emphasizing outward conformity to democratic norms and behavior, she argues, has a greater chance of sustaining a new and fragile democracy than do more direct attempts to punish past misdeeds and alter people's inner convictions.

Anne Sa'adah is Professor of Government at Dartmouth College.

Germany's Second Chance

Germany's Second Chance

Trust, Justice, and Democratization

Anne Sa'adah

HARVARD UNIVERSITY PRESS

Cambridge Massachusetts

London, England

1998

Library of Congress Cataloging-in-Publication Data

Sa'adah, Anne.
    Germany's second chance : trust, justice, and democratization /
Anne Sa'adah.
        p.   cm.
    Includes bibliographical references and index.
    ISBN 0-674-35111-8
    1. Democracy—Germany.
    2. Social change—Germany.
    3. Germany (West)—Politics and government.
    4. Germany (East)—Politics and government.
    I. Title.
    JN3971.A91S23 1998
    320.943'09 049—dc21   98-15511

For Lee

Contents

Preface

No country (or political regime) has a corner on complexity or inner contradictions, but some countries (and regimes) are psychologically more stressful to study than others. Germany is a stressful country to study, and so, even though my intellectual interests have always focused on the sources and variations of democracy and dictatorship in Europe, I avoided writing about Germany. When I was a graduate student, Nazi Germany was not where I wanted to be late at night; even living in the shadow of the Third Reich seemed depressing.

Twenty years have since passed—years in which democratic politics in West Germany often seemed problematic but never artificial or truly threatened, years in which all the major democratic systems encountered serious political and economic difficulties, and finally, years in which countries without strong liberal traditions, including the former East Germany, have sought to establish democratic regimes. It seemed intellectually indefensible to claim an interest in liberal political development and to avoid Germany.

But the Third Reich is still there, and its shadows are indeed long. Germany continues to be, and will perhaps always be, as President Gustav Heinemann suggested upon assuming office in 1969, *ein schwieriges Vaterland,* a difficult fatherland. French landscapes are inscribed in my memory; French literature shapes my understanding of the human condition; the French language is the medium of some of my deepest friendships. Raise a flag on any hill in France, I told a perplexed German friend, and I will gladly die for it; the metaphor was fortunately outdated, but the sentiment behind it was real.

My pulse does not quicken when I see the black-red-gold banner of the Federal Republic (even though it too represents freedom), and German is to me still a foreign, rather than simply an alternative, language. My preferred literary works—Alfred Andersch's *Winterspelt,* Jurek

Becker's *Jakob der Lügner*—are not drawn from the traditional classics, Goethe or Fontane, but reflect on the human condition through the prism (sometimes distorting, sometimes magnifying) of the Nazi experience. Some of my closest friends now are German, but we sometimes come up hard against a wall of misunderstanding that can be explained only by radically different political experiences and cultures. And yet I now occasionally slip into the first-person plural when I speak about the problems and possibilities of contemporary Germany. The Federal Republic is indeed *ein schwieriges Vaterland,* but it is a country in which I feel implicated.

In the course of this process, I have incurred an unusually large number of personal and institutional debts. Institutional debts are always the easiest to acknowledge. They make the other debts possible. I would not have been able to write a book about Germany without the support I received from the National Endowment for the Humanities, the Fritz Thyssen Foundation, and the Harry Frank Guggenheim Foundation. I am also grateful to the editors of *French Politics and Society* for permission to use material in Chapter 1 that originally appeared as "Forgiving without Forgetting: Political Reconciliation and Democratic Citizenship," *French Politics and Society* 10, no. 3 (Summer 1992): 94–113.

Dartmouth College, where I have taught since 1984, accommodated my leave requests and generously supplemented my grants with funds from the Deanery and the Rockefeller Center. The intellectual give-and-take of a collegial department and a fine undergraduate student body helped me clarify my questions and elaborate my arguments. Our departmental secretary, Kathleen Donald, was unfailingly helpful.

Along with the use of computers and e-mail, the Interlibrary Loan system has changed the conditions of research at places which, like Dartmouth, aspire to remain undergraduate teaching institutions while also maintaining high standards of research. The Interlibrary Loan Office, and especially Patricia Carter, were helpful well beyond the call of duty, often locating German material in American libraries when I could not find a copy in Berlin.

Konrad Kenkel, Jocelyne Kolb, and Dieter and Monika Mahncke helped make Germany seem less foreign. My late colleague Henry Ehrmann, whose scholarly career had focused on France but who had remained connected to his native Berlin, helped me bridge old and new interests. Joanne Audretsch's good humor and generosity (and washing machine) eased my first months in Berlin, while our husbands, both academic economists specializing in industrial organization, enjoyed each other's intellectual company.

Charles Maier, hard at work on his own book on the German transition, provided indispensable encouragement. Stanley Hoffmann, who probably would have preferred a book about France, was nonetheless supportive. The immediate impulse to write this book came not from Charles but from Pauline Maier, who drew my attention to Aedanus Burke's plea for political forgiveness (see Chapter 1), and from our common teacher, Bernard Bailyn, who threatened to suggest the topic to a graduate student if I did not follow through on it.

In Berlin, Peter Steinbach arranged a research affiliation with the Gedenkstätte Deutscher Widerstand, giving me access to a comfortable office, a convenient library, and a temperamental copier machine. The French, German, and Polish colleagues and doctoral students who participated in an interdisciplinary research group "Coming to Terms with the Past" alerted me to different perspectives and helped me sharpen my own ideas. Birgit Schwelling and Peter Krause were fine friends and exemplary research assistants. Jürgen Findeisen, in the Presse- und Informationsamt der Bundesregierung in Bonn, forwarded material from periodicals I might otherwise have missed.

While I was in Germany, I had occasion to meet many of the people whose actions and aspirations animate these pages: politicians, journalists, government bureaucrats, former leaders of the citizens' movements in the DDR, intellectuals. These contacts were invaluable: they gave me access to the often unspoken assumptions and frames of reference that structure the way political life unfolds in a given country. Since the list of individuals is long and the setting was rarely a formal interview, it seems best not to name names, but I am grateful to all for their openness and their interest.

Two people played a special role in the genesis of this book and in the development of the arguments presented in it. Georges Lavau died in October 1990 after a long illness. We could never discuss the arguments I elaborate here, but the questions I ask are questions he would have found important, and as I wrote the book, I missed the conversations we would have had about its themes and theses. I met Gesine Schwan in Berlin in October 1992. If Germany is a *schwieriges Vaterland*, a friendship undergirded by shared intellectual interests, political concerns, and personal sympathy and enriched by different perspectives and experiences nonetheless made Berlin feel like home. Without our friendship, I would have written a book, but not quite this book.

Finally, I am grateful to my editor at Harvard University Press, Michael Aronson, who guided this book through to publication with a reassuring mix of enthusiasm and efficiency, and to my superb copy editor, Amanda Heller; I can only wish that she could have gotten to my prose at an earlier stage.

This book was completed in the early summer of 1996. Relevant events—especially trials and developments in partisan politics—have of course continued to unfold. Nothing, however, has happened to make me wish to alter my analysis in any fundamental way, and I therefore decided against changing the manuscript to keep up with the newspapers. What changes I did make are relatively minor. I hope to revisit many of the issues raised here in future writings, and there to take into account both later events and criticisms of the arguments I propose in this book.

Authors can be stubborn people. For all errors of fact or appreciation that may have crept into these pages, I alone am responsible. For all errors expunged in a timely way, I thank all those who helped.

This book is dedicated to my husband, William L. Baldwin. He put up with everything spouses put up with when their spouses write books, in this case including several long separations, dinner conversations in a language he claimed not to understand, and a lot of very vile Berlin weather.

Notes on Translations and Terminology

Except as otherwise noted, the translations from French and German sources are mine. Where a word itself has assumed a particular importance in a debate, I have often left the word in the original language, while also providing a sense of its meaning in English. Examples include *Schlußstrich, Zwangsvereinigung, Rechtsstaat,* and *Unrechtsstaat.* Beginning in Chapter 2, I make frequent reference to what Karl Jaspers called "Nichtgemeinsamkeit," which I have translated as "lack of community."

Throughout the book, I have used "Germany" (unmodified) to denote the Federal Republic of Germany after October 1990, that is, unified Germany. I use "German" or "Germany" modified with a lower-case "east" or "west" to designate the "new" and the "old" Länder of unified Germany. An upper-case "East" or "West" signals the period between 1945 and unification. I have used the names East Germany and DDR interchangeably; likewise, for the pre-unification period, I have used the terms West Germany and the Federal Republic interchangeably. The abbreviation BRD (Bundesrepublik Deutschland), however, has pejorative connotations in German, and is generally employed only by a certain segment of the left. I have therefore kept it as is in translated quotations where it occurs (it is used, for example, by Gregor Gysi), and have otherwise used no abbreviated form to designate the Federal Republic, either before or after unification.

Andrea. Unhappy the land that has no heroes! . . .
Galileo. No. Unhappy the land that needs heroes.
Brecht, *Das Leben des Galilei*, 1938–39

Political Reconciliation
and Democratization

Many visitors to Germany in the decades after 1945 probably caught
themselves, as did this writer, staring into the faces of passersby and
silently posing uncomfortable questions about their pasts. New democracies do not start with new citizens: they take what they get. This is a
book about what such countries can do, and do, with what they get. This
is also a book about Germany, which approached this problem after
unification in 1990 with an understandable, if not always wholly justified, sense of déjà vu.

For want of a better term, I call the process I analyze here political
reconciliation. A democratizing regime may execute or imprison or temporarily disenfranchise some figures from the preceding dictatorship, but
it will not be able to exclude all individuals who supported the fallen
regime. Democracy offers most of the compromised—and many who are
more than just "compromised"—a second chance. The reconciliation
process defines the terms of the offer, which will differ from country to
country. Political reconciliation reestablishes a political community; it
(re)creates the conditions of political trust. Trials and executions, public
debate and truth commissions, forgiving and forgetting, may all be part
of the process.

Although some kind of reconciliation process takes place after any
regime change, the focus here is on reconciliation processes embedded in
democratization efforts. By democratization I mean the creation and especially the consolidation of a liberal democratic political system based
on representative institutions, competitive elections, individual rights,
and limited government. I understand "consolidation" to involve more

1

than institutional stability; it is a complex, multifaceted process, best measured in decades (or generations), not years.[1]

Both theoretically and practically, the tasks of reconciliation represent a particularly complex problem for the would-be founders of a liberal democratic regime. The special difficulties arise because the various means used to achieve reconciliation—limitations on participation and competition, punishment, forgiving, a kind of negotiated memory, or forgetting—often stand in tension with values central to the liberal project: freedom of thought, expression, and assembly; political equality; the neutrality of the state; government by consent; due process and the rule of law; and the moral agency of the individual. Different positions with regard to reconciliation rest on—and, in a fluid political situation, may contribute significantly to—different theories of democratic trust and citizenship, different conceptions of legality and justice, different understandings of the sources of democratic stability, and new definitions of national identity or political solidarity. Through its specific concern with trust and legitimacy, the debate about reconciliation is inextricably tied to the issue of political culture; and because the issues of compensation and punishment are likely to arise in any interaction between former victims and former perpetrators, the reconciliation debate is always at some level a debate about justice. What variations on trust and legitimacy appear within democratizing and democratic political cultures? Are different variations sequential in post-authoritarian settings, or does the promotion of certain patterns of legitimation or trust tend durably to exclude the development of other patterns? Are specific patterns of legitimation associated with specific patterns of trust, or do the two appear to develop independently of each other? How—and how quickly—can different kinds of trust and legitimacy be created? How does the debate over the terms of inclusion in the new community contribute to evolving understandings of justice?

In the chapters that follow, strategies of reconciliation, along with the different actors who, in various arenas, elaborate and pursue them, appear as the independent variable. Understandings of justice and patterns of legitimation, trust, and partisan competition are the immediate dependent variables, and are of primary interest here. These understandings and patterns seem to have long half-lives, and they help account for the diversity among established democracies. No politically traumatic past is easy to "master," as any American who has reflected on the legacies of slavery knows. Thus, types of democratic consolidation (or, potentially, of political instability or democratic breakdown) are the ultimate dependent variable.

In any specific historical case, the approach adopted to reconciliation will have multiple and often contradictory components, with different mixes appearing in different policy and political arenas. A strategy of reconciliation is not typically formulated, debated, and adopted or defeated as such, the way (for example) a government's proposed fiscal policy might be formulated, debated, and voted up or down; and even if a government more or less consistently employs a given approach, that approach does not therefore become binding on the society as a whole. It is the mix that matters, and precisely because the mix is likely to be complex, it is analytically useful to begin by differentiating between two ideal typical approaches to the problems of reconciliation. Throughout this book I use these strategies to identify what is being mixed and to analyze on whose terms and with what results the mix is being made.

In a democratizing setting, any strategy of reconciliation seeks ultimately to create a limited community of behavior (outward respect for democratic rules and institutions) and conviction (internalization of democratic values and norms). Different approaches diverge in their appreciation of how the two types of community can best and most quickly be achieved. I define an *institutional strategy* of reconciliation as a strategy that tends to assign chronological and causal priority to the creation of a community of behavior, and that emphasizes the ability of institutions and procedures to engender a pattern of behavior that may not correspond to the inner convictions or the past political commitments of individual actors, but that can (hypothetically) be expected ultimately to reshape political culture and common conceptions of justice as actors bring their beliefs into harmony with their actions. Advocates of institutional strategies are inclined to concede equal membership in the new community to all who outwardly obey its rules. In contrast, a *cultural strategy* tends to assign greater immediate importance to the creation of a community of conviction, in the sense of a self-conscious constitutional consensus undergirded by a democratic political culture. The proponents of cultural strategies judge individuals, coalitions, and institutional arrangements according to whether or not these arrangements reward past democratic commitments and embody the demonstrably authentic affirmation of democratic convictions: this is the substantive yardstick against which they define justice. They argue that the new political culture of democracy can best be learned through an active and ongoing intellectual and emotional confrontation with the (still fresh) experience of dictatorship—and that in the wake of a dictatorship, that confrontation is in fact indispensable to the creation of functional patterns of legitimation and trust.

In historical cases of successful democratization—including postwar West Germany—institutional strategies have predominated. Institutional strategies accompany successful democratization processes because they create public tolerance for the new regime and facilitate the reorganization of political competition around issues that do not touch the constitutional format of the country: they speak to the immediate political needs of a fledgling democratic regime in search of a majority. They enable young democratic regimes to survive despite nondemocratic electorates; negatively put, they prevent a reversion to dictatorship. In our often ugly world, this prophylactic function is in itself a signal accomplishment.

Institutions, however, do not "create" democracies, and there is a difference between public tolerance for (or indifference to) a political regime and legitimacy, understood as the articulated or potentially articulated belief that the organization of public authority is rightful and just. Many years ago a great student of democratic institutions reminded Americans: "To assume that this country has remained democratic because of its Constitution seems to me an obvious reversal of the relation; it is much more plausible to suppose that the Constitution has remained because our society is essentially democratic."[2]

What then is the role of new democratic institutions in societies that are not "essentially democratic"? Institutional strategies propose a top-down solution to the problems of democratic consolidation. They create space for democratization to occur in two ways. First, they draw a distinction between public and private trust, defining the former as reliability and confining understandings of trust-as-trustworthiness to the private realm. Second, because they envision social relationships in general and politics in particular as decisively mediated by institutions, institutional strategies assume that in a contest between (democratic) institutions and (nondemocratic) mores, institutions *can* win: institutions shape patterns of behavior, and over time these patterns are transmuted into norms. If older generations were shaped by dictatorship, younger generations will respond, culturally as well as behaviorally, to the different incentives established by democratic institutions.

Officially, and despite Robert Dahl's caveat, this view of trust and the central importance assigned to institutions have a long pedigree in liberal theory, and especially in Anglo-American liberal theory—that is, in statements of liberal theory elaborated in societies already most conducive to liberal government, or "essentially democratic." From John Locke to John Rawls, the classic arguments in defense of "negative" liberty, like the liberal response to the republican emphasis on civic virtue, all posit a public indifference to the private identity of individual citizens as the proper liberal stance. In these arguments, liberal institutions do often compensate for the absence of "better motives" (*Federalist* 51), and liberal arguments about justice often center on procedure.

The key problems associated with institutional strategies lie in their linked insistence on procedural justice and on trust-as-reliability, understood here as the expectation of a predictable adherence to prior undertakings or rules, as if trust-as-reliability and procedural justice defined an adequate floor for public interactions in a democratizing—or even a democratic—society. Cultural strategies are bottom-up strategies of democratization: their proponents focus much more closely on the floor, and they worry about the consequences of using rotten boards. They warn that institutions can be emptied of meaning if used by people who do not respect their spirit. However inadequate cultural strategies may be in sustaining new democratic regimes politically, they speak more directly and more powerfully than do institutional strategies to the crucial issues of trust and legitimacy, and they make more immediate room for a substantive redefinition of justice. In societies preoccupied by private and public forms of betrayal, cultural strategies emphasize trust-as-trustworthiness, understood as an internalized, autonomously generated, and reliable personal disposition toward honesty, sympathy, and solidarity. Cultural strategies tend to put victims first; institutional strategies tend to put order first.

The collisions, collusions, and compromises between these two strategies are explored in the chapters that follow. This project was originally conceived, in the late 1980s, as a reflection on a set of historical cases that cut across the boundaries of historical time, geographic location, and national culture. I hoped to show how debates about reconciliation are inseparable from and indicative of the redefinition of political issues and alliances that takes place after a regime change. In the cases I had chosen, reconciliation debates demonstrably provided the forum in

which different liberal understandings of the role of institutions and political participation, the meaning of equality, and the nature of political
obligation became, potentially or actually, the basis of new political coalitions. The cases served to elucidate certain enduring tensions within
liberal political thought, to analyze the construction of new political
coalitions and institutions, and to suggest new paradigms for understanding contemporary processes of political democratization—a task I
had hoped to address in an extended thematic discussion of contemporary cases.

As my research progressed, the pace of political events in what we
used to call Eastern Europe accelerated beyond anyone's prior expectations. After some hesitation, I adjusted the focus of my research to address the challenge that the unfolding events posed to my discipline and
to my own understanding of the dynamics of liberal political development. The book I was writing became primarily a book about political
reconciliation and democratization in contemporary Germany.

Post-unification Germany does not provide a "typical" case of post-
authoritarian political reconciliation and democratization. On the one
hand, the current German process of reconciliation in unified Germany
is uniquely encumbered by the still unfinished business of "working
through" or "mastering" the legacy of the Nazi dictatorship;[3] on the
other hand, the accession of Länder (states) from the former German
Democratic Republic (Deutsche Demokratische Republik, or DDR) to
the Federal Republic through the use of Article 23 of the West German
Basic Law means that the essential tasks of both democratization and
economic adjustment in east Germany are taking place within the framework of an established democratic system—a unique advantage, and one
that simultaneously reassures advocates of institutional strategies that
the institutions will in fact be strong enough to control behavior and
shape culture and allows those more persuaded by cultural strategies to
argue that precisely because the institutional framework is stable, actors
should attend immediately to the cultural dimension of democratization
lest democracy's institutions be durably distorted.

Germany is different in other ways as well: it lacks the pressures
toward ethnic or regional separatism that have complicated reconciliation and democratization processes elsewhere, especially in the ex–Soviet Union and the former Soviet bloc countries of eastern Europe. Yet
the very ways in which the German case is atypical make it a particularly

rewarding focus for comparative study. The themes and problems which arise in Germany but do not appear, or do not have the same importance, elsewhere increase the range and interest of the arguments made: these themes include most notably the interaction between debates on how the DDR past should be worked through and debates on how the National Socialist past was or should have been worked through in both postwar German states, and the simultaneous playing out of efforts to foster a competitive party system in the new Länder and to alleviate dissatisfaction with the established parties in the old Länder. That in Germany economic problems, while hardly negligible, are less urgent than they are in less developed democratizing countries, that questions of national identity are not reflected in ethnic or regional nationalisms, and that there is no skeptical or hostile military elite waiting for a chance to gain or regain power, all make it easier to focus specifically on the political difficulties of working through an authoritarian past, and to analyze the consequences of different choices for the development of party politics and the creation of a democratic political culture. These tasks are further facilitated by the lapse of time since 1945: if "third wave" democratization processes in general and post-1989 transitions in particular are still young, two full generations have passed since the collapse of the Third Reich, providing a richer empirical base from which to venture generalizations.

Democracy—the type of politics that allegedly "won" as communist systems collapsed in 1989–90—is not and never was a static thing. Democratic politics today is everywhere more exposed to the discontents and longings to which cultural strategies respond. State socialist systems could not reform themselves; now the burden of adaptability is on democratic systems. As both survey data about electorates and the appeal of so-called communitarian critiques of liberalism suggest, the understanding of liberalism, and of trust, that is assumed by institutional strategies is becoming harder and harder to sell in any contemporary democratic community, no matter how established that community is.[4] In established democracies, cultural arguments will appear more compelling whenever political representation and party competition no longer seem satisfactory instruments of public debate and choice. And in any community where "victims"—whether of crime, discrimination, alcoholic parents, abusive relationships, or dictatorship—are an important political and cultural category and where the recognition of victims' claims is an important component of prevalent understandings of justice, cultural strategies will have particular resonance. In the increasingly personalized politics of contemporary democratic societies new and old, publics are more and more sensitive to issues of authenticity, identity, and recognition—issues about which institutional strategies and institutional understandings of liberalism quite deliberately have relatively little to say.

In this sense, the adjustment problems of contemporary German democracy speak to our common future rather than to Germany's very particular past. To citizens and scholars alike, regardless of their level of interest in or indifference to matters German, the post-1989 German case is especially instructive because in Germany an institutional strategy was significantly modified by the incorporation of elements normally associated with cultural strategies. East European observers of the German debate often note how much more preoccupied Germany has been with questions of guilt and complicity than other formerly communist countries (Poland, the former Czechoslovakia, Hungary). A comparison to post-Franco Spain invites the same observation. Only in Germany have the files of the former secret police been made available, and—at least as of this writing—only in Germany has there been a sustained attempt to bring diverse categories of old regime supporters and officials to trial.[5] Unified Germany could afford to adopt elements of a cultural strategy precisely because the institutions of the Federal Republic were secure enough to withstand the turbulence thus risked, and it was prodded to so because of the unique character of its past. Since the demands of cultural strategies may well become more and more difficult to defer or deflect, in both democratizing and democratic countries, the opportunities and dangers associated with such strategies seem worth our attention.

In Chapter 1 I draw on a diverse set of cases to establish the terms on which democratizing countries can deal with compromised citizens. I introduce the costs that "successful" institutional strategies entail and the disappointments they engender. I then turn to the contemporary German case. Has disappointment been reduced by the use of elements associated with cultural strategies? Has democratization been served? In Chapters 2 through 6 I use the reconciliation problem to analyze specific aspects of transition politics: the articulation by political actors of an understanding of what democracy means (Chapter 2), the political-intellectual effort to elaborate a democratic consensus (Chapter 3), the legal effort to redefine justice and individual responsibility (Chapter 4), public debates about individual biographies (Chapter 5), and the development of a new partisan system (Chapter 6). The focus is on the post-1989 German experience, analyzed in conjunction with and against the backdrop of the post-1945 experience.

In the Conclusion I return briefly to the problem of trust in post-authoritarian settings. Liberal society may require a kind of trust that liberalism itself cannot create, and that is especially likely to be lacking in the aftermath of a dictatorship. Institutional strategies cannot make people trustworthy, but they can make people reliable in limited arenas. Good institutions can induce people, even "bad" people, to play good roles. This is a troubling notion to those of us who think that identity and behavior are closely related and who would prefer a more robust definition of justice than liberalism typically offers. But institutions may be our best—and even our only—bet. The alternative preoccupation with transparency and recognition is especially compelling in transitional situations, but even there it may be counterproductive. Beyond transitional situations especially, but even in transitional situations, it both betrays our lack of confidence in our institutions and contributes to their further weakening. Not just democratization but also democracy, like so many other good things in life, may disappoint.

One

The Disappointments of Democratization

In the contemporary world, the fall of a dictatorship and the possibility of a transition to democratic rule are normally greeted with euphoria. Successful democratization strategies, however, disappoint even though they succeed. They disappoint because they do not meet the high aspirations of those who had fought most fervently for freedom, and they succeed because, at the price of such disappointment, they enlarge the coalition willing actively or passively to support the new democratic regime. Empirically, the construction of a democratic coalition has always been the result of reconciliation strategies that are primarily institutional in their logic. Such strategies exact a high price: they do not create the "république pure et dure"—the clean and tough republic—that was the goal of French *résistants* during the Nazi Occupation and that is the common dream of men and women who fight, often against the odds, for freedom, and they involve the suppression or distortion of historical memory. Men and women endure prison and torture and exile and ultimately death for the chance to be free, and what they get—if they are fortunate—is not the participatory, compassionate, upstanding republic of their dreams, but negative liberty. What one might call real existing liberalism is then experienced as a partial defeat; the political culture of the new regime's supporters is impugned, the motives of the regime's leaders are questioned, and both are blamed for the failure to achieve a higher standard of political and social justice.

The transition to democracy, from the fall of the dictatorship to the final consolidation of a political system based on individual rights, representative institutions, and free and competitive elections, creates not one but two sets of losers: the defenders of the old regime and the advocates of cultural stategies. The latter define themselves as losers as it becomes clear how cautiously the old regime's elites and supporters will be treated; they compromise their chances of building broad reformist policy coalitions and then spend their political capital in a losing battle to keep the creation of a new political culture at the top of the political agenda. The more they are marginalized, the more insistent they become in their reminders that institutional strategies sacrifice memory, preferring what the Germans call a *Schlußstrich*—putting a question to rest, closing the books—to uncomfortable discussions of a painful past. Such strategies, they argue, blur distinctions between those who acted well and those who acted badly under the old regime and obscure the fundamental, unbridgeable differences between dictatorship and democracy. Without memory, they insist, it is not possible either to distinguish trustworthy from untrustworthy compatriots or to understand why the old regime was illegitimate. Allowing personal and political responsibilities to go unacknowledged, they assert, is incompatible with a democratic political culture. A democracy built on such a foundation may not crumble like a house built on sand, for other factors (external pressure, for example) may hold it erect, but it will not be a pretty building.

The voices calling for memory and accountability may appear to go unheeded, but democracies, unlike the nightmare society of George Orwell's *1984,* do not in fact forget. No public authority, let alone a social group, can ever draw a *Schlußstrich* under the inherited burdens or drop the curtain on the historical memories of a free people. Free societies do not forget because they must, by definition, protect the prerequisites of memory: privacy and property, free access to information, and freedom of thought and expression. After the work of democratic consolidation is completed—and often after the generations most directly compromised by the old regime and most important to the transition have been replaced by younger generations—the barriers to memory can be dismantled, whether by a free press looking for scandal or by scholars seeking promotion as well as understanding. Furthermore, those barriers will always be informal and breachable. The later recovery of memory will be characterized by distortions of its own; the distortions will reflect the characteristics and preoccupations of the society and polity that have developed since the end of the old regime, including those brought about by the particular ways in which memory was sacrificed. Like the initial debate, the later recovery of memory will have a visible impact on partisan competition and political culture.

Throughout the many phases of transition, consolidation, and democratic "normality," disappointment with the process therefore plays an important part. That part can be constructive: even (or precisely) when an institutional strategy is at its height, the stubborn insistence on memory and skepticism regarding trust-as-reliability by disappointed men and women still persuaded of the need for a cultural strategy can help keep the pragmatism of the "institutionalists" from degenerating into a cynicism that could threaten the success of democratization. The disappointed, however, are more likely to perceive the interaction as a competition and the stakes as zero-sum: every step away from memory and the recognition of responsibilities is in their view also a step away from a genuine democratic renewal—with no guarantee that history will provide the community another chance to make good its errors. Their opposition to institutional strategies is therefore vehemently and bitterly articulated. Empirically and in retrospect, however, the interdependent contribution of institutional and cultural strategies to democratization appears more significant than does the theoretical gulf that lies between them. In the short run, the twin results of the relationship are democratization and disappointment; in the long run, the results are democratic stability and memory. At every step the mix of strategies affects the emerging and evolving political game.

Every democratization process is in important ways unique. Disappointment, however, appears to be a common feature, and it is a direct and immediate product of the reconciliation debate. In the first section of this chapter I establish a baseline of what disappointment looks like, using voices from the Federal Republic and France after 1945. Across significant differences of time, political experience, and culture, reconciliation debates resemble one another in terms of the substantive arguments put forward by each side. In the second section I use the postrevolutionary American case to illustrate how the advocates of institutional strategies of reconciliation answer their critics: How does one make the argument for disappointment? In the next two sections I use post-Terrorist and post-Liberation France to consider the democratic viability of different types of institutional strategies: At what point should democratizers stop pushing aside off their disappointment and start worrying about an immediate risk to the democratization process itself? In the final section I review the disappointments of democratization.

"I Can Imagine Another Germany": The Shape of Disappointment

Through the hard and uncertain years of reconstruction and the long decades of international tension, the democratic character of the Federal Republic of Germany was guaranteed by the Western occupying powers: the United States, Great Britain, and France. Between the German capitulation in May 1945 and the beginning of the Cold War in 1947–48, efforts were made to call former Nazis to account. Trials, however, soon gave way to amnesties, and the denazification program was widely judged a failure (see Chapter 4). Within the bounds of the sovereignty conceded to the Federal Republic, West German leaders relied on institutional mechanisms (established by the Basic Law and guaranteed by the Western Allies), a specific national agenda (reconstruction and the so-called economic miracle of the 1950s), and a variously motivated but shared anticommunism to ensure democratic outcomes despite the manifest absence of a democratic political culture. An ugly past, if never successfully forgotten, was deliberately consigned to the shadows. "The Federal Republic," one observer noted, "labored under the obligation to satisfy everyone." Resisters and victims did not have the numbers; perpetrators big and small and *Mitläufer* (the denazification program's term for followers) did. To the latter, the republic extended a "cold amnesty."[1]

The institutional strategy that produced this result was subjected to steady criticism by those who urged the necessity of an immediate, ongoing, and honest confrontation with Germany's past. The demand for self-scrutiny was articulated with particular vehemence by the student movement of the late 1960s, but already in 1950, in an influential article published some fifteen months after the creation of the Federal Republic, the anti-Nazi German intellectual Walter Dirks commented negatively on the political course that events had taken, not just in West Germany but in all the liberated countries of Western Europe: "We are in the process," the left-wing Christian Democrat wrote, "of losing the peace." Dirks's perceptions are virtually identical to sentiments expressed at precisely the same moment by former Resistance activists in France, and they anticipate with arresting similarity the bitterness of former East German dissidents in unified Germany: "Fear, the need for security and comfort were stronger than courage, truth, and sacrifice," Dirks wrote, "and so we live in a period of restoration."[2]

Fear and the need for security and reassurance weave the human fabric from which institutional strategies are cut; they also have a prominent place in liberal theory, however miserable they may appear in the heady days that follow the demise of a dictatorship. Cultural strategies demand "courage, truth, and sacrifice"—a generally unpromising electoral program in a democracy, whether transitional or mature.

The personal and political disappointment experienced by democratic activists in Germany and France is perhaps best captured by two novels, one French and one German, of unequal literary quality, both written and published when disappointment was most bitter: Jean-Louis Curtis's *Les Forêts de la nuit* (The Forests of the Night, 1947) and Wolfgang Koeppen's *Das Treibhaus* (The Greenhouse, 1953).

By 1947, the Free French leader Charles de Gaulle had resigned from office and created a political movement opposed to the constitutional setup of the new Fourth Republic. The tripartite governing coalition of socialists, Christian Democrats, and communists was about to come undone. Curtis's novel conveys the disappointment that accompanied these developments (more fully discussed later in this chapter). Curtis describes a cross-section of social relationships and political commitments in a French town located on the former border between the occupied (northern) and the "free" (southern) zone; the story takes place between the complete occupation of France by German troops in November 1942 and the Liberation. Francis, the deferential son of a bombastic and conservative father and an irreproachable student in a Catholic lycée, represents the pure and youthful Resistance hero who has definitively moved away from a conservative religious milieu traditionally hostile to the republic. Francis is tortured and shot in January 1944 by French collaborators; his naked body, mutilated almost beyond recognition, is left in a ditch near Bordeaux. As Allied armies advance, the German occupation troops depart; they leave the town silently, in the middle of the night.

The town that is thus "liberated" is not a pretty sight—no prettier than it had been during the ugly years of the war and Occupation: among the adults, fear, the desire to humiliate, and opportunism predominate. The town's new leader, Darricade, an engineer with a now forgotten right-wing political past, is a calculator and a climber, devoid of personal and political integrity. He can claim to have been in the Resistance, but during the war he always let others—Francis, for example—take all the risks. Exploiting Francis's name, Darricade successfully pursues the postwar political career his wartime actions were calculated to promote. The real heroes, meanwhile, are dead, or soon retreat to private life. In every social arena, the people who enjoy prominence are, like Darricade, the opportunists and the trimmers. Political rewards, the idealists observe, have not been distributed according to merit. Disappointment is too weak a word to describe the reaction of those who feel cheated of their victory. Gérard, a young man who joined the Resistance after years of compromise and indecision, is mortified by what he sees at the Liberation: "baseness, cowardice, and stupidity winding their dance around a dead enemy."[3]

Gérard is both scolded and comforted by Pierre, the man whose charisma had led him to join the Resistance, and with whom he is now standing in line to enlist in the regular army. The two volunteers have just watched a fat, cigar-smoking, middle-aged man, his expression "indifferent and scornful" (452), come out of the offices of the Comité de Résistance and climb into an official Cadillac. Gérard bristles; Pierre rejects his indignation and his disappointment: "I am glad to give myself," Pierre says, "for a world that is still so imperfect, for a cause somewhat compromised by some of its supporters. I find it all normal, and I am happy" (453).

The knowledge that men like Pierre and Gérard would be exploited and that men like Darricade would end up in power pushes another character, Jacques, earlier too coldly intelligent, too detached, and too lucidly desperate to join the Resistance, over the edge into hatred and self-hatred:

> Jacques was there on the curb, contemplating the crowd . . . "They" were repulsive, repulsive . . . [sic] Their monstrous baseness, their cowardice, their ugliness. This day which could have been beautiful and noble, "they" had disfigured and debased it. It was to save these worms that millions of men had died, millions of men, that France's purest sons had endured torture, that English paratroopers had fallen from the sky like liberating angels; to save these worms, the Russian and American armies had shown themselves prodigies of energy and endurance. Jacques looked at the crowd, and his disgust hurt him like extreme

sensuality. To be of a different blood than theirs, of a different species,
. . . to become a plant or a mineral . . . He wished a German machine
gun would have suddenly have appeared in the square and lashed the
populace with its murderous whip. It would be good to hear them yell
with fear, . . . trample one another in frantic panic! (470–471)

As the book ends, in 1946, the town is dominated socially by Jacques's
mother, the irretrievably trivial, scheming, petty socialite responsible for
Francis's arrest, and dominated politically by Darricade. To make the
scene even more depressing, Darricade is encouraging Jacques's mother
to stand for parliament.

Most of the action in *Les Forêts de la nuit* takes place between November 1942 and August 1944; only the very short "epilogues" are set in
1945 and 1946. Disappointment set in early in France because the Resistance was able to reproduce a version of politics as usual even before the
Liberation. Resistance groups defended different political ideas, and published undergound newspapers and pamphlets in which those ideas were
expressed and debated. De Gaulle's efforts to make the Free French look
and act like a democratic government in exile had the unintended consequence of allowing the old parties of the Third Republic to reassert their
identities. After the Liberation, politics as usual—what de Gaulle, who
resigned abruptly from office in January 1946, when he was unable
to impose his constitutional preferences, scornfully referred to as "the
games, the poisons, and the pleasures of the system"[4]—quickly returned,
as reformist forces lost out to more classic elements in the socialist SFIO
(Section française de l'internationale ouvrière) and the Christian Democratic MRP (Movement républicain populaire, rhetorically Marxist and
anticlerical in the former case, conservative in the latter), as the Communist Party returned to its Stalinist traditions, and as conservative forces
regrouped.

The action in Koeppen's more complex and interesting novel *Das
Treibhaus* takes place later than the action in Curtis's book. Koeppen's
work is set in Bonn during the rearmament debate of the early 1950s,
and it re-creates for the reader what Dirks called the "restorationist character of the epoch": not an event but "a process, a condition, a climate."[5]

Koeppen's hero, Keetenheuve, had been a young journalist during the
Weimar Republic; when the Nazis came to power, he voluntarily left the
country. He emigrated to Paris and spent the war in Canada and London,

but "never ceased to feel German."[6] At age thirty-nine he returned to Germany, a thoughtful but convinced pacifist, "filled with hopes that lingered for a time" (232). He was elected to the Bundestag as a Social Democratic Party (SPD) deputy.

Keetenheuve quickly became uncomfortable with the artificial, constructed quality of the regime, with the social and political hypocrisy prevalent in Bonn, with the fierce partisanship of the politically important actors—and with the rush to rearm. In both public and private ways, he tried to find his bearings in the "greenhouse" where a new Germany was ostensibly being grown, but he suspected the plants he saw of being poisonous, and the main gardeners—the calculating old chancellor (Konrad Adenauer) and Knurrewahn, the figure who represents the SPD leader Kurt Schumacher—did not inspire his trust. The chancellor, Keetenheuve observed, sat through the parliamentary debate preceding the critical rearmament vote looking like a bored actor on whom a tiresome part had been imposed: "He was no dictator, but he was the boss: he prepared everything, made everything happen, and he despised the oratorical theater in which he too had to play" (367). The parliamentary SPD had little better to offer—and Keetenheuve detected no reformist push from below, "no restless desire for renewal, no courage to overthrow the old, dead values" (362).

The metaphors Koeppen uses to describe the Federal Republic vary: West Germany is most often compared to a greenhouse, but sometimes to a hospital ward, and sometimes to a school. In each case Keetenheuve feared that the results of the experiment would not be happy: "The people had of course remained the same, they had no intention of becoming different" (232). He himself was a study in private and public disappointment. He was a nonconformist, "unbelieving, doubting, desperate, skeptical," a "loner," "a man without contacts," an impotent "romantic defender of human rights" who "could desire but . . . never educate" (241, 230, 273, 240, 230). Upon his return to Germany, Keetenheuve had fallen in love with Elke, the homeless, destitute adolescent daughter of Nazis who had committed suicide as the war ended, a girl who "had no idea what to do with freedom" (230). But that private attempt to save something out of the ruins had also failed: the book opens with Elke's death, presumably a suicide. Keetenheuve had lost on every front. Revolution, he now understood, was a "dead concept" (316). He knew himself to be uncertain of what he wanted, other than a more engaged citizenry and a parliament in which reason and persuasion would prevail over partisan reflexes; he also knew that he had "no prescription . . . that would make the patient healthy tomorrow" (369). He was reassured only by the continued presence in Bonn of his former colleague Mergentheim. Mergentheim had known when to desert the Weimar Republic, and then when to desert the Third Reich, and had now "become a sought-after and patronized man of reconstruction." His continued presence signaled that the worst was not yet on the horizon: "So long as Mergentheim was behind his desk, so long as he did not move on to something new, to become, for example, correspondent in Washington, the state appeared secure to Keetenheuve and the enemy far away" (269).

Keetenheuve was increasingly tempted to flee—from the greenhouse with its dubious plants, from his own impotence, from his personal and political failures—mentally by reading Baudelaire, physically either by accepting the government's offer of a diplomatic post in Guatemala or through suicide. As the book ends, "only sadness remained" (389); the Bundestag had voted to rearm, and Keetenheuve was standing on a bridge: "He was a burden to himself, and a leap from the bridge made him free" (390).

In 1967, on the occasion of Konrad Adenauer's death, Dirks, who like Keetenheuve had opposed rearmament, and who, like both Keetenheuve and the French Catholics who went from the Resistance to the MRP, had fervently hoped for a type of democratic political competition close to the people, built on mutual trust and open dialogue, looked back with renewed disappointment at the road that had been missed: "I still know full well," he wrote, "the bitterness with which I experienced the beginning of the Adenauer era."[7] That bitterness, and above all that sense of loss, are already clear in Dirks's 1950 article: "Restorationist times are always times of overdue but missed upheaval. Restoration is fear of revolution."[8] In 1967, without denying Adenauer's achievements, Dirks concluded, "I can imagine another Germany, to which the very old man was an obstacle." This "other Germany" whose absence Dirks deplored, borrowing the term used during the Third Reich by and for anti-Nazi Germans, would have been more compassionate, more participatory, more internationalist, more conscious of its past.

Why had the opportunity been missed? Was the disappointment inevitable? Were the chancellor and "Knurrewahn" to blame? Could

Keetenheuve have found the "prescription" he lacked? Was German political culture simply too corrupted by a tradition of authoritarian rule and a decade of publicly approved criminal bestiality? In 1950 Dirks was more inclined to criticize the failings of reformers, especially Social and Christian Democrats, who had been unable to impose the new politics in which they believed, than he was to attack men of conservative temperament and conviction, from whom better could not have been expected: "The real sin of restoration is the sin of omission," he wrote. "The real guilty are those called on to promote renewal and who are too comfortable to take on . . . the effort and the risk of acting."[9]

By 1967 Dirks seemed more sensitive to the issue of leadership, and he contrasted Adenauer to a contemporary Adenauer had disliked, John Kennedy: "These two very different men present a choice between two different conceptions of politics: between the attempt . . . to mobilize all good forces for great ends, and a statecraft . . . that does not expect much of people and that seeks and holds power against them, coolly and without affectation."[10] Noting the decisive impact that Adenauer's leadership had had on the young republic, Dirks assumed that the leadership would have been just as effective had it been put to less "restorationist" purposes. Keetenheuve's story, so consistent in its basic outline with the stories of disappointment in liberated France and in other comparable historical situations, suggests otherwise. Keetenheuve, sad and tired and isolated as he was on the eve of the rearmament vote, did not imagine that any other system would produce better results, "and the loudmouths who wanted to get rid of the parliament altogether were also his enemies" (360). Keetenheuve did not want to play Saint-Just, nor did he think admiringly and longingly of the DDR's "antifascism" as he stood on the bridge. Yet he knew that he could not find a democratic "prescription" to achieve his goals, not because he had not tried hard enough, but simply because there was no such "prescription." The old chancellor was the better leader, not because he was a better or more dedicated or more intelligent man, but because he had chosen a strategy that *could* be pursued according to a democratic prescription.

Institutional strategies often become identified with leaders because popular trust in the individual with the prescription compensates for the instability and uncertainty otherwise characteristic of political life in transitional settings. But institutional "prescriptions" are complex and flexible, and different leaders understand and apply them differently. In doing so, they are motivated by their own pasts and ideas, but in the particular way they define the old regime, construct the new regime, justify the inclusion of compromised individuals in the new community, and shape the political agenda and alliance patterns of the new regime, they also are responding to and can be constrained by the forces they perceive to be at work in their society and the resources they identify as possible sources of support. Keetenheuve loses, but in politics, the war is never over; Keetenheuve need not have leapt from the bridge. Dirks urged on like-minded compatriots "courage, tenacity, and a cleverness that does not stay caught in the present," and so defined the critical function such men and women play in democratization processes where institutional strategies have won: "What can still happen is work on the consciousness of the time, work on the public conscience, on public opinion. Tell it like it is . . . This is work that can bear fruit when the time comes—if the time comes."[11]

A German bullet paralyzed Gérard's arm, but at the end of *Les Forêts de la nuit,* he and his wife are schoolteachers,working, it could be said, to preserve and prolong their country's "second chance."

What Dirks expressed as disappointment and self-indictment and described as "a scandal and a shame,"[12] younger men and women expressed as anger, and in their condemnation of the road traveled, a not insignificant minority was tempted to reject West German democracy because it was imperfect, rather than to defend it (as Dirks did) because it was a democracy. For many other, less extreme, members of what is loosely called the 1968 generation, the perceived failure of their parents to acknowledge and discuss their own complicities during the Nazi years had irretrievably poisoned the life of the Bonn republic.

More than a half century after the end of the war, this perception of the past's grip on the present is still alive, and in the coming chapters, we will repeatedly take note of its influence. Many Germans continue to argue that the necessary coming to terms with the past has not yet taken place, and that Germany's postwar democratic conversion will not be fully persuasive—even if it is institutionally secure—until that confrontation does occur. Those who make this argument are unimpressed by pre-unification survey data indicating fundamental shifts in German political culture and unreassured by the ability of the political system to weather the challenges posed by political turnover, economic recession, and political violence.[13] They would agree with the writer Ralph Giordano that "the Federal Republic has a Janus head, a double face." Alongside a Federal Republic consciously dedicated to diversity, freedom, and international solidarity, a less attractive Germany remains, marked by "xenophobia, right- and left-wing extremism, right- and left-wing terrorism, as well as a deeply institutionalized antiradicalism that responds solely to left-wing terrorism."[14] Giordano identified these trends two years before the unification process began—and five years before the spectacular anti-foreigner riots in Rostock that seared the conscience of a nation even as they reopened old wounds. Building on the positions elaborated in 1967 by Alexander and Margarete Mitscherlich in their influential analysis of the psychological bases of German collective action,[15] Giordano distinguishes Germany's first guilt—"the guilt of Germans under Hitler"— from its second guilt: "the repression and denial of the first guilt after 1945." This "second guilt," he argues, "shaped, and continues to shape, the political culture of the Federal Republic in essential ways," continually compromising the chances for a genuine and definitive process of democratic political renewal.[16]

Giordano attributes responsibility for Germany's "second guilt" to the political class of postwar West Germany as a whole, "who stole away from a compromising phase of national history that they had lived through and helped shape." Giordano, who is also vehement in his insistence on the need to work through the DDR past, emphasizes the "catastrophic effects on political orientation, moral renaissance, historical lucidity, and rehumanization" of the strategy followed after 1945.[17] But citing a "depressingly large number of examples," he also understands its adoption to be the logical outcome of democratic politics—not of some peculiarly defective German trait:

> The causes of party behavior lie in the nature of the democratic system itself—in the dependence on voters. Whoever says to a Nazi, who would much prefer not to learn anything, that he is a Nazi, is not going to get that Nazi's vote . . . The second German Republic succeeded a dictatorship without parallel . . . Now of course the leaders of a certain period of history can be driven out, but not the people that produced the leaders. With the people, the democratic successor state must somehow make do, it cannot get around them. Clearly there is a kind of law that says that democracies do not overcome the heritage of dictatorial predecessors.[18]

Giordano does not, of course, suggest that dictatorships deal more felicitously with the moral burdens of past dictatorships, and his understanding of the link between the successful introduction of a competitive party system and the reluctance to confront issues of past responsibility suggests the difficulties of translating his positions into policy. At the very least, however, Giordano indicates that, for many observers, the institutional strategy adopted during the Adenauer era had ambiguous consequences.

Willy Brandt fled Germany in 1933 and was later deprived of his citizenship by the Nazis; he could hardly have felt much affinity for compatriots compromised by their actions under Hitler's dictatorship. The contrast between Brandt's nuanced retrospective judgment on postwar choices and his friend Giordano's more forceful positions is therefore particularly instructive: it demonstrates that the institutional strategy Adenauer pursued found defenders well beyond the ranks of Adenauer's coalition, and well outside the circles of conservative tradition and social prominence, where indulgence toward former Nazis might have been predictable. But such support was never free of misgivings. In his famous first governmental declaration of October 1969, Brandt implicitly conceded the persistently problematic character of German political culture by challenging his compatriots to accept a new kind of citizenship: "We aren't looking for admirers," Brandt exclaimed, "we need people who will reflect critically with us, who will share in decisions and in responsibility." Brandt defended West Germany's record, but his positive recapitulation of the Federal Republic's first two decades was in fact double-edged: it was both an affirmation of how far the country had traveled and an evocation of the long road yet ahead. German democracy was not in decline, Brandt argued, but added, "We are just now getting started!"[25]

Two decades later, Brandt reflected critically on how the Federal Republic had dealt with the legacy of the Third Reich. An interviewer asked, "Don't you think that the holes in political consciousness could no longer be filled in, because we didn't start doing it in time?" Brandt replied to the question with another question. To him it was *the* question, and one to which the historical record had clearly not provided an adequate answer: "That may be, but, to put it simply, how was one supposed to make, how could one make, democrats out of nondemocrats, antifascists out of fascists?" Had he remained a journalist, Brandt conceded, he might well have been more critical of the conciliatory strategy adopted by the government. But in the end, he stood by the judgment he had arrived at as a politician:

> One cannot materially rebuild a completely destroyed country or create a halfway decent state, hoping that out of it something like a social democracy and a partner for other peoples will develop, and at the same time bury one's people in their guilt and complicity.
>
> You must try, if you want the first thing, to win over and integrate as many people as is in any way possible, including those who aren't exactly unblemished, including the fearful and the cowardly, to give them the chance to start over.[20]

Neither individuals nor communities can in fact "start over," but institutional strategies of reconciliation give individuals and societies marked by dictatorship a second chance. How the second chance gets used—what sorts of patterns of trust, legitimation, and partisan competition emerge—depends in part on the extent to which it is used as a chance to start over. Brandt's position on this critical question repeats, almost verbatim, arguments articulated after the American Revolution—to which case we now turn, in part in order to have the arguments made in terms we are morally able to hear. They are hard to hear in the postwar German context because they sound like attempts to relativize or minimize Nazi crimes and German complicities, especially since the voices making the arguments normally carried considerably less moral authority in this regard than did Willy Brandt's. But analytically, and in terms of their implications for democratic theory, the arguments in the two cases resemble each other in important ways.

Democracy as a Second Chance

We do not know for certain how many Americans sided with Britain during the Revolutionary War. We do know that throughout the decade and a half of resistance and armed confrontation, revolutionary governments in the rebellious colonies responded to "disaffection" by adopting measures designed to coerce, contain, and finally punish Americans who remained loyal to the British Crown.[21] We know that such "Loyalists" came from every walk of life, and we know that, even as the war drew to a close, they formed a substantial minority: modern scholarship suggests that one fifth of the white population was Loyalist in its political preferences.[22] Finally, we know that the American Revolution was not a peaceful transformation: while it lacked the social dimensions and the orchestrated public violence of other revolutions, it was a bloody, wrenching, and lengthy upheaval.

The American debate about reconciliation is important both because of the arguments it brought forth and because of the revolutionary settlement it promoted. We owe the federal Constitution of 1789 to men who, a few years earlier, had pleaded for an institutional approach to reconciliation. They bequeathed to us the institutions we associate with modern democracy: a binding constitution, the separation of powers, a freely and regularly elected parliament, and a government limited in its functions and powers. But we owe the Bill of Rights primarily to men who had insisted on the need for a cultural strategy. Institutional arguments "won," but cultural arguments did not completely "lose," and they were never ignored, much less silenced.

American proponents of institutional strategies shied away from punishment and spoke reluctantly of "the late controversy" (Benjamin Rush); they sought simply to put the Revolution behind them. This readiness to sacrifice memory prefigured what would become a national pattern: in their political self-understandings, Americans consistently decline to confront their own public tragedies and minimize the place of violence in their collective history. This was a very costly strategy for race relations, but it was much less burdensome to the revolutionary settlement. The postrevolutionary loss of memory did not represent a direct political risk to democratic politics because the Loyalists had never been able to elaborate a compelling ideological defense of their position: revolutionary fears to the contrary notwithstanding, the delegitimation of the "old regime," such as that regime was, could simply be assumed. In this sense, the postrevolutionary debate in America differs significantly from debates in other, more contemporary settings, where a failure to remember may adversely affect the new regime's patterns of legitimation, and where disappointment may be a more reliable indicator of real political danger. The American Revolution created a representative democracy in the former colonies, and the war was followed by a vigorous debate about reconciliation. But it would be an anachronism to call George III's government a dictatorship, even if many Americans did call the king a tyrant. Both ideologically and institutionally, the new American government built consciously on its British antecedents, and American liberalism inherited the rich legacy of seventeenth- and eighteenth-century British liberal thought. The same continuities cannot be wished on successor regimes to twentieth-century dictatorships.

This difference between the American case and more contemporary cases is more obvious to us, however, than it would have been to the revolutionary generation. The revolutionaries were far from believing that their triumph represented the final victory of freedom over "tyranny." On the contrary, most eighteenth-century Americans still believed in a cyclical view of history, and held republican government to be especially precarious. The case in favor of a cultural strategy represented the simple application of then current "Old Whig" understandings of stability and moral unanimity to the political problems of the postrevolutionary political community. It was the position adopted by Americans who did not think the revolutionary agenda could or should be superseded in the postwar republic; they did not think in terms of "democratic consolidation" because they did not believe that democracies could be consolidated. According to the Old Whig account, the Revolution could never be "over"; if the revolutionary community sought to "move on," it could move only onto the slippery slope of corruption and decline. This fall could be deferred, but many believed it could not ultimately be averted. In their pessimistic appraisal of human nature, these revolutionaries were "men of little faith,"[23] "old-fashioned fellow[s]," as Patrick Henry portrayed himself in one of his interminable speeches to the Virginia ratifying convention of 1788,[24] men still emotionally and intellectually wedded to the opposition ideology of the 1760s and 1770s. For them the adoption of a cultural strategy was a matter of survival, and "mere" memory accompanied by scattered examples of punishment would not suffice. The American opponents of institutional strategies did not place much stock in the possible causal importance of patterns of public discourse, and so were much less invested in articulated memory of any sort than later proponents of cultural strategies would be. Rather, they wanted to see Loyalists—"vipers in our bosom," as a New Jersey petition called them[25]—simply *excluded* from the new republic. In their view, the argument was not about whether the republic would be clean and tough or tarnished and disappointing but about whether it would exist: in this sense they were more rather than less desperate and determined than their twentieth-century counterparts. But since we do not believe as a matter of course in cyclical historical patterns, and since to us the Loyal-

ists seem (in contrast to Nazis) ideologically innocuous, we can listen to
the debate with detached interest.

"Justice, policy, and our obligation to perpetuate the freedom we possess" seemed compelling reasons for refusing Loyalists a place in the new
political community, despite the protective provisions included in the
treaty that ended hostilities.[26] The long war, the treaty's revolutionary
critics argued, had given all Americans ample time to choose sides: the
Tories (as the Loyalists were often called) had chosen against American
freedom and independence. Recalling the "treason, murder, and robber-
ies" of which he claimed the Tories were guilty (widespread spying for
the secret police is a more recent invention), the New York publicist
"Brutus" asked rhetorically: "Can you seriously hope, that such outrages
against the principles and feelings of humanity, can either be forgotten or
forgiven?"[27]

The case for an institutional strategy depended in part on the assertion
that the Revolution was over, and in part on the articulation of a new
understanding of the nature of political conflict, political obligation, and
republican citizenship. The proponents of institutional strategies began
to replace Old Whig notions of political cycles and decline with a lin-
ear conception of progress. They argued that the Revolution had been
brought to a happy conclusion, and that its success had created a new
social and political agenda. That new agenda created a political opportunity: it made old loyalties and antagonisms both less obvious and less
relevant, while new tasks offered a means of forging a common identity
among past adversaries. Former Tories could play an important and constructive role in the "apolitical" project of promoting the realization of
the republic's material potential. The advocates of an institutional strategy paid tribute to revolutionary virtue, but they trusted rules and institutional mechanisms to preserve liberty, they envisaged the development
of a society in which private activity would increasingly supplant public
commitments, and they recognized fundamental law and international
treaties as legitimate and indeed necessary limits on more immediate
expressions of popular sovereignty. A republic, "A Planter" argued, was
not like a church, and should rightly cast its nets of membership as
widely as possible: "Faith is necessary in religion," he argued, "but not in
morality; and much less in politics."[28]

In contrast, advocates of cultural strategies saw in "faith" the only reliable guarantee of trustworthy conduct, in whatever arena. In their view, the conflict that had opposed Patriot to Tory was insurmountable because it pitted virtue against vice. Repeatedly they defined the revolutionary conflict as opposing liberty to tyranny, and therefore honor to dishonor, candor to deceit, independence (of mind, conscience, and action) to dependence, courage and virtue to cowardice and self-interest. They understood political commitments to reflect fundamental dispositions of character rather than variable responses to circumstances. They therefore denied that Tories could change. Whether their choices had originally been motivated by the "lust of power and domination" or simply by fear, Tory souls were now lost to the republic; they were "characters who are incapable of ever becoming by any means, miracles excepted, good citizens."[29] They might "show a temporary conformity to a government they can neither abandon nor overturn," but this would be the result of "self delusion" if not "direct deceit."[30] At best, the Tories would always be political dependents: "They will one and all, rich and poor, become the abject tools of the party who favours and procures them a pardon." More likely, they would "remain the same implacable, secret enemies, they have always been to the rights of this country, brooding and waiting in sullen silence, for a favourable opportunity to avow their machinations."[31]

No one who urged an institutional strategy went into detail about the "prison-ships" and "murders" so frequently evoked by their opponents, and they assumed that most people's political loyalties are decisively shaped by context. They minimized the "misconduct or knavery of some people during the late storm"[32] and insisted on the importance of British leadership and natural deference in leading some Americans astray. They reminded their compatriots of the early evacuation of leading (and presumably influential and convinced) American Tories as the outcome of the war became clear. They recalled the difficulties men had encountered as they sought (hypothetically) to behave well under trying circumstances. Alexander Hamilton argued that the Tories left behind on American soil were simply conformists, who would now conform to the norms and mores of the republic:

> The number of the disaffected, who are so, from speculative notions of government, is small: The great majority of those, who took part against us, did it from accident, from the dread of British power, and

from the influence of others to whom they had been accustomed to look up. Most of the men, who had that kind of influence are already gone: The residue and their adherents must be carried along by the torrent; and with very few exception[s], if the government is mild and just, will soon come to view it with approbation and attachment.[33]

Advocates of cultural strategies made citizenship a function of service and merit: even if the Tories could be shown to pose no threat to the safety of the state, they did not *deserve* to be members of the new republic. "They fought for slavery," a press item noted, "let them have it."[34] To the advocates of institutional strategies, this argument was both presumptuous and politically senseless. "Common Sense" warned against the arrogance of assuming the transparency of human actions, let alone motives. "When an enemy suddenly extends his arms and authority over a country, it is impossible for every one to get out of his way," he noted. He meant his remarks literally, but they can also be understood figuratively. That is, where an individual feels materially disarmed in the face of a dominant political force, he may also be ideologically vulnerable:

> The incumbrance of children and families, the insurmountable difficulty of procuring conveyance for so many thousands at once, the embarrassment of private circumstances which none but themselves can know, the intricacy and influence of dependent connections, the want of money to move with, and, at last, the not knowing where to go . . . will unavoidably leave numbers within their power, whose situation having blended with the voluntary traitor, exposes them alike to indiscriminate suspicion. All are not friends or enemies who at first appear so. Misfortune may have the resemblance of guilt, and guilt assume the stile of misfortune; and to distinguish between them, requires observation, temper and prudence.[35]

Benjamin Rush argued that it was in the interest of the republic to give Loyalists a second chance. "There was a progress in the minds of most men upon the subject of the late controversy," he noted. Some had joined the revolutionary cause later than others: Was this reason now to reject the services they might render? "What should we think of part of a crew in a leaky ship, in the middle of the Atlantic, who, out of resentment to one half their ship's company for refusing to take their turn at the pump for one night, should swear, that at no time during the remaining part of the voyage they should take their turn at the pump, even though they repented of their negligence, and shewed a disposition afterwards to share in the toils or danger of the voyage?"[36]

Aedanus Burke, a South Carolina judge, proposed a comprehensive defense of an institutional strategy. In 1783 he urged the repeal of new legislation penalizing the estates and restricting the political rights of men who had collaborated with the British occupation authorities between 1778 and 1781.[37] In the winter of 1782–83, the state of South Carolina was a deeply divided community, still on the edge of violence.[38] Burke articulates a jurist's understanding of the theoretical arguments for an institutional strategy, and he suggests two quite different justifications for such a strategy. He uses the two arguments cumulatively, and seems to have sensed no tension between them. The arguments are, however, distinct in both their assumptions about political community and their implications for political obligation, and they imply two different standards of memory in a transitional setting. The first argument minimizes political obligations, and therefore political guilt, by minimizing the moral importance of political community. This argument is atypical of the reconciliation debate in America; in its failure to define the abandonment of republican values as a culpable act, it illustrates the danger that an institutional strategy can present to democratic legitimacy if pushed too far. The second argument posits political community as a morally important fact, but advocates the reintegration of former adversaries as the precondition of a free community. This argument reappears again and again as an element of successful institutional strategies, in America and elsewhere.

On the first argument, political membership is defined by a set of highly limited contractual relations between the state and each individual citizen or subject. The citizen/subject enters the political community in order to obtain physical safety. He thus trades obedience for protection, and retains at all times the right to judge whether or not the protection he gets justifies the obedience he gives. His sole motive for entering into political society is fear. Self-preservation is both a natural right and a duty, and so as soon as the state withdraws its protective shield or becomes incapable of providing security, the citizen is released from his obligations. He is entitled, even enjoined, to seek protection from whatever power he thinks is most likely to provide it.

Individuals who pledge allegiance to a conquering foreign army or to a triumphant domestic faction are, in this account, morally and politically blameless. In retrospect, their decision may seem hasty, imprudent, or foolish—but never dishonorable, unfaithful, or treasonous. Political society is here conceived as held together from the top down, and it is purely instrumental in nature. Self-government is not a moral asset whose preservation might compete with physical security for priority.

Once the vertical bonds between protector and protected are broken, there are, in this account, no residual horizontal bonds between members of civil society. Members of a political society share nothing but the need for protection—that is, they all fear, but they do not trust. Ignoring Locke, Burke cites Hobbes's claim that "sovereignty is the soul of the commonwealth, which once departed from the body, the members do no more receive their motion from it," and then extends the argument: "Our inhabitants did nothing more than their duty in taking protection [from the British] . . . The sovereign power was in a state of temporary death, the soul was fled and departed, and nothing remained but the carcass; which could no more be injured or violated by any of our former citizens taking protection, or signing a congratulation, than they could be said to commit murder by trampling on the body of a man who had been dead and buried many months."[39] This account fully exculpates citizens who submit to a victorious political enemy—provided, presumably, that they trample on nothing more sentient than a carcass. The soul of the citizen is wholly separate from the soul of the state; if the state is reduced to a "carcass," the citizen should fear for his possessions, not his soul, and certainly not for the carcass. Burke still does not include taking up arms for the British in his list of permissible acts. In German terms, he offers excuses for *Mitläufer* but not for perpetrators.

Where there is no crime, punitive measures have no place. Should a new government adopt such measures, Burke supplies additional grounds on which to reject them. Political prosecutions in general, and ex post facto prosecutions in particular, generate fear and uncertainty among the citizenry. They therefore violate the basic purpose of political society, Burke says, which is to eliminate insecurity. They are wrong both because they create a crime where there was no offense, and because they destroy the reputation the state may have acquired as a reliable provider of security—the only legitimacy to which a state can aspire. The adoption of arbitrary legislation is by definition a subversive act.

The argument from protection is Burke's primary argument. He uses it to condemn the punishment of past political commitments and to plead for political accommodation. Burke cites author upon author—Machiavelli, Blackstone, Bodin, Grotius, Pufendorf, and of course Hobbes—in its defense. Most of the authorities he cites are preliberal or nonliberal thinkers: their words serve Burke's purposes precisely because this argument focuses on the duties of voluntary political subjects rather than on the loyalties and obligations of democratic citizens. In Burke's view, revolutionary South Carolina had witnessed a great deal of violence (which the judge hoped would soon be forgotten), but no political *crime* whose memory might be worth preserving for the future instruction of republican citizens. Burke solves the problem of punishment (and avoids the problem of memory) at the price of dismissing the idea that politics is an arena in which all of us as citizens define, express, and seek to protect not only our physical possessions but also and above all certain moral values. Pushed to this extreme, an institutional strategy can confuse positive law with justice, and fail to take individual moral agency and democratic citizenship seriously.

Burke was, however, writing in the context and in the service of a republican revolution, and intertwined with the argument from protection, his pamphlet suggests an argument for an institutional strategy compatible with democratic citizenship. This second argument openly advocates a politically motivated form of deliberate forgetfulness. Republican government, Burke argues, rests on trust (among citizens, and between citizens and their government), pride, and political equality. The prosecution of political commitments made under a past political regime subverts all three prerequisites of republican government and is therefore inconsistent with republican statesmanship.

Participatory political arrangements require trust among the participants, and the need for trust precludes the use of political justice as a tool of republican government.[40] In a republic, trust—trust-as-reliability—is based on the certainty that constitutional provisions protecting the individual will be respected, no matter how contentious political life becomes (and Burke reminded his readers that political life in a republic is likely to be very contentious). Constitutional protections guarantee that political competition will never endanger the security of persons and possessions. The punitive legislation passed by the Assembly, Burke noted, destroyed the fundamental guarantees on which participatory government rests: by both creating crimes after the fact and violating the right of the accused to a fair trial, the new laws greatly increased the potential costs of political participation while making the nature of the costs unpredictable. The legitimation of political justice meant that political defeat might now have lethal consequences. In the politically flammable atmosphere of 1782–83, the recourse to ex post facto legislation, "which even in arbitrary governments is reckoned tyranny," confirmed Burke in his opinion that political justice is simply masked revenge, "hostility under the shape of justice." Revenge does free government less harm, Burke thought, when it is wrought openly, "in a mobbish way, or by force of arms." In a war, no one expects to trust the enemy, "but our Assembly very peaceably, under the mask of justice, and under the forms of parliament, condemned the citizens in the violation of the spirit and substance of both."[41]

The open-ended character of the punitive legislation would invite abuse by unscrupulous men eager to settle private accounts behind the cloak of indignant patriotism. The laws would threaten more men than were ever likely to be prosecuted, but since the rules of due process had been set aside, men would not wait to be accused before taking measures to protect themselves. Denied the protection of the law, they would seek safety outside the law, in subversive and conspiratorial activity.

The situation would soon escape the control of those who had created it. In the short run, political trials might seem to serve the republic by expeditiously removing its enemies. In the long run, Burke warned, constitutional norms once violated are not easily reestablished. Political justice would introduce the habits of civil war into the politics of the peacetime republic. If the balance of political power shifted, men who now saw only the advantages of political trials might have occasion to regret their choice. Then, Burke wrote, "the sheets on which those [punitive] laws are written, may wrap in winding-sheets some of their descendants."[42]

Having made the republican case against retroactive legislation and political prosecutions, Burke entered another argument against punishment, cautioning against any measure that impugned the virtue of the people. This argument explicitly recommended obscuring the past commitments of individuals in order to undergird the new call to citizenship. Undermining the self-confidence and pride of a free people is, Burke wrote, "a most mischievous policy." He continued, "It breaks that spirit, and generous pride, which is the best guardian of public liberty and private honour. It overwhelms the public as well as the private mind, with conscious inferiority; degrades men in their own opinion, and renders them fit tools for the ambitious designs, and arbitrary dispositions of haughty aspiring superiors." If some South Carolinians had acted dishonorably under the British, Burke argued, it would be in the interest of the republic to "cover over any stain of dishonour" rather than "lay them under the condemnation of treachery to their country."[43] People live up to the expectations we have of them: men whose reputations have been ruined will have nothing to lose by acting badly. Republics require free moral agents confident of their own, and one other's, ability and inclination to act well. Burke argued, in short, that it is better for a new democratic community to have fictitious honor than no honor, better a solid public form of trust (as reliability) than an uncertain if more complete form of trust (as trustworthiness).

Finally, if past political commitments are made actionable, Burke noted, someone must judge. If some citizens are allowed to sit in judgment on the political virtue of other citizens, and this to prosecute crimes defined after the fact, what will prevent the judges from first arrogating to themselves a tutelary authority over their fellow citizens, and then slipping logically toward tyranny? What will prevent the part of the population branded as traitors from rising in rebellion? Self-government requires the assumption of political equality; dividing the community into a virtuous segment with full political rights and an unvirtuous segment deprived of its rights would destroy the republic.

Burke may have understood his two arguments—the argument from protection, and the argument that justifies forgetting the past actions of individuals—to address different political moments. The first argument provides a code of conduct applicable before, during, and after the breach of a prior political contract, but it is of limited usefulness to citizens who take their political obligations and commitments seriously, regardless of the circumstances in which they find themselves. It lays the foundation for the argument that any conduct apparently consistent with a dominant legal-political order is permitted simply because an established order promotes it. In the American states through which competing armies had marched, protection had been notoriously unreliable. Yet what could be called the "no protection–no allegiance" argument was infrequently used, even by Patriots who argued for institutional strategies and the adequacy of negative liberty in the peacetime republic: apparently it did not reflect a widely accepted understanding of the meaning of citizenship in postrevolutionary America, and it would not be better received today. The argument against punishment and in favor of forgetting acknowledges the moral importance of self-government, but Burke applies it only after a legitimate democratic government has been restored or created; he does not even use it to propose a retroactive code of conduct for citizens in countries where constitutional government has collapsed. It defends an institutional strategy as the least noxious of the available options: the alternatives, Burke asserts, are inherently dangerous and inconsistent with republican government. The argument tells us that men who are treated as pariahs will not act honorably; in the name of the republic, it demands that the past be recast in myth and/or shrouded in forgetfulness. The argument does not, however, meet the need of the new regime to legitimize itself and delegitimize its past competition. It does not tell us whether the acts we condemn as dishonorable in fact merit our moral censure. Here, too, it points democratizing elites toward hazardous territory. It limits the extent to which the new community is likely to use the second chance offered by an institutional strategy as an opportunity to start over.

Alexander Hamilton incorporated the different levels of obligation appropriate to different situations into his brief for an institutional strategy, and avoided many of the difficulties Burke's arguments posed. Instead of minimizing the public obligations of citizens, Hamilton distinguished between revolutionary enthusiasm and the inevitably interested character of conduct typical of politically normal times, and insisted on the radical nature of the political rupture the Revolution represented:

> It was the policy of the revolution, to inculcate upon every citizen the obligation of renouncing his habitation, property, and every private concern for the service of his country, and many of us have scarcely yet learned to consider it as less than treason to have acted in a different manner. But it is time we should correct the exuberances of opinions propagated through policy, and embraced from enthusiasm; and while we admit, that those who did act so disinterested and noble a part, deserve the applause and, wherever they can be bestowed with propriety the rewards of their country, we should cease to impute indiscriminate guilt to those, who, submitting to the accidents of war, remained with their habit[at]ions and property. We should learn, that this conduct is tolerated by the general sense of mankind; and that according to

that sense, whenever the state recovers the possession of such parts as were for a time subdued, the citizens return at once to all the rights, to which they were formerly entitled.[44]

The Revolution was over, but the republic still had work to do: liberty had to be secured against new challenges from new quarters, and national greatness and prosperity demanded the energies of all available hands. Old Whig ideology had taught that resistance was justified if—but only if—authority was despotic. The war had necessarily muffled the voice of the law, and years of civil strife had released "the spirit of private revenge, and private assassination." The advocates of an institutional strategy argued that a policy of retribution and punishment against the Tories, by encouraging people to think and behave as though the Revolution were still in progress, would promote licentious conduct, and so be more dangerous to the republic than the Tories themselves could ever be. It would, Burke argued, be "a dishonour to the Revolution." He criticized the "retaliating spirit" that would "keep up the distinction of whig and tory when the cause of it is done away," and attributed the "paltry, wretched policy of worrying each other by mutual hatred, and mutual revenge," to "silly passions."[45]

The Revolution was over, the proponents of institutional strategies argued, both because the Tories had lost the ideological contest and because the republic had effectively reestablished civil authority; in 1983 Hermann Lübbe would make a similar argument about the legacy of the Third Reich (see Chapter 3). However deep disagreements might once have been, they were now irrelevant and self-defeating. The Revolution was over, Burke argued, and the republic had to move on: he saw no need need to look "so far back" as even a few years. "Looking so far back, and bringing on violent enquiries about what was done two or three years ago, prevents the Government from applying a remedy to that which is amiss at present. The rulers of this country, without looking so far back, will have work enough to govern it, and obviate the mischiefs which time and chance will bring about.[46]

The skeptical believed that "time and chance" would simply reintroduce old mischiefs. Less skeptical, the advocates of institutional strategies believed it more prudent to focus on new mischiefs. The possibility that old mischiefs might not recur made possible a new, noncyclical vision of political change. "A Patriot" summarized the conciliatory senti-ments espoused by those who urged institutional strategies. He allowed that his memories of the Tories' conduct still made him feel indignant, "but their disappointment is their sufficient punishment; and nothing is more ridiculous than those idle apprehensions which some affect to feel from their machinations: if America stood firm against the force of Great Britain, aided by the influence of these people, what is to be apprehended from their secret practices now?"[47]

Both sides scored points. Loyalists who remained in or returned to Amer-ica eventually bought forgiveness with public contrition and good be-havior. Anti-Loyalist legislation lapsed or was repealed. Loyalism as a political choice was never rehabilitated, and as a model for the politics of the future, it was never even proposed. The legislative solutions to the Loyalist question were often untidy, but the political results helped seal the revolutionary settlement. In any assessment of the impact of the Loyalist debates on the development of American political ideology and institutions, this untidiness is worth remembering. Minimal and maxi-mal claims on the loyalties of citizens coexisted. The complexities of this solution remained typical of the liberal tradition in America, and thus characteristic of the political self-understanding of most Americans. The ambiguities are perhaps best expressed by Benjamin Rush, who in argu-ing against the maintenance of Pennsylvania's Test Act asserted in 1784–85 that "taxes, and a peaceable submission to all such laws as are not contrary to dictates of conscience, should always be considered as the morality of citizenship," but who three years later claimed, "the revolu-tion is not over!" and declared: "Every man in a republic is public prop-erty. His time and talents—his youth—his manhood—his old age—nay more, life, all, belong to his country."[48] These ambiguities notwithstand-ing, by the end of the 1780s, the dominant logic was an institutional logic. The coalitions that formed around the cluster of issues raised by the Loyalist debate extended through the constitutional debates of 1787–1789, and the federal Constitution embodies the principles initially ar-ticulated by advocates of an institutional strategy of reconciliation. The result, as has been noted too often to warrant repeating, was the consoli-dation of a new kind of republic, one that could be maintained in a large territory with a diverse, competitive population intent on pursuing pri-vate goals.

The Limits of Forgetting

Institutional strategies stress the adequacy of trust-as-reliability as the basis for the everyday operation of a republic. Institutional strategies themselves demand a certain kind of shared self-confidence. They ask a political community to bet together on the consolidation of democratic institutions, and the common bet, rather than shared substantive values, serves as the initial basis of political trust.

In post-Terrorist France the conflicts were too multiple, the blood was too fresh, the competing ideologies were too intact, and the warring parties remained too well organized to make the required bet seem plausible—and no external power stood ready to compensate for the unfavorable domestic circumstances. In many ways, post-Terrorist France would seem to represent the worst-case scenario for advocates of an institutional strategy. For this reason it might not appear a promising choice for extended analysis. It does, however, offer a unique window on a historical case where reconciliation strategies had to take into account a multiplicity of politically dubious pasts (prerevolutionary as well as Terrorist), where a proto-totalitarian dictatorship had placed itself squarely within the then still young Western democratic tradition, and where the "old regime" was toppled from within. The first and last factors multiplied the difficulties of creating a stable coalition. The second factor, however, speaks most directly to the problems of post-communist transitions. How was post-Terrorist France to throw out the dictatorial bathwater without losing the democratic baby? The Jacobins had never repudiated the values, the goals, or even the institutions of the liberal revolution they sought to complete, and yet the politics they created before and while they were in power can meaningfully be termed criminal. On what basis could non-Terrorists and former Terrorists make a common bet on the future? Assessing the complex revolutionary past proved particularly challenging to contemporary actors—as assessing an even more complex, but in many ways comparable, mix of intentions and actions would prove challenging to actors in post-communist political communities.

Robert Lindet was a veteran revolutionary. From 1789 to 1795, from the meeting of the Estates General to the beginning of the Directory, three parliamentary bodies succeeded one another at the center of French political life: the Constituent Assembly, the Legislative Assembly, and the Convention. The first body emerged from the Estates General; it declared the Rights of Man in the summer of 1789 and drafted the constitution that was intended to establish a constitutional monarchy. The Legislative Assembly convened in Paris in the early fall of 1791, in the uneasy aftermath of the king's abortive flight to the border; during its tenure, war was declared, the moderates around Barnave lost control of the Revolution, and the Girondins were purged. The Convention first met on September 21, 1792, after months of street unrest and in an atmosphere of latent civil war. The Terror (including the trial and execution of Louis XVI) followed; the period was dominated by the Jacobins, by the Convention's so-called Committee of Public Safety, and in particular by Robespierre. Robespierre was overthrown by opponents within the Convention in July 1794 and immediately killed.

Lindet sat in both the Legislative Assembly and the Convention. He had been elected to the Committee of Public Safety on April 7, 1793, and had remained on the Committee during Robespierre's tenure. His personal stake in reconciliation was therefore very different from that of Aedanus Burke, who had never offered his services or his congratulations to the British. The man who most forcefully made the political case for an institutional strategy of reconciliation in the months after Thermidor was a revolutionary activist pleading his own cause: in contemporary terms, he resembles a semi-respectable leader of a semi-transformed successor party (Aleksander Kwasniewski in Poland, for example, or Gregor Gysi in Germany or F. W. de Klerk in South Africa), but in a context of extreme institutional uncertainty. With Carnot, Lindet was among the least compromised of the members of the "Grand Comité," but he did not repudiate his own revolutionary record, and after Thermidor he consistently defended former members of the Committee whose Terrorist commitments had been far more extensive than his own.[49] On 3 Sans-culottide Year II (September 19, 1794), two months after Robespierre's fall, Lindet was still a member of the Committee of Public Safety, and it was in the Committee's name that he rose in the Convention to deliver a general report on the political state of the country.[50] In his speech, Lindet outlined a political strategy for "ending" the Revolution and consolidating constitutional government.

Lindet's speech is in many ways an impeccable and thorough brief for an institutional strategy. But it is clearly the brief of a man whose soul belonged to the Revolution, and whose biography was indissolubly tied to the Revolution's most lethal phase. No more promising spokesman for such a strategy was available: Terrorist repression, the heterogeneous character of the Thermidorian coalition, and the dominant political culture of the Revolution ensured that no major revolutionary leader untainted by Terrorist politics would be present in the fall of 1794 to argue for an institutional strategy. Lindet's political identity complicated the argumentative approach he adopted; so too did the mixed identity of his audiences. Lindet made not just the usual and necessary case for some kind of forgetting; he also urged a *type* of forgetting that reflects his own involvement in the events he reviewed. He defined away the criminal character of the Terror itself. While a period of forgetting is inherent to an institutional strategy, this particular kind of forgetting is not. Instead, it compromised whatever slim chance an institutional strategy might have had in post-Thermidorian France. In America, in France and Germany after 1945, and even to some extent in Spain after Franco's death, the politically criminal character of past political commitments was explicitly reaffirmed, even as the past commitments of individuals were often overlooked and the extent to which those commitments were representative of a society as a whole was denied. To the extent that this decoupling between the delegitimation of a regime and the condemnation of its supporters takes place, institutional strategies are not based on the moral ambivalence of which they are often accused. On the contrary, they may become untenable if their advocates *do* base them on a morally ambivalent assessment of the old regime. Lindet could not articulate the necessary decoupling, not just because the events were too recent, and not just because he was too deeply implicated in the events, but because he saw no way to condemn the Revolution's course without condemning its initial values and goals: liberty, equality, fraternity. Two centuries later, similar complications would arise in the wake of communist dictatorships.

Lindet made the case for reconciliation to a political elite whose reputation was at least as compromised as his own, but he also addressed oppositional groups at both ends of the political spectrum whose defeat was not yet definitive. The re-creation of a political community would require the cooperation of all. Speaking for revolutionary continuity to elites in whose ranks he stood, Lindet urged unity and political tolerance on his comrades; speaking for victims of whom he was not one, he preached a brand of forgetfulness that denied the defining characteristics of Terrorist politics. To Lindet, historical memory seemed imprudent because it would undermine support for the new regime; it seemed morally undesirable because, by diminishing the base of support for free government, it would endanger the moral future of the community and its members. "Reason and the public interest [*le salut de la patrie*]," Lindet argued, "do not permit you to glance back at ruins you have moved beyond" (23).

Lindet's proposed strategy for stabilizing a revolutionary settlement that would durably establish freedom rested on an account of the revolutionary past: that account absolved the Revolution in general and the Convention in particular of moral responsibility for the Terror. Republican stability, Lindet in effect argued, required an attitude of moral neutrality toward the Revolution's Terrorist past. He sought to defuse elite divisions and demobilize lesser political actors by vaunting the Revolution's successes and then, by emphasizing the Revolution's alleged achievements, to justify a redefinition of the political agenda. By refocusing energies on private activities, Lindet thought it would be possible to lower the stakes of politics. He hoped the result would be to broaden the possible circles of political cooperation, and so create enough room for constitutional government and new political practices to develop.

The construction of Lindet's narrative reflects his need to reduce the visibility of the Terror, to restore the political confidence of the people, and to shore up the legitimacy of the Convention. The Terror was not, for Lindet, the defining episode of the Revolution, and he did not begin his speech with its history. Rather, he began by affirming that in a Europe dominated by despots, only a strong nation could aspire to freedom. Revolutionary France had acquired the strength necessary to her survival, Lindet asserted, simply by virtue of her liberal political agenda: liberty and equality had engendered solidarity, courage, and resourcefulness. After 1789, each citizen had a clear stake in the nation and an interest in its defense.

The people, understood as a free association of autonomous individuals, are the heroes of Lindet's account. Repeatedly, Lindet assured the people of their political maturity, independence, and virtue—qualities that he, like Aedanus Burke, knew a republic required. Lindet presented revolutionary discipline—"the sublime reason of the people, who have willingly endured so many hardships" (19)—as coming from below, not above. By implication, he argued that France was fully prepared for political freedom, requiring neither a royal Louis nor a revolutionary Saint-Just.

Misfortune had nonetheless struck. In the midst of popular heroism and conscientious public service, disunity had cast its long shadow over the Revolution. Lindet laid responsibility for this disunity at the door of the Girondins. In September 1794, as Lindet spoke, the Gironde's proscribed defenders had not yet been readmitted to the Convention. Far from recommending the rehabilitation of purged revolutionary leaders, Lindet's argument for reconciliation—the terms on which he proposed to reestablish a political community—implied their continued disgrace. Their innocence would have made their judges guilty, and so compromised the legitimacy of prominent political players on whose power and cooperation Lindet's strategy depended. Lindet portrayed the Girondins as an ambitious, self-absorbed, irresponsible faction (19), and accused them of corruption, the only political crime he ever clearly identified.

The country, Lindet explained, had been disoriented by the multiplicity of signals emanating from its elites, and the Revolution's enemies had naturally taken advantage of the conflicts that ensued. Now the Convention moved to the forefront of his account. Having rescued the people from responsibility for the Terror, Lindet sought to restore the reputation of the Revolution's institutional anchor. With chaos threatening, the decisive actions taken by the assembly had reminded people of their duties, saving the Revolution from internal destruction and the nation from external conquest.

The Convention, Lindet noted approvingly, had responded to the emergency created by the Girondins first by drafting a constitution (the Constitution of 1793, which was never applied), and then by giving the nation the institutional means it required for its political self-defense. Lindet evoked only "a plan of surveillance," which he called "wise and necessary" (19); he did not speak explicitly of revolutionary government (although Tallien had already analyzed the Terror as a system, implicitly and explicitly linking its development to revolutionary government),[51] nor did he name the three "comités de gouvernement," of which the Committee of Public Safety had been the most powerful. He did not use the word "terror" until he got to the events of Thermidor.

In overthrowing Robespierre, the Convention had saved France from divisions provoked by Jacobin leaders who, like the Girondins before them, had abused their talents and their revolutionary record (20). Robespierre and his executed co-conspirators were guilty, Lindet argued, of using power for purposes other than those for which it had been granted to them—not of creating an inherently vicious political system. Like the Girondins, they had used public power for private ends. Unchecked, the atmosphere of division, demoralization, and self-doubt created by Robespierre would have destroyed the foundations of freedom. But the Convention had been saved by its own courage and—once again—by "a great nation, cognizant of its rights, its interests, the laws of nature and reason" (20).

Lindet used his account of the Revolution to line up support within the revolutionary camp. Any strategy for ending the Revolution, however, required a much broader coalition. To win the cooperation of less radicalized or committed actors, Lindet tried to reorient the revolutionary agenda. Here Lindet had both to satisfy his revolutionary audience that he remained faithful to the cause and to persuade the politically disaffected that they would benefit from the Revolution's new direction. It was not an easy task.

Lindet recalled that the purpose of the Revolution had been to enable each individual to define and pursue his own life plan. The republic, according to Lindet's argument, is both our shared enterprise and our common home. Its moral character makes it a shared enterprise, and makes us all, always, accountable to ourselves and to one another for its fate. But while we win and preserve freedom together, we enjoy it alone; like Hamilton, Lindet made a fundamental distinction between revolutionary and "normal" political life. Freedom, once achieved, means the right to pursue private goals without the interference of public authority. Mere membership in the republic, Lindet argued, must create a presumption of trust: citizens owe one other automatic respect and solidarity. Lindet used negative liberty both to make the present irrelevance of past commitments seem plausible and to characterize the normal political life of the republic. The time for political mobilization had passed. Governing, he argued, should be left to the nation's elected representatives, who "alone will lead revolutionary actions" (24).

Individuals were entitled to their private lives, and the community was entitled to the prosperity and international prestige that private initiative would produce. Lindet sought to make reconstruction and economic greatness the new regime's primary goals. The "nonideological" goal of prosperity would draw the Revolution's "semi-friends and semi-enemies" first into grudging cooperation with the new regime, and then steadily into a more fundamental acceptance of the new order: Lindet's argument for political tolerance anticipates Bukharin's political defense of the New Economic Policy.[52] A productive individual would qualify automatically as a good citizen; his economic actions constituted his "public" life, whereas his political views and past were his private affair. Lindet recited the long list of French cities (beginning with devastated Lyon) whose productive capacities had been compromised by years of revolutionary strife. "Let your laws and institutions summon men to work," he then urged the Convention. "Let all useful and productive men be assured of their liberty and their independence; let work be honored and sloth shamed" (21).

Economic reconstruction and progress would provide past adversaries with a common project and France with a peaceful means of asserting her international strength. Without directly attacking the political justification for the Jacobins' expansion and centralization of power in 1793–94, the adoption of economic productivity as a national goal would also provide a rationale for reducing the swollen functions and powers of government, since Lindet clearly envisaged economic expansion based on private initiative.

Lindet reminded his revolutionary comrades that free men judge other free men by what they do, not by who they are. Little good would come of raking up the prerevolutionary lives ("so far back," Burke might have said) of citizens whose current conduct gave no offense: "Do not inquire into the illusions that surrounded their cradle, or the prejudices of caste or profession that they have served under the despotism" (20). And he repeated: "Think only about what remains to be done" (23). In concrete terms, Lindet's insistence on inclusion meant the immediate restriction of the power of local authorities to refuse citizens their *"certificats de civisme."* Lindet recognized the need to restore political equality as well as trust, and he repeatedly asserted that the triumph of the Revolution must create a presumption of civic capacity among all citizens, as though each individual past, whether royalist or Terrorist, had passed away with the political structures that had shaped it.

Tyrants destroy, Lindet argued; the policy of free governments is to include as many people as possible in their guarantees of security. A successful revolution, instead of jealously reserving its benefits for the politically pure, should pride itself on the number of free riders it can attract: "It is not for yourselves alone that you founded a republic; it is for any Frenchman who wants to be free; you are permitted to exclude only the bad citizen" (21).

By whitewashing "the people" and the Convention, Lindet cultivated a political fiction, but another version of the same fiction could have accommodated more memory—or, more accurately, a different kind of memory. A different discourse was at least theoretically compatible with the broad coalition Lindet sought to build. Benjamin Constant, who had a political interest but no personal stake in affirming the honor of past revolutionary actors, recognized the folly of dragging the Convention through the mud of its previous commitments: "It is by praising men that one pushes them to do good," he argued; "it is by appearing persuaded that they cannot refrain from acting well, that one forces them to act well."[53] The moral tensions in Lindet's account arise not in conjunction with his characterization of revolutionary actors but in his assessment of revolutionary acts. Constant, while seeking to co-opt the Convention, still spoke of the Terror and pleaded forcefully against the recourse to arbitrary government and political justice. Lindet did not. That it should fall to a Terrorist to justify forgiving other Terrorists was unfortunate. That the Terrorist in question should seem to minimize the enormity of what had happened undermined both the moral legitimacy and the political plausibility of his proposals. Lindet was trapped by his insider status within a revolutionary tradition whose continuity he sought to maintain; we will soon see his contradictions reproduced by people acting in democratizing settings far more promising than post-Thermidorian France.

Lindet did not deny the possibility of criminal political commitments, and he never marshaled the arguments customarily used to excuse them. For example, he never argued that revolutionary actors who had participated in the Terror but survived the proscriptions of Thermidor had previously been forced to chose between following Robespierre's lead and forfeiting their own lives, and his argument is too resolutely secular to include any allusions to the alleged inner depravity of man (or to the adequacy of divine justice). It is clear from his account that he considered the legacy of the Terror to be the chief obstacle to a successful revolutionary settlement. But he consistently declined to characterize the Terror as a morally and politically unacceptable form of government. In his account, Robespierre had indeed betrayed the Revolution, but the Terror was simply part of an unbroken and unimpeachable revolutionary process.

Criminal behavior is defined in Lindet's speech solely by the *motives* of the actor, not by the act itself: "the mistakes, the errors, even the abuses of power and arbitrary acts" were not to be confused with "the crimes of cowardice and greed" (24). Insofar as this distinction provides a definition of political criminality, it decriminalizes precisely what set the Terror apart from other forms of government and made it such a politically and morally destructive episode. Corruption can (and does) happen under any regime, particularly in times of war, but for Lindet it was a crime; arbitrary acts in the service of the Revolution were simply errors—or a cover for corruption. Where they could be considered "errors," the end so effectively explained and excused the means that Lindet saw no need to focus on the means. What was past was past. Lindet did not want to encourage a reexamination of Jacobin ideology, and he explicitly rejected the possibility of rehabilitating the Girondins, much less their more moderate predecessors. His reticence is easily explained, both politically and personally, but it locked his strategy in contradictions.

Nothing was to be gained, Lindet argued, from treating as actionable offenses "the ills [*maux*] inseparable from a great revolution" (21). Men who had (like the "antifascists" who governed East Germany) conscienciously fulfilled their revolutionary duties deserved thanks and compassion, not condemnation: "They defended the sacred cause of liberty, and in stormy times, they used a great power which necessity had created" (20). If they had been overzealous in defending the Revolution, their "errors" should be forgiven and only their zeal remembered. Into an account which otherwise stressed the role of revolutionary voluntarism, Lindet here introduced the notion of historical necessity. It was a historical dynamic, not base fear or respect for orders from above, which had prompted revolutionaries to make commitments they might now regret. Revolutions bring hard choices to all participants, Lindet admitted, but he asked all who had ever wished the Revolution well, and all who might now recognize their stake in its conclusion, to draw the curtain on their sorrows and their anger and perhaps their shame: "The revolution is over; it is everyone's accomplishment. What general, what soldier has done in battle only what needed to be done, and has known how to stop where cool, calm reason would have had him stop? Were we not at war against a most numerous and fearsome enemy?" (23).

Lindet apparently believed that he could not denounce the Terror more specifically without indicting the leadership of the Convention and destabilizing a political situation it was his purpose to stabilize. Perhaps he believed that a stable regime would provide far more effective protection against future experiments in arbitrary government than could a more explicit and public understanding of arbitrary government, and that in the France of 1794, stability and such an understanding were mutually exclusive goals. He may have been right. To avoid a clear statement of why the Terror had been criminal, however, was to compromise the ideological identity of the new regime in ways that were both morally troubling and politically impracticable. The approach was morally troubling to anyone who assigned moral priority to individual rights, personal responsibility, and democratic citizenship: would people unable to reflect on the nature of the Terror really understand what freedom required of them? The approach was politically impracticable because it neither vindicated those who had suffered under the Terror nor rewarded (ideologically or symbolically) those who had acted well. Given the continued presence of the Terrorist elite in positions of political responsibility, it could therefore not induce the Terror's diverse adversaries to bet on the consolidation of liberal institutions. The contradictions of Lindet's particular version of an institutional strategy contributed to the overdetermined failure of the Thermidorian project. Memory matters, and in some contexts its distortions can lead to outcomes worse than disappointment. In the next section I examine an institutional strategy in a different context, and in the rest of the book we will watch political actors wrestling with different perceptions of the context in which they are acting.

The Limits of Memory

In the summer of 1944, the retreat of Nazi forces and the creation of the Provisional Government once again raised the problem of reconciliation and moved the relationship between democratic citizenship, constitutional stability, and historical memory to the center of the French political stage.[54] As in 1794 (but not 1783), a republic needed to establish a clear and radical ideological break between itself and the regime it was replacing. The Provisional Government, led by Charles de Gaulle, did what Lindet had been unable to do: it adopted an institutional strategy, permitting and then pursuing limited purges based on a mix of selective memory and political myth but focusing on the re-creation of a republican institutional order. The mix of memory and myth made concessions to individuals and to the society as a whole, but as a rule, the mix did not include ideological concessions to Vichy and/or to Nazism. If post-Terrorist France represents the worst-case scenario for an institutional strategy, post-Liberation France represents one of the most interesting cases. In 1945, the bet for an institutional strategy could plausibly have gone either way: external guarantees were uncertain, and the substantive values of the society were ambiguous.

The Third Republic, created in the 1870s, contested by critics on both the right and the left, and periodically rent by ideological strife—most notably during the Dreyfus affair at the turn of the century and again during the 1930s—had succumbed to the German military offensive in the late spring of 1940. On June 14 the Germans entered Paris; two days later Paul Reynaud, whose government had fled to Bordeaux, submitted his resignation, and on June 17 the new head of the government, Marshal Philippe Pétain, an octogenarian World War I military hero, sued for peace. On July 10 what was left of the National Assembly elected in 1936 voted full powers, including constituent powers, to Pétain, who was to lead a "national revolution." On June 17 Charles de Gaulle, an undersecretary for war in Reynaud's government who had been made a brigadier general in late May, arrived in England. The next day, using British radio facilities, de Gaulle went on the air: the fight, he told his compatriots, was not yet over.[55] For the next four years, de Gaulle sought both to promote French participation in the war against Nazi Germany, and to maintain himself as the leader of that resistance.

During the four years between the armistice of 1940 and the Liberation of Paris in August 1944, the disparate forces that participated in the Resistance—among them communists, conservative Catholic military officers, and republican administrators—came together in an often restive coalition under de Gaulle's leadership. The diversity of the coalition was praised in Louis Aragon's famous poetic eulogy of Gilbert Dru and Gabriel Péri—"Celui qui croyait au ciel / Celui qui n'y croyait pas"[56]— a believer and an unbeliever, a young Catholic *résistant* and a former communist deputy, both executed by the Germans; it was symbolized politically by the republican *préfet* and martyred Resistance leader Jean Moulin, the first president of the Conseil national de la Résistance (CNR) and the liaison between the Free French and the domestic Resistance. The Third Republic had always had to contend with radical opposition from both the communist left and the Catholic right; because the Resistance coalition included both communists and Catholics, it represented a new chance for French republicanism. De Gaulle meanwhile warded off Allied attempts to deal with more pliable would-be representatives of France, principally General Henri Giraud.

At the Liberation, de Gaulle moved immediately to reestablish republican authority, thus defending the integrity of the republic against the designs (alleged and/or real) of both the Communist Party and American occupation authorities. Many Resistance leaders expected him to proclaim the reestablishment of the republic. De Gaulle dismissed the expectation as inappropriate and ideologically dangerous. To make such a declaration, the general argued, would be to concede legitimacy to the Vichy government—something de Gaulle steadfastly refused to do: "I wanted to establish that the State, after hardships that could neither destroy nor subjugate it, had simply come home."[57] Speaking from the balcony of the Hôtel de Ville on August 25, 1944, de Gaulle based an appeal for unity on constructed pride: "Paris! Paris violated! Paris broken! Paris martyred! But Paris liberated! Liberated by herself, liberated by her people with the help of France's armies, with the support and the help of the whole of France, of the France that fights, of the only France, of true France, of eternal France."[58]

In the critical initial months following the Liberation, the coalition forged in the Resistance held—a briefly hopeful interlude before the disappointment described in *Les Forêts de la nuit*. De Gaulle himself refused to join a party, preferring to cast himself as the representative of the nation united; his tripartite government was supported by the new Christian Democratic party (MRP), whose republican, socially progressive leadership was drawn primarily from the ranks of Catholic *résistants,* the Socialist Party (SFIO), still under the reformist leadership of Léon Blum and his allies, and the Communist Party (PCF), not yet once again rigidly Stalinist. In the first postwar elections, these parties together won nearly threequarters of the vote.

The coalition was quickly disrupted by disagreements over constitutional issues, and it did not survive the beginning of the Cold War. In conjunction with the constitutional debate (and well before May 1947, when the socialist prime minister, Paul Ramadier, expelled the communist ministers from his cabinet), the coalition became the theater for the debate about reconciliation. As the representative body of the Resistance, the CNR had included the "punishment of traitors and . . . the dismissal from public administration and professional life of all those who cooperated with the enemy or who were actively associated with the policies of collaborationist governments" among the planks of the program it adopted on March 15, 1944.[59] In a few spectacular cases, Resistance justice was rendered before the Liberation: Admiral François Darlan was assassinated in December 1942, Pierre Pucheu (minister of the interior at Vichy from July 1941 to April 1942) was tried and shot in March 1944, just days before the CNR adopted its program, and Philippe Henriot (Vichy's minister of information) was killed at the end of June 1944. In the punitive passages of the CNR program, however, the definition of the important terms—traitor, cooperation with the enemy, "active" association with "collaborationist governments"—was left open, and the debate over their definition, as well as over the appropriate treatment of compromised individuals, was joined in earnest at the Liberation. Politically, the most important actors in the debate were de Gaulle and the Communist Party. The party, whose Resistance units de Gaulle had disarmed or integrated into the reconstituted regular army, and whose representatives in the cabinet had been carefully excluded from positions critical to domestic security, argued vociferously for a vigorous and extensive series of purges. Fearing a destabilizing process of public revenge undesirable in itself and likely to redound to the benefit of the communists, de Gaulle moved to end acts of private retribution and to limit public prosecutions. Meanwhile, the most articulate and intellectually interesting noncommunist critics of the government's policies were Albert Camus and François Mauriac.

Events moved faster than either the debate or the new government: some nine thousand summary executions appear to have been carried out by various Resistance groups during the Liberation,[60] and less drastic punitive measures (for instance, the public humiliation of women who had slept, or who were alleged to have slept, with German soldiers) were widespread.

On March 15, 1945, the still provisional government organized a

Haute Cour de Justice (High Court of Justice) to try the most important treason cases. Pétain was tried from July 23 to August 15, 1945, and condemned to death; his sentence was commuted.[61] Pierre Laval, a formerly republican politician who had been Pétain's prime minister from the disastrous summer of the defeat to December 1940 and the effective head of the government from April 1942 through August 1944, was tried from October 4 to 9, 1945, condemned to death, resuscitated after he attempted to poison himself, and shot by a firing squad. Among collaborationist intellectuals, Robert Brasillach, who had turned himself in at the Liberation, was condemned to death on January 19 and executed on February 6, 1945. Charles Maurras, for decades the influential editor of a reactionary paper, was tried in January 1945 and sentenced to life imprisonment.

Throughout his long political career, de Gaulle consistently asserted the power of institutions to bind political communities and to create positive incentive structures, and thus to offer nations burdened by divisive, undemocratic, and/or unstable pasts a second chance at a stable democratic future. This conviction informed his actions during the war, at the Liberation, and again after he returned to power in 1958. The mixed presidential-parliamentary system of the Fifth Republic, for which de Gaulle had argued unsuccessfully at the Liberation, was intended first to neutralize French political culture—"our old Gallic propensity for divisions and quarrels"—and then to change it: "A day will come, no doubt, when our Constitution, with all that it implies, will have become second nature to us."[62] De Gaulle's hope suggests one account of what in fact happened in the decades that followed the creation of the Fifth Republic: institutions shaped behavior, and over time, the new patterns of behavior produced a new set of expectations and habits different from the set French history had "naturally" produced and reproduced. The new, artificially generated political culture then fed back into the system and supported the institutions that had once created it. The French political system today has many dysfunctional aspects, but they are less uniquely French dysfunctions; they simply demonstrate that France is a "normal" advanced industrial democracy.[63]

The same understanding of the relationship between institutions, political culture, and democratic stability explains de Gaulle's conduct at the Liberation: he focused his energies on institutional consolidation (where his success was only limited), and sought (more durably) to rally public opinion by offering an account of French conduct during the war years that suggested a political community both yearning for and capable of political freedom. "Treason," de Gaulle claimed, "was but an ignoble scum on the surface of a body that had remained healthy." He thought that republican self-confidence—"the best guardian of public liberty and private honour," as Burke had called it—would recover only if large blemishes were hidden, and he asked his countrymen to put their national identity and ambitions before their partisan preferences: "France is made up of all Frenchmen. The country needs, and will perish if it cannot have, the hearts, the minds, the hands, of all its sons and daughters."[64]

The Gaullist myth of a France unanimous in its sympathies for the Resistance, "which in the recesses of its soul never, no never! accepted defeat and humiliation,"[65] has been broadly attacked, particularly by the left: it represents, so the argument runs, a deliberate obfuscation of responsibilities. The criticism collapses, intentionally or unconsciously, the two types of historical memory distinguished earlier in this chapter: it identifies the act of ignoring the politically reprehensible character of the acts committed (Lindet's mistake) with that of forgetting (or feigning to forget) who committed them (de Gaulle's choice). De Gaulle and the component elements of the domestic Resistance had different views of what made certain political commitments undertaken after 1940 criminal, but the Gaullist myth of a *France résistante* did not deny that crimes had been committed. De Gaulle tended to define the offense in terms of treason: the Vichy government had relinquished French independence into the hands of a foreign power—and French collaborationists had applauded and supported that power's victory. Freedom, in de Gaulle's view (and not just in de Gaulle's view), could only be guaranteed by a state; Pétain had not simply repudiated republican values, he had surrendered the structural precondition of political freedom. The domestic Resistance in all its diversity tended, in contrast, to judge wartime commitments in terms of the general value system served: collaboration in all its degrees and forms was criminal because fascism denied human dignity and rights. In either version collaboration was held to be radically illegitimate, and complicitous political indifference was a shameful repudiation of responsibility. De Gaulle, however, was less interested in recalling individual commitments. While he avoided Lindet's error of denying the criminal character of the preceding regime, he also remained silent about the extent to which his compatriots had supported that regime, and he was always reluctant to exclude from the new political community individuals whose pasts were far from unblemished. De Gaulle himself never fell dupe to the myth his approach helped engender: in his *Mémoires de guerre,* he makes abundantly clear how lonely a fight the good fight—animated by "this elite that started with nothing"— often was.[66] His political fiction simply reconstituted a public considered morally capable of free government; it was deliberately conceived and intended as an enabling condition of republican government. It was accompanied by political trials. De Gaulle probably believed that the myth served the republic better than the trials, but the trials, however imperfect their justice and however modest their educational effect, helped keep the country honest.

The republican alternatives to the dominant approach were articulated by two Resistance intellectuals who criticized the posture of the government and insistently recalled the criminal character of fascist values and politics. For democrats who found de Gaulle's fiction unsatisfactory, a choice still had to be made between forgiveness and punishment. The republican argument for forgiveness *and* memory, largely absent in prior historical cases, now appeared, and it was framed in explicitly religious terms. It was contested as representing the inappropriate application of private morality in the public sphere. The philosopher Albert Camus, writing in the columns of *Combat,* made the case for a cultural strategy by defending punishment and political justice, along with memory: if the republic could be *pure* only at the price of being *dure,* he would accept the price—and in fact defend its exaction as a necessary step in the forging of a new political community. The substance of Camus's argument is neither very original nor very interesting; what is interesting is that someone who ought to have known better should have made it. That Camus *did* make it should remind us of the role played by raw emotion in reconciliation debates.

In *Le Figaro,* the Catholic writer François Mauriac, quickly dubbed "St. François d'Assise" by his opponents, urged forgiveness.[67] Both Mauriac and Camus explicitly gave the moral integrity of the republic priority over the immediate expansion its political base. Mauriac's argument for forgiveness simultaneously neutralized the need for punishment and created the psychological space for memory; theoretically, it offered a means around both the exclusionary character of cultural strategies and the forgetfulness of institutional strategies. Through forgiveness, Mauriac suggested, a republic could be *pure* without being *dure*—and he feared that a reforming republic stripped of compassion and hardened against forgiveness would soon turn its back on freedom. Mauriac's argument seems to offer the best of both worlds: the inclusiveness and forward-looking character of institutional strategies, and the attention to memory associated with cultural strategies. It was original, but also politically (or perhaps culturally) unpersuasive.

Forgiveness, Camus argued, would be as fatal to the republic as hatred.[68] The dictates of private morality and the desire for a clear conscience would lead republicans astray. To consolidate the republic, it would be necessary for *résistants* to "know how to speak against their instincts and so renounce their peace of mind," for the moral future of the republic depended on the willingness of Resistance elites to "destroy a living part of this country in order to save its soul."[69] "A country that fails to purge itself is on the way to failing to renew itself," Camus warned.[70] Compassion contradicted the imperatives of public morality, and Camus asserted the priority of the latter: "As a man, I will perhaps admire M. Mauriac for knowing how to love traitors, but as a citizen, I will deplore that ability, because such love will bring us a nation of traitors and mediocrities and a society of the sort we no longer want."[71]

Camus, who is better remembered for his later opposition to the death penalty than for the positions he defended against Mauriac,[72] did not wish to see mass executions, and he reminded his readers that just judges always doubt. He nonetheless argued in favor of retroactive laws and swift justice. "A great nation," he asserted, "rises to the challenge of its own tragedies." The occupation of France by a totalitarian power and the uncertain legal status of Vichy's "État français" had created situations unanticipated by the prewar penal code. As Camus admitted, "There is no law that addresses the form of treason we have all known."[73] If the purges were to serve pedagogical as well as punitive purposes, the code would have to be altered to fit the crime.[74] It would be necessary, Camus argued, for Resistance veterans to "seem unjust in order truly to serve justice."[75] He reaffirmed that he had joined the Resistance to defend a certain conception of man. Men create meaning in an absurd world by their choices.[76] Now Camus used this position to reject Mauriac's religiously motivated plea for charity: "We will refuse until our dying breath a divine charity that would rob men of their justice."[77]

Mauriac's political positions reflected his belief in both the universality of sin and the possibility of redemption. Rigorous justice would never purify the soul of a human community, Mauriac warned, and he cited the Terror of 1793–94 to prove that purity through amputation never amounts to more than a bloody chimera.[78] Honest self-examination by those now crying for justice, Mauriac thought, might temper their eagerness to judge and punish:

> What activist . . . can boast without blushing that he has never sinned against his country?
> . . . Each of us can find in his past enough errors [*erreurs*] to enable him to understand the more serious failing [*faute,* which can also mean "sin"] of others, and to forgive it when the time comes.[79]

Some men, Mauriac conceded, certainly deserved punishment: leaders (like Maurras and Pétain) who had consistently led others astray, and men who had freely denounced other men. But even they rarely deserved to die. Rather, it was the task of the republic to offer "fallen" citizens the opportunity to redeem themselves: it was precisely by refusing to write off any human being as irredeemable that the republic would establish its own moral legitimacy and durably distinguish itself from the totalitarian and authoritarian regimes it fought. The fascist disaster, Mauriac wrote, should have reminded men that respect for human dignity was the precarious achievement of centuries of struggle against instinctive human tendencies toward cruelty and exploitation. He recoiled at the idea of retroactive laws, and saw in Camus's cavalier willingness to adopt them the corrosive effect of four years of fascist rule: "Charity is retreating on all sides, and its absence is creating, among enemies who thought they had nothing in common, a disconcerting uniformity."[80]

On Mauriac's account, political justice was both morally repugnant and politically counterproductive. By resorting to retroactive legislation, the Resistance would betray its own moral identity and push a politically confused nation down the slippery slope toward tyranny. The practice of arbitrary rule would corrupt republican elites, and even the appearance of persecution would alienate a hesitant population. Charity, Mauriac concluded, was both right and politic. He urged forgiveness while continuing to denounce fascism, and without pretending that the Resistance had been a mass movement. His political position was inseparable from his religious convictions: in this story as in others, he believed that the courage, honor, and sacrifice of the few were enough to redeem the indifference, opportunism, and cowardice of the many. Psychologically armed with a New Testament understanding of sin and redemption, he had no need to elaborate a political fiction, and many reasons to favor memory. Forgiveness, he argued, would promote a stable republic whose citizens would be bound to one another by compassion, and to self-government by the intact memory of tyranny.[81]

Neither Camus's plea for toughness nor Mauriac's plea for forgiveness was heeded by the provisional government. Political justice of the sort Camus demanded might well have played into the hands of both the extreme right and the Communist Party, and so destabilized the regime. Mauriac addressed a secular community, but his position is unconvincing, indeed almost incomprehensible, if divorced from the religious beliefs that motivate and justify it. His arguments could not assuage the widespread thirst for vengeance, and in the impassioned atmosphere of the Liberation period, he often seemed to his secular audience to excuse attitudes he meant only to comprehend.

The particular controversy over forgiveness prompted by Mauriac's arguments is worth attention, even though the prominence it gained in the French case is not repeated elsewhere. Political forgiveness is a unique tactic, in that it can be used by the advocates of either an institutional or a cultural strategy; in each case, it constitutes a potential means of neutralizing the primary cost of the strategy. In the case of an institutional strategy, that cost is clouded memory—hindering the types of trust and legitimation that depend on full recall. In the case of a cultural strategy, the cost is exclusion—blocking the kinds of expansive coalitions that depend on integration. For our purposes, the significance of the exchange between Camus and Mauriac lies in its demonstration that forgiveness is unavailable as a political option in contemporary democratizing settings. Democratizing elites can only choose their costs (or their mix of costs); no cost-free strategy is open to them, and the choices will not be easy. Different societies, of course, will bear similar costs differently. In each case, disappointment will be part of the story.

The general argument of this book is that strategies of reconciliation shape the process and results of democratic consolidation through their more immediate impact on patterns of trust, legitimation, and partisan competition. Before we turn to processes of reconciliation in unified

Germany, it is worth reviewing what the cases used in this chapter suggest about the impact of institutional strategies. In each instance, it would seem, such strategies challenge democratic activists to sacrifice a certain kind of straightforward moral integrity. Moral dishonesty—the flouting of justice—is a more serious charge against such strategies than is the fact that they disappoint.

Institutional strategies emphasize trust-as-reliability; their critics answer with the argument—or the psychological conviction—that only trustworthy people will prove reliable when the chips are down. To the critics, Burke's argument (repeated by de Gaulle and many others) that fictitious honor is better for the republic than no honor accepts a hollow, superficial concept of trust, frustrating the demand for a more robust concept. Worse still, it encourages democratizers to treat morally unequal people as political equals, and therefore to insult the memory of those who paid with their persons for their attachment to freedom under the dictatorship. Very few people share the equanimity of Jean-Louis Curtis's character Pierre, and not everyone, as Camus's views illustrate, would find the equanimity admirable. Comrades died, and now the rest of us accept as compatriots those who passively or actively connived in humiliating or torturing or killing our comrades: we greet them on the street, even if we do not invite them home for dinner, and we court their votes at election time, simply because there are so many of them. Or we retreat into angry or sullen intransigence. In either case, can we still look at ourselves in the mirror? Keetenheuve could not.

Institutional strategies limit the emphasis on memory and punishment to the minimum necessary to delegitimize the old regime as a regime and to incapacitate its political leadership. Such strategies avoid calling individuals to account—because too many individuals would feel threatened, and because fictitious honor is assumed to be preferable to no honor. Under these circumstances, the temptation to forget responsibilities, to relativize the fundamental differences between free and unfree regimes, and/or to refuse clear standards in judging behavior that was perhaps "understandable" in the context in which it was committed may become hard to resist: even when men less compromised than Lindet take the lead in promoting institutional strategies, the tendencies evident in Lindet's arguments may reappear. To be forced into a pattern of behavior which suggests that the old regime was not all bad, and that blurs the distinction between those who resisted it and those who, in the words of

"Common Sense," could not "get out of [its] way," seems to many democratizing actors politically dangerous, even when the pattern of behavior is accompanied by a public discourse that officially condemns the old regime.

Finally, institutional strategies have predictable effects on participation, partisan competition, and policy orientations in the new democracy. Institutional strategies are by definition demobilizing political strategies, and they are especially demobilizing if, as is true of revolutionary France, Nazi Germany, or the DDR, the dictatorship was a mobilizing regime that managed to spread its nets of complicity across broad sections of the population: faced with a population shaped by a nondemocratic political culture, institutional strategies choose to demobilize the population rather than try to remobilize it on democratic terms. Democratic activists understand democracy in terms of voluntary and sustained individual participation in politics, and they are disappointed when populations decline the opportunity to assume a share of public responsibility and when leaders devise institutions that discourage political activism and dilute or delay the impact of public pressure on public officials. The perceived abdication of responsibility in favor of charismatic leadership is a further disappointment: like de Gaulle's Resistance critics, democratic activists fear that the leader will compromise on the definition of democratization, and they see in the passivity of the leader's followers the demonstration and perpetuation of a lingering nondemocratic political culture.

Alongside the disappointments associated with demobilization, the agenda pursued by proponents of institutional strategies is almost always perceived as "conservative"—"restorationist," in Dirks's words—by democratic activists who would have preferred to see the incorporation of more elements of a cultural strategy. The new agenda makes too many concessions to the old order, whatever that order was. It reflects the price proponents of institutional strategies are willing to pay in order to transform a minority movement into a majority coalition. Advocates of cultural strategies are disappointed both by the new coalition patterns and by the substantive policy results.

The historical record would seem to provide a powerful empirical argument for institutional strategies, and the success of the strategy is its primary moral defense against the charges of transitory injustice. But most empirical cases can be read in different ways. And because democratization is a complex phenomenon, it can always be argued (in some cases more convincingly than in others) that democratic consolidation occurred *despite* the adoption of an institutional strategy—or at least that the resulting democracy would have been "healthier" or more secure or more compassionate if a cultural strategy had dominated; that a more deeply rooted sense of trust would have facilitated creative dialogue and encouraged habits of compromise among social and political actors; that a less freighted legitimacy would have discouraged political actors from using *Feindbilder* (us-them imagery, in which a definition of the enemy substitutes for a positive definition of the speaker) to rally support; and that a clear break with the past would have freed partisan politics from the fragmenting, polarizing dynamic created by the continued presence of elements inherited from the old regime.

The case of unified Germany, which resonates at every turn against the post-1945 experience, does justice to all the complexities of a complex set of choices.

Two

No Trust, No Democracy:
The Citizens' Movements and the
Reconciliation Debate, 1989–90

The focus of this chapter is on the role played by East German citizens' movements—and specifically New Forum—in the initial stages of the reconciliation debate. Honesty, trust, and notions of democratic merit were central to the movements' understanding of democracy, and they therefore adopted many of the positions associated with cultural strategies. The results can be seen in a complicated story of perceived disenfranchisement and real political marginalization—one scene in a play simultaneously about disappointment and democratization. The marginalization can be understood either as the unintended consequence of unpredicted political events or, more accurately, as a predictable product of the stance adopted by the citizens' movements in the critical months that followed the collapse of communist party control in East Germany.

Democracy from the Bottom Up: Establishing a Civil Society

On January 26, 1993, the Christian Democratic mayor of Berlin, Eberhard Diepgen, welcomed the Bundestag's investigatory commission on the "Aufarbeitung von Geschichte und Folgen der SED-Diktatur" (Working-Through of the History and Consequences of the SED Dictatorship) to Berlin. The Enquete-Kommisssion, chaired by the Christian Democratic deputy and former East German dissident clergyman Rainer Eppelmann, was scheduled to hold two days of public hearings on the "power hierarchy of the SED." In his opening remarks, Diepgen sought to redirect public attention away from the entanglements of private citizens in the security apparatus (Ministerium für Staatssicherheit, or MfS,

59

commonly known as the Stasi)—a "false emphasis"—and toward the "essential thing," the party.[1]

Throughout the forty-year history of the DDR, power had been monopolized, both constitutionally and in fact, by the putatively representative Sozialistische Einheitspartei Deutschlands (SED). The SED had been created in the Soviet occupation zone in April 1946 by the forced amalgamation of the old Communist Party (KPD, Kommunistische Partei Deutschlands) and the Social Democratic Party (SPD). Its "leading role" was consecrated in the first article of the East German constitution:

> The German Democratic Republic is a socialist state of workers and peasants. It is the political organization of workers in city and country under the leadership of the working class and its Marxist-Leninist party.

The SED had thus identified itself in advance as the organization responsible for politics and policy in East Germany. When the DDR collapsed, however, the new democratic actors most immediately sensitive to the problems of recasting the political community did not focus on the party hierarchy itself. Instead, they concentrated their attention on the personnel and activities of the party's self-styled "sword and shield," the MfS. A preoccupation with the "unmasking" of former agents and the determination to expose the organizational structures of the MfS were a particularly important element of the political project of New Forum. New Forum was the largest citizens' movement created in East Germany during the turbulent and eventful autumn of 1989, but it became a major loser in the redistribution of power that took place during the transitional period that followed. The increasingly dominant focus on the Stasi in general, and on unofficial agents (Inoffizielle Mitarbeiter, or IMs) in particular, was thus initially the work of political activists who had spearheaded the fall 1989 revolution in the DDR, but who failed to parlay their early leadership of the citizens' movement into electoral support during the busy election year of 1990.

Like the domestic Resistance in France at the Liberation, so soon so disappointed, the citizens' movement leaders were unable to translate their initial moral prestige into a durable political coalition capable of shaping events, and in Germany the attempt to do so failed much more quickly than in post-Liberation France.

The East German citizens' movements resembled the Resistance in other ways as well: in their internal diversity, in their rejection of traditional lines of left-right cleavage and their distrust of routinized politics, in the tension they noted between justice and the rule of law, and in their belief in the morally and politically transforming character of their own experience. Above all, the two groups were alike in their insistence on the importance of democratic values and in their desire to use the "revolution" in which they had participated to create a republic that would be *pure et dure*. Like Camus, the New Forum activists were convinced that a "country that fails to purge itself is on the way to failing to renew itself." Leading members of New Forum consciously chose and consistently defended a strategy of democratization that rested primarily on cultural change rather than "mere" institutional reform. No trust, New Forum argued, no democracy. Diepgen's effort to focus debate on the party, rather than on the ferreting out of individuals who might at some point have served the MfS, thus went against the grain of three years of public debate and discourse. What Diepgen perceived as a deviation in the public argument about the past is best explained by the citizens' movement's particular understanding of democratic ideology and the response of West German political actors to that ideology, and by the DDR opposition's increasingly marginal position, first in the DDR of 1989–90 and then in unified Germany.

New Forum and other movement activists identified three interdependent sociocultural prerequisites to democratic political development in the DDR: transparency, dialogue, and consensus. Only after these patterns of human relations had been created, the activists believed, could political parties and platforms become viable and relevant expressions of democratic opinion. Political competition could not become the defining process of a free polity unless an organized civil society already existed; neither the process of competition itself nor the traditional competitors—political parties—could create the necessary civil society institutionally, from the top down. Civil society, in turn, presupposed civility, the social habits associated with a culture of mutual respect. Absent such a society and such a culture, the institutional forms of representative democracy would be nothing more than a hollow shell, easily available to be exploited by any group seeking a veil of legitimacy to hide its thirst for power.

These views were not universally held by all members of New Forum, but neither were they confined to members of New Forum—or to East German citizens' movements. It is sometimes hard to tell whether the beliefs owe more to Marx or to Tocqueville, but the concern for civil society was common to democratizing elites in all post-authoritarian settings. If Václav Havel was more eloquent and insistent, and more widely noticed in his appeals for civility, he was by no means alone.[2]

Transparency, dialogue, and consensus were precisely what East German society lacked after nearly three generations of totalitarian rule. "People are simply programmed to think in terms of vertical structures,"[3] a Demokratie Jetzt (DJ, or Democracy Now) activist noted, and Jürgen Fuchs, a dissident writer expelled from the DDR in 1977, deplored the cumulative, uninterrrupted legacy of two dictatorships, focusing specifically on how the years of Nazi and communist dictatorship had made individuals incapable of inner honesty and outward sympathy, trust, and responsibility. "Democracy, parliament, the public, human rights," he remarked, "all that is then mocked, scorned, is 'Western-liberal shit.'"[4]

It was perhaps the writer Christa Wolf, whose own past included so many ambiguities, who most powerfully described the handicap facing those who believed in the immediate necessity of a democratic culture. She recalled an incident that had occurred after a reading of her work. A doctor in the audience had suggested that those present should simply articulate their own opinions.

> In the stillness that followed her words, a woman said softly and sadly: That we never learned. Encouraged to develop her comment, she spoke of the moral-political development of her generation . . . : how they had been raised from childhood on to conform, to stay in line . . . A long-term schizophrenia had hollowed them out as people. So, this woman said, now she could not just suddenly "speak openly" or "say what she thought." She did not even really know precisely what she thought.[5]

Hollow people, citizens' movement activists argued, could not possibly be expected to step unchanged into the role of democratic citizens. Change would have to come from below. In mid-October 1989, a DJ activist put succinctly the political challenge he saw facing democratizing forces in the DDR. Only after a vigorous civil society had developed, Ludwig Mehlhorn argued, "only when this society independent of the state is there and also strong, does it make sense to create political parties." History, he feared, might move too fast, short-circuiting the necessary learning process.[6] Several months—and two elections—later, Wolfgang Templin, a man in his early forties who had once been a party member and a Stasi informant before changing his mind, again empha-sized the problem of grassroots apprenticeship in a historical process that was moving with unexpected speed: "We have a deficit . . . For me the question is: How quickly and deeply can a historical deficit be worked through, at what tempo can political learning processes be completed?"[7]

The question of timing was critical to people who seemed to assume that irrevocable choices were being made: institutional change was pro-ceeding rapidly; cultural change seemed painfully slow; and on both moral and prudential grounds, the ideology of the citizens' movements refused to see the dichronic development as an acceptable feature of a complex and drawn-out democratization process. The second chance would come and go before it could be exploited. In 1948–49 the Federal Republic's founding fathers, cognizant of the deficiencies of German po-litical culture, had opted for institutional structures that preserved de-mocracy through checks and balances and institutional filters between public opinion and decision-making bodies. They settled, that is, for the "hollow shell" whose democratic shortcomings seemed so glaring to citi-zens' movement activists—and whose emptiness had driven the fictional Keetenheuve to suicide. The citizens' movements favored a different ap-proach. Opposition activists did not in general conclude from their ob-servations of the sorry state of east German political culture that a "mod-est" intermediate political goal—the construction of what Marxists had always denigrated as "bourgeois" democracy—might be both morally satisfying and politically exhausting. Even as they deplored the lack of a civil society and the absence of democratic experience, they insisted that Western representative democracy (especially in its West German incar-nation) was not the end of the political road, and that it could be im-proved upon through radical decentralization, consensual decision mak-ing, and direct democracy: "We do not want to repeat the twentieth century, we do not want to copy the landscape of the Federal Republic. We want to develop the political culture of the twenty-first century," declared Jens Reich, a molecular biologist and co-founder of New Fo-rum. [8] Borrowing from both the young Marx's critique of bourgeois de-mocracy and the West German Green or "alternative" ideology of the 1980s, New Forum activists articulated their distrust of power, of the state, and of the neutrality of institutional mechanisms, and their desire to bring to life a new kind of citizen. Again like the Greens, and espe-cially like Marx, they expressed their scorn for German political culture in general and German bourgeois culture in particular, while holding out the possibility of a transformation of daily life in which everyone would come out a moral winner.

The first step in the creation of a civil society, New Forum activists argued, would have to be the establishment of transparency through an ongoing exchange of information. Both the information and the exchange would be crucial. The SED dictatorship had, as the opening sentence of New Forum's first public appeal (under)stated, "obviously disturbed the communication between state and society."9 Through its reliance on secrecy, spying, and ideological discourse, the SED had lost all contact with the political, economic, and human realities of the society over which it presumed to rule. In the process, it had denied East German citizens any easy access to such reality. After decades of illusions, half-truths, and lies, New Forum demanded freedom of information in the broadest sense: information about other human lives and choices, information about the economic and ecological state of the country, information about different political solutions to the crisis at hand. Transparency would allow citizens to deal in realities, in both the public and the private sphere.

Transparency would make possible a genuine dialogue. The idea of a "forum"—like that of a "roundtable"—emphasized the need for honest and common conversation. New Forum was designed to facilitate that conversation by providing "a political platform for the whole DDR that will enable people from all professions, milieus, parties, and groups to participate in the discussion and elaboration of critical social questions."10 In early October 1989, New Forum published not a program but an exhaustive "catalogue of problems" for public discussion.11

Thus, instead of being programmatically united, the Forum saw itself as dedicated to a set of procedural values ("Its members rely on nonviolence, reason, and the power of making arguments")12 which together would contribute to the construction of a democratic community from the bottom up. The dialogue that the Forum sought to facilitate would do more than simply restore the destroyed lines of vertical and horizontal communication; in the process, it would also create feelings of political self-confidence, self-worth, and solidarity among newly empowered citizens. In short, political dialogue would teach citizens the qualities that, in Christa Wolf's informed estimation, they had "not learned." The "round table" mechanism, used across Eastern Europe during the transition period, brought opposition figures, representatives of the regime, and mediators together to discuss problems and options. It was the type of institution New Forum wished to promote.

Movement leaders understood that conflicting interests and ideas would be inevitable in a democracy, and their reading of German history had innoculated them against any attempt to create consensus by appealing to a "German" national interest. Yet forty years of regime-imposed political "struggles" had also left their mark. The movement's self-description as simultaneously suprapartisan and committed to grassroots direct democracy implied a critique of political parties, and that critique in turn suggested a complex and sometimes inconsistent view of political competition organized through a party system and around regularly scheduled elections—even where a mature civil society could be assumed.

Political parties, movement organizers argued, tend to divide citizens while oversimplifying their interests and differences. This perception had no doubt been reinforced by SED practices. Activists feared that parties would prove a breeding ground for intolerance and triviality—both fed by the raw struggle for power—and again emphasized that quiet, open-minded self-confidence and a new kind of human relations were more essential to democratic politics than political parties, which "always succumb to the temptation to inflate third-rate questions in order to get publicity and to mask real questions for which they have no ready answer."[13]

The representation of interests through parties suggested government by elites, increasingly removed from the people they ostensibly represented and the realities their decisions would affect. New Forum, arguing that democracy is "above all daily behavior," pleaded instead "for all forms of direct democracy."[14] The definitional assertion was based in part on a prudential argument derived from experience: "After forty years of tutelary thinking, it is essential that we should no longer delegate our responsibility to parties, but shape politics ourselves."[15]

Empowered citizens engaged in dialogue and acting in good faith would eventually find common ground, and the Forum saw the sense of common ground as both the precondition and the product of cooperative action. Common ground seemed to mean a tolerance based on a sympathetic understanding of unresolved differences: it did not mean unanimity, but it did presuppose some fundamental agreement on moral and procedural principles, arrived at more through common experience than by abstract reasoning. It required much more of the participants than that they abide by a sort of armed truce. It presupposed "common speech," but would emerge from "the common elaboration of political solutions and common action."[16] New Forum seemed to distinguish common ground from both compromise (which it associated with interparty bargaining) and false unity (which it viewed as simply the reverse side of the coin of false divisions and, as such, another danger engendered by party organizations and competition).[17]

Opposition activists argued that political participation would reinforce the moral capacities democracy required—but only if it was fully accepted and fully exercised: "We will be really free only when we take to the streets at any time—and not just once every forty years—on our own initiative, to defend our rights and our dignity. When we do not retreat to niches and say: politics is immoral, but when we take our morality into politics, when we constantly get involved and make the affairs of our society our affairs."[18] Direct democracy, loosely structured by citizens' movements and initiatives, would deprofessionalize politics and keep decision making concrete and close to home. On both counts it would be preferable to the party-dominated, nationalized representative politics typical of Western democracies. In party democracies, Wolfgang Ullmann wrote, "the citizen is excluded from concrete substantive decisions." Citizens' movements, the author of the constitution proposed by the Round Table declared, would "permit the replacement of a spectator democracy by a participatory democracy."[19]

From the beginning, the citizens' movements saw the Stasi issue as integrally tied to the cultural transformation they held to be the central process of democratization. Joachim Gauck associated the significance of his own mission with that link. Gauck, a forty-nine-year-old clergyman from Rostock and an early member of New Forum, became after unification the federal government official in charge of the Stasi archives (quickly and permanently dubbed the "Gauck-Behörde," the Gauck Agency). Gauck played a critical and ongoing role in the unfolding public debate about reconciliation. "It is not enough to have crushed the Stasi," he contended; "we must at the same time liberate ourselves from the chains that bind our souls . . . Just as our souls, when we vacation in a strange land, often arrive late, the feelings and souls of people from the former DDR need a longer time to feel at home in the constitutional framework of a democracy."[20]

Gauck's attention to the files indicated how he thought souls could be speeded down the road to the desired rendezvous with previously unfamiliar democratic institutions. But how much patience was appropriate? Many opposition activists believed that the Federal Republic had waited for the student movement of 1968 before beginning to confront its Nazi past, and they knew that in 1969 Willy Brandt had created a sensation with his pledges to "dare more democracy." New Forum activists believed that the two phenomena were linked: the delayed confrontation with the past had perpetuated a democratic deficit. The patience West German elites had shown in tolerating the delay and the deficit had been misplaced and dangerous, the opposition activists argued. Shortly after the March 1990 elections, the New Forum co-founder and former peace activist Bärbel Bohley outlined the Volkskammer's agenda as she saw it: "The new democracy . . . will be no democracy if we do not deal with our past and its questions." For Bohley, a concrete question focused the issue: "How many of the recently elected deputies were or are State Security agents?" The mainstream parties, she alleged, seemed to consider this question unimportant; on the contrary, it was in her eyes "critical." How else, she asked, "can we get the lies and the heteronomy out of our public life? Unsparing accountability is the point of departure for responsible political action."[21]

Bohley recognized the problem of finding appropriate judges—"for no institution in the DDR is wholly credible"—but this simply made the task of creating a credible body more urgent. Were the task to be pushed aside, she argued, the new German democracy would simply repeat the example of the postwar Federal Republic—to Bohley a negative, not a positive, model. "If history is not now worked through," she warned, "then we will repeat here all that was tied after 1945 in West Germany to the survival of former Nazis in the state apparatus—and not just there. We do not want to wait twenty years for our '68 the way you [in the Federal Republic] did."[22]

The emphasis on transparency, dialogue, and consensus guaranteed that the Stasi would dominate the political agenda of the citizens' movements as soon as democratic competition became a reality. The movements' distrust of parties, combined with the public's rejection of the opposition movement's "socialist" programmatic preferences and the hesitations engendered by the moral challenge the dissidents posed to a quiescent population, seriously disadvantaged the citizens' movements as they passed into a system in which the distribution of power depended on partisan and electoral politics. The cultural strategy increasingly favored by movement spokesmen, however, would have established a different mechanism for distributing power in the new democracy. Convinced that their rules were the right rules, the citizens' movements continued to play by them.

"Banishing Bitterness from My Heart"

On first examination, New Forum's effort to identify and confront former Stasi agents would seem to be an exclusionary exercise intended to ostracize men and women deemed unworthy of full citizenship in the new democratic polity. In fact, activists from New Forum and other citizens' movements saw their concentration on the Stasi as part of an *integrating* strategy of reconciliation, one intended to make exclusion unnecessary by rehabilitating former perpetrators. The inclusionary, conciliatory thrust of the approach explains the Forum's insistence on the need for open and honest dialogue between former perpetrators and former victims, a proposal so patently unrealistic except in special cases that its constant repetition deserves our particular attention. Only dialogue could heal past wounds and (re)create the kind of trust that New Forum activists believed to be the bedrock of democratic politics. They were convinced that "genuine" democracy required the prior construction of a civil society; they focused on the Stasi rather than on the party precisely because the job description of the Stasi had been constantly to seek out, to undermine, and if possible definitively to destroy the social, cultural, and organizational underpinnings of a civil society. To many New Forum activists, it seemed that the Stasi had covered East German society with a thick film of distrust. That film would have to be washed away in order for a civil society to be created. Only then—if then—when people could finally "look one another in the face without distrust,"[23] could partisan politics become a meaningful and desirable instrument of public choice.

No episode more vividly illustrates both the type of confrontation New Forum activists thought indispensable and the benefits they hoped would derive from such interactions than the remarkable conversations that Katja Havemann and Irena Kukutz held between March and July 1990 with "Monika H.," the IM who for eight years had spied on them while pretending to be a member of the dissident groups to which they belonged: Frauen für den Frieden (Women for Peace) and Initiative für Frieden und Menschenrechte (IFM, or Initiative for Peace and Human Rights). The content of the dialogue also suggests why such conversations, intended by Havemann and Kukutz to be a model, were in fact such rare occurrences. Katja Havemann, widow of the SED member turned dissident philosopher and scientist Robert Havemann (1910–1983), was a co-founder of New Forum. Irena Kukutz was likewise a New Forum co-founder. In the 1980s both women had helped organize "Frauen für den Frieden—Ost." Their conversations with Monika H. were published in 1990 under the title *Geschützte Quelle* (Protected Source).[24] In addition to transcribed material from the four conversations, the book contains a forward by Katja Havemann; excerpts from a letter written by Monika to Bärbel Bohley, Kukutz, and Havemann on February 23, 1990; an essay by Kukutz explaining why the dissidents had sought out the conversations with their betrayer; a text written by Monika for her Stasi superiors; an unfinished letter from Monika to her mother; and excerpts from a diary kept by Monika as an adolescent in 1960–62. Except for the introductory material, these texts are all printed on the odd pages of the book. On the facing pages are pictures of Monika and her dissident "friends," reports from the Stasi archives explaining (for example) how oppositional activities could be identified and disrupted, and other documentary material.

For both Havemann and Kukutz, the conversations with Monika answered intellectual questions that corresponded to an acutely felt emotional need: "How was it possible?" asked Havemann (6). "How is it possible," echoed Kukutz, "to misuse people to the point of making them into tools to oppress other people" (14)? The questions about personal motivations suggested a question about social and political effects: "How did the poison work" (7)? But Havemann and Kukutz posed that systemic question in personal terms. Dissident groups and circles of friendship had been so effectively infiltrated that dissidents could not know the truth about their *own* personal and political pasts unless the agents previously in their midst were unmasked and encouraged to tell their stories—a point most eloquently made by the experience of Vera Wollenberger, whose own husband turned out to be a Stasi informer.[25] "When I pored over my Stasi files," Wolf Biermann wrote in 1992, "I wasn't interested in whether Erich Mielke was perhaps not completely honest, for I can see the blood on his hands." A songwriter whose expulsion by the DDR in 1976 had provoked public protest, Biermann continued: "I wanted to know which friend had been an enemy, and which informant was again sitting pretty in Parliament."[26] Only if the past were revealed, New Forum activists argued, could people get on with their lives—private and public. Absent such a dialogue, the poison would continue to circulate, whatever happened to the formal structures of power.

Monika was an ideal conversation partner for Havemann and Kukutz because she never doubted her own guilt. Early in the conversations, Kukutz asked Monika if she saw herself as a victim or as a perpetrator. "That is really a difficult question," Monika replied, "I am a victim of my upbringing, of my whole former life. And really only against this background was this whole thing possible" (51). But Monika then made her interlocutors' emphasis on trust her own, and expressed her growing sense of shame at having betrayed the trust placed in her: "Increasingly, I perceive myself as a perpetrator. Today, I feel a huge shame . . . and guilt, for having taken advantage of trust . . . ach, knock it off, I find the whole thing so awful" (51).

The documents that accompany the conversations, and indeed the conversations themselves, provide ample evidence to suggest why Monika might have fallen easy prey to the Stasi's overtures: the child and then the adolescent we meet in the documents longs for the affection, approval, and stability that her family never provided. But Monika refuses to take the easy way out. Repeatedly she accepts her responsibility for the wrongs she committed. At first, she admits, she tried to make excuses—the same excuses other former IMs constantly used—because she did not want to face her guilt: "Somehow, I really didn't want to see what I had done. I also kept telling myself there were excuses: my God, there were so many informants, I really hadn't done anything bad. And so on. I didn't want to accept my own guilt. I was afraid" (173).

But the attempt to escape responsibility was unsuccessful. Once Monika accepted the offer of a conversation, the presence of her former friends and the obligation to deal with their experience forced on her an effort at honesty: "When Katja mentioned the arrests recently, that really got to me. No excuse can help me. I helped put people in jail—it doesn't matter whether the help was direct or indirect" (175).

Monika did not have a strategy for facing her own future; she no longer even had an adequate explanation for her past:

It is so awful . . . I can't get past it . . . No one can excuse it. And there are so many like me. In terms of motives, mine were not exceptional. What makes people do this kind of thing? Sure, you can say the system makes people do it, but that is just hogwash. I ask myself what I can do to put this behind me. Must I run around forever with my load of guilt, looking anxiously around at people I might meet? I try simply to see it descriptively: here I am, you must accept me. But that is just for appearance. I can't maintain it . . . It also doesn't work to say that we had the law on our side. Getting out of it that way would be like what happened after the Nazi period. I have tried to get out of it by telling myself that I acted in accordance with my convictions and with the law. But it just doesn't work anymore. (175)

In her own eyes, Monika appears completely finished, but her affirmation of her own guilt and of the almost irreparable nature of her acts is portrayed by her interlocutors as the first, painful step in a long-overdue process of empowerment. The empowering agents are precisely the dissidents whom Monika had previously betrayed. Havemann and Kukutz accepted that they would have to share their political and social space with people who had betrayed them, but they also assumed their own moral right to prescribe the conditions of coexistence. Those conditions included a hierarchy of power based on moral merit. Monika, who had earlier confessed, "I was always led and directed from without, from above. I never lived according to my own lights" (147), now acknowledged her moral dependence on the judgment of those whose trust she had violated: "It gives me back a bit of my dignity, that you—to whom I did it—will talk with me. I can also understand very well that Bärbel [Bohley] doesn't want to talk with me" (179). Kukutz, who had reached out to Monika, reacted much more harshly to another former agent whose stance she viewed as impenitent. Such people, Kukutz argued, "trample with empty phrases on my wounded soul."[27] Their refusal to acknowledge their guilt perpetuated Kukutz's bitterness, making it impossible for her to move beyond her past and to recover a feeling of wholeness. Having made her a victim under the old regime, her unrepentant persecutors would again make her an outsider in the new regime.

Monika was not unaware of the new power relationships she was implicitly ratifying. Not for nothing did she fear that she would again be used. Even as she validated the hierarchy of merit and power that Have-

mann and Kukutz sought to establish, she added: "Now don't be angry
with me, you mustn't be angry, please . . . Our conversation helps me a
lot . . . At the same time, I am not entirely sure: might I not again be
used?" (80).

Monika was unusual because she was, in essence, willing to write her
own indictment. Her confessions of guilt did not wipe her slate clean,
and her New Forum interlocutors offered her integration only in exchange for self-incrimination and political disqualification. Whenever
self-disqualification failed to occur, New Forum activists tended to advocate exclusion, consistently seeking to remove people with dubious pasts
from positions of influence in political, social, and cultural life.

New Forum's use of guilt and conditional integration as a partial substitute for electoral politics in establishing a hierarchy of power is usefully compared to the philosopher Karl Jaspers's reflections on German
guilt and politics after the fall of the Third Reich. In his influential 1946
work *Die Schuldfrage* (The Guilt Question), Jaspers differentiated between criminal, political, moral, and metaphysical guilt. Criminal guilt is
the violation, established by an impartial court, of a law in force at the
time the act was committed. Political guilt is the responsibility we all
share for the political system in which we live, whether or not we approve of it. Metaphysical guilt is the disquiet we feel in a universe in
which innocent people suffer. Jaspers defined moral guilt, the most relevant category in the present context, as the retrospective self-understanding of individuals who, in the face of evil, whether from fear or
from interest, had silenced or ignored their own consciences, "those who
knew or could have known and yet continued down paths which they
understand under self-examination to be wrong.[28]

Like the citizens' movement leaders of the transition period, Jaspers
argued the necessity of dialogue: "We want to learn to speak with one
another. This means that we want not just to repeat our views, but to
hear what the other person thinks." As Jaspers wrote, his country still lay
in ruins, and memories of the Third Reich and the war remained vivid. In
the short run, Jaspers acknowledged, dialogue would sharpen feelings of
isolation and cleavage among Germans, exacerbating the "lack of community" that was one of the Reich's most important legacies: "Talking
with one another now in Germany is difficult, but it is our greatest task,
because we are extraordinarily different from one another in what we
experienced, felt, wished for, and did."[29] In the longer run, dialogue

would make possible the reestablishment of feelings of social and political solidarity, while at the same time enabling each individual to come to terms with how he or she had acted during the Third Reich.

For Havemann and Kukutz, the conversation with Monika was a social act, and the dialogue was unaccompanied by any pretense of equality among the participants. For Jaspers, whose positions are often reminiscent of Mauriac's, the sort of self-examination that could lead to the realization of moral guilt and responsibility was an intensely personal affair, and one in which only friends had a right—or even a capacity—to intervene. As Jaspers wrote: "One can assign moral guilt only to oneself, not to another, or to the other only in the solidarity of loving struggle. No one can judge another morally, unless they are so bound together by inner ties that it is as though the judge were judging himself."[30]

The process described and prescribed by Jaspers could not be forced. Even more important, it could not be used as a precondition for social trust or as a political resource for establishing a hierarchy of power. Trust would have to be granted; moral self-examination might—or might not—follow. Its very description made it seem improbable. Yet on the results of this infinitely multiplied process of individual self-examination, Jaspers argued, hung the fate of Germany as a political community. In words that might have been spoken by a New Forum activist, Jaspers asserted: "No purification of the soul, no political freedom."[31] The assumption of personal responsibility was, for Jaspers after 1945 as for the citizens' movements after 1989, an ongoing and a defining act; its impact would be collectively as well as individually liberating. Jaspers's subsequent disappointment was measured by the standard he had set. In 1966 he worried about the direction politics might take in the apparently secure Federal Republic:

> In 1945, we stood before the *moral-political task* of founding a new state. This task is *today still uncompleted* . . .
>
> Today it is our good fortune that we possess the Basic Law . . . This is the rock on which alone the free state of the Federal Republic stands, so long as the rock holds . . .
>
> The lies in their foundations are the poison of states.
>
> With us, however, the lies go much deeper, and greet us, so to speak, at every turn. All can perhaps be grouped around one: the Germans were really never national socialists. Through an incomprehensible misfortune, they fell into the hands of an evil criminal. Through terror,

their patterns of thought may here and there have been troubled, as is human. But fundamentally they were always decent, attached to the truth, and eager for peace.[32]

New Forum activists were determined to fulfill the original assignment: they wanted no part of fictitious honor, both because they thought it could not provide a functional substitute for real honor, and because it forced them to deny their own pasts. If a society accepts counterfeit money as valid currency, the distinction between the two becomes hard to maintain. Honesty and honor were therefore bound together, and as essential to the personal identity of individuals as to the political future of the community.

The commitment of New Forum activists to a democratization strategy that required a democratic culture encouraged them to focus almost exclusively on what Jaspers called moral guilt, to the relative neglect of the other forms of guilt Jaspers had identified. The New Forum activists did not object to trials, but they viewed them as secondary, and they rarely advocated legal punishment for people like Monika. Instead of trials, New Forum activists—and many other men and women who had participated in the citizens' movements—advocated "tribunals," in which perpetrators and victims would confront one another verbally across a common table: "A real coming to terms," Werner Fischer argued, "can be achieved only with the joint participation of perpetrators and victims." He wrote: "We think it . . . very important that official and unofficial agents should have a chance to express themselves on their own initiative, so that they can free themselves of their past. We plead for individual or group conversations with absolute confidentiality. Psychologists, jurists, clergy, together or individually, should be available for these conversations."[33]

A few panels did actually meet,[34] but unsurprisingly, perpetrators did not rush to claim the proffered seats. The more obvious it became that conversations which would resemble the one between Kukutz, Havemann, and Monika in both their content and their power relations would be exceptional, the more inclined New Forum activists became toward exclusionary and punitive measures. Between March 20 and April 17, 1991 (that is, several months after unification and several months before the adoption of legislation guaranteeing and regulating access to Stasi files), *Die Andere Zeitung,* the newspaper closest to New Forum, took the unusual—and legally questionable—step of publishing the names of the two thousand highest-paid Stasi officials. The move was, the editors claimed, a last resort, dictated by a concern for public safety: parliamentary politics as usual had not resolved the Stasi issue to their satisfaction, and the matter was too central for the setback simply to be accepted. Jens Reich defended the decision as a lesser evil, in part because he thought it might finally provoke a dialogue that everyone seemed determined to avoid: "After publication, [it will be] easier for Stasi officers to work through the past and to explain old cases. It will also be easier to analyze one's own complicity and its prehistory and motives."[35] A week later, Wolfram Kempe repeated the claim that the publication of the names would open up a public discussion and guard against a repetition of the Federal Republic's postwar mistakes.[36] The editors insisted that their intentions were conciliatory: "Secrecy, silence, rumors are the ground on which distrust, animosities, and hate thrive."[37] It followed that openness, discussion, and a reconstruction of the facts would produce trust and mutual sympathy. But the nature of the conversations sought was best expressed by Bärbel Bohley at a roundtable organized by *Die Andere Zeitung* on March 28, 1991. She brushed aside the focus on the deposed leaders Erich Honecker and Erich Mielke: "Younger men . . . governed the land and led it to its ruin. It is they whom I would like to *force* into a discussion."[38]

The decision to publish the list had a long prehistory, not just in the elaboration of intellectual positions within the citizens' movements but also in actions undertaken during the transition period. Of the actions, the most notable was the occupation of MfS offices in Berlin's Normannenstraße by a group of New Forum activists in September 1990 (just prior to unification). Participants described the occupation as "an act of self-defense."[39]

The decision to publish the list also had sequels, which became increasingly associated with the Manfred Stolpe case (see Chapter 5). In each instance the activists insisted on the need for transparency and condemned the refusal of ostensibly representative parliamentary bodies to confront the past honestly. Since they believed that the fate of the republic depended on the kind of transparency from which parliamentary bodies seemed to shrink—"Only if the population can become conscious of its past," they declared, "will everyone have a chance to build a truly democratic Germany"[40]—they could claim that despite their negligible numbers, they were uniquely qualified to speak for the democratic future of Germany.

Unable to impose their agenda and their solutions, movement activists increasingly explained the course the *Wende* had taken by appealing to conspiracy theories, claiming that the Stasi had helped conservative west German politicians hijack the revolution.[41] They argued that the Volkskammer, having failed to purge its own membership, to relieve Interior Minister Peter-Michael Diestel of his post, and to ensure suitable control over the Stasi archives after unification, had "declared its moral bankruptcy." Alluding to the "bloc" of coopted parties that had governed with the communists, they contended that "the good old National Front—the CDU and the PDS, an experienced team, so to speak—won. The sixty-eight former Stasi people from all the parties who now sit as 'representatives of the people,' they won."[42]

By March 1991 the tone had become even more shrill—and the claim that the revolution had been hijacked had become more insistent. "Law and justice are miles apart," wrote Bärbel Bohley, "and the victims are left behind, gazing with open-mouthed astonishment at the repetition compulsion of the new champions of law."[43] Jürgen Fuchs compared the German transition experience unfavorably with that of Poland and Czechoslovakia, attributing the hollowness of the German achievement to the omnipresence of politically corrupted actors and suggesting that it might again become necessary to defend democracy in the streets:

> And what way of dealing [with Stasi records] is proposed by elected representatives of this German republic? After all the decades of pressures, humiliation, and socially exercised violence? Turn the page, . . . close the discussion, destroy or burn the documents. In any case make sure that no one can get to them for as long as possible . . . How long we yearned for this free election, for a good democracy—in Prague, Havel wins, in Warsaw, Walesa. And here? Bloc parties, IMs![44]

As evidence of the movements' political marginality mounted, the activists' efforts to draw former Stasi agents into "dialogue" were aimed with increasing explicitness at reversing perceived power relations—as though the "revolution" of 1989 had *not* been won. "Those concerned must be spoken to," urged Bohley. "They must see that they cannot now take on any political responsibilities, that only in this way will it be possible to bring trust back into politics. Those concerned must have the opportunity to resign voluntarily. If they are not capable of seeing what they must do, then they must be publicly put in their place."[45]

The intended dialogue was clearly not conceived as an exercise in mutual self-examination; it was not about forgiveness but about power, though it was also about trust. Faced with a "remarkable coalition of silence between the formerly and presently powerful," New Forum activists such as Tina Krone admitted they had lost patience. At last, "those who for decades organized hunts against thousands of people must be forced to confront their deeds."[46]

Publishing the names of those who had made their living destroying trust and depriving others of their freedom was an act of nonviolent revenge, Jürgen Fuchs declared; it was intended at least to provide the politically disappointed with emotional satisfaction:

> Your secret must be broken, like your power. We no longer want to live with this muck, these lies, this poison, this ongoing mockery! The economic and ecological catastrophe is bad enough, we don't want a psychic catastrophe on top of it . . . The archives are closed, the names are unknown, the generals are comfortably pensioned off, the first secretary is abroad . . . what else are we going to be asked to swallow? Now we are naming your names. Not a hair on anyone's head will be touched. No violence . . . And no one should go to prison, not Mielke, not [Harry] Tisch . . . They should live in their little gardens, free, but there to be questioned and challenged, above all people like [Günter] Mittag and [Markus] Wolf, the really clever ones, the dynamic ones, who are ready to appear on talk shows and speak in soft tones: to discuss their deeds, to clarify their responsibility, their orders and who executed them, where, how, when.[47]

The Shaping of Partisan Politics in the Unification Period

The occupation of the former MfS offices appeared in many ways an act of political desperation. In terms of its intended public effect, the action seemed aimed at signaling to the broader society the gravity of the moral and political mistake for which it was making itself co-responsible. It was not inscribed in a coalition strategy; rather, it suggested a recognition of political isolation on the part of those who undertook it.

Precisely because it facilitates coalition building, the myth of a citizenry faithful to freedom during the dark night of dictatorship—de

Gaulle's evocation of "a body that had remained healthy"—is a very valuable political resource in transitional settings, regardless of how closely it reflects past realities. New Forum's insistence on honesty put this resource out of reach. Yet although the citizens' movements were relatively uninvested in the idea of a people uncompromised under the dictatorship, they were heavily invested in the related notion of a population now ready to dedicate itself to the pursuit of social and political justice. They refused to see, or at least to accept, that the second position could have little political appeal if the first was rejected.

The part "the people" actually played in the collapse of communist rule in East Germany is both an objective question and a perception shaped by public debate. The necessary—some might even argue the sufficient—condition that led to the collapse of SED rule in the DDR was the reform dynamic created by Mikhail Gorbachev in the Soviet Union after 1985.[48] As so often in politics, intended and unintended consequences combined to open up possibilities and produce outcomes that no one had anticipated. The unanticipated developments quickly rocked the postwar status quo in Eastern Europe, and the shock waves eventually reached the DDR, where local circumstances, actors, and choices framed the particular cast that events assumed. In the summer of 1989, as neighboring (and formerly "socialist") countries eased their border controls, the outflow of East Germans leaving the DDR became increasingly dramatic. As thousands voted with their feet, others engaged in unprecedented protest at home, where the rigged local elections of May 1989 provided a focus for public anger.[49] While the SED prepared to celebrate the regime's fortieth anniversary with parades and speeches on October 6 and 7, in Leipzig and other East German cities thousands of citizens packed the churches and then the streets to demand reform. Attending the anniversary celebrations, Gorbachev appeared to signal that Soviet tanks would not be available should the SED opt, a mere four months after the Tiananmen Square massacre, for a "Chinese solution" to civil unrest. East Germany, for years one of the most sclerotic of the East European regimes, stood poised before an uncertain future. Within six months the Berlin Wall had been opened (on November 9, 1989), free elections had been held (on March 18, 1990), a noncommunist coalition government was in power—and the future still seemed uncertain. In May 1990 the East German writer Christoph Hein noted that the uncertainty enveloped both Germanys; in so doing, he defined the stakes of German political debate for the next several years: "We are . . . not at an end point. Everything will get even more interesting. It will also get interesting for West Germany, if it comes to federation, union, annexation, whatever; then in three or four years it too will be a completely different country."[50]

Round Table talks were organized in December 1989. Even at that early date, however, the real stake of negotiations was not the shape of politics within the DDR but the nature of the DDR's future relationship with the Federal Republic. There had been no reformist faction with any political weight within the SED. The intracommunist debate, insofar as it occurred, took place within the ranks of the intelligentsia, was more the product of than the prelude to wider political protest, and focused on the rehabilitation of the Spanish civil war veteran and communist Walter Janka, whose literary and publishing career had ended abruptly with his arrest (on the usual charges of counterrevolutionary conspiracy) and trial in 1956–57 (see Chapter 3).

Nor was there an organized underground movement, comparable to Poland's Solidarity, with a broad popular base, tested leadership, organizational strength, and political experience. By its mere existence, West Germany had served as a brake on the mobilizing capacities of an East German opposition: from the late 1940s through the late 1980s, the men and women who might have led such a movement were routinely forced or induced to abandon the DDR for the "other" German state. In this respect (as in many others), the German case is without parallel: nowhere else was a nation split in half, with one half subjected to dictatorship while the other half enjoyed prosperity and freedom. Insofar as an organized opposition existed in the DDR, it existed on the margins of the Protestant churches, whose umbrella organization, the Bund der Evangelischen Kirchen (BEK), had reached an uneasy accommodation with the regime in the late 1960s and early 1970s (see Chapter 5). This explains the disproportionate representation of clergy and church activists among the organizers of the citizens' movements of 1989, but it also helps explain the fragile social reach of those movements: led by intellectuals and caught in the swirl of rapidly evolving circumstances, the movements never consolidated a social base among other segments of the population.

The SED's ability to control events disintegrated in the eight weeks between the fortieth anniversary celebrations of the DDR's founding in

October and the party congress held in mid-December 1989. Erich Honecker, who had ruled East Germany since 1971, resigned on October 18, 1989. On December 1 the constitutional clause that consecrated the communist party's "leading role" was officially dropped. On February 5, 1990, opposition groups joined a government "of national responsibility" under the leadership of the longtime party leader of Dresden, Hans Modrow; Modrow would later be tried (and convicted, though not imprisoned) for electoral fraud. The first—and last—free parliamentary elections in the history of the DDR were held on March 18, 1990; the unexpected victor was the conservative Allianz für Deutschland, led by a Christian Democratic lawyer, Lothar de Maizière; de Maizière would later drop out of public life because of accusations that he had served as an IM. On May 5 the two Germanys and the four Allied powers from World War II met in "two-by-four" talks to consider the future of Germany. On July 1 an economic union between the two German states went into effect. On October 3, 1990, the DDR ceased to exist.

Three causally linked and chronologically compressed features of this unfolding drama sharpened the perception among opposition activists that "their" revolution was being hijacked, and thus made them more inclined to adhere to a cultural strategy that would preemptively disqualify putatively antidemocratic competitors. First, the rapid and definitive erosion of the SED's power and legitimacy took place in a manner that disadvantaged all political groups seeking to define and defend a progressive, left-of-center agenda, either in a democratic DDR or in a new, unified Germany. To the extent that this process damaged the SED's successor party, the Partei des Demokratischen Sozialismus (PDS), it could be seen as favorable to democratization; to the extent that it simultaneously created a handicap for most of the recently created opposition groups, it shaped emerging patterns of political competition in ways that favored political forces—including the PDS—disinclined to confront the past. In addition, the organization of new political groups in the DDR was disrupted both by revelations of Stasi penetration and by the increasingly visible intervention of parties from the Federal Republic in the new electoral life of the DDR. Finally, the hesitant construction of new mechanisms of interest articulation, a process in which the Stasi issue figured prominently, was overtaken by the drive for unification, and the opposition groups were not prepared either materially or ideologically to compete for power in a unified Germany.

For our purposes, the crucial event in the disintegration of SED power occurred on December 1, 1989, when Heinrich Toeplitz of the Christian Democratic Union (Christlich Demokratische Union, or CDU), chair of a committee set up to investigate corruption and abuse of office, and formerly the president of the DDR's highest court, rose in the Volkskammer to read a preliminary report that detailed how the party brass and their relatives had lived.[51] Almost overnight, the accounts of life in the north Berlin suburb of Wandlitz—combined with Kommerzielle Koordinierung (Commercial Coordination, the office overseeing foreign trade and currency) chief Alexander Schalck-Golodkowski's flight on December 6 to the Federal Republic—did what forty years of repression, economic mismanagement, and ecological destruction had failed to do: the revelations of privileged access to housing, Western consumer goods, and health care discredited not only the SED but also the very idea of "socialism."

The most obvious and immediate loser of the "identity crisis"[52] unleashed by the revelations was of course the SED, which now engaged in a desperate attempt to recast itself as a "party of democratic socialism," while at the same time retaining as many of its material resources and advantages as it could. On December 3 the SED Central Committee and the Politburo resigned en masse; Erich Honecker and eleven other top officials were—true to former communist practices—summarily excluded from the party.[53] Several officials were arrested. In the first two weeks of December, the SED rebaptized itself as the SED-PDS; its new leader, Gregor Gysi, would remain at the head of the successor party until his voluntary resignation in January 1993. Through the parliamentary elections of October 1994 and beyond, Gysi would continue to be the preferred PDS intermediary with the general public. His credentials were ambiguous: to some observers he would look very much like a latter-day Robert Lindet. As a lawyer in the DDR, he had defended opposition figures, including both Bärbel Bohley and Robert Havemann, but the suspicion soon emerged that he had also been an IM (see Chapter 6). For all his energy and wit, he could do little to bridge the gulf of disgust and disillusionment that separated the party from the people.

The less obvious, less immediate, but nonetheless important loser as the SED sank under accusations of corruption as well as authoritarianism was the noncommunist and as yet non-party left, that is, the citizens' movements. New Forum gained legal recognition on November 8, 1989, a scant four and a half months before the Volkskammer elections of March 18, 1990. During those four and a half months, as a pluralist landscape hesitantly took shape in the DDR, important organizational options were considered, coalitional patterns were established, and programmatic decisions were made. The growing hostility to "socialism," the skepticism with which SED-PDS efforts at "renewal" were greeted within opposition circles, and the citizens' movements' discomfort with party politics combined to cut off or strain relations between the movements and the three groups most likely to provide them with ideological and/or political support: intellectuals, the PDS, and the newly (re)created SPD.

Although leaders from the citizens' movements were often reluctant to define themselves in left-right terms, they regularly expressed their loyalty to some kind of socialism. The later political commitments of many suggest that the expressions of loyalty were motivated by more than the expediencies of the moment. As we have already seen, many opposition activists did not consider the Federal Republic a particularly attractive political model. New Forum's Sebastian Pflugbeil affirmed: "In New Forum we pretty much agree that we don't want to copy the Federal Republic. We also agree that we want to link up with socialist traditions."[54] On September 12, 1989, the founders of Demokratie Jetzt, including Hans-Jürgen Fischbeck, Ludwig Mehlhorn, Ulrike Poppe, Wolfgang Ullmann, and Konrad Weiß, issued an "appeal to get involved in our own affairs." If socialism could not be rescued, the writers warned, there would be no alternative to "Western consumer society." Like many PDS pronouncements, the appeal seemed to identify "the West" primarily with capitalism and consumerism rather than with political freedom.[55]

On October 2, 1989, the organizers of Demokratischer Aufbruch (DA, Democratic Awakening) wrote: "We want to learn anew what socialism can mean for us."[56] On October 6, New Forum leaders protested "against the government's attempts to represent us as enemies of socialism," and instead reversed the accusation: "It is rather the incapacity of the SED that is endangering socialism on German soil." Like many subsequent statements, the New Forum declaration went over the heads of the SED leadership to propose a coalition of goodwill and common purpose to the putatively dedicated socialists whose idealism and energies the party had squandered and betrayed: "You have enormous reserves of expertise and experience, which we urgently need for the renewal of our society. You demand the leading role: exercise it!"[57]

In this sense and on this point, the opposition leaders hoped that it would be possible to construct a political coalition around the old ideals of the socialist movement: justice and equality. This belief was their version of "a body that had remained healthy." They argued not that everyone had remained faithful to freedom, but rather that even failed socialism had instilled socialist values—making it theoretically possible that a democratized DDR, unblemished by either consumerism or dishonesty, could in fact improve on the quality of political life in the Federal Republic. The hope was short-lived; the myth would have a complicated future. When, on February 1, 1990, Hans Modrow outlined his vision of "Deutschland einig Vaterland" (Germany, united fatherland), the editorial staff of *Die Andere Zeitung* reacted with acid disappointment to the communist-led retreat from socialist ideals. Their editorial statement explicitly rejected "bourgeois democracy" as an adequate political goal, but acknowledged that the retreat sounded by Modrow would win majority approval. Six weeks before the March parliamentary elections, the newspaper's staff had to recognize that its preferences were not shared by a public increasingly eager for the economic and political security that unification appeared to offer.[58] As the opposition swam against the current, seeking to define a democratic but distinctive DDR identity in which socialist values would have their place, it found applause where it did not want it (among intellectuals) and misunderstanding where it could have hoped for support (in the SPD).

Unlike most opposition leaders, intellectuals had established reputations and a high public profile—always a valuable political resource in an emerging democratic landscape. On November 4, 1989, hundreds of thousands of people gathered in East Berlin under the auspices of the East German Artists' Association to protest government policies and to reclaim the rights theoretically guaranteed them by the constitution of the DDR. The speakers were a heterogeneous crowd: they included both the opposition and church activist Marianne Birthler and the former spy chief Markus Wolf, both Friedrich Schorlemmer, the opposition clergyman from Wittenberg, and Günter Schabowski, the Politburo member whose announcement on November 9 that travel restrictions would be lifted led to the opening of the Wall. Several prominent intellectuals appeared; echoing earlier (and anticipating later) statements by citizens' movement leaders, they did not cite the Federal Republic as a political model. Stefan Heym, a seventy-six-year-old writer who had emigrated in 1933, then served in the U.S. Army during the war, left the United States during the McCarthy period to settle in the DDR, signed the November 17, 1976, declaration protesting Wolf Biermann's expulsion, and later became a PDS deputy in the Bundestag, spoke for "freedom and democracy and for a socialism worth its name." Christoph Hein echoed: "Let's build a democratic socialism on a legal basis, one that is accountable! One that doesn't make a mockery of the word 'socialism.'"[59]

On November 8, a group of East German intellectuals and opposition figures appealed to their compatriots to take their stand in the DDR and sacrifice for a better future—more socialist, and therefore allegedly more democratic—than what the Federal Republic could offer them. The signatories included the writers Christa Wolf, Volker Braun (both Wolf and Braun had signed the 1976 protest against Biermann's expulsion), and Christoph Hein, and the conductor Kurt Masur, alongside opposition activists Bärbel Bohley (New Forum), Erhard Neubert (DA), Gerhard Poppe (IFM), and Hans Jürgen Fischbeck (DJ): "We beg you," they wrote, "stay here in your homeland, stay with us! . . . Help us set up a real democratic society, one that also preserves the vision of a democratic socialism."[60]

On November 28 a larger group, far more heterogeneous in both professional and political terms, issued another appeal under the title "Für unser Land" (For Our Country). The title alone was a political statement: it identified the DDR as a viable *Heimat* (homeland) alongside the Federal Republic. This time the signatories included not just intellectuals (among them Walter Janka) and opposition figures but SED leaders as well: Wolfgang Berghofer (mayor of Dresden) signed the initial document, and Egon Krenz, who helped sideline Honecker and then replaced him as head of the government, later added his name to the list of sponsors. In drawing sharp distinctions between the DDR and the Federal Republic, the appeal sought to preserve the moral high ground for the DDR:

> Either we can insist on the independence of the DDR and attempt to develop . . . a fraternal society in our country that could guarantee

peace and social justice, the freedom of the individual, freedom of movement for all, and the preservation of the environment.

Or we must accept a sellout of our material and moral values . . . Then, sooner or later, the German Democratic Republic will be taken over by the Federal Republic of Germany.

The country stood before a moment of decision, and the signatories urged their compatriots not to throw away the political opportunity available to them: "Let's take the first path. We still have the opportunity to develop a socialist alternative to the Federal Republic, in neighborly equality with all states in Europe. We can still reflect on the antifascist and humanist ideals from which we once set out."[61]

The "Für unser Land" appeal would soon be constantly cited as damning evidence in the debate about the political role of intellectuals in the DDR (see Chapter 3), but it was anachronistic by the time it was issued. By early December 1989 at the latest, the moment of decision had passed. The possibility of constructing on German soil a "socialist alternative to the Federal Republic," assuming that possibility had ever existed, had evaporated. In a telling coincidence, the first Bundestag discussion of unification coincided with the Volkskammer report documenting party abuses. Popular patience with social "experiments" had run out. But New Forum did not see in intellectuals like Christa Wolf— or Walter Janka—attractive coalition partners or spokesmen in any event. Already in the fall of 1989, political relations between the opposition and intellectuals were at best ambiguous and at worst tense. Intellectuals tended to look back with nostalgia and regret at what they perceived to be decades of missed opportunities; New Forum activists, while professing their attachment to socialist ideals, looked back in anger at a regime that had both persecuted and disempowered them. That anger increased as the complicated relations between intellectuals and the communist regime became the object of sustained public attention (see Chapter 3). One effect of the fallout, immediately felt, was to discredit further the socialist idea(l)s on which the programmatic appeal of opposition groups depended.

Given their commitment to democratic socialism, the citizens' movements could be expected to look for political allies on the left—with the PDS and/or the SPD—and with one another. In anticipation of the March

1990 Volkskammer elections, New Forum, DJ, and IFM created an umbrella organization, Bündnis 90 (Alliance 90), on February 6, 1990.[62] Left out of the new alliance were three other citizens' movements—Vereinte Linke (United Left), the Greens, and Unabhängiger Frauen Verband (Independent Women's League). Most Bündnis 90 leaders initially anticipated cooperative relations with the SPD and antagonistically competitive relations with the PDS. In the end, the cooperative relations with the SPD did not materialize: despite their common commitment to democratic socialism, the SPD and Bündnis 90 differed significantly in their understandings of how political institutions and processes could and should work. The SPD opted for German unity and then for a "Grand Coalition" with the conservative Allianz für Deutschland; it accepted political parties as adequate instruments of interest articulation; and it increasingly tightened its ties to its West German sister party. New Forum greeted each decision with a mixture of hostility and disappointment.

Nor was Bündnis 90 particularly tempted by an alliance with the PDS, which would be branded during the election campaign as the "Partei der Schuldigen" (Party of the Guilty). The SED-PDS leader Gregor Gysi argued, in December 1989 and later, that the left would stand or fall together. Then and later, he sought to reach out to other progressive political forces—a strategy burdened, as the SPD was quick to note, by a long and unfortunate history, for communist parties had always ruthlessly exploited such alliances to promote their own hegemony. Gysi argued that the PDS could move beyond its past, and he hoped it would become a "modern socialist party," which would draw on "social democratic, socialist, non-Stalinist communist, antifascist, and pacifist traditions" to negotiate a "third way" "beyond Stalinist socialism and the domination of transnational monopolies." He saw this recast party as "the practical homeland of committed democratic socialists, not a class and also not a mass party."[63]

Within Bündnis 90, the PDS was variously appreciated, but alliances with the party were not concluded. Wolfgang Templin (IFM), who was critical of the SPD's inclination "to put democratic socialism in the corner" while chasing after Christian Democratic voters,[64] did not conclude in the PDS's favor. Arguing that democratic centralism was a "deeply rooted" reality and not just a Soviet imposition, Templin questioned the ability of the PDS to engage in meaningful self-renewal.[65]

The triangular relationship that emerged among Bündnis 90, the SPD, and the PDS was characterized by mutual distrust and disappointment. The SPD's faith in the shaping power of free institutions distanced the party from Bündnis 90, and both parties were too committed to delegit- imizing communist politics (even if they understood that process in different terms) to be seriously interested in an alliance with the PDS. In his 1990 book, *Wir brauchen einen dritten Weg* (We Need a Third Way), Gysi argued that the PDS represented both an obstacle and an opportu- nity for the German left. The complications the party brought in its bag- gage were obvious, but Gysi saw as an advantage "that it is a DDR party that owns up to its history and to the great hopes that once attached to this German Democratic Republic." Gysi recognized the contribution made by social movements and citizens' initiatives, but he maintained that "in developed bourgeois societies, parties are and remain the deci- sive channels of political interest articulation and aggregation"—pre- cisely the reality that the citizens' movements sought to transcend. Gysi also made an institutional argument about the transition:

> The clearly different left-wing cultures in the DDR and the BRD are above all conditioned by the two systems. They will move closer in the wake of German unification, above all through broader dialogue with one another. What we need above all is the will not only to deal with one another but also to work together politically. The left in east and west is going to be forced by unification to find a new common point of departure. The faster it understands this, the faster we understand it, the more useful it will be for the German left.[66]

The institutional perspective suggested in Gysi's argument was re- jected by the citizens' movements, which spurned the message along with the messenger. For them, the PDS's SED past decisively defined its present, in ways that institutional incentives were unlikely to change (and that the PDS's preference for partisan structures was, from the point of view of the opposition leaders, unlikely to encourage).

Relations between Bündnis 90 and the SPD worsened after the Volks- kammer elections. On April 13, reversing previous positions, the SPD accepted German unification through Article 23 rather than Article 146 (thus obviating the need for a new constitution, in whose elaboration east Germans could have participated) and opted for participation in a "Grand Coalition" government rather than for opposition side by side with Bündnis 90 (and the PDS).[67] In the end, the SPD decided that its own participation in the government was more useful than its presence in the opposition. In defending the party's contested decision, Wolfgang Thierse warned against "a latent demand for monopoly control" on the part of Bündnis 90 with regard to the representation of forces that had brought about change in 1989. Thierse, a party leader who became chair of the SPD Volkskammer group in August and later served as vice chair of the party in unified Germany, conceded that the government's program represented a compromise, "but not an indecent one, or at least indecent only to those who believe that compromises are always rotten. I believe that the ability to compromise is a fundamental democratic virtue."[68] New Forum's Jens Reich replied that grand coalitions by their nature remove issues from public debate: "A Grand Coalition means that all conflicts will be relegated to backrooms." He rejected the SPD's arguments as "fainthearted," and called on the SPD to take its place in the opposition.[69]

The SPD left the government in mid-August, but the breach between the party and the citizens' movements did not heal. On September 27–28, 1990, the SPD (East) formally merged with the SPD (West). As an endless debate over the future of the movements unfolded, Reich reiterated the argument for an autonomous citizens' movement "not just squeezed in somewhere between the FDP [Freie Demokratische Partei], the SPD, the Greens, and the PDS, but at right angles to the existing political trenches, as an offer to people who don't like the partisan scramble." The citizens' movement could and should serve as a "referee in the political ring." Reich's recommendations in 1990 are reminiscent of the "program" Dirks had assigned to his friends as the revolution for which they had hoped was displaced by the restoration they feared and despised. Reich conceded that the citizens' movement might come to represent "a flash in the pan from that remarkable fall, which already seems so far in the past," but he hoped instead that even in defeat, the veterans of the movement would continue to work in quiet and unspectacular ways for a new political culture: "We must address movement people from all camps. Their sensitivity to democracy and fairness, their human impulses, their humor, their fears."[70]

The electoral results of the decisions and relationships worked out during the transitional months of 1990 were in fact disappointing to the left in general and to the citizens' movements in particular.[71] In the

Volkskammer elections of March 18, 1990, Bündnis 90 garnered a mere 2.9 percent of the vote, while the Allianz für Deutschland won 48.1 percent of the votes and 192 seats. The SPD, perceived as less enthusiastic about unification than the Allianz für Deutschland, won only 21.8 percent of the vote and 88 seats. Looking back in November on the March 1990 elections, Konrad Weiß recalled the shock the results had inflicted:

> Up to March 18, we thought that we had enough support in the population to make it possible for us to work toward a different model, an alternative to the model of West German society. We were also in complete agreement that we wanted to work with the SPD to achieve our goals . . .
>
> I think that the break came on March 18, . . . when we learned to shed the illusion that the citizens' movements are also the people.[72]

The various citizens' movements, often running independently, and relatively absent outside of urban districts, improved their performance in the local elections of May 6, 1990: movement candidates won 13.27 percent of the vote in Berlin (as opposed to 8.99 percent in March), 11.85 percent in Leipzig (7.46 percent in March), and 12.61 percent in Dresden (7.65 percent in March).[73] The partial recovery was, however, ephemeral. In the Bundestag elections of December 2, 1990, Bündnis 90/Die Grünen (Greens) won some 6 percent of the votes. The three citizens' movements originally party to the Bündnis 90 coalition merged with one another on September 21, 1991, and with the west German Greens in the spring of 1993. While the citizens' movements faded from the political landscape, the PDS, which had won 16.3 percent of the March 1990 vote and just under 10 percent of the east German vote in December 1990, was represented in the Bundestag. It remained a political force to be reckoned with, especially in the new Länder (see Chapter 6). After the elections of 1994, Bündnis 90 representatives sat in the state parliament of only one of the five new Länder.

In the view of many New Forum activists, the revolution had in fact lost. How else could the movement's electoral and political weakness be explained? Having staked their strength on an illusory cultural revolution, New Forum leaders watched it evaporate with bewildered and often bitter resignation. Already on September 9, 1990, Bärbel Bohley complained that New Forum's political morality had been turned to its own and the people's disadvantage: while New Forum activists had sought dialogue and promoted reform, others had grabbed for power.[74]

In March 1991, Werner Fischer (IFM) reread the history of a period that had seemed so exhilarating to its actors and speculated that its true meaning might be more somber. Why had the former bloc parties played such a major role, he asked, and had not the new parties and citizens' movements themselves been infiltrated by Stasi informants?

> Is it not possible that the particular way in which the DDR went under, that the preparation for a quick and unconditional annexation by the Federal Republic had a logic to it, and that it happened with the support of the former MfS and its master the SED? That such helpers as de Maizière, Schnur, Steinberg, Viehweger, and Böhme were useful for this? Maybe in Bonn the past, the vulnerability to blackmail, or the thirst for power of such men had long been known . . . One could instrumentalize the former Stasi workers and use them for one's own political ends . . . Now, however, we want to know: Who is who, and where and with what purposes have they found accommodation![75]

The activists' disappointment with what Wolfram Kempe called "the whole parliamentary circus" reinforced their tendency to appeal to the street, and to see in the grassroots politics they believed they represented the great gift that eastern Europe could bring to the Western democracies. Klaus Wolfram wrote: "The cool cluelessness from above obligates us to self-help from below. Democracy will again be attractive and lively. This is what will come out of the East. We started it, we'll keep it going."[76] "Self-help from below," however, proved a poor substitute for the share of power that veterans of the citizens' movements might more easily have won, had they been more interested in power and less interested in trust.

The Legislative Legacy: The Stasi Archives

As the marginalization of opposition activists and ideas became more pronounced through the winter of 1989–90, the visibility of the Stasi issue increased. The insistence on the issue, and the citizens' movement activists' growing sense of political isolation, were sharpened by the steady flow of rumors regarding the alleged Stasi past of public figures. The Stasi does in fact appear to have been remarkably successful in penetrating opposition groups. From the SED's point of view, the stategy was curiously ineffective: the regime lacked the flexibility to respond to the information it obtained on public opinion, and the development of opposition activities continued despite the deliberately disruptive actions initiated by Stasi agents. From the point of view of a democratizing system, however, the impact of Stasi infiltration was devastating: it nourished an atmosphere of growing suspicion, claimed the political lives of prominent east German politicians, and fed the perception that the ex-DDR would be best governed from Bonn. Two of the most spectacular cases marked the days directly preceding and directly following the Volkskammer elections of March 18, 1990. On March 14 it was reported that Walter Schnur, a lawyer whose clients had included prominent dissidents and who was at the time the leader of Demokratischer Aufbruch, had worked for the Stasi. Within days, Schnur was replaced by Rainer Eppelmann, a forty-seven-year-old Protestant clergyman who later became the CDU chair of the Bundestag's commission investigating the DDR past.

Shortly after the elections, Ibrahim Böhme, co-founder and leader of the east German SPD, was accused of collaboration with the Stasi.[77] Böhme, forty-five years old at the time, was widely considered one of the more charismatic of the new leaders. He was also known to oppose a "Grand Coalition" government with the CDU following the March 1990 Volkskammer elections, and initially many hoped the accusations against him would turn out to be "only" political intrigue.

The Schnur and Böhme cases lent urgency to citizens' movement demands that all members of the Volkskammer be certified as uncompromised by past commitments to the Stasi and that access to Stasi files be protected both from destruction and from eventual misuse by the West German intelligence agency, the Bundesnachrichtendienst. The Volkskammer's unwillingness to purge its own members heightened distrust of institutions and representative politics among people active in the citizens' movements. The Stasi issue had been a flash-point in relations between the Round Table and the government through the winter and early spring of 1990; unresolved, it became a flash-point between the grassroots, *basisdemokratische* citizens' movements on the one hand and the elected Volkskammer and government on the other. In the end, still unresolved, it was inherited by the first all-German Bundestag, elected in December 1990.

In mid-November 1989 the Modrow government had officially replaced the MfS with the Amt für Nationale Sicherheit (AfNS, or Office for National Security). One month later, unconvinced by the change and concerned by rumors that documents were being destroyed, New Forum called for the dissolution of the AfNS. In many localities citizens' committees were already attempting both to ensure the security and integrity of Stasi files and to enforce a cessation of Stasi activity.[78] On December 7–8, at its first meeting, the Round Table reiterated New Forum's demand.[79] On December 17 an oversight committee for the dissolution of the AfNS was constituted. During the next several months, however, the tension continued unabated—and so did the Round Table's preoccupation with the issue.[80] On January 15, MfS headquarters in Berlin's Normannenstraße were stormed; the degree to which Stasi forces themselves manipulated the demonstration (originally called by New Forum, with the understanding that the doors to the building complex would remain locked) has never been fully determined. On February 5, Werner Fischer concluded an interim report on the dismantling of the AfNS with a public appeal. Fischer, like Bohley and Templin, had been arrested in the aftermath of the official January 1988 Rosa Luxemburg demonstration, which had been disrupted by dissidents carrying a banner quoting the murdered socialist leader: "Freedom Is Always Measured by the Freedom of Those Who Think Differently." Fischer's words admirably summarized both the difficulties and the stakes of the discussion. A form of politics had compromised the human relations and therefore the political potential of an entire society, he argued; that form of politics would have to be delegitimized, but without undifferentiated condemnations of individuals. The past would somehow have to be confronted, "so that we can at last look one another in the face without distrust." No trust, no democracy. The fundamental human problem so central to the citizens' movements in general and to New Forum in particular now appeared as a parliamentary and legislative challenge. Fischer called it "a very big problem." He continued:

> The former MfS was an anticonstitutional organization that committed crimes against many people.

But: not all Stasi employees were criminals . . .

. . . How should we now deal with these people and with all those who, in whatever way, in the party or in the bureaucracy, in factories, in apartment blocks, or wherever, directly or indirectly, willingly or unwillingly, helped make it possible for this repressive apparatus to function?

We all know it: the entanglements cut straight through all work collectives, friendships, and families.

We must do something, so that we can at last look one another in the face without distrust. We must learn to live with this heritage, without repressing it and without forgetting too fast.[81]

In its final session on March 12, 1990, the Round Table recommended that a parliamentary commission vet all successful Volkskammer candidates, a recommendation reiterated on March 20 by the Normannenstraße citizens' committee.[82] During the period between the elections and unification, parliamentary and ministry committees worked in often uneasy cooperation with one another and with the Normannenstraße committee to oversee the dismantling of the MfS. The anger and suspicion of movement activists often targeted Minister of the Interior Peter-Michael Diestel of the DSU (Deutsche Soziale Union), who seemed to favor both destroying the Stasi archives and keeping Stasi officers gainfully employed.[83]

On August 24 the Volkskammer adopted the "Gesetz über die Sicherung und Nutzung der personengebundenen Daten des ehemaligen Ministeriums für Staatssicherheit/Amtes für Nationale Sicherheit" (Law for the Safety and Use of the Personal Data of the Former MfS/AfNS). The bill's announced purpose was "to guarantee and promote the political, historical, and judicial working through of the activity of the former Ministry for State Security."[84]

The committee recognized that the bill's provisions were in tension with the normal rules of a *Rechtsstaat* (constitutional state; state ruled by law). But where normal rules conflicted with justice, Joachim Gauck argued, responsible men and women were obligated to choose justice. The conflict between the "formalistic" rule of law and the imperatives of a higher justice would become a leitmotiv of efforts to deal with the legacy of the DDR—as it had been a leitmotiv of efforts in the Federal Republic to deal with the legacy of the Third Reich. "Whoever is in a position of responsibility" Gauck insisted, "must increase justice and not diminish it. It mustn't happen that, for formal legal reasons, which in a functioning and secure society may appropriately have the last word, in our situation laws result that would establish legality, but would minimize justice."[85]

The bill stipulated that the Stasi archives would be preserved, and that their use would be supervised by a citizen from the soon-to-be-former DDR. During the final debate, Marianne Birthler (Bündnis 90) insisted "that control [of the Stasi archives] remain with those most directly affected by them." "We . . . perceive the agreement in the State Treaty as it now stands as humiliating," she said, and continued: "The victims and perpetrators live here in the area of the DDR. The duty to work through this past lies here, the burden of working through it lies here, but also the opportunity to work through it."[86]

Speakers from the DSU, the CDU, the FDP, and the SPD as well as the Bündnis 90/Greens parliamentary groups urged that the provisions of the bill be included in the unification treaty. Criticizing the expressed intentions not only of the Federal Republic's Interior Ministry but also of Interior Minister Diestel, Jürgen Haschke, the parliamentary spokesman on this issue for the DSU and its representative on the vetting committee, argued:

> The manner of Bonn's effort at persuasion shows just how little the citizens of the Federal Republic understand about the material in the Stasi archives—if indeed they understand anything at all. This is a part of our history, a part of our fate and of our suffering. We are bringing it with us to Germany.
>
> Only those who dared to begin are entitled to bring a process to a close. The law in its present form bears the mark of those who dared to begin. They have created a memorial, a memorial to a bad time. And one does not destroy memorials without peril. Those who took the Stasi's fortresses will find the bit of courage needed to defend this legislation before an all-German legislature. We support this bill and demand that it be included in the Second State Treaty.[87]

On August 23 the Volkskammer had approved the accession of the DDR Länder to the Federal Republic through the use of Article 23 of the Basic Law. The unification treaty adopted on August 31, however, made no mention of the guarantees provided for by the Volkskammer's Stasi law. Tina Krone, calling the treaty's failure to guarantee east German control over the Stasi archives "another act in the Stasi archive farce," commented, "Cheated again!"[88] New Forum and other citizens' move-ment activists then responded by occupying MfS headquarters in the Normannenstraße, demanding a revision of the treaty. On September 18 an agreement was appended to the unification treaty. The two govern-ments expressed their expectation that the spirit, and for the most part the letter, of the August 24 Volkskammer law would be promptly reaffir-med by an all-German Bundestag.[89]

The final days of debate in the Volkskammer were dominated by an impassioned discussion of how to deal with members found to have been previously involved with the Stasi. On September 28, Gauck delivered the final report for the special committee overseeing the dissolution of the MfS/AfNS; Peter Hildebrandt (Bündnis 90/Greens) then gave the final report of the temporary vetting committee regarding "former em-ployment of Volkskammer deputies by the former MfS/AfNS."[90] The vet-ting committee had been constituted on April 12 and had first met one week later. Not until September 5, however, had it been able to gain access to the files its work required, and only now—five days before unification—was it in a position to issue its report.[91] The critical immedi-ate question concerned whether or not the names of implicated Volks-kammer members, and in particular the fifteen members most seriously implicated, should be released to the parliamentary body as a whole, and possibly to the public. The committee recommended against releasing the names, but the parliamentary leadership offered a motion that pro-vided for their release.[92] A lengthy, impassioned, and procedurally entan-gled debate ensued, punctuated by personal statements made by impli-cated members and by a motion to exclude former high SED officials in general and Hans Modrow in particular from eligibility to serve in the Bundestag.[93] Marianne Birthler (Bündnis 90/Greens), who would resign in October 1992 from Manfred Stolpe's cabinet, arguing that his version of his relationship to the Stasi was no longer believable, pleaded in favor of making the names public, articulating the now familiar argument that reconciliation presupposed honesty and discussion. Former Stasi informants who had concealed their past while running for office had betrayed the trust of their electors, she said, and uncertainty regarding their identity would perpetuate an atmosphere of distrust:

> We owe it to our citizens to see to it that this parliament does not go down in history as a Stasi parliament [applause] and that the shadow . . . does not burden us all.

Or does anyone here believe that whispered names and unspoken suspicions are less harmful than an open discussion? Only this openness . . . makes it possible for a climate to develop here in which former perpetrators too will be able to speak about their past and so dare to make a new beginning.[94]

The amended motion passed, but was immediately referred to the committee on constitutional and administrative reform to see "whether this decision is constitutional and legal." A Bündnis 90/Green deputy exploded, calling the wrangling "a miserable game" and denouncing the assembly as "a disgrace to itself."[95] Werner Schulz (New Forum; Bündnis 90/Greens) argued that absent a constitutional court, the Volkskammer was sovereign, and he reproached the legislature for not following through on the Round Table's efforts to draft a new constitution for the DDR.[96] Konrad Weiß (DJ, Bündnis 90/Greens) likewise protested the bill's referral to committee. "It is a question of survival for many people," Weiß affirmed. The time for patience was over. "I am not in favor of protecting these people now," he said. "They had the opportunity to resign . . . They could have claimed illness, no one would have noticed anything. But now it really will no longer do. Our people are waiting! [applause by Bündnis 90/Greens, the SPD, and the DSU]."[97]

Just as it started to look as if the names might be released, deputies began to request the floor in order to explain the circumstances of their contacts with the Stasi. When the vote came on whether or not to release to the press the names of the fifteen members most implicated by Stasi documents, sixty-eight deputies voted in favor, eighty voted against, and the remainder abstained.[98]

On October 2, 1990, the Volkskammer held its thirty-eighth and final meeting. As the spokesmen for the different parliamentary groups voiced their various appreciations of the transitional period between the fall 1989 protests and unification, two themes regularly resurfaced: each speaker praised the peaceful revolution "from below" that had brought freedom to the DDR, and each stressed the need for a continuing and painful confrontation with the past.[99] To many in the citizens' movements, the words rang hollow. The movement activists had already encountered disappointment: they had been rejected at the polls and were dissatisfied with the treatment of the Stasi issue. "At the end," Jens Reich remarked in *Die Andere Zeitung,* "the Volkskammer was just a solemn corpse." But he also sought to qualify the disappointment he and many of his friends felt. He named four "pluses" as he reviewed the brief history of the freely elected Volkskammer, among them the DDR's confession of responsibility for crimes committed by the National Socialists and the renunciation of the the United Nations' anti-Zionist resolution. He added that the Volkskammer's discussion of and legislative response to the Stasi issue, however incomplete, could be considered a "partial success." Yet "the minuses," he conceded, "weigh more heavily." Among them:

—the constitutional question was taken off the agenda, . . .
—the SPD shouldn't have joined the coalition,
—the issue of the Stasi archives remained unresolved . . .
—in the end, we put up with unofficial Stasi agents as deputies and ministers.

Reich, once again echoing Dirks, concluded by reminding his citizens' movement readers of their common and ongoing mission: "I don't want to leave politics. We must figure out new ways of bringing like-minded people together for effective action. Inside and outside parliamentary bodies."[100]

In November 1991, after nearly a year of public debate and parliamentary deliberation, the first all-German Bundestag adopted the Gesetz über die Unterlagen des Staatssicherheitsdienstes der ehemaligen Deutschen Demokratischen Republik (Law regarding the Documents of the State Security Service of the Former DDR), more commonly known as the Stasi-Unterlagen-Gesetz (StUG).[101] The attention devoted to and the controversy surrounding the StUG greatly overshadowed the intermittent discussion of how DDR "state criminality" might best be prosecuted, and the StUG's adoption preceded the establishment in February 1992 of the Zentrale Ermittlungsstelle zur Bekämpfung der Regierungs- und Vereinigungskriminalität (ZERV, or Central Investigating Authority for the Fight against Governmental and Unification Criminality; see Chapter 4). The bill, which became law on December 20, 1991, regulated access to Stasi files. It was jointly proposed and supported by the parliamentary groups of the governing coalition (CDU/CSU, FDP) and by the opposition SPD. The Bündnis 90/Greens parliamentary group withheld its support; so too, from different motives, did the PDS/Linke Liste group. The stated goals of the new law, which speaker after speaker described as a foray into territory never previously charted, went beyond those articulated in the bill adopted by the Volkskammer. They included:

1. to give the individual access to information about him recorded by the State Security Service, so that he can assess the influence of the State Security Service on his personal fate,
2. to protect that individual, that his individual rights and privacy not be damaged by access to information about him recorded by the State Security Service,
3. to guarantee and promote the historical, political, and legal working through of the activity of the State Security Service,
4. to make available to public and nonpublic bodies the information necessary to achieve the goals set forth in this law. (§1 of StUG)

From the first floor discussion to the final vote, the specific framing of the bill was bitterly contested by Bündnis 90 deputy Ingrid Köppe. In 1977, at age ninteen, Köppe had been forced to interrupt her studies after she refused to sign a declaration condemning the songwriter Wolf Biermann. She had represented New Forum at the Round Table discussions during the last months of the DDR. The bill gave the minister of the interior the authority to order the release of records to state agencies charged with ensuring national security. Again and again, Köppe insisted that such provisions put "the intelligence interests of the Federal Republic above the victims' interest in a full and unsparing working through [of the past]." Again and again, she rejected as unacceptable the centralization of authority over the Stasi records that the bill stipulated. "The reports on victims," Köppe argued, "are . . . a piece of stolen private life,"[102] and they belonged to those from whom they had been stolen; they should be kept easily accessible to victims and beyond the grasp of yet another intelligence service. "We assume," Köppe asserted, "that intelligence services have no place in a real democracy, because they work not openly but secretly." Observation had taught her, she added, that "intelligence services cannot be controlled."[103] Köppe's use of pronouns, as well as the tone and substance of her comments, conveyed the gulf of misunderstanding that separated her from her parliamentary colleagues, especially those who came from the old Länder. "Your proposed bill," she told her colleagues, "is so twisted that official interests have clear priority over victims' rights." The incomprehension was mutual, leading Hartmut Büttner (CDU) to exclaim in the middle of Köppe's speech, "Just what world are you living in?"[104]

Both Rolf Schwanitz, who reported the bill out of committee for the SPD, and Angelika Barbe, a founding member of the East SPD, conceded that elements of the bill gave them "stomach pains"; it was nonetheless, they argued, a necessary and acceptable first step. Schwanitz placed particular emphasis on the fact that the bill would disclose to victims the identities of the informants who had spied on them, and thus would begin to meet the problem of dissolving the atmosphere of fear and distrust in the new Länder. "Not free of charge," Barbe argued, could reconciliation be achieved, and added, "Before forgiveness comes the recognition of guilt." The right of victims to see their files was essential to the process, and its guarantee spoke in favor of the bill: "At stake are the rules of discussion, the opportunities for society to participate in the discussion, an ethic of political action."[105]

The bill's sponsors enjoyed an overwhelming majority in the Bundestag. The files were accordingly opened on January 1, 1992, under the continued supervision of Joachim Gauck. As the controversy surrounding Manfred Stolpe soon demonstrated (see Chapter 5), the files alone could not resolve the fundamental issues created by the existence of a secret police and a communist dictatorship. In May 1990, Ralf Hirsch (another person who had been arrested in the wake of the January 1988 Rosa Luxemburg demonstration), wrongly accused of having worked as an IM, commented: "At the moment, there is nothing worse, either in the east or in the west, than the accusation of having worked for the Stasi. A robbery, even a rape wouldn't cause the same uproar or prompt so much inquisitiveness."[106]

Subsequent developments amply confirmed Hirsch's perception. His observation, like Diepgen's remarks to the Enquete-Kommission reproduced at the beginning of this chapter, again suggested that the issue of individual entanglements and responsibilities might overpower or distort interest in other problems, including the issue of ideological delegitimation.

The fiercely "grassroots democratic" positions of most New Forum leaders contributed powerfully to the movement's emphasis on political culture and personal trust rather than on institutions and political processes. This emphasis on culture and personal relationships can be understood in part as a reaction against the only kind of political party and mechanism of interest articulation that most New Forum activists had ever directly experienced: the SED and democratic centralism. But the Forum's anti-party bias also reflected the activists' perceptions of the disarray into which Western processes of interest articulation had fallen in a "postmaterialist" age. While democracy "triumphed" in the former Soviet bloc and elsewhere, established pluralist systems seemed incapable of resolving their own "crisis of democracy." Why should the new democratizing elites of the DDR have trusted the defense of their interests and aspirations to a party system and political class from which West German citizens themselves, like bodies politic in other advanced industrial democracies, felt increasingly alienated? Most of all, the emphasis on trust was a reaction to a society in which trust had been so systematically violated. It was meant to repair disappointment, and instead it helped to compound it.

Ludwig Mehlhorn had hoped that efforts to create a civil society would not be artificially foreshortened by a premature unification of the two Germanys. New Forum translated this into the motto "First grow up, then marry!"[107] Others expressed this idea by interpreting Willy Brandt's famous and constantly quoted response to the fall of the Wall: "What belongs together will now grow together." Brandt himself would also emphasize another line from his speech: "Nothing will ever be again as it once was."[108] In Brandt's view the circumstances (past and present) called for political creativity, not "reunification," not restoration. But in the DDR many feared—and then complained—that instead of being allowed to grow together gradually, the two societies would be "cobbled" together artificially, to the enduring prejudice of democratic development in the former DDR—and in the Federal Republic. The experiences of the freedom movement in the DDR, wrote Wilfried Geisler, "could provide a strong impulse for a new German democracy . . . We want to co-shape unity . . . What *belongs together* should *grow together.* Nothing should be *cobbled together.*"[109]

The citizens' movements consistently pleaded for "a completely different country," but already in October 1989, Mehlhorn summarized the political danger he saw coming: "As far as I can see, there is a consensus in all the opposition groups that a unification or reunification debate such as has been conducted in the Federal Republic during the last weeks is at least counterproductive, if not actively harmful . . . Many people fear a reunification in the style of an annexation by the Federal Republic; they don't want such a colonization, no matter how glittery it might be."[110]

Before the March 1990 Volkskammer elections, New Forum could (and did) assume that it spoke for "the people," suddenly come to life after years of enforced and/or accepted silence. The results of the elections, however, suggested a marginality that would become more and more pronounced during the succeeding months. As this trend confirmed itself, New Forum activists seem to have used the Stasi issue to explain and to counteract the demoralizing implications of their own political isolation.

For all these reasons, by the summer of 1990, the "working through" of the Stasi past had come to dominate the agenda of New Forum activists. They pressed their case with sufficient vehemence to move the Stasi issue to the center of relations between east and west Germans, where it was soon picked up for other, exclusionary uses by conservative west German intellectuals, themselves on the rebound from a different confrontation with the past—the *Historikerstreit,* or "historians' debate," of the 1980s. In the short run, few of the New Forum leaders who remained active in public life in unified Germany seem to have noticed that their issue had backfired. If unification could not be delayed until a democratic culture could be established in the DDR, New Forum activists had at least wanted a strong voice in the unified state. Instead, their insistence on the Stasi issue was used to disqualify the actors who could have given them that voice and to cast moral discredit on a public that might have pressed for a distinctive agenda.

Three

After the Lie: Democratic Legitimacy without Community?

The Federal Republic brought to the "new Länder" and to the process of German unification established democratic institutions, but also a distinctively brittle, fractured, and defensive sense of democratic legitimacy, born in large part of the interaction between longer traditions of German political culture and the particular ways in which West Germany had worked through the multiple legacies, political and personal, of the Third Reich.[1] The lack of democratic self-confidence and the associated patterns of political argument represent a partial cost of the postwar institutional strategy that also produced stable democratic institutions; they illustrate the "lack of community" that Karl Jaspers hoped dialogue and self-examination would overcome. Instead, political debates suggested a partially blocked political learning process, and tended to reproduce the lack of community. The unhealed fractures left over from the Nazi era created a self-perpetuating logic of political distrust, an underlying assumption that actors would be unreliable despite the increasingly manifest reliability of the system. West Germans (and others) often point to the political, cultural, and especially economic burdens they took on when unification came. The blocked learning process was a negative *West* German addition to the burdens of unification, and it is within the context of that broader and ongoing process that I propose to analyze the controversy that erupted in 1990 around Christa Wolf, one of East Germany's best-known and most productive novelists.

The "basic consensus" of the Federal Republic was often described, by those who thought or wished to assert that such a consensus existed, as "anti-totalitarian": anti-Nazi and anticommunist. The negative formulation of this consensus contributed to or was indicative of its brittleness in three ways. First, its supposedly evenhanded quality, equally anti-Nazi and anticommunist, was often less than obvious: the right argued (or proceeded from the assumption) that the Nazi danger lay definitively defeated in the past, whereas the communist threat was all too real; the left retorted that the communist danger was exaggerated and was being used as a convenient excuse for forgetting about the Nazi experience and its multiple legacies. Second, the fractured nature of the consensus tended to reinforce long-standing patterns of political argument and interaction: the propensity to resort to *Feindbilder* ("us-them" imagery) and polemics, to suspect the (hidden) motives and honesty of one's adversaries (and even of one's putative friends), to avoid a reexamination of anti-Western traditions long common to both the left and the right in Germany, and to adopt a defensive posture that systematically underestimated both the capacity of one's opponents to learn and change and the power and attractiveness of one's own positions. Finally, the insistence on an "anti-totalitarian" consensus created a unique political investment in a debatable category produced by a hardly infallible academic discipline. Long after American political scientists had become cautious in their use of the category, it continued to play a central role, directly and indirectly, in West German politico-intellectual debates. The category had been developed by scholars who *were* evenhandedly anti-totalitarian: Carl Friedrich, Hannah Arendt, and (in Germany) Karl Dietrich Bracher.[2] But by the 1970s, when it was intellectually challenged in Germany by new research interests, it had assumed functions that made its political use relatively impervious to academic critiques.[3] It resurfaced after unification as a major concept structuring debate about the experience of dictatorship; the problems associated with its use contaminated the discussion of what should have been a far less contentious term, namely, *Unrechtsstaat* (a regime not bound by law; see Chapter 6).

The collapse of the Soviet empire, German unification, the legacy of the second German dictatorship, and the simple passage of time invited Germans to move beyond the blocked learning process associated with the "anti-totalitarian" paradigm. Anti-totalitarian discourse had had a great deal to say about "them" and relatively little to say about "us." With "them" no longer in the picture, it was at least conceivable that people would find new ways of talking about "us." The purpose of this chapter is to show how the old patterns weathered the challenge, thus renewing the legitimation problems that had accompanied the Federal Republic since its inception—despite the stability of its institutions and significant cultural change.

In the first and second sections of the chapter, I focus on the abbreviated debate among East German intellectuals about Stalinism and the all-German debate about Christa Wolf (the so-called *Literaturstreit*). In each case an emphasis on issues related to trust and betrayal helped deflect public interest from the systemic features and leading decision makers of the DDR; instead, interest concentrated on morally complex figures whose compromises with the regime might have encouraged a differentiated and nonaccusatory discussion—"in the solidarity of loving struggle," as Jaspers had proposed after 1945—about how people have responded to the threats and temptations associated with twentieth-century dictatorships, and how they later lived, individually and collectively, with the choices they made. Instead, Wolf was pilloried—or defended—using arguments and ways of arguing already standard in the Federal Republic. More was at stake here than the efforts of conservative politicians and some intellectuals to shift the ideological boundaries of public debate in the Federal Republic, although that too was happening. In the third section of the chapter, I suggest that in the repeated and repetitive debates about German history (and especially about the Third Reich) which unfolded between 1983 and 1995, we can discern a pattern of argument that resembled the pattern evident in the *Literaturstreit*. Taken together, these debates suggest that the brittle character of the Federal Republic's understanding of its own legitimacy was self-perpetuating: like the "old" Federal Republic, the new Germany—and especially the new Länder—would get stable institutions and a brittle sense of democratic legitimacy. The cultural strategy promoted by the citizens' movements encouraged an emphasis on trust; that emphasis theoretically created an opportunity for Germans to reach a common understanding of personal responsibility in political life. In the particular political, intellectual, and cultural context of (west) Germany in the late 1980s and the 1990s, however, the opportunity was missed.

In the concluding section of the chapter, we will have to ask whether the kind of blocked learning process described here is a predictable consequence of institutional strategies, or whether it is a particularity of the German case—a cost associated not with institutional strategies in general but with the uniquely terrible nature and extent of Nazi crimes.

The Criminalization of Complicity

Communism, the East German regime never tired of asserting, had liberated East Germans from fascism: from 1945 to 1989, "antifascism" was fundamental to East German communist claims to legitimacy. The claim, along with the constant drain of dissidents who resettled (voluntarily or involuntarily) in the Federal Republic, helps explain why East German communists in general and intellectuals in particular—unlike their Polish, Czech, and Hungarian counterparts—were so slow to break with communism, and so reluctant to do so completely. Communism had represented their second chance, their opportunity to retrieve a collective (and often personal) mistake of massive proportions. As in Poland, Czechoslovakia, and Hungary, communism in East Germany was imposed by an external power; in 1945 its domestic proponents knew only too well how thin their support was. But to East Germans, communism offered a pardon; and given the enormity of the prior offense, the offer was very hard to refuse. In this sense communism was, like Nazism before it, seductive rather than persuasive. When compared to the ties between intellectuals and the regime in other East European countries, the resulting relationship was differently freighted, even for those who rejected it or eventually broke its bonds.

In 1989 a long-overdue public discussion of Stalinism finally began in East Germany. It was a debate about the links between Stalinism and communism, and therefore ambiguous in its stance vis-à-vis communism, whose respectability and reformability some participants assumed and others sought to establish. The debate was led by—and focused on—intellectuals. On October 28 (ten days after Erich Honecker's resignation), the playright Heiner Müller and the actor Dieter Mann organized a reading from Walter Janka's newly published memoir *Schwierigkeiten mit der Wahrheit* (Difficulties with the Truth) at the Deutsche Theater.[4] Janka, born in 1914, had been a lifelong communist: by the time he was in his teens, he had become, as Gustav Just later described him, "the sort of communist who became a hero in partisan struggle: unbending, faithful, a revolutionary to the marrow of his bones."[5] In 1933 he had buried his older brother, a KPD Reichstag deputy murdered by the Nazis in April; shortly thereafter Walter himself was arrested, and spent two years in Nazi prisons and concentration camps before being expelled to Czechoslovakia. When the party, citing his lack of military experience, refused to send him to Spain, Janka allowed himself to be sent instead by the Czech youth organization. Arriving in Spain in October 1936, Janka fought first as a soldier in the Thälmann Battalion. He eventually rose to the rank of major in the Spanish army.

In 1941 Janka escaped from an internment camp in France. Later that year, he and a number of other communists sailed for Mexico, where he remained for the duration of the war. In Mexico City, Janka organized the publishing house El Libro Libre. Among the books he published figured Anna Seghers's well-known novel about Nazi Germany, *Das siebte Kreuz* (The Seventh Cross).[6]

In January 1947, Janka and his wife returned, via the Soviet Union, to Germany. Janka worked initially as a personal assistant to Paul Merker, who had also been in exile in Mexico and who was now a member of the Politburo.[7] After a year Janka resigned. He refused reassignment to the security apparatus, insisting on employment more consistent with his professional capabilities and predilections. During the next several years, he held leading positions in DEFA (Deutsche Film-Aktiengesellschaft, the East German film production company) and in the Aufbau publishing house. In every case his achievements were accompanied by tensions bordering on confrontation with the party hierarchy.

For Janka, the politically defining event of the 1950s was Khrushchev's denunciation of Stalin's crimes in his famous speech to the Twentieth Congress of the Soviet Communist Party in February 1956. Shortly before his own arrest in 1957, Gustav Just—who had grown up the son of a working-class communist from the Sudetenland but had become a decorated officer in Hitler's Wehrmacht before choosing the Soviet zone in 1946—recalled the "wish-dreams" that Khrushchev's speech had inspired among reform-minded communists. Now, he hoped, the Soviets would come to their senses, the reformists would win, and Germany would be reunified.[8]

In this atmosphere Janka openly promoted what passed for a reformist line, and banked on the imminent replacement of the rigid Stalinist leadership represented by Walter Ulbricht. Just as Ulbricht's demise had been prevented in 1953 by the June 17 uprising, however, so it was now precluded by the leadership's reaction to the events in Hungary. Between November 1956 and March 1957, one after the other, Janka and his political confederates (including Just) were arrested.

The book from which Dieter Mann read was an abridged prepublication version of Janka's memoirs. Its three chapters focused on Janka's arrest in December 1956 and on his subsequent show trial and imprisonment.[9] Christa Wolf called the evening a "premiere" because "for the first time, we are discussing, as publicly and as radically as possible, the fundamental evil, from which over the decades almost all other evils in the DDR derived: Stalinism."[10]

The discussion begun in the Deutsche Theater was soon distorted and abbreviated by the rush toward unification. But it was that discussion—essentially both East German and intraleft—and not the subsequent west German attacks on east German intellectuals spearheaded by the conservative daily *Frankfurter Allgemeine Zeitung,* that first elevated the silence and inaction of men and women who could and should have known better into the morally preoccupying feature of Stalinism. This development, like the citizens' movement's focus on IMs, again diverted attention from leaders and institutional structures, and concentrated instead on individuals and their (presumptively freely assumed) choices. Like the citizens' movement's understanding of democracy, it potentially called *all* who had lived under the dictatorship—or a dictatorship—to account, and it privileged the issues of trust and betrayal. It focused on the "crime" which a regime that had *not* engaged in genocide or aggressive war, and that had been more repressive and invasive than it had been murderous, had most often and most consistently encouraged. Silence, complicity, and betrayal were also misdeeds that had outlived the Stalinist period of communist rule, and that could therefore be argued to represent features of communist rule in all its phases. Potentially, this preoccupation could have encouraged a new, symmetrical, all-German curiosity about the complicities of ordinary people—and especially of Wehrmacht (regular army) soldiers—during the Third Reich, thus promoting rather than inhibiting a collective learning process, but this did not happen.

If the public discussion of Stalinism did not begin in earnest in the DDR until 1989, Janka's private reflections on Stalinism had begun much earlier, during his long and lonely years in prison, when his own conscience had been his only interlocutor. Three sets of characters are critical to Janka's description of his political fall, and by extension to his understanding of why reformist forces failed to reshape real existing socialism. The first set includes the politically responsible architects of East German Stalinism, along with their willing tools: among the architects were Walter Ulbricht, the party leader, and Erich Mielke, the head of the secret police, and among the tools, Ernst Melsheimer, the state prosecutor in Janka's trial. The second set includes proven communists left morally disarmed by the ethical suppositions of Leninism: the most prominent representative of this group was Johannes R. Becher, a poet and former antifascist who was DDR minister of culture when Janka was arrested. The final set includes comrades who had identified with Janka's reformist aspirations but who did not rise to his defense when the showdown came: the unforgettable exemplar of this anguished group was the novelist Anna Seghers, whose deafening silence in 1956 seemed still to ring in Janka's ears in 1989.

Janka offered no particular insights into Stalinist rule—Arthur Koestler's *Darkness at Noon,* to which *Spuren eines Lebens* appears in many ways a non-fictionalized counterpart, provides its readers with a far more searching examination of Stalinist patterns of thought, belief, and action—but Janka had no trouble naming the set of "comrades" who perverted socialism: the list included neither Becher nor Seghers. Janka's psychological preoccupation with Becher's betrayal and Seghers's silence did not blind him to the identity of his real enemies: Ulbricht, Hermann Matern, Melsheimer, and Mielke.

Like Wolf Biermann, however, Janka found his real enemies too predictable and too evil to be morally interesting. Janka had first encountered Erich Mielke in Spain, and even then Mielke was a villain. Janka was fighting as a volunteer in the Thälmann Battalion; Mielke, already attached to the party's notorious intelligence service, was wearing a fancy uniform, smoking cigarettes, and sending politically suspect comrades to their death.[11] Janka took Becher's antifascist credentials more seriously, and was correspondingly more troubled by Becher's failure to denounce Stalinist crimes. But Janka explained Becher's conduct by citing a mixture of rank cowardice, normal ambition, and a purely instrumental understanding of law.

For Anna Seghers's behavior, Janka offered no explanation and no excuse. It was Seghers who had insisted that Janka attempt to rescue Georg Lukács after the Hungarian uprising of 1956. All Janka could do is recall her enduring silence, both during and after his trial. He remembered seeing her stare "uncomfortably at the floor," a silent onlooker as Lukács was "slandered and falsely incriminated."[12] From his comrades turned enemies, Janka expected what he got. From his remaining comrades, he still hoped for solidarity, and Seghers's silence stung.

In Janka's assessment of Stalinism, moral interest was thus inversely related to political responsibility: Ulbricht was responsible and repellent, but Seghers was more preoccupying and present. In the course of the discussion unleashed by Janka's book and by the efforts to reverse the verdict that thirty years earlier had sent him and his co-defendants to prison, the hierarchy of responsibility was gradually obscured. The morally interesting case became the focus of attention, debate, and censure. Seghers, who had died in June 1983, became a conspicuous object of moral blame—as though her conduct, rather than Ulbricht's politics, had been the cause of Janka's fall and imprisonment. This pattern would be repeated in the Christa Wolf case, and later again with Manfred Stolpe. In each case the self-examination and questioning of the actor—by Anna Seghers in her posthumously published novella *Der gerechte Richter* (The Just Judge), by Christa Wolf in *Was bleibt* (What Remains), and by Manfred Stolpe in his autobiographical account *Schwieriger Aufbruch* (Difficult Awakening)—would be used as evidence to suggest that the actor was morally culpable, and public debate would focus on the morally interesting characters rather than on the politically responsible figures.[13]

The emphasis on loyalty and betrayal invited an argument that attributed ultimate responsibility for the stability of the regime to the everyday complicity of upright citizens, inside and outside the party, whether the party in question was the SED or the National Socialists (NSDAP), and whether the regime was the DDR or the Third Reich. Janka did not make this argument when he spoke of the DDR, but others soon did. In his lengthy critique of the November 28, 1989, "Für unser Land" appeal, Arno Widmann wrote: "The whole system worked only because everyone—or at least almost everyone—helped. The neighbors, for example, who no longer greeted the young couple that had applied for exit visas, or the school principal, who for years harrassed a female colleague whose companion had holed up in the West, or the decent citizens who reported their neighbors' Western contacts."[14]

The increasing concentration on the complicity of upright citizens obviously broadened and ultimately transformed the initial East German debate about Stalinism. Heinrich Olschowski elaborated on Widmann's theme, and explicitly drew on terminology associated with the analysis of commitments made during the Third Reich: "The *Mitläufer* are among us. And they have a dismayingly good conscience, because they make no use of it. For everything in which they participated, they now do not want to be held responsible. They have internalized the 'organized irresponsibility' of the system."[15]

When, then, had the system become morally indefensible, and when had those who had not resisted it become co-responsible *Mitläufer*? Seghers's defense presupposed that in 1957, loyalty to the party was still a morally tenable position. Erich Loest, who was also arrested in 1957 and who then spent seven and a half years in a DDR prison, argued that Seghers had in fact done what she could to protect Janka. She had tried to use her influence within the party to secure Janka's release—with no visible effect either to Janka's advantage or to his prejudice. A courtroom gesture, Loest asserted, would have "looked good" in retrospect, but would have had "absolutely no effect" on the outcome of the trial. The notion that such a protest could or should have had a different purpose (e.g., to discredit the regime's pardon-and-promise offer) or been aimed at an audience outside the courtroom (e.g., the non-party public), Loest rejected as inappropriate. Loest urged Seghers's would-be judges to recall (or sympathetically reconstruct) the political atmosphere of the 1950s and the psychological impact of Seghers's previous political experiences:

> Now it has become a common game to reflect on whether Anna Seghers was a coward. This is senseless, and it puts the debate on a course where it does not belong. "She could have gone to RIAS [West Berlin radio station] and told everything." A clever young woman suggested this recently in a discussion. Her voice was relaxed, her face was smooth, her eyes were clear. Anna Seghers could have? Right straight down the streets? And then?
>
> The Cold War, crackling with frost, could on any day turn into a shooting war. Two blocs stood with atomic weapons trained on each other, the division of the world cut through the middle of Berlin. There was no third way, certainly not for Anna Seghers. A flight to the Western public would have meant a break with her past, her party, her philosophy, her experience and all her friends, with her books and— still—her hopes. She had not passed blind and deaf by the Stalinist witch-hunts; she suffered from the contradiction like all her contemporaries. The Hitler-Stalin [Non-Aggression] Pact [of 1939] had cut a gash through her understanding of life, but had not exploded it.[16]

Loest's argument makes sense only if communism could be seen, in sharp distinction to National Socialism, as a legitimate enterprise, plausibly providing both a pardon and a promise, a different version of a second chance. Loest would never have argued that Nazi ideals were worth the temporary sacrifice of individual conscience, nor would he have suggested that loyalty to Nazism could be justified by the political context in which it arose. But as the DDR crumbled and the debate widened, Loest's view of Seghers's commitments began to appear increasingly lonely. By 1989, even the search for a "third way" seemed to some observers culpable, and the stalwart loyalty to the party exemplified by well-informed and lucid intellectuals like Seghers seemed indefensible. In early December 1989, Christoph Hein reviewed Just's memoirs for the weekly *Sonntag*. The playright attacked "real existing socialism," saying it was "nothing more than a system in which an entire people was checked and exploited by a small political clique using an all-powerful secret service and an almost solid net of surveillance and denunciation, spying and repression."[17]

What then of those who, living in an actually existing socialist state, had remained loyal to socialism? Hein, a parson's son, had never been seduced by communism; he had, he later explained, been saved by his biography, as others—he named both Christa Wolf and Wolf Biermann—had been misled by theirs.[18] Hein emphasized that a reexamination of the Janka case could only mean the self-examination of everyone who had lived in the country where the case had occurred. He specifically mentioned morally culpable silences and "small everyday betrayals." The discusion would not be easy, but it would have a payoff: "We will," Hein wrote, "learn about ourselves."[19] It seemed fair to ask what part west Germans would play in this process of self-discovery. In the not-so-distant past, they too had encountered the problems of silence, of courage and cowardice, of solidarity and betrayal, and the role of partner was at least a possibility. Whose past would be examined, and on what terms?

Disclaiming "What Remains"

The west German role in the learning process first came into focus during the so-called *Literaturstreit* occasioned by the publication of Christa Wolf's "Stasi story," *Was bleibt,* in June 1990. In the prior (and ongoing) West German debate about responsibilities incurred during the Third

Reich, the role of intellectuals had attracted relatively little attention. No West German court ever brought an indictment against—for example— Martin Heidegger or Carl Schmitt, and Herbert von Karajan and Wilhelm Furtwängler, who had "graced" the Third Reich with their music, later did the same for the Federal Republic.

There were good reasons why, after 1989, the role played by intellectuals would come under closer scrutiny than it had after 1945. First, intellectuals had accepted for themselves—and legitimized to others—the pardon-and-promise package the regime proposed, and in comparison with their counterparts in other East European countries, they had been noticeably slow in separating from the regime when its promise turned out to be empty: "everything," Wolf Biermann recalled in the summer after the Wall fell, "was bewilderingly intermingled." He continued:

> We were intertwined, entangled, and related as if by marriage to our adversaries . . . The deep family ties to our sworn enemies never broke off, because we all carried the contradictions within us . . .
> And so we talked to one another, we were indeed family, torn to the point of blood, but family. And all the hate, the poison, the anger came from this intimate, forced embrace with our oppressors.[20]

Second, because of their own ambivalent feelings and commitments, intellectuals were—as Anna Seghers's biography demonstrated—especially prone as a social group to be caught in the webs of moral and personal betrayal, whose exposure and exploration would become central to the post-1989 transition. And since art does often reflect reality, ambivalence and betrayal appear as themes in the literature produced by East German writers. This was particularly true of Christa Wolf. Wolf, sixteen as the war ended, had had no difficulty giving her childhood allegiance to the Third Reich, and in 1945 she was receptive to the new regime's pardon and promise; later she wrote a widely acclaimed novel about an adult looking back at her childhood in Hitler's Germany.[21] Wolf joined the SED, held responsible positions, and served briefly (in 1959–1962) as an informant for the Stasi. The debate about her commitments was a test of how Germans—especially west Germans—would frame the problem of complicity. It was a measure of how, or whether, they would be able to construct an understanding of "what remained" through which west Germans and east Germans, right and left, ex-'68ers and their parents and their children, would feel commonly and reciprocally challenged, and out of which a common understanding of political obligation, democratic citizenship, and political legitimacy could emerge.

Was bleibt is written in the first-person singular, and it is clearly intended to reflect Wolf's own experiences. A draft of the book was written in 1979, when its publication might have created serious political difficulties for its author, but Wolf did not publish it then. She revised the manuscript in late 1989; it appeared in early June 1990, some three months after the free elections of March 1990 and just four months before unification. The book recounts a day in the life of a female writer in East Berlin who is under secret police surveillance: outside her apartment, three young secret police agents sit in a parked car. Wolf's character, who had found hope in a dictatorship, speaks of inner fear and self-doubt. The account begins with the self-admonition "Just no fear," and it is focused throughout on the narrator's feelings and on the inadequacies of the vocabulary available to her as she seeks, with at most very incomplete success, to overcome her fear and to assess what is happening to her. Not only can she not properly express the political and psychological situation in which she finds herself, but also she is not even sure that if one day she does come into possession of the appropriate language, she will still rightly remember the reality she had once so urgently wished to capture: "In that other language, which I can hear but not yet speak, I will one day talk about it. Today it would still, I knew, be too early. But would I sense it, when the time was right? Would I ever find my language? Someday I would be old. And how would I then remember these days?"[22]

Alongside the narrator's raw fear stands her "shameful need to be on good terms with all sorts of people" (20–21). But the narrator is not simply conflict-averse, and the emotion she evokes here is not a private emotion. Rather, she is caught in precisely the bind that Biermann described. She cannot fully separate herself from the agents who are spying on her or from the political system that put them there, and even her desire to do so is uncertain: she needs, after all, "to be on good terms with all sorts of people." She is, as the story repeatedly demonstrates, a conscious, if always uneasy and often guilt-ridden, participant in the "ritual, facades, and excuses" that Václav Havel—more bluntly concerned with lies than with fear—had identified in 1978 as the fundamental feature of modern dictatorships.[23] Wolf's narrator had met one of the men assigned to follow her at a sausage stand near her apartment building, and early in the story she tellingly labels him "man [*Herr*] or comrade." She must repress her instinct to bring him and his colleagues hot tea (16, 19); thereafter, the agents are always referred to by the wholly neutral expression "the young men." Even at the end of the book, as she reads aloud from her work to an audience partially genuine and partially composed of agents, and as she feels herself almost released from her usual hesitations and paralysis, she tells herself that she must read well for the sake of *both* elements of her audience, the agents as well as the honest listeners: "For where is it written that they are of steel, that they are not also seducible" (93). The use of the word "seducible" in this context is itself interesting: it is the word often used to explain popular support for Hitler, and here it suggests a tendency to think of politics in emotional terms—seduction or fear, pardons and promises. In the book, the only alternative way of measuring political appeal is in purely practical terms. Thus, the narrator is appalled by the waste of social resources that the existence of a secret police imposes on a society—*her* society— with so many needs: able-bodied young men could, she repeatedly observes, be better employed doing things other than spying on their compatriots (13, 23, 29), and the agents who read other people's mail were using the photocopying machines that were nowhere to be found in the libraries, where they were truly needed (54).

Emotional separations, whether public or private, are, as we all know, rarely clean. "One day I grasped," the narrator claims, "that I had no access to the young men there outside. They were not my sort. They were the emissaries of the others" (21). In fact, however, she is deeply uncertain of her own identity. Two years later, in the course of the second controversy over Christa Wolf (centered this time on her relationship to the Stasi), the public would learn that the Stasi's code name for Wolf and her husband, Gerhard, had been "Double-Face" (*Doppelzüngler,* literally "double-tongued"). In many ways, the code name she was assigned as a "victim" seems more appropriate than the impersonal code name that Wolf had, as an informant, earlier chosen for herself (Margarete, her middle name). Wolf never acknowledged deliberately speaking out of both sides of her mouth, but in *Was bleibt,* she did confess to not knowing which words might represent a genuine self: "I myself. Who was that. Which of the many beings, out of which 'I myself' assembled myself. The one that wanted to be known? The one that wanted to spare itself? Or that third, that was still tempted to dance to the same tune as the young men out there in front of my door? . . . That was it, what I needed: to be able to believe that one day soon I would be able to separate myself completely from that third and get it out of me; that I really wanted to do so . . . "(57).

Ultimately, the separation remains incomplete: the narrator's attitude toward the authorities is one of suspicious accommodation—and she remains accommodating even though, like Wolf in the DDR, she knows she would be partially protected by her reputation and her international visibility were she to be less accommodating. Her readiness to compromise stands in explicit contrast to the self-effacing courage of several young people who nonetheless take her for a mentor. One rings her doorbell, manuscript in hand, while inside the anxiety-ridden narrator imagines the visitor to be the police. The young woman has already gone twice to prison "because she did not belong to those who could be blackmailed" (75). Furthermore, she writes well. Here, where the narrator might have refused "to dance to the same tune as the young men" watching her, she instead urges the incautious woman to return to the world of lying. She seeks to destroy the woman's self-confidence and sense of self, and to infect her with the fear that had crippled her own identity (77).

The young woman, however, is more courageous than the model she has chosen: in the book, the difference seems visceral, a matter of character (or perhaps generation) rather than deliberation. The narrator admires the young woman's integrity and strength, without, however, being able to identify with or imitate either. In fact, she seems briefly but explicitly to stand with the other side, with the "young men," suddenly no longer the "emissaries of the others." "*We* cannot save her," she remarks, "cannot spoil her" (78, 79; emphasis added).

Also more courageous than the narrator is another modest young woman who rises to ask a question about "the future" during the discussion after the narrator's open reading. Once again the narrator's instinctive response is to try to neutralize the attempted introduction of the "truth" and to restore the "ritual, facades, and excuses" on which the regime rests. This transpires in the presence of "Kollegin K.," the staff member of the cultural center who is responsible for the evening. Kollegin K. appears in the book as a caricatured, stereotypical representation of fear, submissiveness, and stupidity. She may be real, but (like

Honecker or Mielke) she is uninteresting. In an apparent setup, Kollegin K. has called the police to break up the peaceful, friendly crowd of people who had arrived too late to gain entrance to the reading. The narrator is not yet aware of this development, but we have no reason to think that her response to the young woman's intervention would have been different if she had already been informed. In the end, her conscious attempt to dismantle the bridges to reality that the young woman was seeking to build does indeed seem more culpable morally than the conduct of Kollegin K., a frightened, unthinking bureaucrat, too transparently contemptible ever to be mistaken for a model by someone still morally capable of making better choices. Here, moral culpability becomes hard to separate from political responsibility, for while others—Honecker and Mielke again—made decisions and still others, such as Kollegin K., executed them, it was the narrator who helped see to it that the decisions were accepted.

Assuming the young woman interested in "the future" to be unconscious of the danger in which she had placed herself, the narrator tries to "cover" for her. But others in the audience take up the question, and the narrator "became silent, and listened, as I have rarely listened in my life" (95f). In *Was bleibt* it is—rightly—around the unassuming but fearless young woman (she turns out to be a nurse) who values reality, and not around the narrator who battles her anxieties with lies, that a circle forms as the meeting breaks up. In real life, of course, prominent writers enjoy a broader public platform than do obscure nurses, whatever their relative endowments of courage and lucidity may be—and Christa Wolf, while she may also have been listening, did not choose the option of remaining silent. In interviews and statements, she insistently reaffirmed the political and moral viability of the role she had played in the DDR and described in *Was bleibt*: that of a woman born in 1929, shaped by Nazism before embracing communism, by the mid-1960s increasingly subject to self-doubt, a partially paralyzed character constantly—and to the outside observer perhaps self-servingly—caught between complicity and dissent. Of her complicity there were many signs and symbols: her membership in the SED (from 1949 until June 1989), the leadership positions she occupied in the cultural world, national awards, the right to travel. For many, the most graphic, and ultimately unpardonable, demonstration of her complicity was her brief cooperation with the Stasi, from 1959 to 1962. Already in November 1987, Marcel Reich-Ranicki, at the time the chief literary correspondent of the *Frankfurter Allgemeine Zeitung* (a post he occupied from 1973 to 1988, when he retired to become the moderator of the popular television program *Das literarische Quartet*), and probably then the most prominent and influential literary critic in the Federal Republic, had attacked Wolf for allegedly playing both sides of the political line, siding cautiously with dissidents at one moment and reassuring the political establishment at the next.[24] In 1993 *Der Spiegel* labeled the "fearful Margarete" simply an "irresolute opportunist," and marveled that she could ever have been more favorably considered. The contemptuous surprise suggested as much an absence of curiosity about West German motives as a lack of interest in East German realities.

The signs of Wolf's dissent included, most notably, the integrity of her novels themselves (especially the later ones), her signature on the famous petition protesting the expulsion of Wolf Biermann in 1976 (which Reich-Ranicki wrongly accused her of having subsequently retracted), and the forty-two volumes of reports the Stasi saw fit to keep on her between 1968 and 1980 (by 1992, the reports written after 1980 had been destroyed).

Christa Wolf publicly regretted her cooperation with the Stasi. She was, she wrote Inge Aicher-Scholl, the surviving sister of the Scholl siblings executed for their role in the Weiße Rose (White Rose) resistance group during the Third Reich, "shocked by this part of my past."[25] She also claimed, in private letters as well as public statements, to have forgotten the episode by 1992, when, "completely unprepared,"[26] she accidentally came across the incriminating documents: "A classic process of repression," she said with some understatement, "that gives me occasion to reflect."[27] The person who had assigned herself a code name in 1959 now seemed, she said, wholly a stranger to her.[28] But Wolf's "shock" and contrition never extended to commitments beyond her relatively fleeting entanglement with the Stasi. She never even suggested an apology for, nor did she ever find incomprehensible, her allegiance to the DDR, and, the forty-two volumes of Stasi reports notwithstanding, she rejected the notion that she had ever been a victim, saying, "I felt myself too active."[29]

Speaking in 1987–88 of the early 1960s, Wolf told Therese Hörnigk, her East German biographer, of the hope and excitement that had both motivated and derived from her political commitments. But even more revealingly, she suggested—as had Loest when speaking of Anna Seghers—that she had seen "no alternative": "Should we have considered the West Germany of Adenauer and Globke or Erhard as a possible place to live? This land here was . . . our battlefield, we wanted to prove ourselves here, we wanted it to happen here, and in our own lifetime."[30] Hans Globke had written the authoritative legal gloss on the discriminatory Nuremberg laws. Adenauer did not view this past as politically disqualifying, and appointed Globke state secretary. Wolf did not want to share her second chance with the conservative and the compromised.[31]

The "West Germany of Adenauer and Globke" had many things to offer—and first among them, political freedom. But it could not offer a pardon. It could not even offer a myth on the order of de Gaulle's myth of a Paris "liberated by herself." It could offer only the sorry lie that Jaspers denounced, according to which Germans, "always decent, attached to the truth, and eager for peace," had "through an incomprehensible misfortune" fallen victim to an "evil criminal," or alternatively, the long, difficult, frustrating "work on the consciousness of the time, work on the public conscience, on public opinion" that Walter Dirks had urged on his contemporaries. To Christa Wolf, neither offer was compelling: forced to chose between freedom without a pardon (or a democratic majority) and a pardon without freedom, she opted for the pardon and against freedom. In December 1989—two weeks after signing the "Für unser Land" appeal urging her compatriots to stay put and to prevent the "sellout of our moral and material values"—Wolf repeated and explained her reasons for remaining in the DDR. She spoke now of the mid-1970s, the period in which Biermann had been expelled. "The question was," she allowed, "whether one could stay in the DDR." And again she dismissed the notion that a real alternative had been available: "We did not see an alternative in any other country. Furthermore, I was really passionately interested only in this country. Only here, with all the despair, with all the exclusion, the self-doubt that living here brings, did I feel the strong friction that throws off productive sparks. That was my motive for writing."[32]

More than constituting her "motive for writing" (a common reason for a reluctance to leave one's country, but a surprising criterion to use in assigning one's political allegiances), the mixture of hope and despair, of ideological assertiveness and moral self-doubt, were fundamental to Wolf's identity. Wolf had not forgotten the *Kindheitsmuster* (patterns of childhood) that Germans of her generation shared, and she found it endlessly difficult to shed the solution the DDR had offered her. *Was bleibt* testified to the costs of her choice.

Two broad options were open to Wolf's critics: they could construct her (auto)biography as a German biography and ask what it told them about their own (and about the "West Germany of Adenauer and Globke"), or they could attack her as if she were someone with whom they did not have to live, whose story had nothing to do with or to tell them about their own. In this context, four distinct responses to Wolf's past political commitments emerged.

The "conservative" position, associated with Frank Schirrmacher and the *Frankfurter Allgemeine Zeitung (FAZ)*, but shared by many New Forum ex-dissidents, obeyed the attack logic and denied all respectability to communism. It likewise condemned those—including Wolf, but also including Western politicians and allegedly tone-setting left-of-center intellectuals—who had supposedly served it, believed in it, or compromised with it, whether by professing respect for communist ideals or by investing in détente. During the *Historikerstreit* of the 1980s, the *FAZ* had consistently offered its pages to writers who radically relativized the distinction between Nazism and communism; now that distinction was dismissed without any sustained effort at substantive reflection. The purpose of the critique was to condemn and exclude, not to understand, and certainly not to identify common experiential ground. The former DDR dissidents did not share the ideological project of the revisionist historians and publicists, but they nonetheless viewed insistent efforts to distinguish between Nazism and communism as idly academic or politically self-interested or both. Newcomers to a West German debate with a long history, they either did not grasp or did not care that they were being used by people whose broader agenda they did not share.

The significance of Wolf's ephemeral secret activities, Schirrmacher asserted, paled before her consistently defended public commitments. Schirrmacher accused those who now used contact with the Stasi as an index of moral and political turpitude of deliberately missing the point in order to deflect attention from their own more pernicious complicities; that is, he sought to settle outstanding *West* German political accounts, against the left and against the proponents of détente. For him, Wolf's biography was a new weapon on an old battlefield.[33]

Václav Havel, during his years as a dissident, had also denounced the irretrievably vicious character of communist systems. In its clarity and intransigence, Schirrmacher's position at least superficially recalls the substance of Havel's argument; the resemblance is superficial to the extent that Schirrmacher's formulation conspicuously lacks the dispassionate, compassionate, self-searching commentary that is of more than incidental importance to Havel's exposition, and because for Schirrmacher, the argument's instrumental utility was essential to its appeal. Schirrmacher might have spoken, as Havel did, of totalitarian systems or modern dictatorships, but he did not. He might have constructed Wolf's biography as an all-German biography, but he did not. Schirrmacher's argument was anticommunist, not anti-totalitarian, and like anticommunist appeals throughout the history of the Federal Republic, it owed part of its political resonance to the persistence of a profoundly *illiberal* anticommunism that the Nazis had exploited, exacerbated, and passed on to the Bonn republic, where it was in turn nurtured by the Cold War and the presence of a Soviet-sponsored communist dictatorship in East Germany.[34]

Schirrmacher's review of *Was bleibt* appeared even before the book became available, and helped set the terms of the debate. The "left" responded to the immediate instrumentalization of the discussion in two ways. The second was the more promising, but the first was more important, because it spoke to the essentially west German ideological battle that was emerging.

Left-of-center west German intellectuals, perceiving themselves to be under attack by a familiar adversary, responded in kind: by reasserting the moral hierarchy between Nazism and communism, by defending Christa Wolf's person, and by denouncing an allegedly open chase against the left. As assaults against "foreigners" multiplied and extreme right parties chalked up successes in state elections,[35] the traditional left looked not to its left but to the right for the effective enemies of German democracy. The defensive commentary of intellectuals such as Günter Grass and Jürgen Habermas was as partisan as Schirrmacher's; in Grass's case, it was also substantively rather less compelling. In the 1960s Grass had been constantly and sharply critical of precisely the "West Germany of Adenauer and Globke" that Wolf had found so repellent. But Grass had always laced his criticism of the Federal Republic with an intransigent rejection of the DDR, and in addition to *Die Blechtrommel* (The Tin Drum), he had offered his readers, in *Die Plebjer proben den Aufstand*

(The Plebeians Rehearse the Uprising), an unflattering representation of Bertolt Brecht (and, by extension, of other East German intellectuals who had compromised with the East German regime).[36] In August 1961 Grass appealed directly to Anna Seghers to denounce the construction of the Wall.[37] In a further appeal to the members of the Writers' Union to clarify their position, he wrote: "There is no 'inner emigration,' nor was there one between 1933 und 1945. Whoever remains silent becomes guilty."[38] In later years, however, when Grass looked for danger of either the creeping or the overt variety, that danger always wore brown, and it was on that menace from the right that Grass kept his attention focused during the period around unification, voicing reservations about unification and resigning angrily from the SPD as the party moved toward a compromise with the conservative governing coalition to revise the constitutional provisions governing political asylum.[39] Now Grass lashed out against the "massive campaign," "atmosphere of hate," and "inquisitorial tone" that he perceived in the commentary on *Was bleibt,* and condemned critics who would use a book "to settle all accounts with the author."[40]

Jürgen Habermas had made democratic legitimacy a central concern of his philosophical reflections, had shaped the West German debate about "constitutional patriotism" as a basis for West German political identity, and had been a major protagonist in the *Historikerstreit*.[41] He now reiterated the distinction between the communist regime that had existed in East Germany, whose "innumerable crimes" he deplored, and "that breach of civilization that leaves one speechless," the Third Reich.[42] "The Nazi period," he declared, "is unmistakably marked by its state-sponsored, bureaucratically executed discrimination and its comprehensive, industrially organized extermination of an ascriptively defined domestic enemy."[43] Habermas nonetheless had no difficulty acknowledging the importance of the characteristics shared by Stalinism and Nazism, or in placing both at the opposite extreme from liberal democracy. The "working through" of the past, Habermas argued, should serve three purposes: the replacement of undemocratic elites, the prosecution of crimes sponsored by the dictatorship, and the creation of a democratic culture.[44] He did not think that the process could or should be deferred or avoided, and he rejected the notion (associated with institutional strategies) that working through the past was unnecessarily destabilizing psychologically and politically. In contemporary pluralist societies, Habermas noted, a democratic political culture will *always* be an artificial, constructed achievement; to call the process of creating one destabilizing was to concede ground to the partisans of a more "natural," and much less democratic, political culture, based, for example, on ethnicity.[45] In 1992 Habermas was still arguing that conditions for a successful "working through" of the past were favorable. In contrast to the 1945 generation, most Germans now wanted to come to grips with their difficult past(s), and west Germans at least had some experience with the process. In 1994 Habermas could still sound an optimistic note. The new situation, he suggested, represented a unique opportunity and a possible turning point in the history of German democracy, the chance to make good on the republic's unfulfilled promise of an anti-totalitarian consensus.[46]

The process of "working through the past" could at any moment, Habermas recognized, be derailed by a personalization of targets and themes. Personal cases were certainly not irrelevant; Habermas cited the postwar examples of Heidegger and Carl Schmitt. "But even in such cases," he said, "an individual biography is only publicly relevant to the extent that it helps us explain a representative failure under typical circumstances, or that it is instructive with respect to the mechanisms of oppression."[47]

Habermas wanted to discourage personal, partisan attacks while encouraging an effort at common understanding. Even as he recognized the opportunity that unification theoretically presented and hoped that the younger generation would find the construction of an anti-totalitarian consensus less complicated than had his generation, he identified the obstacle that made the opportunity so difficult to seize: "Anticommunism or antifascism will be unnecessary midwives at the birth of liberal attitudes and democratic beliefs only when political socialization no longer takes place under a polarizing, global suspicion of domestic enemies."[48]

The end of the Cold War did not dismantle the "polarizing, global suspicion of domestic enemies," an achievement which might finally have liberated German democracy from its dependence on *Feindbilder.* Habermas's hopes were disappointed. He deplored the "ugly spectacle around Christa Wolf,"[49] and he was far more specific than Grass had been in his assessment of the broader political agenda behind the attacks on her. Clearly, he did not see any "anti-totalitarian consensus" emerging that could unite Wolf's critics and people such as himself. The critics, he suggested, were glad of the long-awaited opportunity to smear the left in particular and intellectuals in general.[50]

A third argument, less audible than its competitors, was articulated by left intellectuals who had experienced "real existing socialism" at close range, and who, for whatever reason, seemed unembittered. This approach spoke to east German sensibilities and sought to interpret them for west Germans. It proposed a dialogue, but it found few takers on either side. Martin Ahrends did not deny that west Germans had a right to pass judgment on east Germans; rather, he suggested that they simply did not know what they were talking about. He recalled that the DDR had been created by an external power, and that it had collapsed when and only when that external power had withdrawn its support; in 1989 as in 1949, the actions and attitudes of East Germans were causally very secondary in explaining events. Schirrmacher had claimed that *Was bleibt,* had it been published when it was originally written, might have undermined the regime, and others had echoed his views. "Are you really that naive?" scoffed Ahrends. "Would this famous 'Revolution' [1989] really have happened sooner if Wolf and a dozen others who had not left had identified themselves openly as dissidents? The only result would have been that they would now be in the West, with the clear conscience of those who were always 'upstanding.' Christa Wolf can look conformist and opportunistic only to people who have no idea what life inside the DDR was like."[51]

The argument invited a discussion of what "life inside the DDR" had in fact been like for different groups of people at different times—presumably a complex historical question. Ahrends offered an argument about the place he thought Wolf had occupied in the inner life of the DDR. In a situation no one in either German state could change without causing a bloodbath, he said, Wolf had helped people in East Germany establish and maintain some contact with their own reality: "If one wanted as an East German to learn more out of that stifling time than resignation, boozing, and escape techniques of all types, if on top of it one wanted to achieve a human attitude, writers like Wolf were irreplaceable."[52]

Wolf could not have played this role had she not stayed in the DDR and done what was necessary in order to retain the right to publish there, and those compromises she had made. They were not, Ahrends asserted, dishonorable compromises, and they had served an oppressed and powerless people well during the "waiting period" imposed and enforced by external actors. Ahrends's argument suggested a program of dialogue, research, and reflection—not at all what the market wanted.

A final argument, in between the positions of the left and right, drew a clear distinction between communism and Nazism, but asserted that Wolf had nonetheless discredited herself, either by sticking to her early choices beyond any chronological point of moral plausibility, or by talking to the Stasi. It shared the formal traits of the arguments between which it sought to mediate: like those arguments, its primary purpose was to assign blame or innocence, to differentiate between "us" and "them."

Erich Loest, who had defended Anna Seghers, was not similarly indulgent toward Wolf, whom he saw as having been too well rewarded by the East German regime, and for good reason, for too long. "Distrust," he wrote after Wolf had publicly acknowledged her Stasi contacts, "punishes those who come too late with their self-indictment."[53] Sitting down with Stasi agents had been Uwe Kolbe's reproach to Sascha Anderson, the young poet who for years had served as a Stasi informant. The East German public, the unheroic majority, Kolbe asserted, had "recognized only one taboo: getting involved with the Stasi."[54] In this account it was not dishonorable to be or to have been a communist: "Even today I respect honest communists," the literary critic Fritz Raddatz wrote, and explained the distinction: "Not one of them was ever a shake-hands man with the executioner."[55] It was, in fact, the same distinction that Janka had drawn between himself—the genuinely heroic young antifascist in Spain—and Erich Mielke, quietly liquidating men who thought he was on their side.

The argument that conceded moral respectability to communist ideals and to communists who had not succumbed to the lures of the secret police had the advantage of political convenience: it could unite a large group of otherwise heterogeneous political views and interests. It did not frontally challenge the left; it did not call into question the pursuit of Ostpolitik; and no one likes snitches. In the polarized atmosphere inherited from the *Historikerstreit* and renewed by the left-right exchange over Christa Wolf, this argument may have represented the only possible consensus position. Intellectually, however, the argument stood on unstable ground. Since it never sought to shift the purpose of the enterprise away from judgment, its intellectual instability tended to reinforce the political certainties of the right and the left. The ambiguities of the argument were not hard to identify. If cozying up to the Stasi was so unacceptable, why was it permissible to continue to believe in and support a system that so conspicuously depended on the effectiveness of the secret police for its existence? Raddatz argued that by talking to the Stasi, Heiner Müller and Wolf had ultimately sided with the hangmen and "become the construction workers of a persecution system." Such complicities had kept a repressive regime going: "The whole gangster syndicate of Mielke & Co. could stay afloat only because all too many people failed to make theirs the late brave sentence of Brigitte Bardot, 'Moi, je ne marche pas.'"[56]

Why, however, should this indictment be limited to people who talked to the secret police? Informing on comrades may demonstrate a lack of elementary moral elegance, but it is hard to argue that it was of more practical significance than open party activity—as Schirrmacher had noted. Who won more converts to communism or neutralized the potentially liberating doubts of the morally sensitive more effectively: the indomitable, upstanding soldier in the Thälmann Battalion or the sinister intelligence agent behind the lines? It is also not clear why it might be important, in judging the moral significance of collaboration, to maintain any distinction between Nazism and communism. This was the point that the dissident writer Jürgen Fuchs made in his impassioned and often bitterly sarcastic reply to Habermas at the final hearing of Rainer Eppelmann's Enquete-Kommission.[57] Speaking from his gut rather than with his head (and implying that this was, under the circumstances, the proper way to speak), Fuchs said: "I don't want to speak generally about 'systems' . . . I only want, . . . alongside systems and sociological concepts, to remember *people,* to put them for a moment at center stage."[58] During the debate over Wolf, Ulrich Greiner had formulated the point more fully. His statement works only if the task is defined as that of drawing a line between good people and bad:

That the two [Nazism and communism] are not the same, that, for instance, the crimes of National Socialist Germany were immensely greater than those of socialist Germany, is obvious, but is not of importance here. To their victims, forced migration, torture, and murder are always the same reality, regardless of the reasons for them. It is enough that Stalinism on German soil committed frightful injustices against many people, and not by accident, but systematically. And it is an indisputable fact that intellectuals were co-responsible.[59]

Thus the intellectual instability of arguments that sought to draw a line between "good" and "bad" communists reinforced the determination of the right and the left to impose their simpler, more instrumentalized accounts. The instrumentalization of the debate by both the right and the left in turn invited and rewarded a final and particularly unedifying response to the Wolf controversy: the "game" of muckraking and denunciation, whose players could pursue their activities with or without consciously seeking to promote any particular ideological agenda. In an article in *Die Zeit,* the critic Iris Radisch deplored the game of "Stasi and Gendarme" that was being played, not only without any commonly agreed-upon ground rules or even a common vocabulary, but also in such a way as to deepen the cultural gulf between east and west Germans.[60] But *Die Zeit,* too, was a participant in the game. When Robin Detje asked rhetorically in that newspaper whether the playright Heiner Müller might rightly be considered "a pig," Frank Schirrmacher, otherwise hardly suspect of harboring undue sympathy for Wolf or Müller, attacked what he called "a bad game."[61] He called the line taken in *Die Zeit* "nothing other than a justification of and a plea for denunciation."[62] The weekly *Der Spiegel,* without using the word, engaged in the same game—and the popular press could perhaps not have been expected to join in any other.[63] Looking for buried past contacts with Eastern intelligence services became the German counterpart to the American media's thirst for sex scandals; but unlike sexual allegations, the allegations of a Stasi past were ideologically loaded.

The "game" reached its symbolic culmination in the early summer of 1994, when it was learned that Marcel Reich-Ranicki had been the responsible intelligence service officer at the Polish consulate in London in the late 1940s and had been considerably less than candid about when, why, and how he had left the Communist Party. As late as April 1994, Reich-Ranicki had reviewed Wolf's latest book of essays for *Der Spiegel,* using the occasion to call the book whiny "kitsch" and its author "a representative" and "state poet" of the DDR, and to contrast his own break with communism with Wolf's seemingly endless allegiance: "It isn't a question of whether she was blinded, but of whether she still is."[64]

Barely two months later he repeated the tired excuses—he had hurt no one, could not remember, had not done anything significant, had nothing to be ashamed of—which he had previously so savaged when others had used them, and he attacked the style of the television program on which the accusations against him had initially been aired: "The film seduces using the method: Mrs. Schulz lives in Hamburg. There are many whores in Hamburg."[65] He did not feel compelled to reflect on how the method might have become current.

At the end of the second debate over Christa Wolf, Ulrich Greiner said that the discussion had become "a disastrous quarrel." Only if a consensus existed that "socialism had deserved its fall and that . . . the real DDR was nothing for which one should have wished a longer life" could the discussion be constructively pursued. That consensus, he noted, did not exist.[66] The dynamic and terms of the debate itself, which Greiner had earlier helped shape, and whose purpose should have been to create precisely the consensus whose absence he later lamented, had in fact made such a consensus very unlikely. It was a "disastrous quarrel" with both a past and a future.

Dictatorship, Democratic Transitions, and "Lack of Community"

It is tempting to see in the polemic that greeted *Was bleibt* an inevitable development. But it is important to understand why, in the German context, it may in fact have been not only almost inevitable but part of an established pattern of argument as well. Frameworks that would have promoted the use of Wolf's work as an opportunity for collective self-reflection while avoiding the "tout comprendre, c'est tout excuser" trap were available. Václav Havel's political writings suggested such a framework, as did the passages of Jaspers's philosophical writings that had informed his positions in *Die Schuldfrage*.

Havel proposed an intransigent standard of opposition to totalitarian dictatorships of all colors, but one that was simultaneously compassionate and self-critical. The Czech writer, by virtue of his own biography and his country's less compromised past, was wholly external to the family fight that ripped at the conscience and consciousness of postwar East German intellectuals. Havel had never looked to communism for a pardon. A central message of Havel's argument was that modern dictatorships create a culture in which different people may bear different degrees of responsibility, but in which the sides are not usefully defined as us versus them: there is only an us. Havel blurred the line between victim and perpetrator, not in order to pass perpetrators off as victims (as often happens in Germany), but in order to make us all confront the ways in which we take the side of the perpetrators. In their substance and especially in their tone, his positions offered a useful contrast to *all* the positions taken by German participants in the debate about DDR intellectuals.

In his influential 1978 essay "The Power of the Powerless," Havel tried to specify how a combination of coercion and temptation induces people to participate in, and thus appear to lend legitimacy to, regimes that deny them freedom.[67] Havel made his argument by examining the hypothetical conduct of an apparently apolitical greengrocer who exhibits a sign reading, "Workers of the world, unite!" hanging it "among the onions and carrots" in his shop window.[68] The greengrocer's willingness to display a sign which does not express his own considered convictions and which his customers barely notice, Havel argued, epitomizes conduct in post-terrorist totalitarian systems and reveals the underlying logic of such regimes.[69] The pattern of conduct, he asserted, is induced by the system, but is reproduced by greengrocers, intellectuals, factory workers, party reformers, and almost everyone else. Havel's explanation drew on the example of real existing socialism, but was explicitly intended to address the problem of complicity in any modern dictatorship.

By displaying the sign and so conforming to the expectations imposed from above and daily ratified by his customers (who might well notice and feel uncomfortable if the sign were *not* there), Havel's greengrocer becomes implicated in the game established by the regime: he accepts and relays the lie that the regime puts forward as reality. "Classical dictatorships," Havel argued, were specifically political: they were characterized by specific power relations, and they were challenged by people who organized themselves to change those power relations. The line between rulers and ruled (between them and us) was clearly drawn, and it was maintained by "naked discipline," that is, by violence or the threat of violence (134). Post-terrorist totalitarian dictatorships, by contrast, are more aptly described as distinct cultures, maintained not by violence but by a "certain metaphysical order" (137). Theirs is a culture of total manipulation, and the order on which the culture rests is a lie universally made and universally accepted. Ideology—"a world of appearances, a mere ritual, a formalized language deprived of semantic contact with reality and transformed into a system of ritual signs that replace reality with pseudo-reality" (138)—perpetuates the lie and draws everyone, both ostensible leaders and those they purport to lead, into its poisonous embrace. Havel's analysis deemphasized the notion of dictatorship as an injustice inflicted by one group of people on another, but it did so without destroying the categories of personal guilt and responsibility:

> Position in the power hierarchy determines the degree of responsibility and guilt, but it gives no one unlimited responsibility and guilt, nor does it completely absolve anyone. Thus the conflict between the aims of life and the aims of the system is not a conflict between two socially defined and separate communities; and only a very generalized view (and even that only approximative) permits us to divide society into the rulers and the ruled. Here . . . is one of the most important differences between the [totalitarian] system and classical dictatorships, in which this line of conflict can still be drawn according to social class. In the [totalitarian] system, this line runs *de facto* through each person, for everyone in his own way is both a victim and a supporter of the system. What we understand by the system is not, therefore, a social order imposed by one group upon another, but rather something which permeates the entire society. (144)[70]

Havel, writing ten years after the "Prague Spring" but seven years before Mikhail Gorbachev acceded to power, was skeptical of the efforts periodically made by "insiders" to alter the fundamental reality of this system—that is, he denied that the system was reformable. Leaders, he wrote, are "often no more than blind executors of the system's own internal laws—laws they themselves never can, and never do, reflect upon" (140).[71] In the unlikely event that someone who had risen through the ranks still retained some independent conception of his own identity, he would, Havel assumed, quickly lose his leadership position, or be gradually forced to conform to the prevailing norms.

Such regimes cannot tolerate any cracks in the metaphysical edifice that supports them. In order for the regime's pseudo-reality successfully to replace reality, everyone must claim it is real. No individual, and certainly no organization, can be permitted to give public voice to the truth: "Living within the lie can constitute the system only if it is universal" (147). This dependence on a perverted form of consent makes such

regimes peculiarly dependent on the society they oppress. Unlike traditional dictatorships, Havel wrote, a mature totalitarian system "does not
rely on soldiers of its own, but on the soldiers of the enemy . . .—that is
to say, on everyone who is living within the lie and who may be struck at
any moment (in theory, at least) by the force of truth" (149).

In Havel's account, the "soldiers of the enemy" in fact enlist in the
regime's army: "we" become "them." The attraction of living within the
lie is that it absolves the individual of all responsibility. Havel described
the regime's ideology as "a bridge of excuses" (135) and asserted that the
irresponsibility it permits not only feeds on the weaknesses of human
nature, but also builds powerfully on the "foundations laid by the historical encounter between dictatorship and the consumer society" (145).
Post-terrorist totalitarianism is the most extreme form of the "crisis of
contemporary technological society" (206) and of the resulting "general
inability of modern humanity to be the master of its own situation"
(207). This crisis of responsibility afflicts Western democracies as well as
Soviet bloc countries; it is a feature of modernity.[72] The success and
spread of mature totalitarianism constitute "a record of people's own
failure as individuals" (145)—a record encouraged by the forward march
of technology and bureaucratization, but also by the innate desire of
human beings to shirk responsibility for their lives and their world.

Since the system "works only as long as people are willing to live
within the lie" (141), Havel concluded, it is both extraordinarily resilient
and peculiarly vulnerable. On the one hand, it is supported by the inherent weakness of individuals and the constant invidious pressure of technological "progress"; on the other hand, it is continually assaulted by
"the aims of life, that is, the elementary need of human beings to live, to
a certain extent at least, in harmony with themselves" (161), or, as Havel
specified, "in harmony with their better self" (167). The regime is threatened whenever anyone within its reach—such as the young writer and
the nurse in *Was bleibt*—reestablishes contact with his or her own identity and acts independently, whenever there is "an attempt to regain
control over one's own sense of responsibility" (153).

From this account of the origins and nature of contemporary totalitarianism, Havel derived specific ethical conclusions about how men and
women caught in its embrace should seek to conduct themselves. "Living in truth," he asserted, is both the only effective and the only morally
defensible domestic means of resisting and combating a mature totalitar-

ian system. The truth "is a bacteriological weapon, so to speak, utilized when conditions are ripe by a single civilian to disarm an entire division. This power does not participate in any direct struggle for power; rather, it makes its influence felt in the obscure arena of being itself" (149).

Havel's argument suggests that totalitarian regimes can be subverted but they cannot be "reformed" or "improved." Their mechanisms are too resilient—and too impersonal—to be vulnerable to strategies that promote incremental change through dialogue and negotiation. Between the "world of appearances" and the world of reality, there is no room for "mutual understanding" or respect. Compromises always redound to the regime's benefit, since the outside negotiator must allow himself to become implicated in the system. In this account, a half-truth is a lie, and all the more noxious because it is an act of self-deception.

Havel's uncompromising portrait of totalitarianism is not a recipe for total confrontation—political or armed—for two reasons: first, the front lines run through the soul of every individual human being, and second, in the modern world, violence would merely accelerate the technological tendencies responsible for producing totalitarianism in the first place. Before 1989 Havel's preferred method of resistance was the legalistic approach adopted by Charter 77 and VONS, the Committee to Defend the Unjustly Prosecuted. By appealing to the formal legal code to protest the Czech regime's daily violations of human rights, Havel and his friends attacked what they saw as the main prop of the system: the "ritual, facades, and excuses" (189) that guaranteed the regime against reality.

Havel's moral stance contains a prescription for democratic transitions that focuses on the personal and is in many ways anti- or at least prepolitical; it recalls positions defended early on by the East German citizens' movements. If totalitarianism is understood as a culture of lying and individual abdication that is both induced from above and welcomed on all sides, rather than as a power structure entirely dominated by a single political party, then its ultimate defeat can be ensured only by a cultural transformation that would be the sum of a mass of individual moral choices and changes. A new system, Havel argued, "is not something that can be designed and introduced like a new car" (162).

Perhaps unsurprisingly, Havel cautioned against viewing parliamentary democracy as either a panacea or a paradise—again in unison with the citizens' movements (208).[73] He treated modern democratic political parties—which in his view also obscure individual responsibilities, even if less spectacularly and with less lethal consequences than dictatorships—with suspicion, and preferred small, spontaneous, impermanent groups "infused with enthusiasm for a particular purpose and disappearing when that purpose has been achieved" (210).[74] And, rejecting "a return to the spirit and methods of traditional politics" as a goal, he emphasized the need for honesty and integrity in the struggle:

> It is of great importance that the main thing—the everyday, thankless, and never-ending struggle of human beings to live more freely, truthfully, and in quiet dignity—never impose any limits on itself, never be halfhearted, inconsistent, never trap itself in political tactics, speculating on the outcome of its actions or entertaining fantasies about the future. The purity of this struggle is the best guarantee of optimum results when it comes to actual interaction with the [totalitarian] structures. (205)

Havel's insistence on a "never-ending struggle" and on the need for vigilance and purity reflected his own experience. In January 1977, Havel, then serving as one of Charter 77's spokesmen, was arrested. It was his first encounter with prison:

> One evening . . . I wrote out a request to the Public Prosecutor for my release . . . I wrote my request in a way that at the time seemed extremely tactical and cunning: while saying nothing I did not believe or that wasn't true, I simply "overlooked" the fact that truth lies not only in what is said, but also in who says it, and to whom, why, how and under what circumstances it is expressed . . . I sent the request off the following day and because no one responded to it . . . I more or less forgot about it. And then one day lightning struck: I was given to know that I would probably be released, and that in the process, "political use" would be made of my request.[75]

Havel was devastated: "There were weeks, months, years, in fact, of silent desperation, self-castigation, shame, inner humiliation, reproach and uncomprehending questioning." The incident left him "in the sharpest confrontation I had ever experienced with the 'absolute horizon' of my relating, i.e., with the Being of the world and my own being." He continued:

> It enabled me not only to understand . . . but to experience, in a directly physical way, the fact that one's identity is never in one's possession as

something given, completed and unquestionable, as an entity among entities, as something one can husband like anything else, that one can use, depend on, draw on and, every so often, give a new coat of paint . . . The opposite is true: one can, at any time—in the space of a few minutes—deny one's entire history and turn it upside down: all it takes is a moment of inattention, . . . of careless trust that one is what one is, and must be so always. I understood that my identity is what I seek, do, choose and define, today and every day; that it is not a path I once chose and now merely proceed along, but one that I must redefine at every step, wherein each misstep or wrong turn, though caused only by neglecting one's bearings in the terrain, remains an irradicable part of it, one that requires vast and complex effort to set right.[76]

The political counterpart to the personal stance that Havel advocated is a public sphere characterized by civility. If Havel's understanding of political institutions often seemed incidental and vague, his understanding of and commitment to civility seemed quite precise.

Václav Havel was too far away, physically and intellectually, to shape decisively the tone and content of the German debate over Christa Wolf's words and actions, past and contemporary. Havel's substantive positions can be used for instrumental purposes, as "political tactics," but they were not formulated for such purposes, nor did Havel himself ever use them that way, once freedom came and democratic political competition increased the incentives to do so. In a democratizing setting, Havel's positions can provide the foundation blocks of a broad new prodemocratic political consensus only if they are not instrumentalized, that is, only if they are not immediately mobilized as partisan weapons that actors turn against one another. Havel's arguments, formulated underground, were strikingly non-adversarial in tone; they were intended to bring people into confrontation with *themselves,* and in power Havel consistently avoided using them for polemical, exclusionary purposes. Like Jaspers, Havel maintained the categories of guilt and responsibility: he recognized the obvious distinction between people who had had other people imprisoned or shot and people who had hung slogans among the carrots and onions in their shops. But he emphasized a prior and prerequisite failing—the inclination to remake reality so as to avoid responsibility—in which we all participate. Because we are all at least potential (and usually actual) participants in the development of unfreedom, we all share in the same moral universe, and we owe one another assistance in a struggle for freedom that is at least as much personal as it is political. Havel thought not in terms of a dichotomous opposition between victims and perpetrators, but in terms of a spectrum of responsibility.

The "everyday, thankless, and never-ending" process of self-discovery that allows the individual to grasp his or her own identity and keep it, morally speaking, "right side up" seems to invite the type of human relations that Jaspers had described as a "loving struggle." This was the context, Jaspers had argued in 1946, in which people could acknowledge moral guilt, and he suggested "rules" intended to safeguard the reciprocity of the exchange. A "loving struggle" presupposes equal individuals in intimate and sympathetic relation with one another,[77] and in 1946 Jaspers argued that Germans could come to terms with their moral guilt only if they established such relations among themselves. He also argued that only by coming to terms with their moral guilt could Germans achieve political freedom: "No purification of souls, no political freedom."[78] The point of departure was hardly promising: "We have in common," Jaspers acknowledged, "the lack of community" (15). Germans had experienced the Third Reich differently, in and from different "places," both figuratively and literally. Precisely for this reason, the readiness "to talk with one another" (11), "to see questions from the other's standpoint" (12) was their "biggest task" (15). He contended: "No question can be off-limits, no dearly held assumption, sentiment, or illusion can be shielded. But it is also not acceptable to slap others in the face with challenging, unfounded, ill-considered judgments. We belong together; we must feel our common cause when we talk with one another" (13).

With regard to moral guilt, Jaspers argued, the right to judge would be "visible in the acts and attitude of the judger: . . . in whether he speaks from inside or outside the situation, as one who seeks to explain himself or as an accuser, as a close partner looking for a key to self-elucidation or as a stranger on the attack, as friend or as enemy. Only in the first case does he have an unquestionable right [to speak]; in the second case, his right is dubious, at any rate restricted by the measure of his love" (30).

As we have seen, Jaspers belonged to the postwar disappointed. Instead of the difficult dialogue he had urged, people had chosen the easy way out. He readily imagined an individual using his argument about moral guilt as an excuse for complacency: "Moral guilt—I can already hear it: that one's own conscience is the only possible court, that others cannot proffer reproaches. My conscience will be kind to me. It isn't so bad: turn the page [*Strich drunter*], and a new life" (54).

"Turn the page, and a new life" is an oversimplified and pejorative, but not fully inaccurate, description of how institutional strategies play out. The West German one had had benefits. With Allied help, West Germans had used their new life well: starting over, they had built the first peaceful, prosperous democracy on German soil. But it had also had costs, as in other ways, Germans had simply started again. *Strich drunter* had left Germans with their "lack of community." The new life they built generated a limited consensus and sense of community, but both were in important ways superficial. In the aftermath of the Third Reich, Jaspers warned that accusatory and exclusionary interactions would simply repeat the exclusionary tactics of the Nazis (13). But even before the 1930s, modern German politics had been ideological and fragmented, with actors more oriented toward staking out a position than toward finding common ground, and more given to stigmatizing or ridiculing than to persuading the opposition. Now the "lack of community" created a subterranean layer of distrust below the conscious adhesion to democratic values and the reiterated confidence in the stability of the new republic.

This thesis, asserting a link between the unresolved "lack of community" left over from the institutional strategy pursued after 1949 and a brittle sense of community forty years later, was directly denied by Hermann Lübbe in 1983. But it was confirmed, I want to argue, by both the form and the substance of a series of exchanges (including the one of which Lübbe's lecture was an element) ostensibly about contemporary German history that took place in the decade around unification, and among which the *Historikerstreit* of 1986–87 was only the best known.

In his closing remarks—"National Socialism in the Political Consciousness of the Present"—to an international conference organized in the Reichstag in still-divided Berlin on the occasion of the fiftieth anniversary of the Nazi seizure of power, Lübbe made an argument that was both a defense of an institutional strategy and an account of what—in Lübbe's view—the institutional strategy followed in West Germany had looked like. Lübbe argued that the overwhelming character of the military defeat, the proof the war had provided of external resistance to German imperial projects, and the "moral evidence of the terrorist and criminal consequences of National Socialist rule" had definitively discredited Nazism. "The effect," Lübbe claimed, "was a complete discrediting of National Socialist ideology, especially in its central racist and 'living space'–oriented elements."[79] He recognized the persistence of what he called "relics" of Nazism but insisted, "On the normative level . . . National Socialist relics were nonexistent" (332). He specifically denied the political relevance of private and psychological factors, of the "inner state" of the generations that had experienced the Third Reich, for "the inner states of individual subjects tell us little about what prevailed morally and politically. We know what prevailed when we know what fundamental moral and political principles could not be publicly contradicted except at the price of moral and political isolation" (332–333).

Lübbe's argument here seems particularly careful, and his language is worth noting. Except when he attacks the '68ers' attitude toward the Federal Republic [a "delegitimation effort" assisted by theories of fascism (340)], he consistently avoids the family of words related to "legitimacy," preferring instead to speak of "discrediting" in reference to the postwar fate of Nazism and of the Federal Republic as having a "history that one can, indeed must, approve."[80] A legitimate system of authority is a system accepted by its subjects as just and right. Once Lübbe had discounted the importance of "inner states," it would have been difficult for him to make a persuasive case about legitimation or delegitimation. Instead, he cites behavior and public acts as evidence for his claim that the "relics" of Nazism had been politically neutralized.

The normative appeal of the fallen dictatorship, Lübbe claimed, had been shut down: through the regime's own failures, through the public decisions of democratizing actors, and through the creation of new institutional structures. The relative silence which bracketed the Nazi experience in the postwar Federal Republic had been indispensable as Hitler's majority was integrated into the new democracy: "A certain silence was the psychologically and politically indispensable medium for the transformation of our postwar population into the citizenry of the Federal Republic" (334). Like Jaspers, but retrospectively, Lübbe noted the "lack of community" among Germans who had come through the war, and he posed the same question: "How did people deal with one another?" (334). Lübbe did not miss an absent myth of virtue (which Aedanus Burke and Charles de Gaulle had understood as one way of overcoming "lack of community"); rather, he praised what he perceived as a kind of silence constantly verging on speech. Ignoring considerable evidence to the contrary, Lübbe argued that the key leadership posts in the new republic—the example he used was the rectorship of a university (for the irony, see Conclusion)—had gone to men who had acted well under the Third Reich, and suggested that the resulting relationships, between superiors who had acted well and subordinates who had acted less well, were tolerable only on the basis of "asymmetric discretion" (335). Discretion, he emphasized, was quite different from forgetting: "Institutional reconstruction, to which people were bound in common, was achieved in the context of this discretion. After ten years, nothing was forgotten, but a few things were finally completely cured" (335).

Thus Lübbe explicitly rejected the argument, most commonly associated in the public mind with the Mitscherlichs' 1967 study *Die Unfähigkeit zu trauern*, the 1968 protest movement, and Ralph Giordano's *Die zweite Schuld* (1987), that Germans in the Federal Republic had repressed their memories or avoided their guilt.[81] The 1968 generation had, Lübbe claimed, "for reasons that are fundamentally independent of the relationship to National Socialism" (339), distanced itself from the ambient adherence to the Federal Republic, and had then opportunistically exploited the accusation that the past lived on as a convenient and potent weapon in its generational and political battles. In the 1960s "fascism" was put forward as an alternative comparative category to totalitarianism: those who used the concept drew analogies between French right-wing movements, Italian fascism, and National Socialism, emphasized class relations and the crisis of capitalism as explanatory variables, and saw in the movements' anti-Marxism an important common trait. Fascism was a category popular with Marxist social scientists; conservatives tended to reject the category in part because they did not want to be caught in bad company and in part because they refused the association drawn between capitalism and fascism. Lübbe attacked this interpretive school not just for leading scholars down what he saw as a relatively blind alley, but also for undermining the legitimacy of the Federal Republic and for spreading an "atmosphere of intellectual suspicion" (341).[82]

Lübbe's lecture—and the lively discussion it elicited—suggested themes and theses that would inform public debate in general and conservative discourse in particular up to and through the unification period. Lübbe's central argument comforted the convictions and sensibilities of those who believed that Nazism no longer challenged German democracy, and who saw the only threat to the republic as coming from the left—and from a left whose discourse and appeal had, in their view, nothing to do with the complicities and evasions of the older generation. Lübbe declined to distinguish Nazi *ideology* from authoritarian patterns of expectation and behavior (private and public) that the Nazi experience might have engendered or reinforced. He argued (plausibly if debatably) that the former had been definitively discredited, and without exploring the latter, in effect asserted that such patterns were without public or private consequence. For Lübbe, "scandals" such as denunciations of Willy Brandt for having emigrated were not disturbing "because they were, already at the time, appropriately spoken of and criticized as detestable."[83] Thus Lübbe denied both that the truce the West Germans had organized around their "lack of community" after 1945 had been based on repressed memories and that the persistence of the "lack of community" had had any significant costs.[84] In contrast, Hans Maier emphasized that the "source of a distrust, of a loss of trust between the younger and the older generation," lay not in what the older generation had done but in its subsequent silence.[85] But Lübbe retorted that political disaffection among young people had been common to all Western industrial democracies in the late 1960s, and denied that the '68ers' hypersensitivity to—and exploitation of—the Nazi past had causes worth considering. In Lübbe's perception, the '68ers (with whom he seemed eager to settle accounts) had used false charges to indict the prior generation; in the process, they had weakened a democratic order—a "political and cultural system"[86]—whose successful (if imperfect) construction seemed something of a miracle.

The "system" was indeed what was at stake for Lübbe in this discussion, for he understood his account of the postwar treatment of the Nazi legacy to be fundamentally related to the viability of the Federal Republic: "I have tried to show how, all in all, the history of the Federal Republic is a history that one can, indeed must, approve."[87] In Lübbe's view, the '68ers had portrayed German democracy as too ugly to love, on the false accusation of persistent continuities from the Nazi period that the postwar silence had left undisturbed. Lübbe seemed so angered by the attempt that he was unable to see it as a possible cost of the strategy whose necessity he defended.

The discussion in the Reichstag took place within months after Helmut Kohl replaced Helmut Schmidt in the chancellor's office, thereby ending thirteen years of Social Democratic rule. It preceded by two years Richard von Weizsäcker's landmark speech commemorating the fortieth anniversary of the end of the war and by three years the so-called *Historikerstreit*, the politicized and polarized debate that so marked the politico-intellectual life of the Federal Republic in the mid-1980s. The *Literaturstreit*, discussed earlier, is in turn best understood as a sequel to the *Historikerstreit*—and as a prelude to other, equally polarized though more circumscribed debates: over the redesigned Neue Wache memorial in Berlin (1993); over whether or not the resistance of future DDR leaders deserved to be honored in ceremonies commemorating the fiftieth anniversary of the July 20, 1944, attempt on Hitler's life and over the moral status of the Wehrmacht (1994); over the way May 8, 1945, should be characterized and remembered (1995). In each case, German "lack of community" was replayed and reinforced.

Taken together, the debates suggest the blocked political learning process described at the beginning of this chapter, rather than stations on the road to a democratic consensus. In each instance, history and allegedly academic debates about history were instrumentalized for political purposes. This was perhaps not surprising, especially given the content of the history under discussion. But in each case the instrumentalization of the debate prevented certain issues from being resolved, or even from being clearly stated. The debates therefore took on a repetitive quality. Intellectual arguments were faulted for being politically suspect; they were stigmatized rather than discussed. This strategy was used by the "left" as well as the "right"; its impact was amplified by media coverage.[88] It damaged the expectation that debate could include the possibility— much less imply the obligation—of persuasion or common progress. One result seems to have been to weaken the purchase of intellectual arguments in general on public debate, leaving actors free to assert either, as the French would say, "n'importe quoi," or to reiterate arguments that had already been voiced and beyond which it should have been possible to move. Tim Mason deplored the *Historikerstreit* as a "barren cultural episode."[89] Barren it may have been to the historian seeking to understand the Third Reich; but precisely because of its intellectual barrenness, it is indicative to the political scientist of important aspects of German political culture. Jürgen Habermas called it a debate "over the self-understanding of the Federal Republic," and he too was right.[90]

Insofar as the *Historikerstreit* and the *Literaturstreit* had intellectual substance, both debates, like subsequent ones mentioned earlier, ultimately turned on the question of the political and moral comparability of fascism and communism. The debates derived their energy, however, not from the intellectual insights they provided, but from the accusatory and justificatory points staked out by the participants. Ernst Nolte insinuated that the Final Solution had been a defensive imitation of a Bolshevik model.[91] Ralph Giordano asked why it was that "not one of the executioners of July 20, 1944, whether in a judge's robe or a uniform, was ever called to account, not a single one."[92] Alfred Dregger, parliamentary leader of the CDU/CSU from 1982 to 1991 and a wounded veteran of World War II, vehemently defended the honor of "those who fought as soldiers at the risk of their lives for Germany."[93] Looking back at the July 20 debate of 1994, Jens Jessen concluded in the *Frankfurter Allgemeine Zeitung*:

> From their lecterns, historians fight in vain for nuance. Contemporary Germany demands a different picture, one which shows a ditch that no common tradition bridges. For the fiftieth anniversary of the twentieth of July, political adversaries fell on one another's resistance traditions with a hatred that spared nothing: no morality, no dignity, no memory, nothing. They spoke and they wrote as if to kill a second time. Perhaps the old perception still holds, that Germany is a country like Spain: it only becomes fully itself in civil war.[94]

Jessen exaggerated, but he exaggerated in ways that brought reality into sharper focus: forty-nine years after the collapse of the Third Reich and five years after the opening of the Berlin Wall, an anti-totalitarian consensus in Germany had neither been created nor been effectively replaced by a more positive account of democratic legitimacy. Nothing suggested that the pattern was likely to change: it seemed a motor for its own self-reproduction.

"Lack of Community" and Institutional Strategies

In the following chapters we will encounter further illustrations and consequences of this blocked learning process and its supporting forms of noncommunication. Schematically summarized, the consequences of West Germany's postwar institutional strategy have appeared in this chapter under the following guise: a dictatorship left a legacy of experiential and moral "lack of community." The institutional strategy adopted legitimated a large degree of private and public avoidance of the issues and experiences that underlay this "lack of community." The common experience of new democratic institutions compensated only partially for the preceding "lack of community," otherwise perpetuated by the relative silence that surrounded its sources. The lingering "lack of community" undermined interpersonal and political trust, making polemics, *Feindbilder,* and political pessimism constant temptations.

In comparative perspective, the question is whether the institutional strategy is to blame for cultivating and justifying the silence (and the injustices it covered), or whether Nazi crimes (and the complicities that permitted them) were such that more silence was necessary than an institutional strategy normally imposes, and that the consequences of the silence were far more perverse and pervasive than is usually the case. In other words, is the blocked learning process analyzed in this chapter a normal cost of institutional strategies or the unique cost of a unique history?

We do not yet have enough evidence to answer this question; it invites further empirical study in currently democratizing countries. Institutional strategies are frequently defended as promoting the necessary formal integration of former adversaries into the new democratic polity. The foregoing analysis of the German case suggests that such integration is but an incomplete remedy for the "lack of community" that dictatorships leave behind, and that the broader political and cultural dynamic set in motion by an institutional strategy may make it difficult for the polity to move beyond a kind of coexistence to a more substantive integration, even as the experience of dictatorship recedes in time and generations succeed one another. On the personal level, institutional strategies ratify injustice and then deny what they have done. Even if cultural strategies do not represent a realistic alternative, they may be right in their predictions about the dysfunctional aspects of institutional strategies (the point that Lübbe seemed determined not to see).

The German experience, however, would seem to represent an extreme case. The particular characteristics of the case made the margin for maneuver in which an institutional strategy could develop and/or be modified by elements of a cultural strategy especially narrow. In Chapter 1 we saw that institutional strategies are often accompanied by claims that the fallen regime had enjoyed little genuine support. Myths of self-liberation and widespread resistance create their own problems, but they may create fewer difficulties than their unavailability engenders. In Germany, such myths were unsustainable: the weight of the country's nondemocratic traditions would have made them seem implausible, and they would have been in too evident contradiction with the reality of support for Hitler. The horrific nature of the acts committed and the breadth of involvement in those crimes, as well as the suddenness with which the regime collapsed (defeated by foreign forces and without a prior period of opening), lent a particular significance to the silence that an institutional strategy sanctioned.

If institutional and cultural strategies of reconciliation represent the two broad options on which democratizing elites can draw after a dictatorship, the heritage of the West German postwar experience left *both* options burdened as Germany again faced the tasks of reconciliation after unification. Institutional strategies were burdened by their negative associations with the post-1945 experience, and so were suspect on the democratic left. Since in this case the fallen dictatorship was a communist one, cultural strategies were distorted and annexed as a polemical weapon by the right (which might otherwise have been inclined toward a more resolute preference for institutional strategies).

"There was no 'zero hour'" in 1945, no blank slate on which anyone could write as he pleased, President von Weizsäcker reminded his compatriots in 1985. "But," he continued, "we had the opportunity to begin anew. We used that opportunity as well as we could. In the place of unfreedom, we put democratic freedom."[95] That unified Germany could cope with the difficult double heritage evoked in this chapter—and with unprecedented unemployment—without lapsing into a political crisis any deeper than that of any other major Western democracy should remind us of the strengths and benefits of institutional strategies, even at their worst.

Four

Successor Justice: The Appeal to Common Sense and the Redefinition of Justice

No claim may be more powerful in a democratic environment than the claim to articulate a position that represents "common sense." In a political argument, the invocation of common sense may either articulate a consensus or seek to create one. Common sense, I suggest in this chapter, is the ultimate—but morally ambiguous—political arbiter of norms in a democratic society.

Common sense is an ambiguous yardstick because it does not offer a standard measure indifferent to time, place, and circumstance. It normally derives from accumulated experience; where that experience is nondemocratic, it too will be nondemocratic, and it will always be resistant to voluntaristic manipulation. One important defense of democratic government is that the freedoms it protects leave it exposed to the voices of those who want common sense to include more rights for more people. Democratic politics, that is, always seeks to recast disappointment as aspiration.

Resistant though it may be, common sense must change if political culture is to change. In nondemocratic as well as democratic settings, and especially in transitional settings, political actors use politics to turn (or to try to turn) the political position held by a part of a political community into the common sense of a whole community. In this respecct, successful democratization redefines the common sense of a community in two stages: in the short run, it changes the community's constitutional principles (that is, its spoken rules and assumptions), and in the long run, it changes the community's political culture (its habits and values). The more direct the logical and chronological relationship between these two steps, the less the disappointment.

Political trials are often one aspect of this process, in part because, with C. S. Lewis, we believe that pain may "[plant] the flag of truth within the fortress of a rebel soul."[1] The power to (re)define common sense is what is most fundamentally at stake in a political trial, and different prosecutorial strategies go about the task of redefining it in different ways. Whatever strategy is adopted, however, political justice raises complex problems. It invites retroactive legislation, and it gives full play to the tensions between the utilitarian and retributive justifications for punishment. Utilitarians justify punishment by invoking the imperatives of deterrence and prevention; retributionists, beginning with Kant, appeal to the notion of moral desert.[2] Even in established liberal communities, punishing a person without particular regard to consequences, simply because the person's conduct deserves censure, is often attractive. It does justice to what Joel Feinberg has called the "expressive function" of legal penalties; that is, it "expresses the *judgment* (as distinct from any emotion) of the community that what the criminal did was wrong." At the same time, it takes into account the emotional needs and desires of the victim(s) and of the offended community: "It is . . . a symbolic way of getting back at the criminal, of expressing a kind of vindictive resentment."[3]

The "expressive" potential of legal proceedings makes them especially tempting in democratizing settings. But where the courts respect liberal rules of due process, and especially given the problems of prosecuting crimes defined after the fact, the "expressed" moral sentiment of the court may not send the morally clear message of reprobation sought by the prosecution (and/or demanded by victims); it may then contribute to both resentment and disappointment.[4]

Different kinds of trials involve different kinds of long-term political risks to the new democratic norms they are intended to promote, and they prejudice in different ways the conception of justice likely to emerge in the new democracy. In the first section of this chapter, I briefly review liberal understandings of the relationship between law and justice, especially as those understandings are reflected in our views of ex post facto prosecutions. In the second and third sections, I show how the appeal to common sense was used by the prosecution in the Nuremburg Trial before the International Military Tribunal in 1945–46 and by the defense in later West German trials of National Socialist crimes, especially in the crucial Auschwitz Trial (November 1963–September 1965). I argue that different prosecutorial strategies in the two cases—an institutional strategy at Nuremberg and a cultural strategy at Frankfurt—in fact put different sides at an advantage in the battle to (re)define common sense. In both cases, however, it proved very difficult to use the courtroom (or, as denazification demonstrated, a questionnaire and paralegal chambers) to force a reassessment of the commitments ordinary men and women had made during the Third Reich. In the final section, I explain and assess the prosecutorial confusions that have marked legal efforts to deal with crimes associated with the communist dictatorship in East Germany.

Political Justice and Revenge

When a fledgling democracy brings former dictators and their henchmen to trial, is it justice or is it something else—revenge, for instance, or persecution, a continuation of armed hostilities after one side has been materially disarmed, or simply the illegitimate use of public force to punish politically objectionable actions or opinions? Trials try to make right an unjust past. "When we face actions that not merely express the message that a person is degraded relative to the wrongdoer but also try to establish that degradation," Jean Hampton argues, "we are morally required to respond by trying to remake the world in a way that denies what the wrongdoer's events have attempted to establish, thereby lowering the wrongdoer, elevating the victim, and annulling the act of diminishment."[5]

This is not an easy task. In a subsequently much quoted statement, the former East German dissident Bärbel Bohley expressed her disappointment with the legal and political treatment the Federal Republic had accorded former servants of the East German dictatorship: "We wanted justice," Bohley said, "and we got the rule of law."[6] Bohley's words echo the anger Albert Camus expressed after the Liberation in 1945, when he remarked, "There is no law that addresses the form of treason we have all known."[7] In a transitional setting, the primary legal fight is usually over the issue of retroactive legislation and two small words in Camus's statement: "we" and "all." Whatever the statute book says, Camus and Bohley suggest, a crime is a crime, provided that "we all" recognize it as crime. That common recognition, Camus implied, is what differentiates justice (which democrats favor) from vengeance (which they stigmatize) when punishment is not prescribed by existing statutes.

We are rightly suspicious of political actors who claim a special, extralegal knowledge of what "we all" know and want, and the idea that state power can legitimately be used against individuals only to uphold the prescriptions of existing statutes has long been a cornerstone of liberal theory. Thus Locke, in the *Second Treatise,* makes the respect for "established and promulgated Laws" a hallmark of legitimate government (§137). The legal principle *nulla poena sine lege*—reaffirmed in the Basic Law and in the first paragraph of the Federal Republic's penal code—upholds liberal political principles in three ways.[8] First, it guarantees that no one accused of a crime can reasonably claim to have been caught by surprise by the accusation brought against him: we all know in advance the rules against which our conduct will be judged by the only authority legitimately permitted to use physical force to punish delinquent conduct. Second, the requirement that laws be "established and promulgated" makes it easier to determine whether or not a given law applies equally to all members of the community; that is, it makes exceptional legislation (revenge disguised as justice) easier to discern, and presumably to denounce and resist. And finally, the requirement that authoritative rules be passed as legislation by a representative body decreases the chance that laws will depart from common understandings, to serve instead a fleeting impulse or a partial interest under the guise of an imperative vox populi. This is especially true in a system characterized by checks and balances. It was the Federalist argument in favor of a representative republic: the legislative process as a whole was seen as a way of protecting the community against the usurpation of public power by a faction, which Madison defined as "a number of citizens, whether amounting to a majority or minority of the whole, who are united and actuated by some common impulse of passion, or of interest, adverse to the rights of other citizens, or to the permanent and aggregate interests of the community" (*Federalist* 10). In this account, common understandings define the law and the law defines justice. In other words, a procedural rule (no ex post facto legislation) is viewed as an essential guarantee about what justice will look like substantively (it will protect our rights as individuals and reflect the common understandings of our "permanent and aggregate interests").

Locke, however, also proposes a complementary but potentially alternative account of justice, to be used in exceptional circumstances—circumstances he associated with the external defense of the commonwealth, where the executive might need to act quickly, decisively, and secretly. In this second account, substantive criteria prevail over procedural considerations. In exceptional circumstances, Locke writes, "whatsoever shall be done *manifestly for the good of the People,* and the establishing the Government upon its true Foundations, is, and always will be just Prerogative" (§ 158, emphasis added; cf. Chap. 14). As in the Camus passage quoted earlier, the assumption of common agreement about the just nature of the measure is essential to Locke's position: extraordinary measures are justified not by a leader's claim that they benefit the people, but rather by the public perception that the measures do indeed promote the common good. The action taken by the executive reflects or anticipates a decision which for practical, accidental reasons—the special constraints on foreign policy making for Locke, the loss of national independence and political freedom for Camus—cannot be adopted through the usual legislative channels. In contrast, where prerogative is invoked and exercised in violation of a community's common sense, Locke warns, it may (and, if it becomes a pattern, even should) lead to armed rebellion. Its use always represents a political risk. In retrospect, it may be praised as an act of leadership that anticipated and encouraged the crystallization of a new understanding of justice; but it may also be condemned as a move toward dictatorship, the opening scene of a coming civil war, an attempt to push a political community down a path of injustice.

This discussion suggests a first approximation of how established democratic societies use substantive and procedural criteria to distinguish between justice in the public arena and revenge. Both are responses to perceived injustice, but they are different responses. Substantively, an act of justice responds to the violation of a shared and specified understanding of what constitutes criminal activity. A person who commits a criminal act is "guilty." For most of us, he or she is guilty in a double sense: guilty "as charged" of having violated a statute to which all members of society are subject, and guilty in the sense of having violated a shared moral norm sufficiently important to the society as a whole to be enforced through the state. Ideally, the convicted person comes to recognize his or her own guilt. Procedurally, an act of justice is defined by the protections accorded the alleged perpetrator: prior knowledge of the rules, the presumption of innocence, the right to counsel, the assurance that his alleged victims will not be his judges, and so on. Finally, an act of justice pursues a mix of goals—retribution, reparation, prevention, (re)education—in which personal retribution and direct reparation (by the perpetrator to the victim), while not necessarily excluded, typically do not dominate. In this last point substantive and procedural criteria merge: the depersonalization of the ends pursued tends to promote a dispassionate and fair use of the means prescribed.

We typically qualify as an act of revenge any retributive action which differs substantively or procedurally from an act of justice: substantively, it may not be supported by a shared understanding of what constitutes criminal behavior; procedurally, it may be the work of non-state (or non-sovereign) actors, and/or it may disregard the rights of the accused. Revenge is always an act of retribution and is intended to produce emotional and/or material compensation for the person or group whose previous suffering is being avenged. Thus, justice presupposes a community whose norms the criminal violates; revenge takes place in an atmosphere of unmediated—though not necessarily (or even typically) unlimited— enmity.

In transitional settings, the procedural rule against ex post facto legislation often appears to an important segment of opinion as an obstacle to justice, while at the same time the substantive expectation that exceptional measures will enjoy consensual support is rarely realistic. In the context of our post-authoritarian "lack of community," "we" are unlikely "all" to agree on what constitutes criminal or even moral responsibility. The regime change, especially if it comes suddenly, disrupts the life plans of the old regime's supporters and opponents alike, disappointing the former and raising the expectations of the latter—and thus creating a situation in which both sides, for opposite reasons, are likely to criticize legal measures as unjust. Furthermore, as Aedanus Burke's arguments remind us, political justice has never enjoyed good press in liberal circles: it violates important principles, and it seems part of a political dynamic hostile to liberalism. Political justice, we usually assume, is simply a vehicle that permits judicial murder (and therefore all lesser penalties) in the service of partisan causes, and we are inclined to see in it one of the preferred propaganda instruments of dictatorial regimes, or of transitional regimes on the verge of betraying their liberal aspirations (England in 1649, after Pride's Purge, or France in 1793–94, as the Jacobins struggled to consolidate their control over the revolutionary movement). Political justice often looks more like revenge than like justice—and that is certainly how its "victims" perceive and portray it, whether they are democrats being railroaded by dictators or dictators being tried by democrats. *Siegerjustiz* (victors' justice) was the term used in Germany to discredit efforts to bring former Nazis and their collaborators to justice after World War II. After unification the term was used to criticize attempts to hold former East German officials legally responsible for the roles they played in the DDR: indicted, as a former member of the Politburo, for manslaughter for the shootings on the border, Egon Krenz angrily told a court whose authority he rejected, "This is victors' politics."[9] The expressions recall Thrasymachus' cynical definition of justice at the beginning of Plato's *Republic*. Blurring the distinction between justice and vengeance, Thrasymachus defines justice as "nothing other than the advantage of the stronger" (338C), suggesting that any act of retribution sanctioned by public authority would meet the definitional requirements of "justice." In every country, Thrasymachus argues, rulers demand obedience, and they are the people who write the laws (339A).

Thrasymachus' argument denies the existence of anything resembling natural law or what we have increasingly come to call human rights. Contemporary Western jurisprudence, and more especially post-1945 efforts to establish international norms of lawful behavior, represent (among other things) an effort to answer Thrasymachus' outburst—and Camus's anger: power may shift, regimes may come and go, but certain acts are inherently wrong and in theory actionable, even if institutional shortcomings prevent their actual prosecution and punishment. On certain fundamental issues, we now assert, common sense is always common—even when a political regime seeks, through law and/or sheer force, to impose a different standard. The philosophical validity of this statement remains contested, and the international community's willingness as well as its ability to enforce articulated standards are very imperfect, but politically the claim has become harder and harder to circumvent. Thus, communist governments signed the Helsinki Final Act (1975), pledging themselves to respect a long list of important rights, and the Constitution of the DDR acknowledged the legal significance of "recognized norms of international law," in violation of which no legal order could be given (see, e.g., StGB/DDR §258).

Two decades after the defeat of the Axis powers and twenty-five years before the demise of communist regimes in the Soviet Union and its former satellites, Judith Shklar suggested that political justice might contribute to the establishment of liberal norms, especially after a regime change. Shklar defined a political trial conventionally, as one "in which the prosecuting party, usually the regime in power aided by a cooperative judiciary, tries to eliminate its political enemies." In an analysis explicitly informed by the experience of postwar Germany, she then argued a less conventional position, implicitly distinguishing between justice and revenge:

> It is the politics of persecution which political trials serve that is the real horror, not the fact that courts are used to give it effect. There are occasions when political trials may actually serve liberal ends, where they promote legalistic values in such a way as to contribute to constitutional politics and to a decent legal system. The Trial of the Major War Criminals by the International Military Tribunal at Nuremberg probably had that effect. To be sure, within a stable constitutional order political trials may be a disgrace, a reversion to the politics of repression, but it is not the political trial itself but the *situation* in which it takes place and the *ends* that it serves which matter. It is the *quality of the politics* pursued in them that distinguishes one political trial from another.[10]

Even the most cursory comparison of Pierre Laval's trial in October 1945 and the Nuremberg Trial would make clear that democratizing elites exercise some control over the "situation" in which a political trial takes place, and that the trial situation they create matters. Laval was condemned to death after a rowdy ten-day trial, during which the normal procedural rules of justice were openly flouted and little attempt was made to insulate the proceedings from the political passions of the moment.[11] He was then revived after he attempted to poison himself, in order that he might be shot by a firing squad. Whatever one thought of Laval's conduct between 1939 and 1945, the lasting impression left by the trial was one of revenge rather than justice. In contrast, the American architects of the Nuremberg proceedings were, despite persistent and important differences of opinion within the American government about how the charges should be framed, in agreement about the sort of "situation" the trial would have to represent.[12] The American position was that "if we are going to have a trial, then it must be an actual trial."[13] Thus Henry Stimson, the secretary of war, admonished Henry Morgenthau, secretary of the treasury, against the summary measures Morgenthau preferred, arguing the necessity of "careful thought and a well-defined procedure" that would respect "at least the rudimentary aspects of the Bill of Rights."[14] Supreme Court Justice Robert Jackson, in a speech to the American Society of International Law some two weeks before he was appointed to lead the American team in Nuremberg, put the point even more sharply:

> Courts try cases, but cases also try courts.
> You must put no man on trial before anything that is called a court
> . . . under the forms of judicial proceedings if you are not willing to see him freed if not proven guilty.[15]

The "situation" Jackson and his colleagues sought to create at Nuremberg was one intended to hold the perception of unfairness—of *Siegerjustiz*—to a minimum. The picture of "justice" presented by the trial differed significantly—and positively—from the picture presented by Laval's trial. Three of the twenty-five individuals indicted at Nuremberg were in fact acquitted, among them Hjalmar Schacht, for whose conviction Jackson had pleaded with particular (if misplaced) vehemence. The organizational indictments were qualified by the tribunal, and even under the qualified indictments, three of the six indicted organizations were acquitted. Thus, the record suggests that a political trial can be made to resemble an "actual trial" in ways that extend well beyond the cosmetic. Far from feeling uncomfortably constrained by Shklar's "situation" requirement, Jackson saw its fulfillment as the precondition of a politically successful trial.

In Shklar's argument, not the "situation" of the trial but the ends it serves are ultimately crucial. Shklar suggests that we look to the "quality of the politics pursued" before reaching a judgment about political justice: "Ultimately," she argues, "it is the political results that count."[16] But how are we to know in advance what "ends" a political trial will in fact serve? Shklar's argument is a much more permissive one than Locke's argument about prerogative, which makes the existence of a latent consensus in support of the measure adopted the condition of its legitimacy. In Shklar's argument, political results are decisive, but in the real world, political results are notoriously hard to predict and almost equally difficult to trace back to their causes.

Shklar's more precise formulation of the argument—that the test of political justice must be whether or not it serves, in immediate and tangible ways, "the prospect of tolerant society"[17]—does not resolve the problem, but it does bring us back to the fight over the definition of common sense. The argument could be restated in the following way: in a transitional setting, the justification for political trials is not that the end (a change in regimes) justifies the means (the hasty elimination of opponents), but rather that the means (the identification and punishment of perpetrators, the vindication of victims, and the delegitimation of a dictatorship through legal and paralegal measures) can contribute to the end (the creation of a tolerant society). Where the latter link exists, where political justice represents part of, and is consistent with, a process of ideological change rather than an embarrassing but transitory loss of control, it may be useful. The battle over the redefinition of political common sense is a central element in this process of ideological change, and both its means and its motor may offend liberals. Ex post facto legislation (the means) obviates the need to manipulate existing codes in order to put "the form of treason we have all known" within the reach of the law. It gives democratizing elites a chance openly to state their values and to define the ensuing public debate. And the desire for revenge (the motor), which rightly makes liberals nervous, may in fact be an important force driving the process—no matter how often prosecutors and witnesses insist that it is not.

Thus, in a 1946 speech to the American Historical Asssociation, Herbert Wechsler, assistant attorney general as postwar legal strategies were being mapped in Washington, treated the thirst for vengeance as a legitimate motive as he justified the U.S. decision to press for a trial of Nazi leaders:

> Certainly only the firmest conviction that punishment in this situation could serve no adequate temporal purpose would have sanctioned dismissal of the millions of complainants with the admonition that "vengeance belongs to God." In truth, *the volume of accumulated passion sufficed in itself to establish such a temporal purpose*—for who can doubt that indiscriminate violence, a blood bath beyond control, would have followed an announcement by the responsible governments that they were unwilling to proceed? If nothing else was to be accomplished, it was essential that some institutional mechanism be provided that would reserve the application of violence to the public force, to cases in which punishment might serve a constructive purpose and in which reason would conclude that it was deserved.

Even more explicitly than Shklar, Wechsler emphasized the importance of the ends that trials might serve: the "constructive purpose" he wished to promote was the "tolerant society" Shklar also advocated. Punishment would serve that end by performing a deterrent function. Since men in power must reckon with the chance that they may someday lose power, the possibility and precedent of punishment, Wechsler hoped, might gradually eliminate certain political options from consideration, "the dark shadow of organized disapproval eliminating from the ambit of consideration alternatives that might otherwise present themselves in the final competition of choice."[18]

But Wechsler expected a trial to provide an even more immediate service in the construction of a tolerant society: he hoped that it would offer sufficient satisfaction to those calling for revenge to obviate the possibility of a "bloodbath" or the renewal of what Shklar called "the politics of persecution." Wechsler's formulation—"a blood bath beyond control"—raises the question whether a bloodbath that somehow did not get "beyond control" might contribute to a new sense of justice.[19] The more usual term for a "controlled" bloodbath is a purge, marked by summary executions and/or special courts. France experienced such a purge in 1944–45; predictably, it is remembered as just by those who supported it and as vengeance and persecution by those who were its "victims." Its lasting impact—positive or negative—on the development of democracy in postwar France is difficult to assess.[20] At a minimum, it should remind us that revenge often seems a psychologically more adequate response than legal justice to the sense of injustice that former subjects of a dictatorship may feel. Justice, Judith Shklar notes, "lacks the emotional punch" that revenge supplies, and therefore usually disappoints those who have endured injustice.[21] We should not expect legal justice to substitute for revenge. Can we nonetheless organize legal justice (as Wechsler suggested we could and should) in such a way as to dull the demand for revenge? Can legal justice validate and vindicate the suffering experienced by those who lived under a dictatorship?

These are, of course, political questions at least as much as they are legal dilemmas, for prosecutorial decisions in these areas are always political decisions. Different trial strategies, consistent with either institutional or cultural logics of reconciliation, may privilege different parties in the struggle to redefine common sense, and therefore disappoint or anger different groups in different ways. In a transitional setting, prosecutors may choose to focus their energies either on the prosecution of the former regime's leadership (an institutional strategy) or on bringing a broader spectrum of actors to trial (a cultural strategy). In choosing between these two options, decision makers draw, consciously or unconsciously, on different accounts of both the nature of the dictatorship and the requirements of a democratization process. Each choice sends a different message to the public. If the decision is made to concentrate on the prosecution of prominent leaders, the message is that the leaders bore decisive (though not necessarily exclusive) responsibility for the dictatorship and its crimes, and that democratization will not be impeded by the assumption that the rest of the population remained as uninvolved as possible. If prosecutors cast their nets more widely, the message is that meaningful responsibilities were more broadly distributed, and that democratization requires a careful examination of the commitments made by people who may perceive themselves simply as having made the best of a bad deal under the dictatorship.

Each of these strategies encourages a different public discourse about common sense; each burdens the redefinition of justice and the democratization process in a different way. Of course, the choice between the strategies will not be made in a vacuum, and the same circumstances that influence the choice—the particular character of the dictatorship, the length of time it remained in power, the base and breadth of the support it enjoyed in the society it ruled, the reasons for its ultimate demise, and the process that led to its replacement—will also tend to lend more or less plausibility to different accounts of common sense. By focusing on the experience of postwar West Germany, we can hold many contextual factors constant. The Nuremberg Trial is an example of the first strategy; the so-called Auschwitz Trial is an example of the second.

"Crime in the Moral Sense"

The spotlight in Nuremberg was on men who had played important roles in politics, the economy, and the military between 1933 and 1945. "We have no purpose," Robert Jackson argued, "to incriminate the whole German people."[22] As we shall see, the prosecutorial strategy at Nuremberg was not fully consistent. Its major thrust, however, supported what Karl Jaspers would later deplore as the sort of founding lie of the Federal

Republic, its "common sense" of its own moral worth, so detrimental, in his view, to the development of German democracy (see Chapter 2).

Jackson's strategy, however, accepted the deal that Jaspers denounced. Jackson sought to enlist the German public in his commonsense denunciation of the Third Reich by conceding ground to the public's commonsense affirmation of its own innocence. "If the German populace had willingly accepted the Nazi program," Jackson argued, "no Storm-troopers would have been needed in the early days of the Party and there would have been no need for concentration camps or the Gestapo." The prosecution would focus, Jackson promised, on "the brains and authority back of all the crimes," on "men of a station and rank which does not soil its own hands with blood," on "men who knew how to use lesser folk as tools." These men, he asserted, had literally built criminality: they were "the planners and designers, the inciters and leaders without whose evil architecture the world would not have been for so long scourged with the violence and lawlessness, and wracked with the agonies and convulsions, of this terrible war." The defendants had turned Germany into "one vast torture chamber," annihilating "the decent and courageous," intimidating "the decent but weak." The clear implication was that most Germans had once been, had longed to remain, and could again become decent men and women. The individuals responsible for the escalating indecency of the Third Reich were the "twenty-odd broken men" Jackson observed in the dock, and of whom he asserted, "their personal capacity for evil is forever past . . . Merely as individuals their fate is of little consequence to the world." The defendants were, however, on trial as "symbols," as representatives of "sinister influences that will lurk in the world long after their bodies have returned to dust."[23]

Jackson was making an argument from prevention: "Civilization can afford no compromise with the social forces which would gain renewed strength if we deal ambiguously or indecisively with the men in whom those forces now precariously survive." But the case was not based on preexisting statutes. The indictments of Nazi leaders, Jackson argued, were justified by common sense—even if the London Charter had created crimes after the fact. "Plain people with their earthy common sense," Jackson argued, had extended the meaning of unjust war after 1918 to include "not merely uncivilized ways of waging war, but also the waging in any way of uncivilized wars—wars of aggression." The Nazis had chosen to ignore such norms, which were clearly discernible in interwar treaty agreements. Now the London Charter had declared aggressive war to be a crime. Raised in the common law tradition, Jackson argued that common sense suggested that in a system based on precedent, constituted "through decisions reached from time to time in adapting settled principles to new situations," there always had to be a first case; Nuremberg was that case. Some degree of unfairness was unavoidable: "When the law evolves by the case method, as did the common law and as international law must do if it is to advance at all, it advances at the expense of those who wrongly guessed the law and learned too late their error."[24]

The law could not afford, Jackson maintained, to stand in opposition to a widely and clearly held perception of justice. The higher purpose normally served by the injunction against ex post facto legislation was the belief that the rule of law and justice were coterminous. Here, however, the rule of law itself would be undermined were law to "lag so far behind the moral sense of mankind that conduct which is crime [sic] in the moral sense . . . be regarded as innocent in law." The argument worked only if Germans themselves were assumed to participate in the general community whose "moral sense" was defining a new statutory crime. But if the argument could not be made to work, then courts would be powerless in a situation where their presence might be desperately needed, as calculated instruments of both retribution and prevention: "Civilization asks," Jackson told the court, "whether law is so laggard as to be utterly helpless to deal with crimes of this magnitude by criminals of this order of importance."[25]

Jackson's approach assumed that once Nazi philosophy was discredited and Nazi leaders were eliminated, it would be possible to neutralize the "social forces" that had supported Nazism through institutional engineering—a position close to the one Lübbe defended in 1983 (see Chapter 3). The International Military Tribunal (IMT) proceedings were intended in part to disseminate information, and so to show Germans what had been done by Germans in the name of Germany; but Jackson repeatedly made clear that in the prosecution's view, the defendants were stand-ins for a political system, not for a guilty population. Erik Reger, who covered the Nuremberg Trial as editor of the Berlin newspaper *Tagesspiegel*, immediately recognized the implicit bargain the indictment represented, and identified the danger it created: "The murderers are right there in the dock. With every document the prosecution produces, another blemish on the soul of the average German disappears, and while the gallery, from Göring to Keitel, looks black as pitch, the average German looks as pure as a romantic full moon over the Heidelberg Castle."[26]

Jackson (like Lübbe) understood "social forces" to be politically dangerous only if they were or could easily find organized expression. Such expression presupposed a legitimizing, mobilizing ideology, a set of appropriate institutions, and a group of capable leaders: Jackson's strategy—in the promising context set by total military defeat and occupation—focused on eliminating all three. Reger's worries went in a different direction. He explicitly denied the underlying "decency" of Germans who had acted badly out of weakness or interest, and (like Lübbe's critics) he questioned the ease with which they could be used as constituent units of a new democracy. Assigning guilt to all who, from whatever motives, had followed Hitler, Reger argued, "This is not a story of error or misunderstanding or blindness, but of character faults."[27]

Jackson, however, was not interested in the misdeeds of average Germans—and as the failed case against Hjalmar Schacht would show, the court could not successfully prosecute "character faults." Even with regard to the men before him, Jackson had no intention, he said, of losing his way in "a wilderness of single instances"; instead his overriding goal would be to establish the overall criminal nature of the Nazi regime. It was not a picture in which the average German was likely to recognize his or her own place: "My emphasis will not be on individual barbarities and perversions which may have occurred independently of any central plan . . . Nor will I . . . dwell on the activity of individual defendants except as it may contribute to exposition of the common plan."[28]

The legal device of the "Common Plan or Conspiracy" allowed the "twenty-odd broken men" to be tried as representatives of a system that indeed could not itself "be produced for trial, cannot testify, and cannot be sentenced." The first count of the indictment charged that "all the defendants . . . participated as leaders, organizers, instigators, or accomplices in the formulation or execution of a Common Plan or Conspiracy to commit, or which involved the commission of, Crimes against Peace, War Crimes, and Crimes against Humanity . . . and . . . are individually responsible for their own acts and for all acts committed by any persons in the execution of such plan and conspiracy."[29]

The indictment went on to define the Nazi Party (NSDAP) as the "central core of the Common Plan or Conspiracy," and to summarize succinctly but thoroughly Nazi ideology, political practices, and policies. In its "statement of individual responsibility" for crimes committed, the indictment spelled out the relationship of each individual to the regime, with the purpose of showing the defendant to have been a key architect of Nazi politics by placing him within an institutional context and by describing his connections to other top decision makers. The description of Hermann Göring is indicative of how the prosecution sought to portray all the defendants: it began with a summary of the positions Göring had held ("Supreme leader of the SA, general in the SS, a member and President of the Reichstag . . . and Successor Designate to Hitler"), followed by the argument that he had first used his influence to promote and consolidate the power of a criminal regime and then used his power to plan or commit the criminal acts cited in the indictment.[30]

Avoiding the "wilderness of single instances," Jackson used his opening statement to describe the Nazi program, the party's seizure of power, the consolidation of the regime, the process of rearmament, and finally the pursuit of Nazi goals through warfare. The arguments of the chief prosecutors often resemble impassioned lectures on contemporary history. But the lectures might have an old-fashioned ring in today's academic world: they focused, so to speak, on kings and princes.

If the defendants were to be brought before the court as "symbols," the court itself would also be a "symbol." The defendants would enjoy the right to a fair trial that liberal nations guarantee to accused individuals. Their individual responsibility and guilt would have to be established according to the normal rules of judicial procedure.

Preliminary investigation soon allayed the prosecutors' fears that their case would founder for lack of evidence: in July 1945, two months after assuming his post, Jackson wrote, "I did not think men would ever be so foolish as to put in writing some of the things the Germans did put in writing."[31] The focus on the "Common Plan and Conspiracy" meant that the Nuremberg Trial produced an extraordinary volume of evidence about the Nazi regime. The essential elements of the evidence were reported in the press and brought ordinary Germans into forced, if fleeting, confrontation with the crimes the Nazis had committed; the rest of the evidence nourished scholarship on the regime for decades.

Given the purpose of the trial—to establish the criminal character of the Nazi regime—the absence of Hitler and Goebbels was of little importance. They were, so to speak, present in spirit. What mattered was the power of the blows delivered to the murderous edifice they, together with the men who were tried at Nuremberg and with others, had conceived and built. How powerful, then, were the blows? Even before the trial was concluded, there were three indicators that the version of common sense it tended to promote was less than satisfactory. The inadequacies of the trial's dominant logic were evident in the presentation of the case against Hjalmar Schacht, in the controversy surrounding the case against Nazi organizations, and in the relief with which some American prosecutors greeted the denazification program.

Most of the defendants at Nuremberg were convicted. Three were acquitted. One of those acquitted was Hjalmar Schacht, who had been minister of economics and president of the Reichsbank. Schacht's role in the regime was obviously less central than that of (for example) Göring; it was also far more ambiguous, since Schacht resigned as Economics Minister in 1937, could prove his later connections to the July 20 resistance circles, and ended the War as an internee at Ravensbruck. Telford Taylor, a prosecutor at Nuremberg who considered the process used to single out which Nazis should be prosecuted by the IMT careless and often uninformed, was particularly critical of the decision to indict Schacht: "The idea that a man who had ceased to play any important part in Nazi affairs months before the war and who ended the war as a dissident concentration-camp inmate was the best possible candidate for conviction as a war criminal, was preposterous."[32]

Jackson, however, saw the Schacht case differently. In his closing argument, Jackson used Schacht to summarize the contradictions and moral depravity that first explained why men might have been drawn into collaboration with a criminal regime, and then allowed such men to maintain their innocence. Jackson condemned Schacht in personal terms for moral cowardice and criminal irresponsibility. Here, Schacht is not a "symbol" or a stand-in for a state that cannot be placed in the dock; he is an individual who, faced with moral choices, repeatedly chose poorly, and then, when confronted with the reality of his actions, persistently denied that he bore any responsibility. Given the dominant logic of the trial, it is no accident that Schacht was acquitted. Jackson's overdrawn but nonetheless damning description of Schacht, however, suggests that the logic was not fully satisfying, even to those who were its most stalwart advocates.

In Jackson's speech, Schacht seems to be on trial not as a key decision maker but as a spectacular stand-in for the average German: someone perhaps weak but, in Jackson's account, neither particularly intimidated nor particularly decent, who had adapted to the opportunities and constraints created by the Third Reich, and whose objections to the regime came late and were pragmatically motivated, a representative of "the most dangerous and reprehensible type of opportunism—that of the man of influential position who is ready to join a movement that he knows to be wrong because he thinks it is winning."[33]

The Schacht case was by no means the only case that presented problems for the tribunal. The ambiguities of the prosecutorial strategy followed at Nuremberg are most obvious in the difficulties that arose in conjunction with the indictment of six organizations: the Reich cabinet, the General Staff–High Command, the NSDAP "Leadership Corps," the SA (Sturmabteilung, Stormtroopers), the SD (Sicherheitsdienst, security service), and the SS (Schutzstaffel, secret police). The most important legal memorandum drawn up during the planning stages of the trial was penned in September 1944 by Colonel Murray Bernays, a New York lawyer whose wartime work in the personnel branch of the Army General Staff had included tracking the treatment of American prisoners of war.[34] Bernays wanted to snare the men who had executed Hitler's orders. Since these men numbered in the millions—the SS alone had some 700,000 members, the Leadership Corps 600,000[35]—it was clearly unrealistic to demand that each individual be granted a trial. If the organization could be convicted, however, the need to grant individual trials would be obviated; proof that the individual had belonged to the criminal organization would suffice, and the court would need only to deliberate on the penalty appropriate to the individual's level and degree of involvement. Thomas Dodd, summarizing the American position on the organizational charges before the court, reminded his listeners of the purpose these charges were meant to serve. Dodd insisted again on the preventative function of the trial, but here the message targeted not future ministers and generals but every housewife and army private. Dodd's statement was expressly at odds with the otherwise dominant logic of the trial: "By a declaration of criminality against these organizations, this Tribunal will put on notice not only the people of Germany but the people of the whole world. Mankind will know that no crime will go unpunished because it was committed in the name of a political party or of a state; that no crime will be passed by because it is too big; that no criminal will avoid punishment because there are too many."[36]

The principle that undergirded the organizational indictments rested on dubious precedents: among the American precedents cited was the anti-subversive Smith (Alien Registration) Act of 1940, which had been sharply criticized in liberal circles.[37] From the beginning, the charges against the indicted organizations seemed problematic to members of the American prosecutorial team and to several of the judges. In mid-August 1945 (six weeks before the trial began), Bernays left the prosecutorial team. In March 1946 the tribunal specified the sort of evidence that it would consider relevant to a determination of guilt, emphasizing the need to establish shared purpose and sufficient information among members and voluntary membership.[38]

The tribunal later focused even more sharply on the criteria that could be used to assess individual responsibilities within criminal organizations. Right to the end of the trial, the American member of the tribunal, Francis Biddle, who had served as attorney general after Jackson was appointed to the Supreme Court, maintained his distaste for the organizational indictments: "I suggest throwing them all out," he wrote a month before the end of the trial, "a shocking thing, this group crime." Telford Taylor later recalled his own misgivings regarding the practical consequences as well as the legal implications of a guilty verdict: "It must have been apparent to all the other participants, as it certainly was to me, that judicial proceedings, even giving full effect to Bernays's vision of summary process, could not possibly deal with such numbers without hundreds of courts and years of hearings." Justice could not be produced, Taylor remarked, "on such an assembly-line basis."[39]

Assembly-line murder, however, invited assembly-line justice; otherwise, guilty men and women would walk free. This was the problem which, in Taylor's perception, the denazification program promised to solve: "I was, therefore, greatly relieved when, in mid-January [1946] I was visited by a deus ex machina in the form of a letter from Charles Fahy enclosing a document entitled 'Draft Report of Denazification Policy Board.'" The board, of which Fahy was the chair, had been created in November 1945 (six months after the capitulation of German forces) by General Lucius Clay; its task was to outline an overall denazification program that would lend structure, coherence, and consistency to the policies being implemented by American occupation forces. It produced what became the definitional document of the American denazification program, the Law for Liberation from National Socialism and Militarism (March 5, 1946). Taylor responded to the draft report in a memorandum to Justice Jackson, confirming the report's assessment that prosecutors would "not be able to prosecute more than a few hundred, or at the outside, a few thousand major and sub-major war criminals" and approving of the paralegal alternatives created by the denazification program.[40]

Unlike the IMT trial, the denazification campaign was fundamentally dependent on German support and cooperation. It suggested a cultural strategy of reconciliation, but it did more even than demand self-examination and change at the grassroots level. It demanded that the *demand* for exposure and change come in part from the grassroots level—and this even as it abandoned the presumption of innocence, obligating all adult Germans to demonstrate a lack of complicity with the National Socialist regime. Denazification was in many ways a direct assault on contemporary common sense, not a reflection of it or an effort to adjust it in marginal ways. Unsurprisingly, and despite the bitter disappointment of many Germans who had hoped that the country would somehow participate in its own liberation, the necessary grassroots support was not forthcoming.[41] Most Germans who had come through the Third Reich were ready to participate in what Jackson had called the "moral sense of mankind" only if, as Telford Taylor put it much later, "the finger of guilt pointed nowhere in particular."[42] Absent cooperation and support from below, the program became a *Mitläuferfabrik* (a *Mitläufer* factory)[43] rather than an instrument for forcing individuals to confront and take responsibility for their past commitments. American interest in resisting this outcome diminished as the perceived unavailability of alternative German elites became more preoccupying. A web of complicity and what the Auschwitz court, some twenty years later, would still deplore as a "wall of silence"[44] then classified men and women who had been major and minor offenders as mere "followers," possibly contributing to the delegitimation of the fallen regime (identification with which people were forced to deny), but probably inhibiting meaningful dialogue or reflection (whether private or public) about their experiences.[45] "Turn the page [*Strich drunter*]," as Jaspers had anticipated the situation, "and a new life." Unlike trials of former National Socialist perpetrators, which continued for a half century after the Third Reich collapsed, denazification was a passing episode, viewed universally (although for different reasons in different cases), at the time and later, as a failure.[46]

In studies of postwar democratization in West Germany, the stories of the IMT Nuremberg prosecutions and denazification are often separated.[47] In part, this may reflect a division of labor and interest among academic disciplines: Nuremberg has attracted the particular attention of legal scholars and people interested in the development of international law, whereas denazification is a topic for historians and political scientists. But the separation has important substantive implications. In this section I have deliberately tried to link the two stories. In the Nuremberg Trial an institutional strategy of reconciliation dominated, and in part disappointed, though few considered or consider it a failure. The denazification program was an effort to supplement or correct an institutional strategy with a cultural one. It too disappointed, and most observers have found it a failure. Common sense is a stubborn thing.

Ordinary Men, Extraordinary Crimes, and Common Sense

Between 1959 and 1971, three of the Federal Republic's most prominent literary figures published novels that explored the behavior of ordinary Germans—*Mitläufer* and *Anpasser* (adapters, conformists, trimmers)— during the Third Reich. The three books—Günter Grass's *Die Blechtrommel* (The Tin Drum, 1959), Siegfried Lenz's *Deutschstunde* (German Lesson, 1968), and Heinrich Böll's *Gruppenbild mit Dame* (Group Portrait with Lady, 1971)—were quickly recognized as classics. The novels by Lenz and Böll are also indicative of how West German commonsense understandings of guilt and responsibility had begun to shift in the two decades following the war.[48] Among the central figures in Böll's *Gruppenbild mit Dame* is Walter Pelzer, a sort of lesser Schacht, who joins the NSDAP at the right time, profits materially during the Third Reich from the persecution of Jews and the prosecution of the war, carefully avoids getting blood on his hands, and leaves the NSDAP in time to be able to pose as clean when the Americans arrive. "Old Nazi, war profiteer, opportunist" is how his children view him—so he tells us when we meet him, "deep in a state of defensive melancholy that could almost pass as repentance."[49] Even before the war ends, the phrase "I am really not a beast [*Ich bin doch kein Unmensch*]" becomes Walter Pelzer's verbal tic: "Really, he said it so often that one almost didn't hear it anymore," another character observes. "It was like 'The Lord be with you,' or 'Have mercy on us' in church, and later he had two expressions for it: 'I'm really not a beast' and 'Am I then a beast?'" (212).

Another character remarks with some understatement: "It was psychoanalytically pretty interesting, what was going on inside Walter Pelzer" (212). It would also be psychoanalytically and otherwise interesting to know how different groups in German society dealt with assertions like Pelzer's.[50] Pelzer sought maximum material profit at minimum political risk, and was so successful that he had not so much as broken a window during the pogrom of November 9, 1938. For all Böll's sarcasm, would the common sense of the 1960s side with or against Pelzer? Men and women who had been thirty in 1940 were still only fifty in 1960, sixty in 1970, still active professionally, still telling their children how to behave: What would they think?[51]

Siggi, the narrator in Lenz's *Deutschstunde,* is serving a sentence in a detention center for boys.[52] The protagonist of the novel is Siggi's father, Jens Ole Jepsen, whose wartime commitments as the sole police official in Rugbüll, a small village near the Danish border, are reconstructed ten years later by his son. The lad is provoked by the topic he receives as an assignment in his German class: the boys are told to write an essay about "the joys of duty." Reminded of his father, whose every action and relationship was dominated by an utterly undiscriminating conception of duty, the son, who in the end argues persuasively that he is in detention "in the place . . . of my old man" (432), has so much to say that he does not know where to begin. He turns in an empty notebook, and is punished by being confined to his room to write the essay. He is left to decide when the essay is finished. Having begun to plumb his memories, the boy cannot stop—and does not want to stop. Thanks to the assignment, he "returns voluntarily," as he puts it, "behind the bars of my past" (193). Siggi had been born in 1933. Now he tries to draw consequences from his own experience so as to come up with a morally grounded understanding of duty. "I am not talking about just any place," the youth writes, "but about my place; I am not trying to identify just any misfortune, but my misfortune. In sum, I am not telling just any story, because what is indifferent to us creates no obligations" (193).

Siggi's common sense leaves him trapped behind the bars of his father's unacknowledged and unpunished injustices. Jepsen was not a soldier on the murderous eastern front or a concentration camp guard; he was not even a member of the NSDAP. But, as his son's account suggests, neither was he simply a decent man ("decent but weak") caught in the wrong place at the wrong time; he was someone whose common sense was fundamentally impervious to democratic norms. In the spring of 1943, Jepsen receives an order from Berlin: Max Ludwig Nansen, a village resident, expressionist painter, and lifelong friend of Jepsen, is no longer to be allowed to paint. Jepsen reluctantly imparts the news to Nansen: "Here, Max, something's here from Berlin" (30). He had nothing to do with the order, Jepsen says, but he cannot change it and will enforce it. Over the course of the next two years, enforcing the order becomes Jepsen's obsession: the order specifies his duty, and he recognizes no alternative claim on his moral loyalty, no external substantive standard that would allow him to differentiate between orders that should be carried out and orders that should be resisted. He dismisses the painter's resistance as the reaction of a man who thinks himself above the laws that apply to ordinary people ["He with his own laws. With his superiority. With his contempt for everyone who just does their duty" (385)], and he parries the postman's repeated conciliatory admonitions as cowardly (e.g., 279–281). Shortly after the war, representatives of the British Royal Academy visit Nansen to present him with an honorary membership. In Jepsen's presence, they ask how the local police had conducted themselves. Nansen shrugs: "What options did someone who wants only to do his duty and who expects nothing else of himself have?" (359)

Unlike Pelzer, Jepsen is not an opportunist. After the first British soldiers have come and gone, Jepsen receives an order to defend the village ["Gather weapons, yes sir!" he repeats into the telephone, "all able-bodied men, yes sir, the men have been instructed" (289)]. Together with three neighbors—among them the painter—Jepsen builds a trench and prepares to defend the streets. As night falls, the painter decides it is time to go home. Jepsen invokes military hierarchy, calls Nansen a deserter, and draws his pistol. "The way his hand held the high-caliber, hardly used service pistol—it was so calm!" the son observes; "Standing there armed like that, it bothered him so little" (303). As the tension mounts, one of the other men appeals to Jepsen's nonexistent sense of proportion and prudence: "Those are big words ["deserter"], Jens, you ought to rub your eyes a bit" (304). But Jepsen does not have even the flexibility of an opportunist: "I don't ask what one will gain from doing one's duty," he says, "whether it is in one's interest or things like that . . . One's duty, one can't just do it according to one's mood or when it seems prudent, understand what I mean?" (280).

The few months that Jepsen spends in an Allied internment camp have as little effect on his patterns of thought and behavior as does the instruction booklet that he receives to help him find his way in the putatively new Germany. He becomes again, the son reports, "what he always was and also what everyone expected him to be . . . For three months, Rugbüll simply didn't have a policeman, and then there he was again, with his parched face and his ill-fitting pants and he went back to doing his job as though it was the most natural thing in the world, as though he hadn't been off on a forced leave, but just on vacation" (343–344).

Among the things that Jepsen simply continued were his rejection of his older son, Klaas, who had shot himself in the hand to avoid military service, and his efforts to sabotage Nansen's work. Siggi catches his father burning paintings, and is overcome by fear and hate as he observes his father's "unwavering single-mindedness" and "vacant happiness" (351). "You mustn't do that," the boy insists. "What was in the past is out and gone, everybody says so" (351–352). But the father replies first with a blow and then with a lecture about duty. The lecture, accompanied by the "vague gestures that one makes when in conversation with oneself," is nonetheless laced with threats directed at Siggi: "I finished Klaas, and I'll finish you" (352). Siggi now decides that "nothing is safe" from his father (380), and he begins compulsively to steal and hide works of art—the crime for which he is then sent to the detention center.

There is no happy ending in Lenz's novel. Who invented them? Siggi wants to know of his parents (388). National Socialism, it is clear, had not invented the mother, who was prepared to denounce her older son, who looked on with pleasure as her husband beat her younger son, and who is addicted to tranquillizers. National Socialism also did not invent the father, whose content-free understanding of duty enables him to shut out all other emotions and values. As Reger put it in his critique of the Nuremberg prosecutorial stategy, "This is not a story of error or misunderstanding or blindness, but of character faults." Perhaps we could trade them in, Siggi bitterly suggests to his sister in a conversation about their parents (388). But the parents cannot be traded in. Siggi is in the detention center, in his father's place, because his society has declined the challenge Jaspers identified: "Because nobody dared to impose a detoxification program on the policeman from Rugbüll. He can remain

addicted and do his damned duty like an addict" (433). In the end, Siggi
is released from detention, but sees himself unable to escape his past:
"Surrounded by my people, hedged in by memories, soaked in the events
that happened in my town, undermined by the experience that time
heals nothing, but I mean nothing, I know what I have to do and what I
will do tomorrow morning. Fail and fall because of Rugbüll? One could
put it that way" (448).

Siggi's father's world is a universe exhaustively defined by what the
Frankfurt court that heard the Auschwitz case called "a devotion to
orders and a wrongly understood concept of duty."[53] In legal settings,
this led defendants to plead that they had acted in a *Befehlsnotstand:* they
had obeyed orders backed by compulsory force. The Nuremberg Trial
prosecuted men who had given orders. The 1958 Ulmer Einsatzgruppe
trial, and especially the two-year trial in Frankfurt of twenty-two men
who had performed various functions at Auschwitz, put men in the dock
who had been many notches down the chain of command.[54] Unlike the
men tried at Nuremberg, the defendants in the Auschwitz Trial had not
been major decision makers during the Third Reich. They had led "normal" lives—usually under their own names—since the end of the war.
The orders they had executed were far more lethal in character than the
orders Jepsen carried out, and the defendants normally stopped short of
defending the orders they had received. In their court statements they
suffered from the predictable lapses of memory, but they also used their
subordinate position to excuse their actions: they had been in a *Befehlsnotstand.* The effort to call them legally to account represented a
fundamental shift in prosecutorial strategy—and a very different stage in
the redefinition of common sense in postwar West Germany. After a long
decade during which official voices in the Foreign Office had sought a
"final solution [sic] to the so-called war criminal problem," and in which
the minister of transportation, in a letter to the chancellor, could refer to
convicted Nazi criminals as "political prisoners," the shift had been signaled by the creation in 1958 of a central office for the investigation of
Nazi (NS) crimes in Ludwigsburg.[55] Now the men who had done the
dirty work would be brought to trial as alleged murderers and accesso-
ries to murder. "The trial should demonstrate to the world," the anti-
Nazi prosecutor Fritz Bauer told the press, "that a new Germany, a German democracy, is resolved to protect the dignity of every individual."[56]

The results lacked the clarity Bauer worked so tirelessly to achieve.

"The peculiar feature of these proceedings," the court acknowledged, "lies in the fact that we are concerned with state-ordered mass murder." Ex-Captain Robert Mulka, like his co-defendants, the court affirmed, had been "a spoke in the overall 'machinery of extermination.'"[57] Would common sense make this a declaration of innocence or of guilt? This was a question Hermann Lübbe had chosen not to entertain. "I was ordered to that place," the camp pharmacist, Dr. Viktor Capesius, told the court, "without the slightest initiative from my side." He reminded his listeners that he was married to a woman who was half Jewish. And he concluded, "I brought no guilt upon myself in Auschwitz; I ask you to acquit me."[58]

Mulka, born in 1895, was a decorated World War I veteran who had been stripped of his officer status in 1920 after being convicted on a corruption charge. Since as a result of his conviction he would have had to join the Wehrmacht as an enlisted man, his "only" option in 1941 was to join the Waffen-SS. In early 1942 he was posted to Auschwitz, where he soon became acting deputy and then, in July 1942, deputy commander of the camp. He was relieved in 1943, when the wife of another SS officer denounced him for calling Goebbels an "idiot," a statement that turned out to refer to Goebbels's tactics, not his character.[59]

Mulka's testimony asserted three not necessarily consistent arguments: he was never in the camp; he knew what was happening but never participated in a reprehensible action and certainly never issued any reprehensible orders; and he was appalled by what he knew, but believed that he would be killed if he objected. He was of course conscientious—"He [camp commandant Höß][60] had in me someone who was painfully precise and paid attention to everything"—but he insisted that he had never been in the camp ("It is almost incomprehensible, but it is nevertheless a fact") and above all was never on the ramp where arriving deportees were "selected." He wanted the court to believe that he had "had nothing to do with the prisoners and the camp." He was aware of "the things that were going on there"; because of the smell, he continued, "the entire population knew what was happening." But then again he did not know: the commandant "considered me a reactionary, and not suitable for work [in the camp]. He therefore gave me unbelievable mountains of paperwork and responsibility for the economic plant." The prosecution insisted that as an officer responsible for forwarding recommendations for promotion or punishment, Mulka must have known something about the actions that had led to the recommendations. He responded: "Oh yes. I was informed in a general way about what was happening; I have never denied that I knew. But I couldn't possibly have known the details. Those I never knew. All that I heard for the first time only here, during the trial."[61]

Mulka repeatedly reminded the court that he had suffered from stomach trouble throughout the war, and claimed that his experience at Auschwitz had brought him to the brink of collapse. But he "knew" that resistance would be both futile and fatal—futile because others would carry out any orders he might refuse, and fatal because "the heaviest penalties, up to and including death, were attached to not carrying out orders." He knew that there were gas chambers in the camp, but he could not approach the camp commandant, who was "a hard man to read," and he dared not press any questions through military channels: "I was 100 percent convinced that I would have been signing my own death warrant if I had made any such move."[62]

The court took care to explore the plausibility of Mulka's fear: the evidence suggested that camp officers who refused orders could expect to be transferred to the front and/or to a punishment battalion, but no other penalties were likely.[63] During the twenty-month trial, defendant after defendant nonetheless repeated a variation of defendant Josef Klehr's claim: "I had deep sympathy for the innocent victims, but I was a soldier under orders."[64] Klehr maintained: "I was really in a straitjacket. I couldn't just go to the camp physician and say: 'It's a beastly thing, what's being done here [killing inmates with lethal injections].' He would have stood me up against the Black Wall [where prisoners were routinely shot]. I had all sorts of thoughts, but we little drones [*Scharführer*] were really only numbers, just like the prisoners."[65]

The perpetrator as victim, imprisoned in a straitjacket, as anonymous as the camp inmates, similarly helpless and exploited; the commitments made in the "merciless situation of a dictatorship" as a terrible but unavoidable "fate": in his closing argument, defense attorney Hans Laternser would claim that "these defendants too became Hitler's victims."[66] The court itself, in its characterization of how Mulka "became harnessed in the apparatus of extermination," invoked a "chain of unfortunate circumstances." He did, the court acknowledged, "join the SS voluntarily, as a mature adult, and at a time when he should have known that he risked being drawn into criminal acts. It is, however, not certain . . . that he actually considered that he might be misused for criminal purposes."[67] In April 1969, at the beginning of the second parliamentary debate to extend the statute of limitations on murder, Günther Diehl, the government's press secretary, called men who had murdered under orders "victims of the Nazi system."[68] These arguments would echo for decades in German public discourse about guilt and responsibility during the Third Reich, profoundly affecting reformulations of common sense in enduring ways. The arguments were consistent with the vocabulary the Frankfurt defendants took for granted when they recalled their experiences: their adherence to National Socialism had been motivated by a horror of "Bolshevism"; Allied bombing raids were "terror attacks"; and the war's end, which Federal President Richard von Weizsäcker would try (with only limited success) in 1985 to define publicly once and for all as a "day of liberation," was understood as a "collapse."[69]

The court argued that the acts committed at Auschwitz were murder under existing law, and that the illegal and unjust nature of those acts should have been clear to all actors: "For all their differences, there is in the understanding of all civilized peoples . . . a certain central core of justice, which in accordance with a common conception of justice must not be violated by any law or governmental measure."[70]

But the prosecution of ordinary men—even of ordinary men who, unlike Jens Ole Jepsen, had participated in extraordinary crimes—opened up the possibility that the defense might capture the argument from common sense, especially in a culture which recognized Jepsen as a plausible figure. This was all the more likely in the context of a murder trial taking place in a legal system that made murder dependent on the inner disposition of the alleged murderer at the time of the act: "Whoever kills a person out of the desire to kill, in order to satisfy sexual interests, out of greed or other base motives, treacherously or cruelly or in a humiliating manner or in order to facilitate or cover up another crime, is a murderer" (StGB §211).

The court itself was hesitant in its assignment of guilt and responsibility. On the one hand, the court reiterated the argument not only that killing defenseless men, women, and children violated commonsense notions of justice, but also that the defendants knew their actions to be in violation of that common code.[71] On the other hand, the court took seriously its own assertion that men like Mulka, let alone men still lower down the chain of command, had been "ordered into" a criminal enterprise, for actions in the service of which they then bore only limited responsibility: "Only if they showed an eagerness that went beyond fulfilling their assigned tasks, if they participated in extermination actions in a particularly unreserved fashion, urged their subordinates on, or otherwise gave to understand that they considered the mass killings right and necessary should we conclude that they were willing perpetrators."[72]

Furthermore, the court conceded that the defendants might in fact have been externally stripped of the moral compass that would otherwise—"normally"—have given them an imperative reminder of the dictates of common sense. After the Third Reich as before, they had lived "orderly, industrious," law-abiding lives. But National Socialism had created "an unexampled spiritual confusion," "bring[ing] into question previous values and [erasing] the boundaries between right and wrong." The accused had been "misused by a criminal regime to which they had sworn unconditional obedience," even if this misuse attenuated their responsibility.[73]

Common sense, the court suggested, was common only under "normal" circumstances, and the Third Reich, with its "unexampled spiritual confusion," did not meet the standards of normal circumstances. As one defendant who had been thirteen when Hitler came to power put it: "If a superior said, 'This is black!' then it was black, even if it was white."[74] On the one hand, the court was stating, if not the obvious, then certainly a plausible and respectable interpretation of what the Third Reich had meant to those who had lived through it. On the other hand, the description comforted Germans in the conviction that they too had been victims—"One must think honestly about the conditions that prevailed then, under that dictatorship!" Laternser argued, in support of the *Befehlsnotstand* thesis—struggling in extraordinarily adverse circumstances to preserve themselves and their honor: "The percentage of decent individuals is after all no greater and no smaller among our people than it is in other great nations!"[75] To punish a victim for being a victim, however, is at best an act of persecution or revenge, not justice. "That all [Hitler's] beautiful words were falsehood and betratyal we did not understand at the beginning," one of Primo Levi's German readers wrote in 1962 in response to Levi's memoir of the year he spent in Auschwitz, *Se questo e un uomo* (If This Is a Man). The reader went on to assert that "no guilt can . . . be attributed to the betrayed: the traitor alone is guilty." He lamented, as would several defendants in Frankfurt, that resistance in a totalitarian state is hopeless, and concluded—to Levi's indignation—by inviting Levi to feel sorry for the perpetrators ("my poor, betrayed and misguided people") and to get on with his life.[76]

"Do you feel yourself innocent though condemned?" the presiding judge asked Franz Hofmann, who (in his own account) had joined the SS in 1932 because he was jobless and because his brother's unused uniform was sitting in the closet. For his activities in Dachau, where he was posted from 1933 through 1942, Hofmann had already been sentenced to life in prison. Now, two years later, he was on trial for what he had done in Auschwitz between the end of 1942 and April 1944 when he was transfered to another camp. "Do you feel yourself innocent though condemned?" Hofmann did. He was then asked to explain his promotions. He replied: "I did my job. Wherever I get put, I do my work." Hofmann pointed the finger of guilt at higher-ranking officers: "Anyone who knew Höß, who knew Aumeier and Schwarz, knows what was up. They are the people who landed us here. No one could tell them anything. Too bad, that they are no longer here. Someone had to say this! [Wipes away tears.]"[103] But Höß and Aumeier and Schwarz were dead, and Hofmann, who had—he insisted—only done his duty, was, as he saw it, unfairly left holding the bag: "I have no idea what people want from me," he said. "It almost seems as if I had been the main force behind what happened."[77]

"Wherever I get put, I do my work" was a powerful argument in—and after—Hofmann's generation, and the bitterness felt by men who perceived themselves unjustly censured for having done their duty was deeply felt. At worst, they argued, they had been unwitting or unwilling tools, not "the main force" of a criminal regime. A half century after the war's end, suggestions that the Wehrmacht had been massively involved in war crimes, especially on the eastern front, would still suffice to unleash a public polemic.[78] Were German perpetrators also victims, and if they were, was their punishment—legal or moral—a case of justice or revenge? In the ongoing struggle to settle these questions and to redefine common sense in postwar Germany, the Auschwitz Trial may have played an ambiguous role. For the first time, the public was provided with a vivid description not just of the machinery of extermination but also how the machinery worked at the individual level: how children's heads were smashed against walls, how people were crowded into gas chambers, of how some people played "games" in order to kill other people.

The trial proceedings were well covered in the German press, especially by the *Frankfurter Allgemeine Zeitung.*[79] The documentation gathered made it difficult—impossible, defense attorney Laternser optimistically thought—to assert that the gas chambers had never existed or that the Nazis had not deliberately exterminated millions of people. But the trial may not have made it any more difficult for the *Anpasser* and *Mitläufer,* decades after the war's end, to resist democratic intrusions on the alleged common sense the Nazis had endeavored to impose; it may not have made it more difficult for the Jens Ole Jepsens to compromise a new generation's chances of acquiring a new, democratic common sense. In sum, despite a prosecutorial strategy intended to call individuals to account, the trial, like the Nuremberg proceedings, may have contributed to the delegitimation of the Third Reich while at the same time offering ordinary citizens an excuse for their behavior between 1933 and 1945. "I have always thought," Telford Taylor wrote in 1970, "that the enormous enthusiasm in Germany for the motion picture about Anne Frank was largely due to the fact that the finger of guilt pointed nowhere in particular. At the end, one hears footsteps on the stairs and knows that her captors are German, but they are never seen. Thus, the drama provided a universal catharsis which could be enjoyed in safety and without individual embarrassment."[80] The *Frankfurter Allgemeine Zeitung*—like the Frankfurt court that heard the Auschwitz case—thought that the limits of the trial spoke in favor of German democracy:

> A criminal court in our system of liberty and law can do nothing except determine whether an accused person committed a specific crime, and if he did, seek an appropriate penalty. For other tasks, courts lack reliable means. The means are lacking because the court has no legal legitimacy for the things that would be the goal of such means. The all-powerful tribunal that avenges, educates, that inspires fear, regret, and enthusiasm, that reads the past and the present, that shows the people the road to the future—such a court is a creation of the totalitarian state, part and parcel of such a state. It must remain foreign to a free order.[81]

Inge Deutschkron, who had moved from one hiding place to another in wartime Berlin and had managed to evade detection and deportation, saw the question differently. Deutschkron, who covered the Frankfurt trial for the Israeli newspaper *Maariv,* noting that the sole purpose of the death camps had been mass murder, commented: "Only a criminal code according to which anyone who had served in an extermination camp would have to prove his innocence could have meted out to the guilty a just punishment."[82]

Thirty years after the Auschwitz Trial, a Berlin law professor, Bernhard Schlink, published a novel, the first-person account of a relationship between an adolescent (the narrator, Michael Berg) from a polite academic family and Hanna, a thirty-six year-old woman who is working as a ticket puncher for the public transportation system.[83] The two see each other daily for months, then the woman disappears—without warning and without explanation. Years later the boy, now a law student, attends a trial in connection with a seminar on Nazi crimes, and recognizes in one of the defendants his former lover. The woman, who had never wanted to speak about her past or to think about the future, the narrator now learns, had been an SS guard at one of the camps associated with Auschwitz. As the camp was evacuated, she had stopped with a column of prisoners in a village. The prisoners were locked in the local church. An Allied aerial bomb hit the church, the guards refused to open the doors ["How would we have managed to keep order?" (122)], and the prisoners burned to death. "We didn't know," Hanna tries to explain to the court—and to her former lover—"what we should do" (121). Earlier, the judge himself had been unable to provide an answer, as Hanna, thinking out loud in open court, asked, "What would you have done?" The judge, we are told, wore irritation on his face like a mask. Confronted with Hanna'a personal question, he hesitated too long, then responded with an abstract answer—an answer that struck the waiting courtroom audience as "helpless, pathetic" (108–109).

Like Lenz's *Deutschstunde, Der Vorleser* (The Reader) is a book without a happy ending. Hanna refuses to give the court the one piece of information (the fact that she cannot read and write) that would refute the aggravating circumstances alleged against her, and Michael is too conflicted to intervene on her behalf. She goes to prison; Michael reads books aloud onto tapes for her, but will not otherwise communicate with her; she, meanwhile, learns to read, and reads everything she can get about the Holocaust. On the day she is to be released (Michael has arranged an apartment), she commits suicide.

Michael has no direct memories of the Third Reich, and his parents are far less burdensome than Siggi's. But like Siggi's, Michael's life is deeply marked by the difficulties he encounters as he seeks to navigate among the emotional and moral shoals that remained as the legacy of the Third Reich. "The finger pointing at Hanna pointed back at me," the narrator tells us. "I had loved her" (162). He was a '68er ("Work though it! Work through the past! We students of the concentration camp seminar saw ourselves as the avant-garde of those working through the past"; 87), and he envied contemporaries who could take out their feelings of shame and guilt on the parents they nonetheless loved, since for that love they could not be held responsible (162). What, however, was he to do with the bonds that tied him to Hanna?

Schlink's novel suggests an account of the motives and difficulties of the '68ers rather different from the one Hermann Lübbe had offered a decade earlier. The narrator recognizes in his own inner conflicts "the fate of my generation, a German fate" (163). Common sense had—and has—not yet evacuated those conflicts. The courts would continue to play a role in the process: in 1969 the Bundestag passed legislation lifting the statute of limitations for genocide, and in 1979 it finally lifted the statute of limitations for murder. In 1969 Hamburg had proposed federal legislation that would have lifted the statute of limitations for both crimes. "The wounds that such crimes create cannot heal with the passage of time," the state government argued. "The very fact of a murder, through the complete destruction of the victim, also destroys the only possibility of an act of forgiveness."[84]

In 1996 the federal minister of justice, Eduard Schmidt-Jortzig, reported that cases against 5,570 individuals accused of crimes related to National Socialist rule were still pending. The minister reported further that 106,178 individual cases had been investigated since 1945, resulting in 6,494 unreversed convictions.[85] The wounds remained unhealed.

"The Penal Code Is Not Made for Revolutions"

As the foregoing discussion suggests, political justice is at best an imperfect instrument for bringing commonsense understandings of justice into conformity with democratic norms after a dictatorship, no matter what prosecutorial strategy is adopted.[86] In his oral presentation of the verdict in the Auschwitz Trial, Justice Hans Hofmeyer recapitulated the limits within which the court had had—and had wished—to remain:

"The court's job was not to master the past, nor was it the court's job to consider whether this trial was expedient. The court could not prosecute a political case and certainly it could not conduct a show trial . . . The length of the trial and the several presentations of the case that were heard show that the search for the truth stood alone at the center of the proceedings."[87]

The recourse to legal proceedings against former National Socialists, for all its difficulties and disappointments, seems an indispensable station on postwar West Germany's journey to democracy: after the commission of unspeakable crimes by a regime whose decisions and institutions were not well understood, the trials provided some measure of emotional satisfaction to opponents and victims of the fallen regime, developed a massive documentary base, and at least challenged a common sense left over from Nazi Germany. The difficulties courts face increase as one moves away from the extreme case represented by the Third Reich: the crime to which Robert Mulka was an accessory was still genocide, and it was described as such in open court, even if the formal charge was murder. When the crimes committed are less massive, their subsequent prosecution becomes more problematic—and the benefits more elusive.

After the collapse of the DDR, circumstances and decisions combined to produce something close to a worst-case scenario for the use of the legal arena to (re)establish democratic norms as commonsense understandings of justice. First, the most crying abuses committed by the communist regime had taken place during the worst period of Stalinism, in the 1950s, three full decades before the regime's demise. Responsibilities were hard to disentangle (What had Moscow ordered? What had the Germans undertaken on their own initiative?), and many of the individuals most deeply involved were already dead. Second, the type of crime committed was different from the type of crime that had characterized the Third Reich: men and women were hauled from their homes in the middle of the night and tortured and killed in East German prisons, but the regime did not commit genocide and did not launch an aggressive war. Third, communist crimes posed a challenge to democratic notions of justice that was different in kind from the challenge Nazi crimes posed: Nazism explicitly rejected fundamental democratic values (e.g. human equality), whereas communism reaffirmed in theory the values that it violated in practice. In the courtroom struggle to recapture common sense for democratic norms, racially motivated murder is a more vulnerable defendant than is the leading role of the party, and concentration camp guards cut a more sinister profile than do border guards.

These circumstances were further complicated by the way unification was achieved. Given the rapidity with which events moved in 1989–90, there was no time for a democratic DDR to try its own former dictators. The unification treaty maintained in force the Basic Law's constitutional clause forbidding ex post facto prosecutions; this decision may reflect in part the leverage communist elites still possessed as unification arrangements were being negotiated. This power diminished rapidly, however, once unification was completed, and especially after Mikhail Gorbachev fell and the Soviet Union disintegrated. As courts tried to bring former East Germans to trial, it became easy for critics to argue that the courts were "West" German courts, that they were exercising "victors' justice," and that those sitting in judgment had not had to face the practical difficulties and moral dilemmas they now presumed to judge. The particular circumstances that surround the DDR case help explain the universal unhappiness with the results, as well as the pressing calls for amnesties and a *Schlußstrich* which punctuated the process.[88]

Prosecutors, already handicapped by the prohibition against ex post facto prosecution, aggravated their own situation by failing to adopt any coherent prosecutorial strategy: this seemed particularly true of the Berlin Arbeitsgruppe Regierungskriminalität (Working Group on Governmental Crime), constituted in 1991 and led by Christoph Schaefgen. Each of the new Länder created special groups to prosecute crimes related to the maintenance of the communist dictatorship in East Germany. Schaefgen's office was unique because it was in Berlin, and thus responsible for the prosecution of alleged crimes committed in the former capital of the DDR, including those allegedly committed by the former regime's leaders. The office (later reconstituted as a second public prosecutor's office, or Staatsanwaltschaft II) was therefore central to efforts to use the courts to accomplish certain transitional tasks, and even though it was a Berlin authority, it was staffed in part by lawyers seconded from other state governments.[89]

Instead of focusing their figurative (ideological) fire, Schaefgen's prosecutors targeted a wide spectrum of individuals—political decision makers, judges, intelligence agents, border guards, economic profiteers, postal clerks—on a broad range of charges.[90] Several of the cases appeared deliberately to test the applicability of the constitutional injunction against ex post facto prosecutions, and many were overturned on appeal.

Legally, the most interesting cases may be those that were brought, beginning in early 1992, against former East German border guards involved in fatal shootings on the so-called inner-German border, between the DDR and the Federal Republic. Many of these cases were tried in Berlin, but cases were also brought in the new Länder. Numerous convictions were won and upheld on appeal. The charge was manslaughter. The men convicted generally received sentences of under five years' imprisonment, and almost without exception the sentences were suspended. Slowly, the prosecutions moved up the chain of command. The trials continually probed the origins and history of the DDR's border regime and the *Schießbefehl* (order to shoot), but the thrust of the prosecutions was to establish individual responsibility for specific deaths. In 1994 the former defense minister Heinz Keßler, the former army chief of staff Fritz Streletz, and a former member of the National Defense Council, Hans Albrecht, were convicted on manslaughter charges. In September 1996 a Berlin court found the last chief of the East German border troops, Klaus-Dieter Baumgarten, and five other generals guilty, again of manslaughter. In November 1996 the Constitutional Court confirmed the convictions of Keßler, Streletz, and Albrecht and spelled out its position on the constitutional ban against ex post facto prosecutions. That prohibition, the court held, had limits, and it formulated those limits more expansively than prior jurisprudence had allowed. The court had already found that "clear, unbearable violation[s] of the elementary commands of justice" were always actionable, especially given the DDR's formal adherence to international human rights treaties, and it maintained this position even in a case where it acknowledged the role played by youth and indoctrination: common sense, it argued, was always common, at least when it came to knowing that it was wrong to shoot an unarmed person who was simply trying to get out of the country. [91] Now the court held that the ban on ex post facto prosecutions was meant to apply to acts committed in the Federal Republic, that is, in a liberal democratic state. Only in such a political system could the ban's purpose of making the law reliable and predictable for citizens serve justice. The ban could not apply fully to acts committed in a state that "promoted injustice . . . and flouted human rights generally recognized by the community of nations." The court therefore concluded:

> A justificatory appeal cannot be considered when it would excuse the intentional killing of people who wanted simply to cross the inner-German border, unarmed and without endangering commonly recognized interests. Such a justification, one which gave the enforcement of the prohibition against crossing the border clear priority over the right to life, is invalid on account of its obvious, unbearable infringement of human rights as protected by international law. The infringement is so serious that it violates the beliefs about justice held in common by all people and based on the value and dignity of the individual. In such a case, positive law must give way to justice.[92]

The opinions rendered in the border guard and military cases prepared the ground for the so-called Politburo trial which began in February 1996. That case resulted in August in the convictions of Egon Krenz, Günter Schabowski, and Günther Kleiber; they too were found guilty of manslaughter.

At Nuremberg, the International Military Tribunal had set aside the ban on ex post facto prosecutions in order to, in effect, try a regime. The judge in the Baumgarten case, however, denied that courts could play this role, and argued that the part was in any event unnecessary: "At the latest in the aftermath of our historical experience with the so-called Third Reich," the magistrate asserted, "dictatorship is 'delegitimized' in our culture."[93] Politically, it is unclear what the focus on individual responsibilities in these trials accomplished. It is also uncertain how durable the Constitutional Court's interpretation of the ban on ex post facto prosecutions will prove, and how applicable the understanding it articulates may be beyond the German context. While in each case considered here the verdicts were front-page news, the trials themselves did not seem to excite much public interest. They preached to the saved—or further alienated the already alienated, some of whom faithfully showed up in court to cheer on their fallen heroes.

The two court cases that captured the most public attention—both because of when they were held and because of the prominence of the defendants—were the cases against Erich Honecker and Erich Mielke: "two broken men," Robert Jackson might have said, before moving on to indict the system to which the two now old men had dedicated their long lives. It did not happen. Honecker's trial (November 1992–January 1993) quickly became a lamentable spectacle during which the debate focused more on the likely course of the defendant's liver cancer than on either Honecker's personal responsibilities or the type of regime he had led; the trial was finally aborted, and Honecker flew into exile in Chile. Mielke was tried from February 1992 to October 1993 for the murder of two policemen in 1931—a charge hardly likely to expose either individual responsibilities during the DDR or the reality of the secret police world over which Mielke had presided. As Peter Jochen Winters succinctly put it, "The trial of Erich Mielke . . . really has nothing to do with a working through of the past through the legal system."[94] The trial was also unlikely to persuade east Germans of varying political orientations either that the judicial system could vindicate victims or that "west" German justice was dedicated to justice and not to revenge. If the purpose was justice rather than revenge, why dredge up charges more than half a century old?

The fact that the Berlin Arbeitsgruppe Regierungskriminalität remained understaffed and underfunded made the incoherences all the more glaring. It is tempting to recall that West German justice was less than energetic in prosecuting NS crimes during the first decade after the creation of the Federal Republic, and that the lost ground was later partially recouped in trials such as the Auschwitz Trial. The analogy, however, is unpersuasive, once again because of the differences in the scope and nature of the crimes committed, and because fewer constituencies are likely to press for prosecution as the original events recede in time, or to take particular notice of prosecutions that are pursued.

The strategy adopted by the Arbeitsgruppe Regierungskriminalität may simply have been an accident: the product of an understaffed office working under conditions of high political visibility and led by an individual with a particular view of his job. The strategy was not, however, pursued without debate, and alternative models were available. State authorities in Brandenburg, explicitly critical of the so-called Berlin Line adopted by Schaefgen's office, elaborated a strategy different in both its legal-philosophical and its political assumptions.[95] The Brandenburg attorneys limited their efforts to cases they believed they could win: for both legal and political reasons, they were not interested in testing the latitude of the ban on ex post facto prosecutions. Legally, they saw the *nulla poena sine lege* principle as fundamental to the legal order of a democratic political system, and they argued that the only legitimate purpose of a trial is to convict a criminal. They did not believe it appropriate to use trials to cast social and political opprobrium on people whose activities may have been "worthy of punishment," but who nonetheless could not be convicted of crimes under existing statutes. Politically, they argued that limited but successful prosecutions would be far more likely to delegitimize the old regime and win allegiance for the new legal order than scattershot prosecutions that would be overturned on appeal.

The Brandenburg strategy might well have been harder to defend in a politically more exposed environment. While Schaefgen's choices may have been in part an accidental product, they may also tell us something important about the conflicting demands we now place on democratic legal institutions when we are confronted with a breach of democratic norms. Nuremberg set an example—but it set that example in a specific political environment. In 1945 the Allied victory was total, the German capitulation unconditional, and the nature, scale, and consequences of the crimes that had been committed defied the imagination of normal men and women. Germans were at the mercy of whatever legal decisions the Allies might choose to make. The situation after 1989 was quite different: in this context, the DDR can be understood to have tendered a conditional surrender, and there were treaty and other constraints on what sorts of prosecutions could follow.

At the same time, the expectation that political crimes committed under the dictatorship would prove actionable and would be brought to trial was probably far greater after 1989 than it had been in 1945. Verbally articulated standards had become much more rigorous. In the German case, this was true partly—but only partly—because of the perceived partisan usefulness of the issue. It was also true because international standards of behavior had evolved and been repeatedly reaffirmed: in constitutional texts, international treaties, and statements by heads of government, and in the work of organizations such as Amnesty International. That articulation had come about in large measure as a response to the remembered experiences of the 1930s and 1940s. In the international arena it resulted in more anguish than action; there was always an argument—or an excuse—for inaction. Violations of human rights went unpunished because the costs of punishing them were perceived as too great. The verbal inflation of rights to be protected nonetheless proceeded unchecked.

As we have seen, using the legal system for political purposes is always a risky endeavor. After 1989, the inflated expectations collided with unchanged institutional and political constraints, symbolized by the *nulla poena sine lege* principle. One result was the strategy adopted by Schaefgen, which seemingly tried to achieve both the goals tied to an institutional logic of prosecution and those associated with a cultural logic—as though experience did not indicate that one or the other would have been difficult enough.

Even as the events at issue recede further in time, a steady stream of cases will in all likelihood continue to be prosecuted or heard on appeal, and some of those cases—like the case against Egon Krenz and his Politburo colleagues—may involve formerly prominent people.[96] But the political interest of the Krenz trial peaked during its opening phase, when Günter Schabowski, while holding himself "not guilty in the sense of the indictment" and expressing skepticism regarding the usefulness of the trial, nonetheless acknowledged the authority of the court ("I have no use for rhetorical flourishes like 'victors' justice'") and criticized the regime he had served. Schabowski paid tribute to those who had done what they could to make the best out of a system in which they had been forced to live and who therefore continued in some way to identify, if not with the regime, then at least with the life they had led under it. Leaders like himself, he said, were in a different situation: "Only those who were in positions of responsibility in the DDR are obligated to recognize and acknowledge the fundamentally unsuccessful and flawed character of the system." This he tried to do, and the effort led him to acknowledge moral "shame and guilt" for the shootings on the border between East and West Berlin—the crime for which he and his colleagues had been brought to trial. He asked the relatives of victims for forgiveness, acknowledging that he might be refused. "But without this sort of awareness," he added, "it would be impossible for me to go on living."[97]

Schabowski qualified his sense of responsibility by denying that any effort from within the Politburo to alter the DDR's border regime could possibly have succeeded. His statement nevertheless contrasted sharply with the statement made by Krenz, and even more starkly with the statement that Erich Honecker had made to the same court in December

1992. Honecker's declaration had been unapologetic and openly pro-vocative. West Germany, Honecker asserted, had always persecuted com-munists, and it was simply continuing to do in the 1990s what it had done in the 1950s: "The *Rechtsstaat* BRD is not a state ruled by law, but a state ruled by the right." The effort to make his trial into a "Nuremberg Trial against communists" was in Honecker's view laughable: "There were no concentration camps in the DDR, no gas chambers, no political executions, no Volksgerichtshof [a reference to Roland Freisler's deadly People's Court during the Third Reich], no Gestapo, no SS. The DDR did not launch a war or commit war crimes or crimes against humanity. The DDR was a consistently antifascist state, whose dedication to peace brought it international prestige." The Wall, Honecker claimed, had de-fused an increasingly tense situation in the midst of the Cold War, and he felt no guilt—legal, moral, or political—for his part in maintaining it.[98]

Krenz, who had helped depose Honecker in 1989, was far more mod-erate in his claims than had been his former boss. He understood, he said, the irreparable pain of those who had lost loved ones on the border (the shootings had also "affected" him), but he stopped short of admit-ting guilt, whether moral or legal.[99] Krenz attributed the border regime to the "harshness of the Cold War" and to superpower politics. A reporter noted the irony of the arguments made by the defense and the prosecu-tion: "All those who once claimed with pride and fervor that the DDR was absolutely sovereign now assert the contrary. Their critics do the opposite. Those who only spoke of the DDR using quotation marks now retrospectively declare the country to have been an independent state."[100] Increasingly, the trial focused on the issue of where imperative political decisions had been made—arguably not a topic best consigned to a court of law, and not one which, when pursued through subpoenas and accom-panied by technical legal arguments, was likely to retain public interest for long. Krenz admitted to being preoccupied by the past: "I have . . . in the past years reflected again and again on the objective and subjective reasons for the failure of our societal project," he told the Berlin court. "Today more than ever, I am conscious of my share of responsibility for what went wrong in the DDR." But he felt accountable only to a public ("the citizens of the DDR") unable to hold him to account, and not to what he claimed was a partisan court. The court's point of departure, he asserted, was that "the only good socialism is a defeated socialism," and to such a court he did not feel answerable. When the verdict was delivered, Krenz was seized before he could leave the courtroom; the authorities claimed, against the evidence, that he might flee the country while his case was on appeal. The move, though quickly reversed by another court, seemed to confirm Krenz's view that "victorious power [was taking revenge] on the representatives of the defeated power."[101]

If the Krenz trial, despite its prominent personalities and the heavy investment of prosecutorial energies, did not capture the public imagination, it seems improbable that any future case will contribute significantly to common understandings of justice in unified Germany.[102]

As we saw in Chapter 2, the German effort to use nonjudicial "tribunals" as a substitute or supplement for trials was overtaken by other measures: the opening of the Stasi archives, the creation of a parliamentary commission of inquiry, and judicial proceedings (administrative purges will be considered in the next chapter). But in recent democratization processes elsewhere, democratic activists have sought to establish publicly the facts of who did what to whom during the dictatorship through "truth commissions" and nonjudicial fact-finding endeavors, equating this process of reality recovery with justice and claiming for it an indispensable role in the process of democratic consolidation.[103] Truth commissions tend to accompany contemporary noncommunist transitions from authoritarian rule. Their establishment seems to correlate not so much with the type of transition (with different types producing arrangements in which former elites retained more or less leverage over decisions regarding justice) or with the condition of civil society, as with the type, level, and timing of violence characteristic of the old regime. Where regime-sponsored physical violence against putative opposition groups and/or individuals was at its most lethal, or even (as in South Africa) accelerating just before the transition began, but where it nonetheless never reached the point of wholesale massacres, the effort to name names and recover information seemed particularly compelling.

Germany did not meet these criteria, and the German Enquete-Kommission established by a nearly unanimous vote of the Bundestag in May 1992 (and renewed less unanimously in 1995) was not a truth commission. Its creation had first been pressed in parliamentary circles during the debate over the Stasi archives; the commission was to ensure that the DDR did not become reduced in the public mind to the Stasi. The commission called a large number of witnesses, but it did not gather personal testimonies or seek to clarify individual destinies. The charge to the commission was explicitly didactic, and in keeping with the Federal Republic's ongoing attention to "civic education" *(politische Bildung)*. The parliamentary act creating the commission assigned the body "the task of working on contributions to a political-historical analysis and to a political-moral assessment." It was to help people who were "struggling for their bearings" and reconsidering questions of peronal and political responsibility.[104]

In two years of hearings held throughout the republic, Rainer Eppelmann's commission heard testimony about the structures of power and the decision-making processes of the DDR, about ideology and strategies of integration and repression, about the impact on the DDR of West Germany's policies toward the rival German state, about the role of the churches, about resistance and opposition, and about the Stasi. Hearings were typically structured around expert testimony, with actors then called upon to respond and participants free to pose questions or make observations. Further expert testimony was entered into the written record. The hearings were reported regularly in the national press, and the investigatory record was published in 1995 in an eighteen-volume set. The extent to which the commission helped people "struggling for their bearings" by contributing to the reshaping of commonsense understandings of justice, responsibility, and legitimacy remains a very open question. The testimony lacked the drama of a courtroom trial; nor was the atmosphere in the hearings that of an academic seminar. From a scholarly point of view, the commission provided a service by eliciting statements from well-known actors and experts and making them readily available. The statements themselves tended to be repetitions of arguments (political or academic or both) made elsewhere; unlike Nuremberg and later trials of Nazis, the Enquete-Kommission did not produce significant new information or analyses. From the point of view of the former victims and opponents of the regime, the commission may have offered an opportunity to elaborate preliminary substitutes for the "honest and objective history books, written from the perspective of the affected, of the victims," whose necessity Eppelmann had urged during the March 1992 debate on the organization and mission of the commission.[105] From the point of view of the average former East German citizen, the effect (direct or indirect) of the commission's activities was probably minimal. In its final report the commission's majority claimed:

"The experiences of the commission lent increased weight to the maxim 'No reconciliation without truth,'" but it offered no evidence, and it also admitted that "the working through of the DDR past and the discussion regarding the consequences of SED rule are still stuck in the early stages" and that "there are already indications that historical experiences are being repressed and even turned into legends."[106]

The immediate goal of the truth commissions set up elsewhere has been exposure, not the reconsideration of political structures and policies, but also not legal punishment. Instead of legal proceedings as a way of placing certain forms of conduct beyond the pale of common sense, this strategy proposes a kind of nonadversarial process of reestablishing democratic justice by exposing the truth of what happened under the dictatorship. Because the process is putatively nonadversarial and because its object is not to send individuals to jail, its advocates see in it a way of avoiding the dilemmas that attach to political justice: here, no ex post facto laws are required, and the strategy's partisans can argue that their purpose is reconciliatory (see Chapter 2). Understandably, their political opponents from the old regime tend to see it differently. For us, however, the critical question is how the large mass of relatively uncommitted citizens—people who were neither victims nor perpetrators but *Anpasser* or *Mitläufer,* and who now, by sheer weight of numbers, arbitrate the new society's redefinition of common sense—respond to the effort.

The retrospective public description of a reality that could not be openly described so long as the dictatorship lasted is supposed to serve three broad purposes: it vindicates the victims of the dictatorship (especially those who died at its hands) by restoring to light their faith and their suffering; it instructs the society that had previously succumbed to the dictatorship and willingly or unwillingly participated in its lies; and it holds a mirror up to that society in which the new image reflected is one of courage.[107]

The reconstruction of who did what to whom, by identifying anonymous torturers and hidden torture cells and by "hearing" the screams of men and women who were told their screams would never be heard,[108] simultaneously honors the suffering of the victims and warns prospective torturers not to bank on anonymity. It recalls Herbert Wechsler's justification of political prosecutions ("the dark shadow of organized disapproval eliminating from the ambit of consideration alternatives that might otherwise present themselves in the final competition of choice"). Ripping away the veil of anonymity restores the human dignity of the tortured (persecuted, imprisoned, executed) and destroys the security of the torturer (persecutor, etc.): "Your secrecy must be banished," Jürgen Fuchs said of the former oppressors, "like your power."[109] It is hard to read the prose and not sense a secondary thirst for revenge: those who had deprived others of their privacy would now also be made to feel exposed.

The reconstruction of how an entire society (with more or less numerous exceptions) organized its life, at both the individual and the collective level, so that forbidden topics would not be discussed is supposed to remind citizens that we are all individually responsible for "living in truth" (as Havel put it), and that dictatorships appeal to the tendency we all have to avoid responsibility.

Finally, this strategy argues that a postdictatorial society that can face the truth about itself is, whatever its past cowardice, a society with the strength and will to be free. Thus it is important that the process of recovery be as broadly based in society as possible; a parliamentary commission like the one established by the Bundestag appears in this context as a poor substitute for a citizens' movement.

It is too early to tell what effect the "Nunca Más" effort on behalf of the "disappeared" will have on political culture and common sense in countries such as Argentina, Brazil, and Uruguay, where the dissuasion of potential dictators is of far more importance than it is in unified Germany, or in South Africa, where the social cleavages run deeper and will be much more difficult to overcome (and where willingness to testify was tied to an offer of amnesty). What does seem clear is that the effort itself represents an understanding of democracy different from the understanding that prompts democratizing elites to punish former dictators through the use of law. Trials suggest a top-down strategy of redefining a society's common sense. This is true even if the prosecutorial approach is informed by the logic of a cultural strategy of reconciliation, since the new direction comes from the state. Compiling and publishing an account of who did what to whom suggests a bottom-up strategy, another example of "self-help from below." The process is meant to reestablish a civil society, and the assumption is that the common sense of a civil society will in fact be civil—that its conception of justice will line up with democratic norms. It is perhaps not surprising that the country that relied most heavily on trials was also the country where a top-down strategy was most easily adopted: the old Länder, still politically dominant in unified Germany, represented the "top."

In this chapter I have tried to elucidate the difficulties and costs, as well as the limited benefits, of *any* legal strategy. In the post-1945 situation, those costs, however perplexing, pale in comparison to the message that would have been sent had trials not been held. In the post-1989 situation, the verdict is less clear.

Five

Compromising Compromises: The Stolpe Case

While the legal proceedings against Erich Honecker focused on the progress of his liver cancer and a court sought to determine whether or not Erich Mielke was guilty of two murders committed in 1931, a far more interesting trial by public opinion and parliamentary inquest was taking place in the national media and in Brandenburg, where a tumultuous two-year debate unfolded regarding the political past and future of the state's Social Democratic minister president, Manfred Stolpe. The debate centered on Stolpe's conduct under the DDR—and on the explanations he gave after unification, and especially during the controversy itself, for his actions prior to 1990. The debate began in January 1992, when Stolpe himself declared in print that as the top lay official and legal representative of the Bund der Evangelischen Kirchen (BEK), he had frequently met with officials from the security apparatus.[1] As the debate unfolded, it became clear that Stolpe's account had been less than candid and complete, and many observers who found his effort to influence developments in the DDR defensible were disturbed by the evasiveness of his explanations.

The Stolpe debate raised issues that were compelling beyond the context of the immediate case in which they were articulated, and it suggested ways of responding that were also relevant elsewhere. Stolpe's actions under the DDR (and the reactions of both his critics and his defenders) were informed by a certain conception of political ethics and a specific understanding of the possibilities of political action under communist dictatorships. The debate about his actions was particularly resonant in part because it paralleled a similar debate occasioned, in Germany and beyond, by détente policies in their various phases.

189

Stolpe sought to effect change from within the system. This is a strategy that anticipates an institutional strategy in the sense that the actor is not allowed to be morally fussy in his choice of interlocutors, and also by its assertion that openness, confidence building, and bargaining can be infectious habits, even in a dictatorship. Where such elements are introduced, it is argued, they are likely to take on a life of their own. In the first section of this chapter, I analyze the debate about how Stolpe put these principles into action. This debate was multifaceted: it put into play arguments about political ethics, détente, and the cultural foundations and institutional flexibility of dictatorships. In the second section I place Stolpe's conduct during the inquiry in its immediate political context, highlighting the bargains implicitly struck between cultural and institutional logics of reconciliation, especially as illustrated in vetting or "lustration" policies. In the final section we consider the model of political leadership that Stolpe proposed to his Brandenburg public, more generally to his former East German compatriots, and at least potentially to an all-German public.

Political Efficacy and Ethics under Communism

Václav Havel's understanding of totalitarianism—as a cultural development involving the mental manipulation and self-deceit of an entire population—both posits the distinction between authoritarian ("classical") dictatorships and totalitarian regimes and departs in significant ways from standard descriptions of totalitarianism. In Havel's account, the mental dismantling of reality has replaced the monopolization of power by a single party, and complicity (not just coerced participation) has replaced terror.

Manfred Stolpe, by training a jurist, understood and treated the DDR as a power structure, not as a culture. By his own admission, Stolpe was not a dissident in the DDR. If his account of what he did is to be believed, he leaned on what Max Weber once called an ethic of responsibility, arguing that political actions should be gauged to produce results and that actors should be judged by the results actually produced, not merely on the basis of their articulated principles. Stolpe assumed both that the USSR would never relinquish control of the westernmost outpost of its empire without a bloodbath, and that even under the oppressive conditions of life in the DDR, a positive-sum game could be created between the regime and its subjects. On these assumptions he chose to play the system. His description of the DDR contrasts sharply with Havel's description of post-terrorist totalitarian regimes: the DDR, Stolpe wrote, "was a dictatorship, but one that wore velvet gloves, and despite everything, it was possible to do a great deal."[2]

The unsuccessful workers' uprising of June 1953 taught Stolpe that open confrontation with the regime would be at best futile and at worst counterproductive.[3] Until shortly before the *Wende* of 1989, he subscribed to the common view that the international power relations that guaranteed communist rule in the DDR would not change within the foreseeable future; the status quo represented "a situation whose evolution we hoped for, but in which direct change was not on the horizon."[4] Stolpe did not, however, conclude that the only alternative to symbolic acts of conscience and defiance was passive compliance or resigned complicity. Against both the dictates of communist ideology and the assumptions of Western students of totalitarianism, the Protestant churches in the DDR had retained a certain organizational and ideological autonomy. Stolpe believed that by entering into a dialogue with the regime and becoming a player in the political game, the churches could hope to modify the domestic power relationships on which the regime rested. The result of this learning process[5] would be a materially and morally improved life for those unable or unwilling to leave the country. The solution—expressed in the BEK's chosen posture as a "Kirche im Sozialismus" and in Stolpe's relations with the regime—may have been (and certainly now appears) morally untidy, but it was, as Stolpe later put it, "oriented toward success," and as such, he maintained, it paid off.[6] Stolpe remembered what he saw as necessary patience and "many, many small steps."[7]

In the late 1960s and early 1970s, the Social-Liberal coalition under Willy Brandt—who also spoke of small steps—adopted a new posture toward the DDR and the communist bloc countries. Two decades of confrontation, the new government noted, had promoted neither the liberalization of communist regimes nor a more humane regulation of the division of Germany. The main achievements of the first phase of West German Ostpolitik included landmark treaties with Moscow (August 12, 1970) and Warsaw (December 7, 1970) and the Vertrag über die Grundlagen der Beziehungen zwischen der Bundesrepublik Deutschland und der Deutschen Demokratischen Republik (Treaty on the Basis of Relations between the Federal Republic of Germany and the German Democratic Republic), or Basic Treaty (December 21, 1972).[8] In the Moscow Treaty, the two parties renounced the recourse to force to settle differences and forswore any territorial claims beyond their borders (Article 3). The Warsaw Treaty reiterated the recognition of the Oder-Neiße Line, thus putting to rest German claims to former territories in Silesia, Pomerania, and East Prussia. In the Basic Treaty, the governments of the Federal Republic and the DDR declared their determination to develop "normal good-neighbourly relations with each other on the basis of equal rights" (Article 1) and their willingness to exchange diplomatic representatives (Article 8). As stipulated by the UN Charter, they renounced the use of force to change borders and recognized the territorial integrity and independence of each state. Neither state would presume to speak for the other (Article 4). After the treaty's ratification, both German states were given seats in the UN General Assembly.

It was no accident that two of the key architects of the new posture were from Berlin. Willy Brandt (1913–1992) served as mayor of the city from 1957 to 1966. Egon Bahr (b. 1922) had been *Chefredakteur* of the radio station RIAS in Berlin during the East Berlin uprising of June 1953; from 1960 to 1966, he served as Brandt's press secretary in Berlin. Adenauer, himself a Rhinelander, preferred to look West; Brandt and Bahr were daily confronted with the reality of the Wall, and with the "feeling of powerlessness" they remembered from 1953.[9] Adenauer's policies toward the East, tailored to the needs and conditions of the 1950s and marked by an intransigent refusal to establish a dialogue with the DDR in the absence of free elections ("the all or nothing approach"),[10] had led, the Berlin leaders argued, to a dead end. For them, the construction of the Wall represented a "turning point"[11]: it was time to consider a new approach.

The assumptions that informed the new policies were outlined by Bahr in a speech to the Evanglische Akademie in Tutzing on July 15, 1963. The policy became known by the title Bahr had given to his speech: "change through rapprochement."[12] Some thirty years later, in his testimony before the Eppelmann Enquete-Kommission, Bahr, with his usual combination of precision and irony, put the formula more starkly: "destabilization through stabilization." The later formula, and Bahr's elaboration of it, suggested the inherent ambiguities of the strategy. "Destabilizing intentions could not be realized," Bahr explained, "without stabilizing moments. Positive inter-German ties or new relations were not possible for the SED regime without stabilizing moments."[13]

Willy Brandt spoke constantly of the need to build trust among adversaries.[14] A relaxation of East-West tensions and the adoption of a less confrontational stance vis-à-vis the East German regime would create breathing space for the communist regime. The Social-Liberal coalition hoped that that breathing space would be passed on to East German citizens, making daily life more livable (for example, through the loosening of controls on communication between East and West) and opening up the possibility that less repressive elements would slowly gain the upper hand in the party leadership. Brandt emphasized that his government's policy not only did not exclude but in fact presupposed a continuing ideological competition with communism. "This government has no intention," Brandt declared, "of recognizing injustice," and by "injustice" he understood both dictatorship and the forced flight of Germans from Poland after 1945.[15] But ideological competition would be pursued without endangering peace—and without excluding cooperation. "The fundamental intellectual debate with communism as an ideology and as a social order must be continued," he said. "But the forms in which the debate occurs must be subordinated to our interest in securing the peace."[16]

Commenting on the policy from the perspective of 1993, Bahr thought it had succeeded. He admitted that he had not taken the East German dissident groups of the late 1980s as seriously as he might have. Younger observers—Bahr cited Timothy Garton Ash—who had turned this fact into a reproach, Bahr suggested, viewed events through a different and distorting lens. Ash's views had been shaped by the successes of the Polish Solidarity movement; but viewed against the experience of dissident or reform movements in postwar Eastern Europe, Bahr argued, Solidarity represented the exception, not the rule. The policies of the Social-Liberal coalition were meant to address the rule, and the rule was that internal opposition movements had been crushed while the West looked on helplessly.[17]

Politically significant and durable dissident movements, Bahr argued, were the product not simply of moral courage and political discontent (in which case communist regimes in Poland, Hungary, Czechoslovakia, and East Germany might have had a very short life), but of new policies that had discouraged the most suffocating forms of repression and had created political room in which dissident movements could live: effective movements emerged, Bahr noted, only "after 1975, after Helsinki."[18] Destabilization through stabilization had worked.

Under morally much more complex and politically much more constricted circumstances, Stolpe took an analogous approach to the regime in the DDR. Born in Stettin in 1936 (also the year of Havel's birth), Stolpe earned a law degree at Jena and went to work for the Protestant Church of Berlin-Brandenburg in 1959. He rapidly became a privileged intermediary between the church and the party/state. Stolpe contributed to the creation of the BEK in 1969 and led the federation's secretariat from 1969 to 1981. As deputy chair of the BEK from 1982 until he assumed political office in united Germany in 1990, Stolpe was the highest lay official in the church. From the late 1960s on, he was one of the main architects of the BEK's self-definition as a "Kirche im Sozialismus," as he put it, "alongside, not against, but in socialism . . . [participating] in the problems and achievements of the surrounding society . . . [striking] the necessary balance between conformity and rejection."[19] The new definition of the church's approach to the regime can be seen as a domestic translation of Ostpolitik.

The church's position—the formula itself does not appear in any formally binding church document—was neither intended nor understood as a simple repetition of Romans 13, the famous passage in which Paul appears to urge submission to "governing authorities." It was a statement not about the "governing authorities" but about the church and its mission. Christians are not free to define the arena in which they are called upon to act out their faith; Christ did not instruct his disciples to confine their proselytizing to democratic societies. Drawing on the experience of the Confessing Church during the Nazi years, the BEK maintained that for Christians who find themselves in an arena not to their liking, the precondition of hope and empowerment is acceptance of the idea that God has placed them where they are and remains there with them. By adopting the posture of a "Kirche im Sozialismus," Stolpe argued in 1978, the church had moved from the phase of "resignation" (accompanied by "paralysis, despair, retreat into oneself"—all clearly pejorative words in Stolpe's vocabulary) through which it had passed in the 1950s and 1960s, to a phase that Stolpe described as one of "regeneration."[20] Dictatorships reduce margins for manuever, but they do not eliminate all choices and all possibilities for constructive action. Stolpe rejected political passivity as a kind of cowardice or dereliction of Christian duty.

Havel spoke of the truth as the "power of the powerless"; the truth could, at least theoretically, destroy the regime. The power the BEK sought to exercise, often using what Havel might have described as the spirit and methods of traditional politics, was of a different nature and dedicated to a different purpose. In exchange for a relaxation of social and political repression, the church could offer the regime a recognition that seemed to border on a concession of legitimacy; indeed, its mere willingness to negotiate often seemed to imply a prior acceptance of the regime. The same dilemma plagued West German governments (as well as West German political parties and social organizations) seeking to walk a narrow line between de facto recognition of the DDR as a negotiating partner and any kind of recognition that could be construed as conceding legitimacy to the communist regime or accepting the permanence of the border between the two Germanys.

The church's policy was meant to encourage change in the DDR in two ways: from above, by securing recognition for the church both as an institution and as the bearer of a set of values and then using that recognition to engage the SED in dialogue and negotiation, and from below, through the participation of committed Christians in every aspect of social life.

It was in the context of the "modus vivendi" summarized by the formula "Kirche im Sozialismus" that Stolpe's interactions with the regime took place.[21] In ethical terms, the validity of the approach rested on the assumption that the regime's elites could learn, that the regime could be made "better," and that its improvement would promote rather than foreclose or delay its eventual replacement, should that option ever become available. The "Kirche im Sozialismus" approach initially appeared as an "integrating formula" that meant different things to different people (both within and beyond the church), "a usable, tactically clever formula that sounded almost like a declaration of loyalty, but on closer examination left everything uncertain."[22] It was debated in church circles before and after its adoption, and official church pronouncements never fully clarified its ambiguities.[23] Like Ostpolitik, it was contested again after unification, by men and women who had never accepted it and were finally free to express their views, and perhaps also by men and women who wished in retrospect to withdraw their support for a policy that had come to appear morally dubious. In 1992 Stolpe summarized his view of the "Kirche im Sozialismus" debate, and drew the connection to the controversy then swirling about him: "The debate around Stolpe mirrors another debate that predates the fall of the Wall: between elements of the opposition and a set of people from leading church circles, the tension between, on one side, the search for truth and a fundamentalist approach to action which placed principles above success, and on the other side, a more pragmatic approach which tried to achieve small steps in order to get closer to grand goals."[24]

The "Kirche im Sozialismus" approach, like Ostpolitik, was the product of a specific generational experience. Like Bahr's generation, Stolpe's contemporaries reacted to the perceived immobility of their elders and were then criticized as spineless by younger men and women. Like Bahr, Stolpe saw the older generation's principled intransigence as understandable but in the end unproductive, and he argued that his young critics, so much less inclined to compromise than he had been, had profited from precisely the political space his approach had been intended to create—and had in fact created.

By 1988, the usefulness of the "Kirche im Sozialismus" formula already appeared "exhausted."[25] It is nonetheless possible that in 1992, Stolpe believed the plausibility of the position he had taken during the earlier period to be so self-evident that he did not anticipate the storm his account of his conduct would unleash. But the often bitter politics of Ostpolitik might have counseled caution. The foreign policy consensus in the Federal Republic had always been relatively limited. The policies initiated by the Brandt government, developed by the government of Helmut Schmidt (1974–1982), and then continued by the Conservative-Liberal coalition under Helmut Kohl, illustrated some of the limits; the policies had left deep scars in both the Christlich-Demokratische Union/Christlich-Soziale Union (CDU/CSU) and the SPD. In addition, Ostpolitik was critically remembered by the same elements of the DDR opposition who had lost patience with the "Kirche im Sozialismus" formula.

Initially, opposition to Brandt's policies had come from the then-opposition Union parties, and especially from the CSU and its powerful chair, Franz Josef Strauß. The Moscow and Warsaw treaties were ratified by the Bundestag on May 17, 1972. The votes on the two treaties were virtually identical: 248 SPD and FDP deputies voted to ratify the Moscow Treaty,

10 CDU/CSU deputies voted against, and 238 CDU/CSU deputies abstained.[26] The Basic Treaty was ratified on May 11, 1973; 268 SPD and FDP deputies and 4 CDU deputies voted in favor of the ratifying legislation, 217 CDU and CSU deputies voted against. The Bavarian state government, under CSU leadership, then appealed to the Bundesverfassungsgericht (the Federal Constitutional Court), alleging that the treaty violated the Basic Law.[27]

Throughout the discussion, the new policy's critics brought two major arguments to bear. First, they asserted that the Brandt government was "selling out" to the communist bloc, in ways that were both objectionable in themselves and contrary to the stipulations of the Basic Law, which (the Bavarians claimed) made German unification an official goal and the Federal Republic the only legitimate representative of the German people. Brandt spoke frequently of the necessary "normalization" of relations between West and East in general and between West and East Germany in particular, and pointed to pragmatic benefits—including peace—to support his position. To his critics, the "normalization" of an allegedly abnormal situation was anathema. But the critics acknowledged that international circumstances made West German intransigence a lonely position, and that alternative policies deserved a chance. They then mustered a second argument against the proposed treaties: "Treaties that cannot occasion ambiguous interpretations—let alone contradictory interpretations," Strauß declared, "such treaties will meet with our approval," but the treaty arrangements the government was proposing were subject to different interpretations by the signatory parties, and were as such suspect.[28] Article 6 of the Basic Treaty illustrated the kind of language that gave the treaty's critics pause: "The Federal Republic of Germany and the German Democratic Republic proceed on the principle that the jurisdiction of each of the two States is confined to its own territory. They shall each respect the other's independence and autonomy in its internal and external affairs." In fact, "destabilization through stabilization"—like Stolpe's "Kirche im Sozialismus" approach—*was* a policy built on ambiguities and partial concessions. Its value, its advocates never tired of arguing, was to be measured by its concrete results. The only alternative, they asserted, was to wait for a miracle, "and that is no policy."[29]

Without support from important elements within the Union parties, the Brandt and Schmidt governments would have been unable to implement the new policies—and the policies would not have survived the demise of the Social-Liberal coalition in 1982. Hans-Dietrich Genscher remained foreign minister after the change in government majorities; his continued presence signaled fundamental continuities in foreign policy. The Kohl government did not seek to undo what preceding governments had achieved, but the rhetorical accent changed. Under Brandt and even under Schmidt, government spokesmen had generally favored an optimistic account of what the policies had already accomplished and might yet achieve. By the early 1980s, both the international and the domestic contexts had changed. Ronald Reagan and Margaret Thatcher were in power, and both preferred a confrontational, ideological language in their public pronouncements on East-West relations. The returns on détente policies seemed disappointing: the Soviet Union had invaded Afghanistan (December 1979), martial law had been declared in Poland, and the "normalization" of relations between the two German states had not prevented East German border guards from continuing to shoot people seeking to slip across the border. Given these developments, and the persistence of elements within his coalition fundamentally opposed to Ostpolitik, Kohl had every incentive to accompany the policy's continuation with a tougher rhetoric. That rhetoric in turn comforted the opinions of those who had opposed the policies from the beginning.

Within the SPD, the divisions over Ostpolitik were slower to develop (and developed around different issues), but were especially deep. They were occasioned by the NATO two-track decision of December 1979, and exacerbated by the SED-SPD dialogue that led in August 1987 to the publication of a joint document, "Der Streit der Ideologien und die gemeinsame Sicherheit" (Conflicting Ideologies and Common Security).[30] The first controversy took place as the Green movement was gaining momentum. Mass demonstrations against new missile deployments—especially the June 1982 demonstration in Bonn, in which between three hundred thousand and one-half million people participated and at which Erhard Eppler, a prominent Social Democrat, spoke—showed that Schmidt's policies were sharply contested by a broad segment of opinion on the political left, within the SPD and among its potential supporters. The politics of the NATO decision, and especially its implementation, were complicated, and were seen differently by people of otherwise similar political convictions in different NATO countries. To the Social Democratic supporters of Schmidt's policies, their left-wing opponents seemed to be undermining the Federal Republic's attachment to the democratic West—a perception encouraged by the fact that some leading opponents of the two-track decision (Eppler, Oskar Lafontaine) were also hostile to continued German membership in NATO. The party's left, partisans of the decision claimed, had an ambivalent attitude toward the USSR—and toward freedom, if the "price" of freedom included the acceptance of a "capitalist" system. As Gesine Schwan protested: "Only someone who shuts his eyes to the Soviet threat can abandon the two-track policy as effortlessly as is at the moment being done by parts of the SPD. Whoever does this does not value the preservation of western freedom very highly."[31]

The suspicion that parts of the party were ideologically unreliable was reinforced by perceptions of the relations that developed during the 1980s between the SPD and the SED and that culminated in the "Streit der Ideologien und die gemeinsame Sicherheit" common paper, in the elaboration of which Eppler, as chair of the party's Grundwertekommission (Principles and Platform Committee), played a central role. The paper argued that an active defense of the peace was the precondition of the ongoing and fundamental competition between Western democracies and state socialist countries. It tried to specify the terms of the ideological competition between West and East, with the SPD articulating Western positions on democratic institutions, individual rights, and political action, and the SED supplying the Marxist-Leninist response. "The conflict over such contradictory basic positions," the paper noted, "cannot be ended by compromise formulas or appeals to the desire for peace." Change could come about only through persuasion, and the paper sought to lay down the rules of a "culture of conflict and of conflictual dialogue." Dialogue presupposed reciprocity, mutual respect, and goodwill between the participants, and a shared assumption that the other side could be persuaded: "Neither side can deny to the other the right to exist. Our hope cannot be based on the idea that one system will dismantle the other. Hope has to be based on the notion that both systems can be reformed and that competition between the systems will strengthen the will to reform on both sides. Coexistence and mutual security are therefore not subject to temporal restrictions."[32]

The Union parties were especially critical of the paper, but it also made some people within the SPD uneasy. In November 1993, Hans-Jochen Vogel defended the paper as consistent with the logic of West German détente policy, which he saw as developing in an unbroken line from Brandt's initiatives through the Kohl government. Vogel, citing the same historical scenes that both Bahr and Stolpe had found unforgettable, reminded his listeners of the events that had shaped his political consciousness: "I was a young man during the Hungarian uprising of 1956. I cannot forget the fired-up words of encouragement that came from the West and then the complete inaction, as Imre Nagy's last, desperate appeals for help came over the radio."[33]

The 1987 common paper, Vogel argued, had forced the SED to accept the principle of political pluralism, and the SPD had repeatedly and unambiguously reiterated its attachment to Western democracy in the text.[34] The text was published in *Neues Deutschland,* insuring its accessibility to the East German population. "Not German social democracy, but the other side, had to worry about 'ideological contagion,'" Vogel asserted.[35] Even Rainer Eppelmann, Vogel reminded the Eppelmann Enquete-Kommission, had thought the paper helpful, arguing; "The paper wasn't in the end very useful to the SED, but gave us tactical advantages in our dealings with the state leadership."[36]

The substance of these complex debates was far from exhausted when unification overtook the participants, and the intraparty splits, especially in the SPD, were only superficially healed. The debate over Stolpe's version of "destabilization through stabilization" was therefore, especially for west German participants and for some ex–East German dissidents, in part a continuation of the détente debate by other means. Like the détente debate, the Stolpe debate did not always follow party cleavages, even among west Germans. But Stolpe's CDU opponents could use the ex-dissidents' critique both to settle accounts within their own political camp and to exacerbate lingering tensions within the SPD.[37]

Stolpe may have hoped that the divisiveness of the debate over Ostpolitik had ended with the end of the Cold War. His critics tended to credit an alternative explanation of why he chose to go public with his story: he may have hoped, by launching a preemptive strike, to limit the damage any evidence found in the recently opened Stasi (MfS) files might cause.[38] Stolpe was not the first important German politician—or church figure—to be accused of improper dealings with the SED and the security apparatus of the DDR. He was, however, the first public figure to be brought to grief by his own deliberate revelations. The controversy began when the weekly newsmagazine *Der Spiegel* published an extended but edited excerpt from an unfinished book by Stolpe in its issue of January 20, 1992.[38]

Stolpe begins his account of the means he employed while serving as the intermediary between the BEK and the regime with a short lesson in the structure of power under communism. This account is remarkable only for its unoriginality—and for the extent to which it departs from Havel's description of mature totalitarianism. The regime, Stolpe reminds us, rested on three pillars: the state, the party, and the security apparatus. He had relations with each of the three, but of the three, the security apparatus seemed to him the most efficacious: in Stolpe's first experience, its assistance was "quick and uncomplicated." In short, "what the state apparatus was unable to do and the party did not want to do, could, via the State Security Service, be brought to the party for a decision and in the end to the state for implementation."[40] Stolpe then recites the story of his interactions with the MfS, which included perhaps a thousand conversations over the course of nearly three decades. The meetings often took place without a third person present, and were sometimes held in secret locations of the Stasi's choosing. Stolpe's hierarchical superiors were not fully informed of his activities. Church guidelines, which differed from district to district and were particularly unclear at the Bund level, did not explicitly support these procedures, but Stolpe claimed that the church had given him "full powers" to deal with matters for which he was responsible.[41] After a three-year investigation of its own, the Evangelische Kirche in Deutschland (EKD) concluded in Stolpe's favor, confirming the Berlin-Brandenburg Church's October 1992 judgment that Stolpe had never ceased to render "extraordinary" service to the church and his fellow citizens. At the same time, both the EKD and the Berlin-Brandenburg Church held that his Stasi contacts, "in view of their type and their extent, were not in harmony with his duties and tasks as a church official." The final report criticized Stolpe's willingness to accept gifts from the regime, his readiness to give the Stasi information considered confidential, and his failure to inform his own superiors of his conversations, but acknowledged that a more conventional course of action might have diminished Stolpe's effectiveness. In a statement adopted by the Berlin-Brandenburg Synod on April 10, 1994, the church had warned against the breach of trust that conversations with the Stasi had entailed, no matter how well intentioned the representative of the church may have been.[42] In 1995, the church nonetheless decided against initiating any disciplinary action against its former official.[43]

The factual debate about Stolpe's past actions hinged on two questions: Did he know that he was the IM the Stasi called "Sekretär," and was anyone hurt (intentionally or unintentionally) as a consequence of his conversations with Erich Mielke's men—or with people from Klaus Gysi's office?[44] In other words, how far had he gone in playing the Stasi's game, and had his strategy involved human costs? Despite two and a half years of unremitting investigation and debate, these questions were not resolved, and given the nature of the available evidence, it is possible that they will never be definitively answered. In his critical report on Stolpe, Ehrhart Neubert, a former dissident minister and co-founder of Demokratischer Aufbruch who was serving as an adviser to the Bündnis 90 parliamentary group in Potsdam, argued that Stolpe, whatever his intentions, had engaged in the political equivalent of reckless endangerment. Stolpe's tactics, Neubert argued, had given the Stasi what the Stasi wanted. "Stolpe's service as a conduit for information was itself blameworthy," he asserted.[45]

Stolpe conceded that the surviving Stasi records relevant to his case were open to multiple interpretations, and during the course of the controversy, he modified his own public assessments of his effectiveness in his dealings with the regime. While he initially portrayed himself as in control of the game he had played, he later retreated, declaring (like so many others identified as IMs), "I was used, deceived, overheard."[46] He acknowledged that he had "remained silent too often and about too much, because I wanted to keep the conversation with those in authority going and did not want to scare them off."[47]

Rainer Eppelmann and Bärbel Bohley were among those who believed that they were personally hurt by Stolpe's actions. Here again, the evidence is inconclusive.[48] The former dissidents seem to have been unable to distinguish between being from time to time instrumentalized—a tactic Stolpe did employ—and being betrayed and materially injured. In their book, being used was equivalent to being betrayed, and betrayal in turn was an injury of the worst sort. This view made a substantively searching exchange between Stolpe and his most vehement critics all but impossible. The debate about facts therefore tended to obscure the fundamental ethical question that even a complete and immediate disclosure by Stolpe of all his actions could not have evacuated: Was the position Stolpe acknowledged having taken—and which he helped elaborate but which was also the official position of the church—a morally defensible position? Can regimes like the one that existed in the DDR be incrementally improved? Did Stolpe's posture make the regime more bearable while it lasted, while preparing the ground for its ultimate demise? Did it, in other words, promote destabilization through stabilization, and this at a moral price acceptable to those who hoped ultimately for destabilization?

In part because this aspect of the Stolpe debate in many ways mirrored the past and recently renewed debate about Ostpolitik, Helmut Schmidt went to Potsdam in mid-February 1992, "in order to stand very publicly by Mr. Stolpe."[49] In contrast, both Joachim Gauck, the chief custodian of the Stasi files and former dissident clergyman from Rostock, and Christoph Stier, bishop of Mecklenburg since 1984, took exception to broader interpretations of the "Kirche im Sozialismus" concept. Both viewed the question from a more limited perspective. Stier denied that Stolpe was authorized to negotiate with the Stasi, or that such negotiations were either necessary or advisable: "I . . . do not share the view that contacts between the Stasi and the church were necessary. Many people now even speak of their contacts with the Stasi as a partnership. I find this word impossible and scandalous. The Stasi was no partner of ours. To my way of thinking, speaking, and acting, that was beyond all possibility."[50]

Stier conceded, however, that while people under his authority refused even to talk to party officials, they did maintain contact with the state apparatus—which of course was controlled by the party: "That was clear to us. But nonetheless for us the distinction was important, because in my opinion it demonstrated a necessary distance from the regime. We spoke with state authorities whose competence included the church, but not with those who pulled the strings behind the scenes. The Stasi was in my view not competent. It had power and influence, but no legitimacy."[51]

What exactly he understands by "competent" here Stier did not specify; he did not, in fact, propose an alternative understanding of the regime to replace that offered by Stolpe. Havel would never have argued that Czech state institutions were competent. Stier's position recalled the arguments made during the *Literaturstreit* that conceded respectability to communist allegiances but condemned conversations with the secret police; like those arguments, Stier's argument seemed to sit on a slippery slope.

Two of Stolpe's early defenders specifically linked their defense to an understanding of the nature of the regime under which Stolpe acted. The former SPD mayor of Hamburg, Klaus von Dohnanyi, Dietrich Bonhoeffer's nephew and also the son of a man executed after the failure of the July 1944 plot against Hitler, intervened in the debate within a week of Stolpe's original article.[52] Reserving final judgment on the specific case, Dohnanyi instead addressed the underlying ethical question. His definition of the East German dictatorship, like Stolpe's, was political. The DDR was not the Third Reich, but it was in certain respects a close cousin: "Both regimes disposed of absolute power. In both cases—in that of the DDR, at least as long as the Soviet Union went along with the regime—open rebellion could not topple the regime." And he immediately drew the conclusion that "the exercise of influence therefore demanded camouflage." The requisite camouflage left little room for moral delicacy:

> Whoever wants to be effective in a dictatorship must wear its colors, where necessary even its hated uniforms and insignia. The open resistance fighter cannot reach the circles of power, and so cannot change the regime's political course. He ends up in prison or in exile.
>
> An unpardonable pride is manifest in those who believe that in order to prove one's decency and morality under a dictatorship, one must be imprisoned, or banished, or hanged. Whoever is prepared to compromise himself in order to limit the damage and help the persecuted proceeds down an honorable path. No one should condemn him—and certainly not someone who has never himself been forced to act and be accountable in comparable circumstances.

Unless evidence could be produced of specific denunciations or crimes, Dohnanyi saw nothing objectionable in Stolpe's contacts with the Stasi: "Contacts with and reports to the Stasi were as unavoidable for people with public responsibilities as were, for example, the reports to the Abwehr [military intelligence] by the Resistance during the Nazi years." And he concluded rather sharply: "Ethics is, in the last analysis, a moral and not an aesthetic category."[53]

Richard Schröder also came to Stolpe's defense.[54] Schröder was an uncompromised east German theologian who had served as the parliamentary leader of the SPD in the freely elected Volkskammer of March 1990. There he had accepted and defended a grand coalition with the CDU, and had argued in favor of rapid unification with the Federal Republic. Searching for standards against which to judge Stolpe's actions, Schröder compared dictators to hostage takers:

> One can somewhat unwillingly comply with their commands, one can cozy up to them, one can take their side. One can simply accustom oneself to the situation. One can say: We don't talk to hostage takers, let them do what they will. But one can also talk to them, in order to succeed in getting them to loosen the chains or to release the women and children or even to end the kidnapping. In that case, however, one cannot say: "You are hostage takers and I despise you." One will say instead: "I can understand you, but . . ." One gets on their wavelength.[55]

Schröder recognized that the kind of interaction needed to secure the release of women and children might land the hostage-turned-negotiator in an uncomfortable moral and psychological position:

> If the kidnapping lasts a long time, empirically a curious and in no way simply hostile relationship establishes itself between hostages and hostage takers . . . One cannot negotiate with anyone absent a certain relation of trust, without a minumum of predictability. If one side has all the power, it is of course hard to assess whether that side is showing real openness or whether with an appearance of openness it is, so to speak, doubly deceiving the other side.[56]

Schröder did not, however, conclude that the position was morally untenable: for him, the bottom line was that the women and children had gone free. For Schröder as for Stolpe, the decisive question was that bottom line. If Stolpe had faithfully sought "through contacts with the Stasi, to protect the church's independent space, to alleviate human hardship, and to bring some movement into frozen relationships,"[57] and if the results were that the church did enjoy a greater margin of manuever than would otherwise have been the case and that hardship had been relieved, then his actions were justified. The actions should not, Schröder added, be judged retrospectively either from the point of view of dissident groups within the church whose less prudent agenda Stolpe might have frustrated, or from the point of view of "Western normality," which obviously did not obtain in the DDR.[58]

The fundamental question was indeed whether the pursuit of influence itself was a morally defensible act. The critical words in Dohnanyi's article are "exercise of influence" and "people with public responsibilities." Stolpe was an influential man in the DDR not because he bore witness to the truth from a prison cell, but for more conventional reasons: because he was a recognized participant in the country's official public life and knew people on the Central Committee. Friedrich Schorlemmer argued that Stolpe was the "long arm of the resistance."[59] Joachim Gauck, however, retored that Stolpe consciously or unconsciously played into the hands of the SED: "The argument that the church or the opposition could only be effective because there were good 'diplomats' at work overlooks the danger that the 'diplomats' would set the norms for activities within the church, and that it was then child's play for the state to limit those activities. It also overlooks the fact that in church discussions of individuals and issues, the 'diplomats' had often internalized the ideas and behavior of SED comrades."[60]

Was Stolpe's public life indeed his original and irreparable error, morally disqualifying in and of itself whatever the Stasi files might reveal about his secret dealings? In the parliamentary debate on his past, Stolpe's critics repeatedly argued that Stolpe had gone beyond "the ordinary compromises that we all made."[61] Indeed he had, and he had done so precisely because he was not, as Peter Wagner, another parliamentary critic, noted, an "ordinary DDR citizen." Wagner, the parliamentary leader of the Brandenburg CDU, acknowledged that he too had had to speak with Stasi agents, "but I was never considered by those gentlemen as a prospective recipient of gifts."[62] Wagner was a medical doctor; Stolpe was the top lay official of the only semi-independent institution in a dictatorship with totalitarian pretensions. The former was indeed an "ordinary citizen," the latter was not; the former had tried to remain decent alongside the system, the latter had tried to change the parameters of the system. That the Stasi cultivated its relations with Stolpe may say more about the position he occupied and about what he was trying to achieve than about the man's moral character—unless it was wrong simply to move away from the status of a normal citizen. Stolpe never thought the move was wrong. "I stand by my attempt," he reiterated in June 1994, "to increase the church's room for manuever and to help people, even if this meant exploiting the possibilities for conversation with the MfS."[63] Schröder acknowledged that hostages sometimes develop complicated but complicitous relations with their captors, and Dohnanyi cited a wrenching letter written by Dietrich Bonhoeffer at Christmas in 1942: "We were silent witnesses of evil deeds, we have washed in many waters, we have learned the arts of pretense and ambiguous speech; through experience we have become distrustful of men . . . , in unbearable conflicts we have been battered and have perhaps even become cynical. Are we still usable?"[64]

Manfred Stolpe read from Bonhoeffer's letter at the conclusion of his speech to the Landtag at the end of the long investigation into his past.[65] He withstood the pressures on him to resign, and remained minister president of Brandenburg. He was both useful and usable: the real question is, for whom and in what ways? This was also the question Stolpe's most bitter—and embittered—critics posed.

No "Ordinary Compromises"

On October 29, 1992, Marianne Birthler resigned her post as education minister in Manfred Stolpe's government. The Bündnis 90/Green activist had concluded, after "careful consideration," that she could no longer sanction Stolpe's conduct by her silence. Declaring that her "main political interest is fighting for public transparency and the public exchange of opinions," she called her resignation the "expression of my personal responsibility for political action and my effort at political authenticity." Birthler implicitly criticized Stolpe's conduct under the DDR, suggesting that had he been a teacher in Brandenburg instead of the state's top elected official, he would have lost his job. That he should remain in his job seemed unfair, and that she should continue as his education minister therefore seemed to her impossible. But she was especially critical of Stolpe's conduct during the investigation itself. "Excuses, dubious explanations, halfhearted concessions that come too late" she said, "destroy our political culture."[66] No trust, no democracy. To some ex-dissidents, it seemed that Stolpe was simply continuing the kind of politics he had practiced under the DDR. Within days, one hundred political and cultural figures had signed a statement calling for Stolpe's resignation. The group praised Birthler's "civic courage" and called her resignation "a logical reaction" to Stolpe's "tactic of delaying and covering up." In the group's view, the wrong person had resigned.[67] The list of signatories included former dissidents from various political parties who shared a preference for cultural strategies: Angelika Barbe [Mitglied des Bundestages (MdB) 1990–1994 and co-founder of the east-SPD], Rainer Eppelmann, Jürgen Fuchs, Martin Gutzeit (also a co-founder of the east-

SPD, later on the staff of the Gauck-Behörde), Ralf Hirsch, Freya Klier, Stephan Krawczyk, Ehrhart Neubert, Ulrike Poppe, Arnold Vaatz and his Saxon colleague Heinz Eggert, Hans-Joachim Schädlich, and Wolfgang Templin.

Birthler's resignation followed by seven months an inconclusive but unfavorable report issued by the Gauck-Behörde; the report sought to establish that Stolpe and the agent identified in MfS documents as "IM-Sekretär" were identical and suggested that Stolpe had known he was being used as an agent.[68] More important, the resignation came seven weeks after the revelation that Stolpe had been awarded a Verdienst-medaille (service medal) in November 1978 by the communist regime.[69] From precisely whose hands he had received the medal remained a hotly contested and ultimately unresolved issue: Stolpe insisted that he had received the medal from Hans Seigewasser, the state secretary for church affairs (Seigewasser died in 1979); the former Stasi agent Claus Roßberg claimed that he himself had given Stolpe the medal. It turned out that Stolpe had also received a valuable Bible and an atlas from MfS officials. He had not informed his BEK colleagues of the gifts.

Stolpe's response to the crisis caused by the discovery of his medal was typical of his conduct throughout the controversy. Having declined to disclose the award before the press discovered its existence, Stolpe then minimized its importance and conceded as little information as possible. Not telling anyone more than the person needed to know was one of the lessons Stolpe had learned under the DDR. Stolpe was a warm, courteous, and articulate interlocutor, but he did not confide easily in others and was widely regarded as guarded and private.[70] "He trusts few people," state party chair Steffen Reiche was quoting as saying, "because he doesn't want to lose control."[71] Under democratic conditions, his reserve made him look at best like a footdragger and at worst like a liar. In the fall of 1993, as a Brandenburg parliamentary investigatory commission sought to wind up its work, Stolpe conceded that he had made mistakes during the course of the investigation. If he had it to do over, he said, he would do it "differently and better": he would "let it all out and go into detail, but be tougher about slander and invective."[72] Not everyone believed him. Was the problem his reserve, or were secrecy, deception, and manipulation the political rules with which Stolpe felt most comfortable—or at least with which he had made his peace? Stolpe himself said, "One must play in all registers and engage all one's troops."[73] In the DDR, had the game been more important than the mission, and was Stolpe now interested primarily in maintaining his own position?

Birthler's resignation marked an important moment in the Stolpe debate—and in the life of the first Stolpe administration. An eight-member parliamentary investigatory commission had been created in February 1992. Its charge focused on factual questions: Had Stolpe been an IM? Who had known of his activities? Had he changed sides? Had he violated the confidence of his church colleagues? Had he worked against the opposition or harmed the interests of East German citizens who sought his assistance in order to leave the DDR?[74] The commission was chaired by Lothar Bisky, the leader of the Brandenburg PDS parliamentary group and later the chair of the federal PDS. Bisky, despite his party affiliation, was widely accepted in state politics as a fair-minded and relatively nonpartisan figure who preferred consensus to polemics.[75] He remained sympathetic to Stolpe throughout the controversy, overseeing the elaboration of the final report delivered to and accepted by the state parliament on June 16, 1994—by coincidence, the day before Eppelmann delivered the final report of his commission to the Bundestag. The Stolpe report was inconclusive; it was adopted by the commission in a five-to-three vote only after months of bitter wrangling, with the CDU and Bündnis 90 dissenting. The most important expression of minority opinion was an eighty-six-page report drafted by Ehrhart Neubert for the Bündnis 90 parliamentary group.[76] Neubert's report was made public in September 1993—twenty months after the controversy began, eleven months after Birthler's resignation, nine months before the formal end of the debate, and one year before Stolpe won an absolute majority in the Landtag elections of September 11, 1994.

The politics of the investigation were as complicated as the politics of the state parliament that created the committee.[77] The state elections of October 14, 1990, returned an assembly composed of 88 deputies: 36 SPD, 27 CDU, 13 PDS/Linke Liste, 6 FDP, and 6 Bündnis 90 (for percentages, see Table 5.1). Stolpe put together a so-called "Ampel" (traffic light) coalition—red (SPD), yellow (FDP), green (Bündnis 90/Greens)—leaving the CDU and the PDS in opposition.

Of all the parties, only the SPD had a clear partisan profile—in part owing to Stolpe's leadership, and in part because the party was not burdened by a DDR past. Stolpe's electoral victories, however, like those of Kurt Biedenkopf in neighboring Saxony, were more the product of per-

Table 5.1   Elections in Brandenburg, 1990–1994 (percent)

	Landtag 14 Oct. '90	Bundestag 2 Dec. '90	Kommunal. 6 Dec. '93	Eur. Parl. 12 June '94	Landtag 11 Sept. '94	Bundestag 16 Oct. '94
Participation	67.1	73.8	59.8	41.4	56.2	71.9
CDU	29.4	36.3	20.6	23.4	18.7	28.1
SPD	38.2	32.9	34.6	36.9	54.1	45.0
PDS	13.4	11.0	21.2	22.6	18.7	19.3
Bündnis 90/Greens	9.3	6.6	4.2	4.6	2.9	2.9
FDP	6.6	9.7	7.1	2.7	2.2	2.6
Bürgerbündnis	—	—	—	—	1.0	—

sonal popularity than of partisan mobilization.[78] With the exception of the PDS, no party could boast a strong local organization. In 1996 the Brandenburg PDS alone had more members than all other parties combined: it had claimed 42,662 members in 1990; 24,998 in 1991; 22,864 in 1992; 20,679 in 1993; and 18,258 in 1994.[79] In contrast, the Brandenburg SPD, although it was the strongest SPD state organization in the new Länder and was energetically (if sometimes controversially) led by another young ex-dissident minister, Steffen Reiche, counted only some 6,500 members in 1992.[80] The FDP was numerically weak at every level and had no easily identifiable partisan profile. During the Stolpe investigation, the party leadership was distracted by the machinations of Rosemarie Fuchs, a deputy and commission member who was excluded from the party in June 1993.

Birthler's Bündnis 90 was the third component of Stolpe's Ampel coalition. In early 1993, Bündnis claimed about seven hundred members:[81] like its counterparts in the other new Länder, its electoral base was narrow and its organization was loose. The diversity of the small Bündnis 90 parliamentary group became increasingly clear during the Stolpe investigation. The trials and tribulations of the party are part and parcel of the marginalization story whose sources we considered in Chapter 2.

In January 1993, Bündnis 90 and the Greens proposed a merger at the national level; the move was intended to maximize the group's chances of overcoming the 5 percent hurdle in the 1994 Bundestag elections. The merger was put to a referendum in the spring of 1993 by both parties, whose memberships voted separately: among the Greens, a simple majority sufficed to approve the merger, but Bündnis 90 required a two-thirds majority. The membership referenda were held in mid-April; 91.8 percent of the Greens who participated in the vote and 85.9 percent of the Bündnis 90 participants approved the merger, which was then consummated at a common party conference held in Leipzig in mid-May. In Brandenburg, however, the results were different. The state party had gone on record in December 1992 as opposing the merger; Günter Nooke, the parliamentary leader of the Bündnis 90 group and one of the two Bündnis 90 members of the investigatory commission, was among the opponents. In the April referendum, 45 percent of the 331 Brandenburg participants voted against the merger, effectively splitting the already small party.[82] While Marianne Birthler went on to become the spokesperson for the merged federal party (where she would frequently complain that east German interests and sensibilities were ignored), Nooke left Bündnis 90. The two state parties formalized their merger in late June 1993.[83] Nooke, however, remained the leader of the shrinking parliamentary group, which dropped the "90" from its name. Nooke, born in 1959, had been active in the peace movement in the DDR and was a co-founder of Demokratischer Aufbruch in 1989 before joining New Forum. He had sat in the freely elected Volkskammer as a Bündnis 90 deputy and had headed the Bündnis 90 list in the Brandenburg Landtag elections in October 1990. By 1993, he was distinguished not only by his hostility to Stolpe but also by his opposition to the planned merger of Berlin and Brandenburg, the terms of which were under negotiation.

The Brandenburg CDU was exceptionally heterogeneous, plagued by personal and substantive quarrels among its leaders, and organizationally weak. It owed its heterogeneity in part to ambiguities it inherited from its past as a DDR "bloc" party, and it owed its leadership difficulties in part to the well-founded perception that opposing Manfred Stolpe would not be a good way to accumulate a favorable electoral record. The party's first parliamentary leader was the controversial maverick Peter-Michael Diestel, who often supported Stolpe. When Diestel finally relinquished his leadership post in May 1992, a bitter and complex fight ensued for the leadership of the state branch of the CDU.[84] Ulf Fink (a west German) was selected despite Kohl's open support for Fink's rival, Angela Merkel. The party's internal rifts were expressed not only in the local CDU's vacillating response to the unfolding Stolpe affair, but also in its Landtag delegation's split vote on the state constitutional draft presented by the SPD–FDP–Bündnis 90/Green government in April 1992.[85] Fink was highly critical of the constitutional draft, but survey data suggest that 80 percent of the CDU voters who participated in the June 14, 1992, constitutional referendum voted to approve the document.[86] By the 1994 elections, the state leadership of the party had again changed, but Carola Hartfelder was no more able than her predecessors to unite the party or its parliamentary group. Hartfelder was forced to resign in May 1996, after a particularly unedifying two-week power struggle during which she tried to oust her critics from other leadership posts.

The Ampel coalition unraveled in late March 1994, when Bündnis 90/Greens split over the Stolpe issue: on March 14, Günter Nooke accused Stolpe of having lied to the investigatory commission. For months Nooke had been attacking Stolpe—and the commission—with increasing vehemence. On March 22, 1994, the two Bündnis 90 ministers, Matthias Platzeck and Roland Resch, left the parliamentary group. In early April, the deputy Rolf Wettstädt followed. The group, now composed of Nooke, Wolfgang Pohl, and Peter Schüler, no longer had the necessary four members. Stolpe initially proposed to lead a minority government with the FDP, then opted instead to seek a dissolution of the Landtag in April and new elections in mid-June. After more than three hours of verbal finger-pointing and ad hominem debate in the Landtag on April 13, the proposed measure failed: the forty-nine SPD, PDS, and Bündnis votes in favor of a parliamentary dissolution were ten short of the necessary two-thirds majority.[87] Even though the CDU had called for a dissolution at the beginning of the crisis, nineteen of the group's twenty-one members now voted against, as did deputies from the FDP; they may have suspected (and they were certainly suspected of suspecting) that they would lose their seats in new elections. Only eighteen deputies— Nooke and Grabert from Bündnis and sixteen members of the CDU— supported a CDU motion calling for Stolpe's resignation.[88] Two months later, on June 16, 1994, after a debate in which Nooke called Stolpe "cowardly" and "interested only in staying in power" and was himself reprimanded by the independent Justice Minister Hans Otto Bräutigam ("You speak as if you enjoyed sole possession of the truth"), the Brandenburg Landtag brought the formal controversy to a close.[89] On September 11, 1994, the SPD gained nearly 16 percentage points over its total in the

Landtag elections of 1990, an unprecedented achievement in the history of the Federal Republic for a major party. Nooke's "Bürgerbündnis Freier Wähler" (Citizens' Alliance of Free Voters), created in late May ("We are a serious alternative for all those who don't want to vote for the SPD and Stolpe"),[90] won a mere 1 percent of the vote; Bündnis 90/Greens, as well as the FDP, fell short of the 5 percent hurdle and were thus also unrepresented in the new assembly. As the results were announced, Petra Weißflog, the state Bündnis 90/Greens party chair and leading candidate on the party list, gave an unofficial but eloquent reaction: "Scheiße."[91] For over two years, Stolpe's Stasi connections had been a major news story. They did not appear to have damaged the minister president's relationship with his constituents.

Such was the broader political and partisan context in which Marianne Birthler made her decision to resign. With regard to the specific issues raised by the Stolpe case, Birthler was in a particularly difficult position: she had spoken out against compromised Volkskammer deputies (see Chapter 2); and above all, as the cabinet officer in charge of Brandenburg's school system, she had been responsible for developing and enforcing the post-1990 version of denazification—or "Entstasifizierung," as administrative purge measures in unified Germany were sometimes called, using an expression that showed the centrality of the Stasi issue— in the sensitive area of education. For Birthler, given irresolvable uncertainties about how "destabilization through stabilization" had in fact affected the evolution of communist regimes, the issues of honesty and fairness seemed decisive. On Birthler's watch, teachers were required to complete a questionnaire, and they were systematically vetted by the Gauck-Behörde; those who lied on the questionnaire or who turned up in the Gauck-Behörde's files as Stasi collaborators (formal or informal) were subject to disciplinary action, usually dismissal. Birthler suspected Stolpe of dishonesty and, given his record of action in the DDR, considered his continued presence unfair. In essence, Birthler argued that it was both politically and morally untenable to pursue a cultural strategy at the civil service level and an institutional strategy at the electoral level—and her own preferences were for a cultural strategy in both arenas.

Denazification did not provide the post-1989 advocates of cultural strategies much positive guidance. After 1945, Western occupation authorities had moved very rapidly from sweeping internment, prosecution, and denazification measures (i.e., a cultural strategy) to more limited forms of punishment and correction, coupled with an emphasis on institutional construction and consolidation. The American Joint Chiefs of Staff (JCS) Directive 1067 (April 26, 1945) and Allied Control Council Directive 24 (January 12, 1946) had sought to exclude all "members of the Nazi Party who have been more than nominal participants in its activities, and all other persons hostile to Allied purposes" (Directive 24) from important positions in public and private life; Germans who had "voluntarily given substantial moral or material support or political assistance of any kind to the Nazi Party or Nazi officials and leaders" fell under the ban, and were to be excluded from any public position above the level of "ordinary labour."[92] But the Western Allies' long-drawn-out and ultimately losing battle to democratize the German high civil service, combined with the rapid demise of the denazification campaign, told another story. By the early 1950s, many of those who had lost their jobs in the immediate aftermath of the war had been rehired.[93]

Denazification was imposed on the entire adult population by a central authority, even though it was enforced differently at different moments and from place to place. The requirement that all German adults submit to the process reflected its wide-ranging goals. Recent transitions from dictatorship to democracy have avoided centrally imposed blanket measures. Instead, more directed attempts have been made to keep individuals implicated in the old regime from stepping into positions of power and influence in the new one. On October 4, 1991, for example, the Czechoslovak parliament passed a so-called "lustration act" automatically excluding various categories of people—individuals who had served in the People's Militia or in a wide array of other organizations—from certain positions of authority or influence (communications, upper-level administrative posts in the public sector) for a period of five years.[94] For both political and legal reasons, the measure was controversial. Václav Havel, president at the time of the bill's passage, considered refusing to sign it, since the proceedings it envisaged judged people collectively and relied on the records of the secret police. Like many, though by no means all, of the most committed former dissidents in non-German eastern Europe, Havel was cautious in his assessment of how responsibilities incurred under the old regime should be judged in the new world of democracy.[95] He was perhaps dissuaded from judgment in part by his own temperament; but his conviction that the old regime had fed on moral shortcomings that all individuals share must have encouraged his compassion. That conviction can be supported either (as in François Mauriac's case) by religious beliefs or by remembered personal experiences.[96] For Havel, both factors seem to have played a role. Where Havel's account of individual responsibility is divorced from a confession of personal guilt, however, it will necessarily tend to place the former, nondissident subjects of a totalitarian regime in a category of moral inferiority. Richard Schröder reiterated the arguments of Aedanus Burke and Charles de Gaulle, noting that descriptions of contemporary political culture, however objective they may be in intent, have political implications:

> It makes a difference whether one advances hypotheses about wholesale moral corruption in the time of Louis XIV, or whether one does the same with regard to 16 million DDR citizens minus 800 dissidents, all of whom are still alive.
> For that means: depriving them of air.[97]

After 1989, both the point of departure and the point of arrival were more ambiguous than they had been after 1945. As a program centrally imposed and applicable to the whole population, denazification has had no counterpart in unified Germany. Such a program would have been incompatible with the primarily institutional thrust of the strategy adopted by the men and women who negotiated unification in 1990, which reflected in part the different level of the "crimes" associated with the communist regime (as compared to the Third Reich), the different breadth and depth of complicity imputed to the population, the absence of an all-powerful occupying army, the early marginalization of the most determined advocates of cultural strategies—and the memories of denazification's failure. It also reflects Germany's federal structure, which leaves broad legislative powers to the Länder (see Basic Law, Articles 30, 70–74).

But as we have seen, the initial emphasis on an institutional strategy was quickly modified by pressures to incorporate elements of a cultural strategy. The first important concessions to a cultural strategy appear in the clauses of the Unification Treaty and the Stasi-Unterlagen-Gesetz that concern the employment of public officials and civil servants. The relevant clauses of the Unification Treaty were to govern civil service employment in the Länder until the new states could pass their own civil service codes, which they were required to do before the end of 1992. This period, which coincided with Birthler's cabinet tenure, was the period in which the least leniency was shown to public servants who had worked for the Stasi or who sought to evade disclosure of their prior commitments. The officials in charge of the vetting were typically either west Germans seconded to posts in the new Länder or (like Birthler) east Germans with ties to the citizens' movements. The former had no experiential knowledge of what it was like to live in a dictatorship, and often belonged to the so-called second generation, born between 1935 and 1950, who perceived their parents' silence about complicities during the Third Reich as a mistake not to be repeated. The officials with ties to the citizens' movements inclined toward cultural strategies. Both groups believed that a cultural strategy corresponded to the preferences of most east Germans—and would later feel, as one of them put it, "baffled" when it became clear that popular preferences were at best quite different.

An appendix to the Unification Treaty specified the conditions under which civil servants could be let go. "Ordinary," formally nonpunitive, grounds for dismissing a civil servant included inappropriate or deficient professional qualifications, lack of need for the skills offered, or the dissolution (*Abwicklung*) of the office or institution that had previously employed the individual.[98] These were very expansive categories, and the rules and procedures that would govern how they were applied were not stipulated. The academic staff of ex-East German universities and research institutes was especially hard hit. Under conditions of general budgetary contraction, many people lost their jobs, and it was often difficult to know whether they had been relieved of their functions because their professional qualifications were genuinely wanting or for more political reasons. Past research records were often taken as indicators of future potential—a customary academic practice, but particularly risky when applied to individuals whose professional development and research possibilities had been manifestly constrained by the political system in which they lived.[99]

"Extraordinary"—that is, punitive—grounds for dismissal were declared by the Unification Treaty to exist when the employee had "violated the principles of humanity or of the rule of law [*Rechtsstaatlichkeit*]" or "worked for the former Ministerium für Staatssicherheit/Amt für Nationale Sicherheit."[100] The treaty had little to say regarding how decisions about who had violated human rights or worked for the MfS were to be made. With the passage of the Stasi-Unterlagen-Gesetz in December 1991, a legal mechanism was set up for checking the archives for evidence of formal or informal employment by the MfS (see esp. §20). The process, however, was controversial, both because the value of the records themselves (those that remained) was contested and because the Gauck-Behörde's interpretation of the records was, like any interpretation, never beyond challenge.

The Gauck-Behörde, with satellite offices in the new Länder, could offer a judgment about whether or not someone had willingly served the MfS; others had to make the decision about who would be employed and who would not. In the two years following unification, each new federal state adopted legislation regarding elegibility for state-level electoral office and civil service qualifications. This legislation tended to expand on the criteria for "extraordinary" dismissal contained in the Unification Treaty. Thus, Mecklenburg–Western Pomerania, Saxony, and Thuringia adopted civil service codes that included—alongside the readiness to support and defend the "free democratic basic order" that is a standard requirement in all German civil service codes—language about past political commitments. The codes excluded from civil service elegibility people who had violated human rights or worked for the MfS. The Saxon code also expressed the "assumption" that other commitments would prove disqualifying:

> It is assumed that former employees or members in the upper echelons of the parties and the mass organizations, the armed defensive forces or fighting groups as well as other state or local authorities or factories in the DDR, especially section leaders in the ministries and in the district councils, district counselors, graduates of the central party schools, political functionaries in the armed defensive forces or fighting groups, ambassadors and heads of diplomatic and trade missions as well as leading members of district and local action groups do not possess the aptitude expected for entry into the civil service. This assumption can be contested.[101]

Brandenburg and Saxony-Anhalt adopted civil service codes that did not contain language about the sorts of past commitments that would be considered disqualifying in the new democracy. The Brandenburg code was adopted just in advance of the legal deadline, and may already have reflected a leniency whose advent Birthler had apparently feared. Vetting officials, whatever their own background, were becoming more experienced: they had developed a more differentiated sense of the biographies they encountered during the individual hearings that always preceded a disciplinary action; they had fewer illusions about public interest in and support for purge measures; and they worried about tradeoffs between professional competence and political qualifications. The Stolpe controversy, one official seconded from west Berlin to Potsdam in 1992 remarked in 1996, had put Brandenburg officials in a difficult position, but ultimately it had also been "a learning experience." The lessons learned confirmed Birthler's fears and marked a movement back toward an institutional strategy.

The effective decisions regarding the criteria and procedures for firing, retiring, and/or penalizing individuals whose commitments under the old regime were deemed incompatible with the continued exercise of their professional responsibilities in a democratic Germany were typically made at a highly decentralized level: within each state, different ministries and agencies adopted different standards and procedures, and local government units also used their own procedures. In 1993 competent officials from the five new Länder had met, hoping to develop a common set of guidelines to govern the vetting process. The Stolpe controversy was then at its height. The effort failed. At stake were two different but intertwined issues: what discretionary power top-level bureaucrats had to make personnel decisions in their departments, and how the criteria for disciplining a civil servant would be defined. Within the Brandenburg government itself, top-level bureaucrats were predictably reluctant to surrender their discretionary power, and different officials applied different substantive standards.

Among the state governments, a rift soon appeared between Saxony and the four other new Länder on the definition of criteria. The Saxons argued for the application of the strict criteria in use in Berlin, where intransigence was facilitated by the on-site availability of alternative (western) officials. Officials from the four other Länder argued for more flexibility on three issues. First, they argued against the so-called *Regelanfrage* (blanket inquiry rule), under which all public employees, from ministers to janitors, had to be vetted by the Gauck-Behörde. They differed among themselves about how to specify who would have to be vetted. Second, they argued against automatically releasing any public employee whose Gauck-Behörde report came back "positive" (i.e., indicated that the individual had worked for the Stasi). Instead, they proposed to consider the content of the information given by the individual to the MfS: if no one had been harmed, or if the intent to harm clearly seemed absent, further employment could be considered. Finally, arguing again against automatic dismissal, officials from the four Länder argued that the age of the individual at the time of collaboration, and the length of the individual's cooperation with the Stasi, should be taken into account.

The interstate discussions ended without the adoption of common guidelines. In Brandenburg, officials tried to work out procedures that would apply throughout the state government.[102] The effort accelerated as the Stolpe controversy wound down. At the conclusion of the debate over the final report of the Stolpe investigatory commission, the Landtag adopted a set of principles proposed by Wolfgang Birthler (SPD), Peter-Michael Diestel (CDU), Siegfried Lietzmann (FDP), Michael Schumann (PDS), and Rolf Wettstädt (ex–Bündnis 90).[103] The principles represented a clear preference for an institutional strategy, and seemed an indictment of the cultural logic that had driven the Stolpe debate. The first two points, both adopted unanimously, attempted to describe the type of context in which debates about past commitments could most fairly and usefully be conducted; they invoked the need for understanding. The third point, adopted by a majority vote, urged mutual respect as a necessary basis for dialogue.

The remaining points—the fourth was approved by a majority, the fifth was adopted unanimously, and the sixth was accepted unanimously with scattered abstentions—sought to articulate a differentiated set of criteria that could do justice to the diversity of motives and individual experience. Whereas the Saxon civil service code "assumed" an incompatibility between objectively defined past commitments and present qualification for public service, the criteria adopted by the Brandenburg Landtag tended to reverse the burden of proof. Individual cases had to be considered on their own merits; motives mattered, proportionality was to be respected, and no one was to be peremptorily denied the right to a second chance.[104]

The new Landtag renewed the discussion of appropriate criteria in April 1995.[105] On the basis of the June 1994 and April 1995 parliamentary actions, the government then published on October 10, 1995, a new set of criteria.[106]. A candidate's "anticipated functions and position in the administration will be considered and the inquiry will concern a specific period of time," the new text stipulated (§1). It confirmed the relaxation of criteria and maintained the decentralization of decision-making power. Inquiries were to go forward if a "well-founded suspicion of cooperation" with the Stasi existed or if the candidate was applying for a particularly important or sensitive position, and these judgments were left to the hiring authority (§2). Normally, only Stasi work begun or continued after January 1, 1980, would be considered relevant (§4). No other past commitments (e.g., SED functions) were specified that might be considered disqualifying; Brandenburg continued to limit its already limited purge to people who had worked directly for the security apparatus.[107] In practice, the new standards also confirmed a further change: no one would be fired simply because he or she had lied about previous contacts with the Stasi on the civil service questionnaire. Now not only did the story of the contacts matter, but so too did the story of the lie. People who had lied out of fear that they would lose their jobs or out of a kind of numb bewilderment at the changes taking place and who now understood why the lie was a wrong, would not necessarily be let go. If by lying they had stolen a second chance, and had then used it well, now their title to the second chance would be granted. They might be demoted or transferred, but they would not be dismissed. The clever and cynical, it could be objected, would learn to simulate a change of heart. Under the new Brandenburg guidelines, cynicism could still be punished. But the fundamental bet was that civil servants were far more likely to internalize democratic norms if their most immediate experience of the new system was one of inclusion rather than rejection.

What the official from Brandenburg described as a "learning process" forced on officials by the complexities of the Stolpe case, Birthler and others experienced as a betrayal of democratic ideals. Between Birthler's resignation in March 1992 and Stolpe's reelection in 1994, a crescendo of voices from the former citizens' movements called with increasing vehemence for Stolpe's resignation. Stolpe was by no means the sole target of their anger; they also criticized west German politicians who (they claimed) preferred Stolpe's company to their own, either because the politicians were all insiders or because they had all believed in the efficacy of Ostpolitik.[108] Germany, the ex-dissidents argued, was repeating the same mistakes that had been made after 1945. Stolpe's electoral victories left them unimpressed. After a dictatorship, they argued, democratic legitimacy cannot depend solely on electoral results, since the majority must be assumed to be compromised: "It should not be the case that those who were essentially responsible for the politics of the DDR should now play the role of arbiter. They now point to their status as elected officials, but who would have been elected in 1945 if the Allies had not imposed their will? Who would the criminals of the Third Reich have called to the witness stand?"[109]

Just as Inge Deutschkron had found liberal rules of legal procedure inadequate in the aftermath of a dictatorship, so did some ex-DDR dissidents question the legitimacy of electoral results in post-authoritarian settings. The Stolpe investigation would make clear, Bärbel Bohley, the peace activist and partisan of a "Kirche von unten" (grassroots church) whose statements and activities in the tense early months of 1988 had embittered relations between the church and the movements on its periphery, asserted in March 1993, whether east Germans had learned anything, "or whether they are so twisted that they need lies, because they can't bear the truth that is also their truth."[110] Günter Nooke conceded during the debate on the commission's final report, "The voters can of course confer legal power on you," and added, "but the voters who trust you are long since more emotionally motivated than informed."[111]

In the ex-dissidents' view, if elections meant that Manfred Stolpe would be resoundingly reelected, both the process and its participants were discredited. Deutschkron had finally adopted Israeli citizenship: "I felt myself a stranger in Germany, insecure and alone. Even friends who understood me and who shared my views could not remedy the situation."[112] Beyond their continuing struggle to discredit Stolpe (and their willingness to meet with Helmut Kohl), the ex-dissidents did not suggest an alternative.[113] They could not exchange Germany for another political home; they did not wish to do away with elections; and by adhering to a cultural strategy, they had opted out of occupying positions where they might have wielded constant leverage against people who did not share their views. Alongside their continuing criticism of how the DDR past was being treated, their efforts focused increasingly on the creation of support networks for former victims. Ehrhart Neubert became a co-founder of support groups for church workers against whom other church workers had informed; Bärbel Bohley sought to set up a "citizens' bureau" with vaguely defined goals and Helmut Kohl's support.[114] "Our concern here is above all for the little people," said co-founder Jürgen Fuchs, "who rebelled in the old DDR and now already see that we are once again the last assholes."[115]

The Ambiguities of Empowerment in Post-Authoritarian Settings

"What belongs together," Willy Brandt declared after the Wall fell, "will now grow together." The growing pains proved more acute and persistent than many had expected. In a November 1991 poll, 47 percent of the east Germans in the sample said that in their view, the west Germans were treating east Germany "like a colony."[116] Three and a half years later, 72 percent of an east German sample said that ex–East Germans were second-class citizens in the Federal Republic, although far fewer—17 percent—counted themselves among the "losers" in the unification process.[117] In April 1996, Stolpe worried about "a whole mix of negative feelings."[118]

Efforts to define the exact nature of the alienation felt by east Germans were inconclusive, in part because east German alienation never spoke with one voice, and in part because even individual subjects might not have given an intellectually coherent (as opposed to an emotionally understandable) account of their discontent. It was therefore probably a mistake to use "Ostalgie" as an indicator of persistent antidemocratic patterns of preference or culture, and to try to measure the putative continuities by using survey questions modeled on those used during the 1950s to track the legacy of National Socialism in the Federal Republic. The East German regime had been viewed differently by its subject population than had been the Third Reich, and while popular discontent would have been impotent against the regime in 1989 had international circumstances been different, in the event, popular discontent—from whatever mix of motives—had been decisively expressed. The east Germans who felt "colonized" did not want another communist dictatorship; the vague sense of loss felt by so many had other objects. East Germans felt disoriented, destabilized, uncertain, devalued. They missed the security and predictability of their former lives—a feeling empirically and analytically quite distinct from wishing for a return to the political conditions that had made life secure and predictable. The general sources of these feelings were not hard to identify: not their presence but rather their absence would have posed the explanatory problem. Within months, without warning, without the self-evident destructiveness of a war, the environment in which 16 million men, women, and children lived their lives and envisioned their futures had changed radically. Value scales were revised; the rules and the very language used to conduct political and social relations changed; borders opened; the sleepy, run-down villages and cities of the DDR acquired a new face; consumer goods became available; the crime rate increased. That most of these changes signaled broader opportunities did not make them any less un-settling, and people viewed the new opportunities from quite different material and psychological points of departure.

Not all the changes were favorable: the world of work had been pro-foundly disrupted. Factories were boarded up, property titles were un-certain, and the environmental disaster created by East Germany's com-munist leadership was now measured by west German standards. Jobs vanished (one third within three years after unification); indeed, a whole way of life seemed to collapse.[119] In a culture where work was a central value and where unemployment had been unknown, the unemploy-ment figures climbed steadily. In April 1996, 3.967 million people (10.4 percent of the work force) were without work in Germany. The unem-ployment rate in the former East Germany, where 1.2 million people were without work, was 16.0 percent: this was a far cry from the "bloom-ing countrysides" that Kohl had promised in 1990. Between October 1995 and April 1996, 425,500 apprenticeship positions were available to 415,900 applicants in ex–West Germany; 68,300 positions were available for 178,000 applicants in ex–East Germany.[120] In Brandenburg, 191,100 people (15.6 percent) were without work. Available apprenticeship posi-tions in Brandenburg fell by 8.3 percent between April 1995 and April 1996; 27,140 young people competed for 9,090 positions.[121] Unemploy-ment rose more quickly in the five new Länder and in ex–East Berlin between April 1995 and April 1996 than it did in any of the old Länder: joblessness rose 2.4 percent in east Berlin and Saxony-Anhalt (to 13.7 percent and 18.0 percent, respectively), 2.1 percent in Brandenburg and Saxony (to 15.6 percent and 15.4 percent, respectively), and 1.9 percent in Mecklenburg–Western Pomerania and Thuringia (to 17.0 percent and 16.1 percent, respectively).[122]

To the disorientation was added a sense of disempowerment: normal citizens felt buffeted by forces beyond their control. In the spring of 1995, east Germans described themselves as relatively "insecure," "not enterprising," "provincial," "not good at decisions," "dependent," and "modest," in contrast to west Germans, whom east Germans viewed as "self-confident," "enterprising," "open-minded," "good at decisions," "independent," and "superior."[123] New elites—even those not marginalized in electoral competition—seemed to feel out of place in the various corridors of power in united Germany, where the economic needs of their constituents did not provide them with an attractive visiting card. Efforts to organize bipartisan parliamentary caucuses to defend the specific interests of east Germans fizzled, overwhelmed by the partisan logic of (west) German politics. In 1996, Stolpe expressed a sentiment widely shared by other east Germans in public life: "We often feel that it is relatively hard for us to get our point of view across in Bonn . . . I often feel as though I had flown straight in from the Congo."[124]

The perceived disenfranchisement of east Germans contributed significantly to the "nervosity" of the German body politic in the years following unification,[125] and to the development of distinctive forms of electoral behavior in the new Länder. Before the investigation of Stolpe's past began, the minister president was certainly the most powerful and articulate east German in national politics, and was often mentioned as a possible successor to President Weizsäcker. The drumbeat of accusations leveled against him after January 1992 raised enough awkward questions to leave him politically handicapped in the national political arena. During the seemingly endless leadership crisis that afflicted the SPD in the mid-1990s, no one mentioned Stolpe as an alternative to the west Germans who dominated (if only by their ineptitude) the party's stage. Stolpe became instead the chair of the party's new Forum Ostdeutschland, a body created in January 1996 and meant to serve in part as an amplifier for airing east German problems and perspectives and in part as a transmission belt between the party and potential supporters in the new Länder.[126] Would the integrity of the democratic process have been better served by less curiosity about Manfred Stolpe's personal past? No one, after all, had accused Stolpe of subscribing to a genocidal ideology or of stocking concentration camps with victims. Nor was either his personal record or his present discourse as dubious or contradictory as those represented by Robert Lindet. What kind of politics did Stolpe in fact encourage, and how did various audiences respond? What can his appeal and its reach tell us about the "common sense" of contemporary Germany?

Stolpe's record before and after unification suggests a pragmatist with principles, little inclined to prolonged introspection.[127] Courted from all sides, Stolpe joined the SPD in the summer of 1990. He explained his choice by citing the overwhelming importance of social questions (employment, housing, and so on) in the transitional period after unification and the "decisive role for social justice" that the SPD had historically played.[128] Before 1989, Stolpe looked for possibilities where others saw only dead ends. After 1989, he did the same: not for nothing is a collection of his speeches and writings titled *Den Menschen Hoffnung geben* (To Give People Hope). Empowerment—of Christians in the hostile environment of the DDR, of east Germans in the difficult environment of the new Federal Republic—has provided a constant theme of Stolpe's politics: a collection of Stolpe's speeches appeared under the title "Daring Democracy: Awakening in Brandenburg."[129] The empowerment theme was always coupled with a call to effort and the demand that people take responsibility for their shared fate. Rhetoric, of course, is not everything: it cannot replace the ability to set priorities, to judge human beings, to construct coalitions, to drive bargains, or to make decisions. But as political leaders in crisis situations have repeatedly demonstrated, rhetoric matters: it helps define the public agenda, it can mobilize energies, it can change the incentives to join a coalition, and it can shape a sense of community.

Just as Stolpe once insisted on the possibility of a learning process in the DDR, after unification he came to insist on the moral and material "readiness and also ability to learn" of his fellow citizens.[130] In his governmental declaration of December 6, 1990, Stolpe acknowledged that the sudden change "from dictatorship to democracy, from a centrally planned economy to a social market economy surprised us and overwhelmed us." Old strategies and prior experiences were now uncertain guides, and Stolpe saw in the "insecurity" (*Verunsicherung*: the word implies a process rather than simply a state) of his fellow citizens an important challenge to the political class. "Perhaps the most important task we face in political life," he said, "is to reinforce the self-confidence and self-esteem of our people!"[131]

Stolpe sought to foster the sense of capacity and self-worth of his fellow citizens in two related ways. Ex–East Germans, Stolpe argued, must not feel themselves or allow themselves to become "second-class Germans." Unlike the PDS, Stolpe made this argument without denigrating the Federal Republic or regretting unification. Instead, like de Gaulle, he did it by extending to the general population the credit rightly due only to the resistance. Also unlike the PDS, Stolpe portrayed his fellow citizens as subjects, not objects, of their own history:

> The breathtaking changes in Germany, the bloodless revolution that led to freedom, is our achievement; we resisted usurpation and shook off the tutelage to which we had been subjected. We did it on our own, not without fear, but with courage and determination.
>   . . . We will seize the opportunity that freedom and unity offer us. And we will perceive that opportunity with the advantages we gained in the shadow of our disadvantages during the last decades: with our will to survive and our patience, with our adaptability and our social ties, with our tenacity and our proven courage.[132]

A strong sense of identity normally contributes to feelings of self-confidence. Stolpe had little sympathy for what already in June 1990 he was calling the "melancholy memory of the good old DDR," identified with intellectuals whose vision of a reformed but independent DDR had been defeated.[133] He did not support the November 1989 appeal "Für unser Land," which sought to forestall the dissolution of a separate DDR entity and identity (see Chapter 2). In March 1990, during the debate over whether the ex-DDR should simply "accede" as new Länder to the Federal Republic under Article 23 of the Basic Law or whether unification should await the elaboration of a new, all-German constitution as provided for under Article 146, Stolpe spoke in favor of Article 23, even though he acknowledged that this choice would simply defer more difficult adjustments to a future moment. East Germans were in no mood for further experiments, he declared, and any recourse to Article 146 would necessarily involve both time and uncertainty. The adjustments themselves required a stable domestic and international environment, and Article 23 was more conducive to stability than Article 146.

In the place of an inappropriate "Ostalgie," and in lieu of equally unavailable pride in being German, Stolpe reminded his constituents that as Brandenburgers, they had a long and distinguished history; he spoke willingly of local history, and did not shy from its symbols. He warned against Prussia's dark side: militarism, expansionism, authoritarianism. Even more insistently, however, he recalled Prussian virtues: selfless dedication to duty and the public good, thrift, organizational capacity, reliability, but also—lest these virtues seem politically neutral and therefore open to abuse—tolerance.[134]

After the Berlin-Brandenburg merger referendum failed, Wolfgang Birthler suggested that Brandenburgers refusing the merger may have in fact been voting *for* Stolpe (whom they did not wish to lose in a new political configuration), and Stolpe himself called the result a vote for Brandenburg, rather than against Berlin.[135] Disentangling the many reasons why different people found Stolpe attractive is as difficult as characterizing the discontent felt by east Germans, and for many of the same reasons. Thus, it is hard to know whether Stolpe won support most effectively by appealing openly to his fellow citizens' good side (through a discourse of responsibility and empowerment) or by appealing subconsciously to their bad side (because his ambiguous record served as a justification and/or excuse for their own past compromises). Stolpe's critics suspected the latter form of attraction, and were appalled when Egon Bahr, claiming that it was the SPD's special mission to reclaim the PDS's electorate for the republic and arguing for a judicial *Schlußstrich* under the record of the DDR, retroactively justified Adenauer's stubborn refusal to retire Hans Globke: "The external symbol of reconciliation with Nazi followers was of course the presence of Globke in the chancellor's office. At the time I thought it was wrong. In retrospect I have to say: Today I see it as one of Adenauer's great achievements as a statesman."[136]

It may well be that the *combined* appeal—to empowerment and to bad conscience—was a significant part of what made Stolpe such a popular figure and compelling mediator between former and present political realities. Survey data suggest a mixed picture of how east Germans view their own past. In 1995, an overwhelming 97 percent of an Emnid sample agreed with the statement: "The only people in a position to talk about life in the DDR are people who lived there." Presented with the statement "I can be proud of my life in the DDR, because I made the best I could out of it and got only as involved with the regime as was unavoidable," 75 percent of the sample said that the statement applied fully (36 percent) or in large part (39 percent) to them. Furthermore, those questioned also said that the statement applied to others: to "almost everybody" (8 percent), to "most people" (41 percent), and to "about half the population" (30 percent).[137] While most east Germans continued to believe that the Stasi archives should be preserved, a steadily increasing proportion agreed with the statement "One should close the books on those forty years": in 1990, 23 percent agreed, in 1995, a majority of respondents (54 percent) agreed. By 1995, only 42 percent agreed with the alternative statement proposed, "First we have to clarify who acted shabbily" ("wer sich schuldig gemacht hat"); this was down from 73 percent in 1990 and 55 percent in 1992.[138] Whether the support for a *Schlußstrich* represented primarily disappointment with how and against whom accountability had been assessed (in trials, bureaucratic proceedings, or in the media) or a rejection of the notion of accountability itself was unclear—and the first kind of disappointment itself embraces many possible motives and meanings.

Like Kurt Biedenkopf, Stolpe was described as a sort of monarch.[139] Democratizing communities have known other republican monarchs: Charles de Gaulle was often so described, and Gordon Craig wrote of Konrad Adenauer that he "was the first German stateman who was able to overcome the unconscious tendency of his countrymen to believe that leaders could only be taken seriously when they wore uniforms."[140] Unlike de Gaulle and Adenauer, however, Stolpe did not practice an authoritarian style of authority. For all his eagerness to make things happen, he was more comfortable as a moderator than as a decision maker and consistently preferred consensus to confrontation.[141] It is also not clear that the former East Germans who voted in such overwhelming numbers for Stolpe and Biedenkopf were satisfying a potentially undemocratic thirst for authority or stability, as was often alleged. Both men exemplified a style of leadership that was also applauded in the old Länder—and which Helmut Kohl did not represent: like Richard von Weizsäcker (CDU) and Johannes Rau (SPD), both of whom enjoyed consistently high ratings, Stolpe and Biedenkopf were men who sought to integrate rather than to polarize, but who nonetheless took clear stands on issues they considered important.

Stolpe's governmental record was mixed, marred by the usual financial scandals (including one centered on mismanagement by the popular minister for social affairs, Regine Hildebrandt) and budget deficits and marked after 1994 by constant tensions between Stolpe and the SPD parliamentary group, which commanded a majority of seats in the Landtag after that year's elections. In his government declaration of November 18, 1994, Stolpe presented a laundry list of sixty goals—too long a list to focus energies or to facilitate accountability. But two issues seemed central to Stolpe during both his administrations: reducing unemployment, and creating a single federal state in Berlin-Brandenburg.

In 1996 unemployment was over 15 percent in every one of the five new Länder. In 1994 Stolpe had set bringing the Brandenburg rate below 10 percent as a goal of his second administration. It seemed unlikely that this goal would be met; the government's economic strategy was at any rate tied to plans to merge Berlin and Brandenburg. Those plans failed.

On May 5, 1996, Stolpe suffered his first major political defeat: by a margin of 62.7 percent to 36.5 percent, Brandenburg voters rejected a proposed merger between their state and Berlin (Table 5.2). The merger was approved by Berlin voters 53.4 percent to 45.7 percent, but since the merger required the approval of voters in both states, the Brandenburgers' refusal was decisive.[142]

The referendum brought to naught four years of negotiation; Stolpe spoke of a "rubble heap." Berlin's CDU mayor, Eberhard Diepgen, and Stolpe had signed the merger treaty on April 27, 1995; the first formal discussions between the two parties had been held on February 29, 1992, shortly after Stolpe confirmed his contacts with the Stasi in the *Spiegel* article. In the late fall of 1994, the Brandenburg CDU and PDS, but also the SPD, demanded changes to the draft treaty as it then stood. By the time the treaty cleared the Brandenburg Landtag (by a vote of 64 to 24) and the Berlin assembly (by a vote of 188 in favor, 43 against, and 2 abstentions) on June 22, 1995, it was clear that important elements within Stolpe's SPD and Diepgen's CDU would resist the treaty's final ratification. From the beginning, Berlin's powerful CDU parliamentary leader Klaus Landowsky barely disguised his opposition, and three days before the referendum vote, Wolfgang Birthler, the SPD parliamentary leader in Potsdam, voiced his reservations in an interview carried in the *Tagesspiegel*.[143] In April 1995 (i.e., a year before the vote), a poll had

Table 5.2   Berlin-Brandenburg Merger Referendum, May 5, 1996 (percent)

	Berlin	Ex–East Berlin	Ex–West Berlin	Brandenburg
Participation	57.8	54.7	59.8	66.6
Yes	53.4	44.5	58.7	36.5
No	45.7	54.7	40.3	62.7

6666666 indicated that 62 percent of voting-age Berliners favored the merger treaty, 25 percent opposed it, 10 percent had no opinion, and 3 percent did not care. At the time, support was actually higher (69 percent in favor) in ex–East Berlin than it was in the western part of the city (57 percent).[144]

The treaty's supporters then made what proved a fatal tactical error. The Brandenburgers had pressed for a referendum date in early October, before the scheduled Berlin elections, and for the presentation of the treaty as part of the completion of German unification (whose anniversary would be celebrated on October 3). Elements within the Berlin CDU, however, preferred a later date, and the vote was finally set for May 5, 1996. In the intervening months the atmosphere soured, especially in Berlin, where the electoral campaign sharpened inter- and intraparty tensions: the CDU claimed that a vote for the SPD (its coalition partner) would be an invitation to an SPD-PDS city government; the character of the CDU campaign plus the SPD's poor electoral performance strengthened elements within the SPD hostile to a continued grand coalition with the CDU; the formation of a new government took months of intra- and interparty negotiation; and Berlin's budget deficit became front-page news. The advertising campaign launched on behalf of the merger was perceived as either empty (as in a poster showing two naked toddlers smiling at each other, with the words, "Together we are strong": "too many pink clouds," Stolpe commented self-critically as he cast his ballot on May 5[145]) or perfidious (as in the CDU poster that proclaimed, without other comment, "For a Christian Prussia," most immediately a hostile reference to Brandenburg's recent incorporation of a course on lifestyles, ethics, and religion into its school curriculum, and more generally a reminder that in a merged Berlin-Brandenburg, the left would enjoy a political majority). By April 27, 1996, a *Tagesspiegel* poll indicated deepening opposition to the merger, with only 45 percent in Berlin and 33 percent in Brandenburg favoring it, and 39 percent and 47 percent opposed.[146] "The biggest proposed political innovation in the Federal Republic, Stolpe's most important strategic goal," the *Tagesspiegel's* Potsdam correspondent reported, "now hangs by a thread."[147]

Stolpe and Diepgen had both campaigned relentlessly for the merger, and Stolpe continued to make its acceptance his cause, even as it became clear that the referendum was likely to fail in Brandenburg. Asked one week before the vote whether he would view a negative vote as a "personal defeat," Stolpe replied simply, "Yes."[148] A Brandenburg campaign poster sought to exploit loyalty to Stolpe while urging voters to think of the future: showing Stolpe's self-confident face, it read, "Those who think ahead say 'Yes!'" But the merger's Brandenburg opponents voted against the merger, not against Stolpe. "I'm for him," a middle-aged woman told a reporter at a rally the day before the vote, and added, "but this time I'm voting no." The reporter asked for her reason: "Brandenburg should remain Brandenburg."[149] It was as though Stolpe had provided his constituents with an island of psychological security, and now—too soon—had asked them to give it up. Already in late March, Stolpe had acknowledged that the merger decision was both a substantive question and "a very emotional matter." As he explained, "The existential experience from the DDR period was that the capital city, Berlin, had to be supported by the rural population or by the population of the whole country, that everything worth anything went to Berlin and that one just had to work more. That feeling sits deep." He added what later became his primary explanation for the referendum's failure: "After these five years of enormous disruption and change, there is something like a need for a rest."[150] Brandenburg had voted against experiments.

In fact, the results were more complex than the crude opposition between ex-East and ex-West suggested. On closer examination, the data revealed two more subtle patterns. First, and expectedly, the proposed merger fared poorly in districts where the PDS was strongest (e.g., Hohenschönhausen in east Berlin, where 62.7 percent voted against the merger). Claiming that a merger was a good idea but that the treaty before the voters was a bad treaty, the PDS had campaigned with closed ranks in favor of a no vote. But PDS opposition alone, no matter how unanimous, would not have sufficed to defeat the proposition. The second pattern suggested that support for the merger correlated positively with perceptions of material and psychological security, with experiences of mutually beneficial cooperative relations with "outsiders," and possibly with the ability to reach back to memories of the region before 1945. This second pattern seemed to explain why west Berlin's wealthy western suburb, Zehlendorf, produced the highest total for the merger (67.9 percent), while Brandenburg communities gripped by the dislocations of unification and too far from Berlin to have engaged in cooperative problem solving—as well as less privileged neighborhoods in west Berlin— voted overwhelmingly against the merger.[151] It also accounted for the opposition among younger age cohorts in both Berlin and Brandenburg (see Table 5.3).[152] Young people would allegedly have benefited most

Table 5.3   Berlin-Brandenburg Merger: Support by Age Group (in percent)

	18–24 years	25–34	35–44	45–59	60+
Berlin	46	51	53	68	70
Brandenburg	24	27	33	50	61

from the merger's long-term positive effects, but they were also more likely to be exposed to the harsh realities of the labor market in the present. They experienced what Stolpe rather bluntly called "something like competition anxiety compounded by a feeling of inferiority."[153]

Such was the fight Stolpe chose to fight—and the fight he lost. Despite its apparently technical character, the merger was an important question, and the battle on its behalf was one of the more honorable ones in recent German politics. Stolpe and Diepgen, across party lines and over significant opposition from within their own political camps, had conceived a project and negotiated an agreement that in the nearly unanimous opinion of Germany's political and socioeconomic elites not only would have had a positive effect on the future development of Berlin and Brandenburg, but also might have had a positive ripple effect across the republic, encouraging the reconfiguration of other federal states (increasing, for example, the pressure on Bremen to merge with Lower Saxony)[154] and the revitalization of German federalism. The merger had been an imaginative, constructive attempt to respond to the opportunities and the challenges created by German unification. Its advantages were treated as almost self-evident by the elites—mainstream political figures, business and trade union leaders, the Protestant bishop of Berlin-Brandenburg, journalists—who supported it. "It is crazy," Diepgen argued, "a state—Brandenburg—with a hole in the middle."[155] While more reasoned, Walther Stützle's "Merger—What Else!" was indicative of this sense of the self-evident nature of the case. Stützle spoke of the future: "It is crucial to avoid the losses that would certainly follow a refusal to merge, and to preserve at the same time the opportunity for economic expansion. No one can argue that Europe needs a common market plus a political union, but that Berlin-Brandenburg can get by fine as ministates. It is that simple."[156]

But it was not so simple. Stützle's plea, willfully or not, ignored the fact that the necessity and benefits of European integration were also more obvious to the country's elites than to its larger population, and he overestimated the voters' inclination to disregard memories of ill-advised elite decisions in the past and to heed sound elite advice in the present. In this case, Stolpe's undiminished personal popularity was an inadequate counterweight to the distrust many voters felt toward more distant, more anonymous elites. The referendum experience illustrated a vicious circle with broader validity, not just in national politics but across the advanced industrial democracies: public distrust of politicians hindered the elaboration and implementation of innovative policy responses to problems, and the lack of innovative policies compounded public distrust of politicians.

In this scenario, and despite the many shortcomings of his administrations, Stolpe seemed on balance more part of the solution than part of the problem. At the very least, Nooke's description of him as an unprincipled backroom intriguer "interested only in staying in power" seemed wide of the mark. Nooke himself had sided with the merger's opponents, making the same appeal to anxiety that the PDS, more experienced in the genre, made much more loudly and effectively.[157]

In the hours following the announcement of the referendum results, Stolpe appeared to be contemplating resignation. He did not, however, resign (and only isolated voices called for his resignation); he was not, he repeated, one to run away.[158] It was an interesting formulation, and again a constant theme of Stolpe's politics, to which different observers could assign a different moral value: to Stolpe, the "Kirche im Sozialismus" had also represented a way of not running away, as had his conversations with the Stasi. No matter how unfavorable the terms of service, Stolpe would stay at his post: "The word 'resignation' is not part of my vocabulary!"[159] Asked very late on the night of the returns how he felt, Stolpe replied, "Tired, and full of ideas about all the things we must do tomorrow."[160] However rehearsed the response may have sounded, it also expressed a genuine attitude.

Stolpe linked his post-unification practice of politics as the art of the possible to his earlier political commitments, and reiterated his appreciation of other, more intransigent approaches. When Bärbel Bohley called for Stolpe's resignation, Stolpe responded:

> I have no adversarial feelings toward Bärbel Bohley . . . In her call for my resignation I can only recognize an old quarrel—almost a religious

war—between purists and pragmatists. What is tragic about it is that
the desire for change had for long years united us. I said to myself: it is
good that we have such people, who without pausing to think about
what can be achieved at the moment, nonetheless say what kind of day
after tomorrow they hope for. I wish that Bärbel Bohley and her friends
would tell us today what they hope the day after tomorrow will be like,
as they told us from 1983 to 1989.[161]

Later, after the controversy surrounding his own past had subsided,
Stolpe succinctly summarized an anger he could understand—and assessed the political costs the anger had involved:

I think that some of the prominent representatives of the opposition
movement feel cheated out of their inheritance. They say: we risked our
heads—but Stolpe first made compromises and then on top of it made a
career. Unfortunately, the former dissidents haven't been able to influence the new Federal Republic much—contrary to what I would have
hoped. We could have used their imagination and their energy—but
many of them are still turning circles around the past.[162]

In the Federal Republic as in the DDR, Stolpe would in all likelihood
have used the ex-dissidents rather than joined them, had they remained
more central players in the political game: he would have used their
goals as orientation markers (alongside others), and he would have used
their militance as a bargaining chip to promote a more moderate program. This is a standard story in the history of successful reformist
politics; the instrumentalization it involves understandably disappoints
those who are instrumentalized, but the result is often the adoption of
reforms that might otherwise have been blocked. Later, we remember the
reforms and forget the instrumentalization that facilitated their passage.

The debate about Manfred Stolpe resonated in ways that the courtroom
trials of political figures did not. It resonated despite the inevitable but
distracting chase after the elusive piece of paper that would definitively
prove Stolpe's guilt or innocence, the partisan distortions, and the lamentable spectacle of journalists paying former Stasi officers for their supposed knowledge of the case. Germans both east and west faced the
moral dilemmas Stolpe faced, and so too, in a less urgent way, did non-
German citizens of NATO countries who took part in the debate over
détente. Stolpe almost certainly practiced something less than full disclo-

sure when discussing his past—whether with the Landtag, the public, or possibly even himself. But Stolpe's stance in the DDR also indicated a coherent ethical position: he chose to press as effectively as possible within the system for whatever reforms could be achieved. His conduct was hard to judge in part because the uncertainty over exactly what he did in private was compounded by an incomplete understanding of what the consequences of his public actions, or of Western détente policies, really were. In what ways did the type of dialogue Stolpe fostered in the DDR make dissent more possible and a "Chinese solution" to the protests of October 1989 less likely, and in what ways may it have helped stabilize a regime while compromising its subjects? In what ways did détente accelerate or retard the demise of communism on the European continent? Stolpe's choices challenge our ideas about the moral compasses we carry, and may remind us to heed Havel's warning that our moral identity is never something "completed and unquestionable . . . something one can husband like anything else, that one can use, depend on, draw on and, every so often, give a new coat of paint." But his choices should also remind us that political decisions are always contextual, and that our knowledge of politics is incomplete. If the debate about Stolpe's past was inconclusive, it was perhaps inevitably and appropriately so.

The debate about Stolpe's present and future, by contrast, had immediate practical consequences and implications. In a political system confronting the daunting task of integrating 16 million new citizens whose economy was in collapse and who had no prior experience of democratic government or a market economy, the type of leadership Stolpe exemplified was, it would seem, both "usable" and "useful." The controversy reduced the sphere in which Stolpe himself could exercise leadership, depriving the German body politic as a whole of an important resource. At most Stolpe became, as his position as leader of the SPD's Forum Ostdeutschland demonstrated, an ambassador of east German interests—and one many west Germans viewed as compromised.

Calculating that only some 300,000 East Germans worked for the Stasi, Joachim Gauck concluded, "We weren't a people of informants, and the well-meant excuses are as inappropriate as the slanderous judgment."[163] Stolpe's call to democratic participation, in contrast, did not prejudge the question whether working for the Stasi constituted the only meaningful form of collaboration or source of enduring identification with the fallen regime; rather, it sought, within limits, to separate past commitments from present duties. It gave people, individually and col-lectively, a second chance—not because they deserved it (that question is simply not posed), but because giving people second chances is part of the job of a democracy. The empowerment Stolpe proposed recalls, but in far more favorable circumstances, Hamlet's appeal to his mother, as the young prince begs Gertrude to part from the man who had become her husband and king after murdering his own brother and sovereign—which in turn recalls how West Germans learned democracy in the fifty years that followed the war: "Assume a virtue, if you have it not." As-sume a virtue, if you have it not; assume their virtue, if they have it not: these are the standard recommendations of an institutional strategy, "for use," as Hamlet adds, "almost can change the stamp of nature." The conflict over different mixes of institutional and cultural strategies is in part a conflict over the significance of the word "almost."

Six

The Crisis of Democracy, the PDS, and Party Politics in Unified Germany

By the mid-1990s, communist successor parties had carved out important political roles in a number of countries that had experienced communist dictatorships—most notably in Hungary, Poland, and Russia. In Germany, the continuing strength of the PDS in the five new Länder and th former East Berlin had finally provoked a substantive debate among other political actors. Successor parties may represent risks to democratic politics—most obviously because of what they are, and less obviously because of the responses they sometimes elicit. The relationship between a successor party and the broader partisan environment is critical in shaping the impact of the party's presence on democratic consolidation, understood in this context as indicated by the type and level of competition characteristic of the party system, the type and level of trust that citizens appear to invest in the mechanisms of representative politics, and the willingness of citizens to embrace the values of a democratic political culture. How the relationship between the successor party and the partisan environment develops depends at least as much on the leadership, resources, and referential world of political figures *outside* the successor party and on patterns of cleavage within the society as it does on the specific character and political record of the successor party; that is, it depends in part on the inclination and ability of political elites in competing parties to pursue different mixes of institutional and cultural strategies with regard to the successor party and its electorate. In post-Terrorist France, ex-Terrorists participated in and sought to control the debate about reconciliation. Gregor Gysi may sometimes sound like Robert Lindet, but in post-communist Germany other players, firmly anchored in a well-established democratic system, are masters of the political field.

An institutional strategy makes democratic normality a result of inclusion; a cultural strategy makes it a precondition. In the partisan politics of unified Germany, a cultural strategy represented the course of least resistance, but not the optimal course.

In the first part of this chapter, I analyze the impact of the crisis of representation in pre-unification Germany on leadership and public discourse during the transition period. I argue that the preexisting crisis of representation raised the political costs of certain leadership options, making it difficult to pursue an optimal mix of cultural and institutional strategies. Most important, the crisis of representation made an argument from state capacity during the unification period nearly impossible. Absent the belief in a "can-do" state, it was very difficult to argue for unification and significant material sacrifices. Instead, Helmut Kohl made promises. The promises he made left the CDU potentially exposed. Kohl responded, as I show in the second section, by using the PDS as a weapon to discredit the SPD—which in turn made the pursuit of an institutional strategy by the SPD seem politically suicidal. In the third section of the chapter, I argue that the central element of the PDS's message, the one that undergirded both its ideological ambiguities and its emotional appeal, is what could be called its alibi culture. Previous experiences with anti-system and extremist parties in established democracies—and the Federal Republic is an established democracy—suggest that German democracy would be well served if its elites decided to overcome an alibi culture with an institutional strategy.

Structural Obstacles to Democratic Leadership

Democracies, it is often said, do not make leaders the way they used to. Since the explanation presumably does not lie in the genetic pool, it must lie elsewhere: in the way leaders are recruited and/or in the setting in which leadership is exercised. In this section I offer an argument about how the setting shapes leadership possibilities in contemporary democracies, and specifically about how the setting shaped leadership strategies during the period around German unification.

There are two common accounts of Helmut Kohl's leadership during that period. Somewhat oversimplified, they could be summarized as follows. According to the first account, Kohl moved decisively and brilliantly, taking advantage of a unique set of international circumstances, adjusting quickly to the rapidly evolving situation in the DDR, and leading West German opinion; the result was unification, to the accompaniment of well-deserved external and domestic applause. On the second account, Kohl achieved unification by selling both West and East Germans a false bill of goods: motivated by nationalist sentiments (however muted their public expression), he promised unification without pain ("in four or five years, blooming countrysides"), even though the coming difficulties were already discernible.

Hans-Jochen Vogel, at the time both the party and parliamentary leader of the SPD, offered a more analytically sensitive account, fundamentally (though politely) critical of both Kohl and his unsuccessful SPD challenger in the December 1990 Bundestag elections, Oskar Lafontaine. Lafontaine, Vogel recalled in late 1995, had shown characteristic disregard for party discipline during the unification process, and in his insistence on the possible detrimental effects of unification on the social safety net protecting West Germans, he had seemed mean-spirited and narrowly partisan. While Lafontaine, "with his pessimistic prognoses, was right on several points," his failure to propose "a realistic alternative" to the government's strategy was politically fatal.[1] In his willing embrace of partisan argument, however, Lafontaine mirrored his CDU opponent.

The SPD's failure to articulate a "realistic alternative" is partially explained by the speed at which events moved during the spring and summer of 1990, but it was also in part the product of a structure of political opportunity that encouraged certain kinds of political discourse (e.g., Lafontaine's appeal to concerns about economic security) and strategies (e.g., Kohl's partisanship) and discouraged others. That same structure of political opportunity shaped both the political environment the PDS then entered and the way other actors responded to the PDS. Political leadership may always be unique, but it is never truly an accident.

Modern political democracy has at least two important definitional aspects. Together they make citizenship, or the personal expression of popular sovereignty, meaningful. First, we recognize a democracy in part by the set of rights it guarantees and the institutions typically constructed for the task of guaranteeing those rights. The rights include freedom of expression, thought, and assembly, the protection of private property, due process and equality before the law, and the right to vote. The institutional arrangements we associate with the preservation of these rights include politically responsible executives, freely elected parliaments, independent judiciaries, and "market" economies.

But modern democracies are also, and just as important, defined by a type of political life. The key actors of contemporary democratic politics are competitive political parties; in contrast, both corporatist mechanisms and personalized, media-driven campaigns undermine the kind of accountability that democratic politics seeks to ensure. Parties socialize elites and electorates; they articulate demands, compete for votes, organize public choices, and, at different times, either mobilize support for the government or propose alternatives (both human and programmatic).

Institutions and even rights are easier to "export" to countries formerly ruled by dictatorships than is a type of political life. Furthermore, while individual rights have in some ways been more and more expansively understood and protected in the established democracies since the 1960s, political parties seem increasingly inadequate agents of public choice, and the complex political culture that combined participation and deference, equality and authority, solidarity and self-reliance, discipline and autonomous responsibility, seems less and less descriptive of social reality in any democracy. The increasing emphasis on private rights and the declining effectiveness of public actors are mutually reinforcing trends: the waning faith in public actors helps explain both the hypersensitivity of large portions of democratic electorates to "law and order" issues and the renewed attention to questions of political membership. In the absence of notable collective political endeavors and achievements (both announced and recognized as collective efforts), the old liberal emphasis on personal security has reemerged triumphant. As the institutions in which membership was played out (parties, trade unions, citizen armies, the school system) have weakened, people have become less certain of the bonds that tie them to others whom they do not "know," but with whom they feel thrown together and whom they now perceive to represent primarily a potential burden. "Friendship," whether private or public, always represents a potential burden, balanced in a voluntary relationship by some mix of pleasure, affection, habit, and solidarity; in a forced acquaintance, attention focuses on the potential burdens because the compensating or countervailing factors are absent. The resulting emphasis on security and the shrinking circles of solidarity in turn complicate the tasks of public actors seeking to organize choices and justify sacrifices. Political parties still "represent" particular interests, as indeed they always did; only rarely, however, can they mobilize popular energies around a redefined set of public priorities with clear and immediate costs and only future benefits.

The "crisis of democracy," in Germany as in the other advanced industrial democracies, is therefore more accurately termed a crisis of democratic party systems, in part the cause and in part the product of a crisis in democratic political culture. It is one of the ironies—and inconveniences—of history that communist successor parties became participants in newly competitive party systems at a time when established competitive party systems were in what many observers considered a crisis, and it is Germany's dubious privilege to be the only country simultaneously confronted by the challenges of democratization and by a "crisis of democracy" otherwise typical of the advanced industrial democracies since the mid-1970s. In Germany the party system was at the center of federal President Richard von Weizsäcker's controversial critique of public life in the spring of 1992; Weizsäcker accused the "party state" of being "obsessed with power during elections and unconscious of power when it comes to the perception of the substantive and conceptual tasks of leadership."[2] Party politicians, Weizsäcker alleged, showed a "constantly resurfacing defense mechanism against bipartisanship [*Überparteilichkeit*: suprapartisanship]," and viewed problems not as opportunities for finding solutions, but as potential weapons to be used against political opponents.[3] The perceived inadequacies of the parties were lamented by the chorus of media voices that declared 1992 to be the year of *Politikverdrossenheit* (a combination of impatience with, lack of interest in, and disdain for politics), and those voices were regularly sanctioned by the electorate in public opinion polls and elections.

The political tasks associated with unification—including political reconciliation—thus had to be fed through a system already under significant pressure. In this context, institutional strategies were too demanding to be sustained: they presupposed an institutional self-confidence that was not present, and a readiness on the part of political actors not to use the PDS to discredit their traditional competitors. But cultural strategies compounded the pre-existing problems, reinforcing a tendency to emphasize identity issues centered on either immigration or alleged Stasi connections and further weakening the bases of constructive party competition. Politicians already lame in one foot shot themselves in the other foot. Mutatis mutandis, this context, and indeed these results, are not unique to Germany. They provide a useful window on the complications of democratic politics in both democratizing countries and established democracies. The view through the window should temper any lingering traces of the triumphalism unleashed by the supposedly definitive "victory" of democracy over its competitors that so excited some observers in 1989.

The main features of the crisis afflicting democratic party systems have become familiar to students of politics in the advanced industrial democracies: they include partisan dealignment; the sudden rise (often followed by an equally sudden fall) of new parties and new leaders; declining confidence in political processes, institutions, and public figures; increasing recourse to nonparliamentary, nonelectoral forms of political action; and rising abstention rates. These phenomena are not as unilinear, universal, or clear as is sometimes asserted, but their existence and their cumulative effect are hard to overlook.

Everywhere, major parties have found it increasingly difficult to win and keep voters—let alone members. Between 1974 and 1995, the SPD's membership shrank and aged: membership dropped by over 10 percent, from nearly a million to 829,000, while the proportion of members under thirty-six dropped from 31 percent to 15 percent (this age cohort represented 16 percent of the general population in 1974 and 17 percent in 1995).[4] In the Bundestag elections of 1976, 74 percent of the electorate voted as it had voted in 1972; 17 percent changed their vote, and 9 percent did not vote. In 1990 the corresponding figures were 56 percent, 23 percent, and 21 percent: voter loyalty had fallen steadily, and abstentions had steadily risen.[5]

Trust and different kinds of political satisfaction (distinguishing between assessments of leaders, parties, policies, institutions, and processes) are notoriously hard to measure and evaluate. Certainly the common perception among opinion makers and decision makers is that trust and satisfaction have declined. Early in the "electoral superyear" 1994, *Der Spiegel* published a lengthy article investigating "why citizens despise their politicians." The article included the results of a survey question asked in 1984 and repeated in 1993: "What traits do you think are typical of politicians? Please name all the traits that occur to you." In 1984 the ten character traits included, in order, "eloquence, experience, honesty, polemics, credibility, duplicity, tenacity, arrogance, corruptibility, ability to compromise." In 1993 the list had changed: "dishonesty, corruptibility, self-interest, inability to act, lack of credibility, lack of courage, obsession with power, incompetence, no positions, shortsightedness." To an open question about the qualities they wished to see in a politician, 63 percent of those polled responded "honesty."[6]

Wolfgang Schäuble, former federal minister of the interior and parliamentary leader of the CDU/CSU in the Bundestag in the mid-1990s, tried to introduce a positive note into the discussion by arguing that at least the German situation was not as bad as the Italian one. Italy could nonetheless serve as a useful warning, Schäuble acknowledged, "for here too, the reputation of parties and politicians has hit a low point."[7] Few contradicted Schäuble's perception—and whatever the "facts," politicians and voters alike base their strategies on their perceptions.

Political scientists have characterized the crisis of representation as the by-product of governmental "overload," of a new "postindustrial" social structure and shifting values, and/or of the demise of the ideologies that once structured public debate and justified long-term loyalty to a specific political family.[8] The "overload" argument has been exploited by conservative parties, now eager to dismantle policies and programs put in place during the years of relative consensus around the ambitions and obligations of the welfare state. The argument has also been to a large extent conceded by social democratic and left-liberal parties. On this account, the expansion of political participation in the 1960s and the simultaneous diversification of groups able to press their demands directly on decision makers led governments to take on too many tasks, and too many contradictory tasks, in an environment where national governments in fact have less and less leverage over important policy results (especially economic performance). The argument asserts a connection between "overloaded" government and the decline in public trust. The alleged solution is to cut back on governmental programs, or at least on the resources available to governments: thus the radical unpopularity of any suggestion that taxes might have to be raised. President Bill Clinton, in his January 1996 State of the Union address, accepted that "the era of big government is over."[9] The same perception is evident in the evolution traced by the Socialist Party in France after 1983, and by the efforts of Tony Blair in England and of Rudolf Scharping, leader of the SPD from 1993 through 1995, to steer their respective parties toward the political "center."

Significantly, there is much more talk about rolling back government than there is about revitalizing the institutional mechanisms charged with the tasks of interest aggregation, enabling them to cope better with new types and levels of political participation, or about rethinking the means of policy implementation, harnessing new actors or new combinations to achieve old (or new) goals. Reimagining the mechanisms of representative government is indeed a daunting task.

Potentially part of the solution, political parties are instead at the center of the problem. Parties no longer serve as effective agents of democratic discipline, in large part because changes in social structure and the cultural environment have greatly complicated the disciplinary task. Subcultures once delivered voters to parties with relative reliability; now the subcultures are gone. The working class is a shrinking social group because working-class employment is no longer so common. But it is a shrinking subculture not just because working-class jobs are vanishing, but because of factors that help explain why other subcultures— regional, religious, ethnic—are also disintegrating or fragmenting: geographic mobility, access to education, less sturdy family structures, the demise of subculture-specific channels of information and the proliferation of individually controlled means of communication (from fax machines and photocopiers to the information highway), and the homogenizing omnipresence of television. In the place of large organizations—trade unions, churches—that stood at the interstices of specific subcultures, interests, and ideologies and commanded significant resources, a plethora of smaller but well-endowed organizations now vie for public influence.

The ideologies that organized Western political parties in the twentieth century have less and less mobilizing power, a development compounded by the end of the Cold War. The new "post-materialist" values, with their emphasis on individual fulfillment and the quality of life, do not offer the same disciplinary possibilities as the values they are allegedly replacing.

In this atmosphere of fragmented demand and dispersed resources, parties, and especially candidates, have come to rely increasingly on media strategies, and often on negative campaigning. Negative campaigning is hardly a new invention, but it assumes a different importance when it is the main political event, rather than a sideshow in a competition fundamentally organized around stable loyalties. Schäuble's account of how and why parties worked when they did may be schematically stated, but it is not idealized: "There were clear political alternatives on all the urgent problems and unresolved questions . . . Debate between the political parties was not a ritual exercise but a fight over basic questions and the future orientation of the country. Debate—the struggle over the definition of the right path—never appeared as an end in itself or as a self-absorbed therapy for the party."[10]

Schäuble wrote these words in 1994, before the "Summer Theater" performance of the SPD in 1995, during which the party's already long-standing preoccupation with itself and its family troubles eclipsed all efforts to focus on substantive problems. Schäuble's account suggests that parties sank into triviality—and therefore disgrace—because the grand questions to which they had proposed alternative solutions either had been resolved or had faded in importance. Absent collective projects with which broad segments of the public identify, public and private scandals dominate the news. The public seems increasingly disinclined or unable to differentiate between a public and a private scandal—and for many reasons, reporters, especially but not exclusively American reporters, feel less and less compelled to respect any limits on what they may ask or say. But the growing sense, often fed rather than fought by the left, that the state *could not* solve problems also distorted and trivialized public debate. Changes in political rules—the increased importance of presidential primaries in the United States, the use of referenda by parties and polities to decide political issues—tended to compound the process of fragmentation instead of bounding it. Unable to put together coalitions to support the provision of social services—from education to bridge repair to welfare—politicians, including politicians on the left, justified their impotence by arguing that the services were wasteful, thus further reducing their own margin for manuever.

The overall result has been a de-organization of political opinion, reflected simultaneously in the personalization of political competition and in the demise of the sort of political leadership that involves persuading publics to accept positions not immediately to their liking. It is almost certainly no accident that the only major Western political figure to have engaged consistently in the latter sort of leadership since the mid-1980s—trying to win people over to relatively unpopular positions—was Richard von Weizsäcker, who did not owe his position to popular election and whose alienation from his own political party in the 1990s became increasingly evident. The de-organization of politics is also visible in the (re)emergence of antiparliamentarian and/or extremist parties (e.g., the Front National in France or the Republikaner in Germany), of often ephemeral middle-class protest parties or movements (e.g., the German Statt Partei or Ross Perot's 1992 presidential campaign), of political groups (e.g., Greenpeace) that deliberately work through channels outside electoral and representative politics, and of mass protest movements that pride themselves on their organizational decentralization and informality (e.g., the demonstrations against the Front National and xenophobic legislation that took place in France in the winter and spring of 1997).

This environment has made state-mediated solidarity and sacrifices hard to organize everywhere, and it vastly increases the incentives politicians have to appeal to the politics of identity and to emphasize issues related to economic and physical security. Germany was in this respect no different from other advanced industrial democracies, but unification suddenly increased the need for sacrifice, the need for parties capable of organizing and socializing opinion, and the opportunities for engaging in the politics of identity.

Taken together, these developments—some supportive of liberal politics, most not—suggested that the Federal Republic of the 1980s and 1990s had become a "normal" advanced industrial democracy: it had been tested and had proven its stability under circumstances of political crisis (the terrorism of the 1970s) and economic difficulties (first in the 1960s, and again from the mid-1970s on), and it had demonstrated its ability to integrate potentially disruptive political forces (most notably the Greens). The possibilities for leadership had narrowed, and its electorate was as disgruntled as the electorates of its sister democracies. At the same time, like all other "normal" advanced industrial democracies, the Federal Republic had particular traits all its own: principally, a politically charged set of questions about German identity and a disinclination to allow those questions to be resolved by liberal values and by the everyday processes of a democratic community.[11]

Excluding the PDS: Preserving Democracy or Poisoning Its Wells?

In the developing relationship between the PDS and the established parties of the Federal Republic, the inclination to engage in cultural strategies seemed more powerful than the objective capacity to pursue institutional ones.

The results of the various elections held during the electoral superyear 1994 suggested—in addition to the general distemper described in the previous section—that the conditions of political competition in the Federal Republic were shifting, and more specifically, that the coalition options available to the CDU/CSU and to the SPD were changing. Two trends were visible in the electoral results: support for the FDP seemed increasingly thin, while the PDS seemed to be establishing an electoral base in the new Länder.

The continuing electoral difficulties of the FDP created, by anticipation, strategic complications for the CDU/CSU and the SPD. Neither party could realistically hope to achieve a parliamentary majority of its own. In the absence of the FDP, the CDU/CSU would have to choose between opposition, the formation of a minority government, and a grand coalition. The SPD, meanwhile, would have to look for support to the Bündnis 90/Greens—and possibly to the PDS—if it wished to return to power at the Federal level.

The solution adopted by Helmut Kohl could be summarized as follows. The CDU would maintain its coalition with the FDP as long as possible. It would preserve its future options by describing "grand coalitions" as undesirable but sometimes democratically necessary solutions to problems of parliamentary arithmetic. And above all, it would seek to weaken the opposition by constantly suggesting that a vote for the SPD would open the door to a government that would include "communists."

Kohl's strategy "worked" in the sense that it allowed the CDU to maintain its power and to keep the SPD off balance. The SPD refused to enter into a debate about alliance options, and could therefore respond only defensively—and ineffectively—to Kohl's strategy. The price was, first, a reinforced tendency to use cultural arguments and a corresponding denigration of the capacity of public institutions to socialize new political players. Second, the strategy further weakened the competitive character of the party system while contributing to support for the PDS in the new Länder.

Kohl's strategy—and the SPD response—unfolded in the long election year of 1994. Brandenburg held communal elections in December 1993. These were followed by state elections in Lower Saxony and communal elections in Schleswig-Holstein on March 13. Federal President Richard von Weizsäcker's successor was chosen by an electoral college on May 23. European elections were held on June 12. State elections were held in Saxony-Anhalt on June 26 (Baden-Württemberg, Mecklenburg–Western Pomerania, Rhineland-Palatinate, the Saarland, Saxony, Saxony-Anhalt, and Thuringia all held communal elections in June) and in Saxony, Bavaria, and Brandenburg on September 11. The second post-unification Bundestag elections were held on October 16 and accompanied by state elections in Mecklenburg–Western Pomerania and Thuringia. One year later, on October 22, 1995, Berlin went to the polls.

The Brandenburg communal elections of December 5, 1993, provided a warning signal: the PDS won 21.20 percent of the vote, coming in well behind Manfred Stolpe's SPD (34.51 percent) but just ahead of the CDU (20.55 percent). In the following months the PDS would emerge as a major issue.

As an indirect election, the selection of the new federal president could not serve as an indicator of voter preferences, but it did provide a sort of ideological preface to the general election campaign. In early September 1993, Helmut Kohl unexpectedly proposed Steffen Heitmann for the office. It was important, Kohl said, to fill the symbolically important position, which Weizsäcker had held since 1984, with an east German. Heitmann, born in 1944, was from Dresden. He had not been a hero under the DDR, but he had kept his hands clean. Like Stolpe, he had been a church official and a lawyer, but unlike Stolpe, he had tried to stay away from politics, and he had avoided the types of situations in which Stolpe had compromised himself. He did not become active in the opposition movement in Dresden until October 1989, but neither did he rush to join the CDU as the party system opened up. Only in December 1991—more than a year after unification—did he join the Saxon CDU; his adherence followed the departure of the party's compromised East-CDU leadership. When Kohl's unsolicited nomination came, Heitmann was serving as justice minister in Kurt Biedenkopf's cabinet; he was the only east German justice minister in the new Länder.

Heitmann's nomination immediately ran into a storm of criticism, not just from the opposition parties, but also from the FDP and from within the CDU. Only the CSU—and the extreme right—seemed pleased with Kohl's choice. Had Kohl reflected on Germany's double past and looked for a presidential candidate *less* likely to promote national integration or the development of an anti-totalitarian consensus, he would probably have been unable to find one. On the one hand, Heitmann's view of the DDR was uncompromising: he demanded "the prosecution of criminal guilt and the identification of moral guilt," and argued that "the concept of reconciliation is not useful to the process of social integration that we need in Germany."[12] In September 1994 he argued that the 1989 *Wende* had in fact been a "revolution," and he regretted the "weakness" that had marked that revolution: "There was no systematic purge [*Beseitigung*] of the former ruling elites; instead, with as much care and as little harm as could come to them, they were brought over into the *Rechtsstaat*." By the fall of 1994, Heitmann no longer believed, as he once had, that the institutions of the Federal Republic could compensate for that early weakness because he no longer believed that commumism as an ideology was dead: "Communism is still alive in people's hearts and minds, and in both the east and the west." The most telling symptom of communism's persistent and menacing presence, Heitmann argued, was the continued appeal of the PDS, and the willingness of democratic parties to accept the PDS as a potential "partner." Heitmann concluded: "We must question the ideology aggressively. Communist teachings were not poorly translated into practice; they are simply wrong. Making this clear is difficult but indispensable."[13]

Heitmann's uncompromising view of the DDR past may have accounted in part for his relative unpopularity in the new Länder, where Stolpe, with his more ambiguous past and his more nuanced views, remained a popular figure. In the old Länder, and among more liberal elements in the new Länder, it was the lessons Heitmann appeared *not* to have learned from Germany's Nazi past that shocked a broad cross-section of the political class. Heitmann was not simply highly conservative on social issues such as the role of women—"not intelligently conservative, but banally restorationist," as Robert Leicht remarked in *Die Zeit.*[14] More important, he dismissed the subjects on which a tentative consensus against the extreme right might have been thought to have formed, arguing, "The remarkable thing in the Federal Republic is that there are a few subjects that have been made taboo." Heitmann's arguments recalled in several respects the grievances cited in the 1994 book-manifesto of the "new right," *Die Selbstbewusste Nation,*[15] and his list of allegedly taboo subjects was revelatory, as was the accompanying assertion that ordinary citizens did not subscribe to the taboo: "There is an intellectual field

of debate that does not necessarily correspond to the feelings of a majority of citizens, but that one cannot overstep without penalty. The subjects concerned include: foreigners, the German past, the Nazi past, also
women."[16]

Heitmann seems not to have understood that views on the social role
of women and views of the Nazi past were not, in fact, equally open
to debate, though in fact they were increasingly debated. A taboo—a
position or view that a human community has classified as beyond the
bounds of acceptable belief or practice—is a synonym, albeit pejorative
in tone, for a negative consensus. Certain views of women might be seen
as "restorationist," but they were not "taboo." The *Historikerstreit,* however, had been in part about whether certain views of the Third Reich
were, or would continue to be, taboo. Heitmann hoped not, and that
hope was embedded in a cluster of views that could hardly appear reassuring to those sensitive to right-wing totalitarian legacies. Heitmann
criticized the Maastricht Treaty and European integration, pleaded the
need for "identity-creating elements,"[17] spoke of "Überfremdung" (being
overrun by foreigners),[18] lamented the moral decline of the West, and, in
a constantly reprinted statement, argued: "The time has come—with
German unity, the postwar period is finally over—to put this event [the
Third Reich] into its place in the general history that we as a people
have."[19] As Friedbert Pflüger, CDU deputy and longtime aide to Richard
von Weizsäcker, put it, were Heitmann to be elected president, "Ernst
Nolte's *Historikerstreit* arguments" would threaten "to conquer the [pres-
idential] Villa Hammerschmidt."[20]

Heitmann withdrew his candidacy on November 25, 1993, and the
CDU eventually proposed Roman Herzog, the then fifty-nine-year-old
president of the Federal Constitutional Court and a west German, as a
replacement candidate. In the subsequent struggle between Herzog, Johannes Rau (the popular SPD minister president of North Rhine–Westphalia), Hildegard Hamm-Brücher (the grand old lady of the FDP), and
Jens Reich (the ex-DDR dissident molecular biologist and co-founder of
New Forum), party political calculations rather than substantive questions prevailed. On May 23, 1994, Herzog was elected president on the
third round of voting.

The next important episode of the electoral superyear took place after
the Saxony-Anhalt state elections, which were held on June 26, 1994,[21] a
month after the presidential balloting and two weeks after the European

parliamentary elections in which the FDP (4.1 percent) had trailed the PDS (4.7 percent) and fallen short of the 5 percent threshold. In 1990 the Christian Democrats, in alliance with the Free Democrats, had carried the Saxony-Anhalt state elections; the CDU had won 48 and the FDP 14 of the 106 seats in the Landtag. The first two CDU minister presidents were forced from office by their political pasts or by more conventional scandals: Gerd Gies resigned on July 2, 1991, after it was alleged that he had used Stasi records to blackmail other deputies; Gies's west German successor, Werner Münch, was accused of improperly padding his income and resigned with his cabinet on November 27, 1993. Münch was replaced by Christoph Bergner, a former member of New Forum. Bergner led the CDU in the June 1994 state elections. This time the Christian Democrats won only 37 of 99 seats (34.4 percent of the vote). With a popular vote of only 3.6 percent, the Free Democrats fell below the 5 percent threshold and were therefore excluded from representation in the new assembly. The SPD won 36 seats (34.0 percent of the vote), up from 27 in the previous Landtag. The Bündnis 90/Greens won 5 seats (5.1 percent of the vote). The PDS won 21 seats (19.9 percent of the vote), up from 12 seats.

The parliamentary arithmetic suggested two possibilities: a grand coalition of the CDU and the SPD (which together held 73 of the 99 seats), or a minority "red-green" government (41 seats) that would depend on PDS votes (or abstentions) for its existence. The national leadership of the SPD was deeply divided on the question of alliance strategies at the federal level; even in the face of the FDP's renewed expressions of loyalty to the CDU-led coalition in Bonn, SPD party leader Rudolf Scharping had consistently refused to entertain an open and organized intraparty debate on the issue of a possible alliance between the SPD and the Greens. He had, however, given assurances that there would be no alliance between the SPD and the PDS at the federal level. Now the party leadership opted for a red-green coalition in Saxony-Anhalt, apparently overruling the preferences of the state party leader, Reinhard Höppner.[22] There would be no negotiations with the PDS prior to the installation of the new government, and no formal coalition at any time, but the minority government would accept support from wherever it came. On July 21, 1994, Höppner became minister president of Saxony-Anhalt, inaugurating what became known as the "Magdeburg Model."

In December 1993, responding to the results of the local elections in

Brandenburg, the CSU interior minister of Bavaria, Günther Beckstein, had called the SED's successor party "clearly anti-constitutional," and had demanded that it be banned throughout the Federal Republic.[23] Christoph Bergner, at the time newly promoted from state parliamentary leader of the CDU in Saxony-Anhalt to minister president, had disagreed. Like Vogel in the early 1980s, Bergner emphasized the integrative, educational capacities of democratic institutions: "I believe these demands [to ban the PDS] are inappropriate. There is in the PDS a Stalinist and a left-anarchist group. This fact alone, however, does not justify a ban. Our democratic culture of dialogue would look poor indeed if we chose this way of dealing with the PDS. What we really need is to go on the offensive with a substantive discussion. Demonizing the party won't get us anywhere."[24]

Six months later the CDU national leadership's response to the elections in Saxony-Anhalt was quick and sharp, and it did in fact demonize the PDS. It also set the tone for the remainder of the national campaign for the Bundestag elections of October 16, 1994. Calling the PDS "rot-lackierte Faschisten" (fascists painted red, perhaps the most memorable line in an otherwise lackluster general election campaign)[25] and the election a "Richtungsentscheidung" (a decision about which direction the country would take), adopting advertisements that recalled the "PDSPD" slogans of 1990, the CDU leadership argued that the SPD could not now be trusted not to enter into an implicit or explicit coalition with the PDS at the federal level after the Bundestag elections, no matter what Scharping said. Hadn't Höppner also given preelection assurances that there would be no coalition with the PDS?[26] In a letter to the CDU/CSU parliamentary group, Wolfgang Schäuble characterized the stakes of the election as he saw them: "The issue is whether a free, democratic, cooperative Germany is going to continue down the path toward an increasingly united Europe, or whether a red-green left alliance is going to throw us into instability at a moment in our history that calls for reliability and predictability."[27]

The CSU party leader and finance minister, Theo Waigel, called the SPD's attitude toward the PDS the "greatest scandal" in the history of the Federal Republic.[28] Schäuble, like Kohl and other Christian Democratic party leaders, accused the SPD of recklessly betraying the democratic values of the republic: "The SPD's capitulation to the PDS is equivalent to the end of the Federal Republic's democratic consensus not to get involved with radical forces."[29] In a campaign pamphlet titled "Future Instead of Leftist Front: PDS—Danger on the Left!" the CDU defended ten theses—all intentionally or inadvertently pitched to west German sensibilities—asserting the communist character of the PDS and the deleterious effect the party would have on the economy, on security, and on immigration controls.[30]

The CDU's strategy deflected attention from policy areas where the government's record was less than stellar and from the political uncertainties occasioned by the erosion of the FDP. Most important, the strategy sought to create the impression that the SPD was an unreliable party, ready to conclude any alliance that would bring it back to power. Thus in Bavaria, where state elections were held in September, a CSU poster reproduced a portrait of Karl Marx with the caption: "I'm coming back! Via Saxony-Anhalt. Thanks to the SPD & PDS."[31]

The same strategy was adopted a year later in Berlin, in the elections that delayed the Berlin-Brandenburg referendum (see Chapter 5). A grand coalition under CDU leadership had governed Berlin since 1991. Now CDU posters around the city warned voters; "When it rains it pours: Whoever votes red-green risks getting the communists" and "With red-green and communists, you are risking the future." Sitting in a field of grass and flowers, a bear (symbol of Berlin) inspected his foot and proclaimed, "Just no red-green louse in my fur."[32] Only when it was too late did the SPD's mayoral candidate, Ingrid Stahmer, condemn the strategy; on the eve of the vote, SPD leaders attacked the CDU's "slander campaign" and warned that Diepgen's party "poisons the well out of which it wants to continue to drink."[33] The results (Table 6.1) pleased only the Greens (Christian Ströbele said, "We are among the electoral victors") and the PDS (Lothar Bisky called it "a very good day")[34]. On the day after the election, Berlin's incurably irreverent taz could not resist; its front-page headline read, "SPD clearly over 5 percent" (referring to the electoral point below which parties receive no representation).

Had the CDU's strategy of excluding the PDS and smearing the SPD in fact dropped poison not only into the wells of the municipal grand coalition but also into the wells of German democracy? Commenting on the political development of the Federal Republic during the 1970s, the political sociologist Rainer Lepsius had argued that in an essentially bipolar, centripetal party system, the recourse to polarizing ideological slogans (e.g., labeling an election a *Richtungsentscheidung*) is a normal

Table 6.1   Berlin Election Results, October 22, 1995 (percent)

	1995	1995—West Berlin	1995—East Berlin	1990
Participation	68.6	71.4	64.1	80.8
CDU	37.4 (-3.0)	45.4	23.7	40.4
SPD	23.6 (-6.8)	25.5	20.1	30.4
FDP	2.5 (-4.6)	3.4	1.1	7.1
Bündnis 90/Greens[a]	13.2 (+3.9)	15.0	10.0	9.3
PDS	14.6 (+5.4)	2.1	36.3	9.2
REP[b]	2.7	2.6	2.9	3.1

Official 1995 results in *Deutschland Archiv*, 12/1995, 1237.
a. Figures for 1990 include votes cast for Alternative Liste.
b. Die Republikaner.

strategy: it allows parties that in reality pursue middle-of-the-road policies and compete against one another for critical centrist voters to satisfy the identity needs of more ideologically oriented voters. Ideological exaggeration, Lepsius argued, is an enabling condition of pragmatic politics, and is functional so long as it is not taken too seriously by the political elites who use it or by the voters who respond (or do not respond) to it. But, he cautioned, "this conflictual rhetoric does become problematic when those who engage in it get trapped by the symbolic exaggerations when it comes to acting. In these cases, the practical alternatives become freighted with symbolic value in a way that may hinder the development of a consensus."[35] The appeal to polarizing symbols through deliberately exaggerated rhetoric was harmless from a democratic point of view only if it enhanced competition within a centripetal framework and did not get in the way of pragmatic politics.

The CDU's approach to the PDS in the years following unification did not meet either condition. In the immediate aftermath of the 1995 Berlin elections, Weizsäcker sharply criticized the CDU's electoral strategy, succinctly summarizing its impact on the party system: "The larger of the two democratic catchall parties [*Volksparteien*] fights the smaller catchall party using the PDS theme, with the result that the smaller democratic party gets weaker and the PDS gets stronger. This really can't be pure coincidence."[36] Two points were implicit in Weizsäcker's remarks: first, that the CDU's strategy had weakened a clearly democratic party while benefiting a less democratic party; and second, that the strategy had compromised the overall competitiveness of the party system. Kohl's response was curt and contemptuous, and demonstrated that he saw no reason to reconsider strategic choices.[37]

The disastrous Berlin electoral results accentuated the leadership crisis within the SPD. At the Mannheim party conference in November 1995, party leader Rudolf Scharping was suddenly and unexpectedly replaced by Oskar Lafontaine. Almost immediately, and for diverse reasons, the relations between the SPD and the PDS showed signs of becoming more supple. At the top, Lafontaine shared neither Scharping's ideological refusal to deal with the PDS (along with Gerhard Schröder, and against Scharping's preferences, Lafontaine was said to have encouraged the SPD leader in Mecklenburg–Western Pomerania to explore the possibilities of an arrangement with the PDS) nor his reluctance to mount a frontal assault on the CDU. Scharping had shown little combative spirit during his stint as party leader. Combative spirit was not what Lafontaine lacked: "Yes, indeed, we are a left-wing party," Lafontaine affirmed.[38] Furthermore, he concluded, "We're coming back."[39] Lafontaine seemed to understand that, absent more flexibility in the party's coalition preferences, his challenge would be mere bluster. "We no longer tremble," Reinhard Höppner said, "when the CDU shouts 'PDS.'"[40] Significantly, it was the PDS that now expressed nervousness: "I am not completely naive about this," Gregor Gysi told Neues Deutschland in late November 1995; "the SPD wants our voters."[41] "We need to pay attention," Lothar Bisky said in early December 1995, "so that we don't get smothered by the social democrats' embrace."[42] Gysi added: "I would warn against any precipitous pace."[43]

The SPD's new willingness to reconsider its coalition options brought attention to the PDS as a party and to the likely impact of different patterns of partisan competition.

The "Real" PDS: Alibis as Ideology

In the years following unification, the PDS sent a mixed ideological message and a comparatively clear emotional message. Its particular mission as a successor party was to provide former East Germans with an alibi for the greater or smaller complicities they may have contracted with the fallen regime. What made the PDS especially troubling was not its positions on the ideological and institutional issues of the day but rather its positions on issues of responsibility for what happened in the past, under SED rule. The alibi was the real life of the party; the occasional ideological backsliding was the superstructure. In some cases the alibi absolved gross abuses of power (though nothing on the order of genocide); in many cases it absolved ugly acts of everyday betrayal; in most cases it absolved real or perceived conformist cowardice. It insulted the courage of those who had not conformed and had suffered, and it expressed what could generously be termed a defective democratic self-image. It did not represent a threat to the safety of the republic.

Ideologically, the PDS was, with regard to democratic institutions and values, a "yes, but . . ." party. This stance was open to two interpretations. In the less reassuring interpretation, the party was ideologically opportunistic: thrust into a new environment, it adopted the discourse most likely to maximize its influence. Had circumstances changed, it would have reverted to its previous ideological positions. It might then have lost the protest voters who supported it, but it could have relied on the efficiency of the cadres it had inherited from the SED. In the second interpretation, the party was—at both the collective and the individual level—genuinely uncertain of its own identity. The main mission of an institutional strategy is to ensure that the "circumstances" do not change: it focuses on keeping the incentives for playing within the system, and the costs of playing outside the system, high. Under these conditions, the PDS's opportunism—if that is what it was—would become a trap in which the party itself was likely to become ensnared: if maintained over time, patterns of behavior adopted for opportunistic reasons nonetheless become habits. It might even be argued that the new patterns will become habits all the more quickly the less the subject is reminded (by partisans of a cultural strategy) that he has been forced into new forms of behavior.[44] And if the party collectively and its members and sympathizers individually were genuinely uncertain of their political identity—a predictable and indeed normal reaction to rapid and radical political change—habitual action could slowly resolve the feelings of doubt and disorientation.

Beyond its announced adherence to the ideals of liberty, equality, and fraternity, the PDS defined itself as "a union of diverse left-wing forces," an "opposition force" united by its dislikes: "What unites us is the determined fight against political disempowerment, the dismantling of the welfare state, and the destruction of human dignity."[45] The negative self-definition was a further sign of disorientation and uncertainty; as a type of self-understanding, it should have been uncomfortably familiar to west Germans self-aware enough to recall their own postwar history. The PDS did not challenge parliamentary democracy or market mechanisms or even the Western Alliance outright or on principle. Rather, it couched its support for these moral and institutional choices in terms that suggested an underlying longing for an undefined, or only vaguely defined, alternative.

The PDS did not refer disparagingly to "bourgeois democracy" in general, but it frequently denounced the suspect character of (West) German democracy, born in sin out of the incestuous relationship between capitalism and fascism and itself always in danger of spawning militarist, racist, and neofascist elements. The PDS emphasized the importance of extraparliamentary action; it advocated a new constitution for united Germany; and it constantly demanded "a fundamental extension and a qualitative development of democracy in all areas of common life."[46]

The PDS condemned state socialism as it was practiced in Soviet bloc countries but also used "capitalism" as a pejorative, polemical term and argued, "Radical market-oriented policies also failed as a solution to the economic problems of German unification." The party demanded a "new social and ecological orientation," with more democratic control (the mechanisms of which were unspecified), more public attention to job creation, and more respect for the environment. The party adopted a pacifist stance, justifying that position by referring both to the nature of modern conflicts and armaments and to the particular burdens of German history. Within the context of its general pacifism, it recommended the eventual dissolution of the Bundeswehr, as well as of NATO and of the Western European Union, and it vehemently opposed the deployment of Bundeswehr troops in Bosnia.[47]

Beyond and through its programmatic positions, the PDS appealed to, and often cultivated, the feelings of disorientation and wounded dignity described in Chapter 5. Its opposition to the proposed merger of Berlin and Brandenburg showed the party's fundamentally opportunistic side in action. The PDS fed, and fed on, anxieties, feelings of rejection, and pessimism; it claimed only to oppose a bad treaty, but proposed no alternative. Party documents consistently referred to German unification as an *Anschluß* (annexation) and emphasized the negative effects of unification on east Germans. The party argued that the "policy of the established parties has turned the former citizens of the DDR into people who, for years if not decades, have only limited fundamental rights." Not surprisingly, the PDS responded to this alleged "destruction strategy" by proclaiming, "In contrast to the established parties, we do not want the westernization of the east, because we do not want a two-thirds society, mass unemployment, prosperity at the expense of less-developed countries, and the destruction of nature."[48]

The function of the party's criticism of West German democracy was to exculpate the DDR; it did not announce a preference for some less burdened example of liberal democracy (as theoretically it might have). It was part of the alibi. According to the PDS:

> Millions of people set out after 1945 to construct a better social order and a peace-loving Germany that would overcome its fascist heritage. This requires no apology. The antifascist-democratic changes in the eastern part of Germany and later the effort to build a socialist society stand in justified contrast to the West German rescue of a capitalism that had been weakened and discredited by the unprecedented and unique crimes of German fascism. To the socialist attempt in the DDR belong worthwhile results and experiences in the struggle for social justice . . . There were also, however, mistakes, errors, omissions, and even crimes.

The distortion and ultimate failure of the socialist project in the DDR was *attributed* to the failure of the socialist project in the USSR, which was in turn blamed on the underdeveloped character of Russian society and on the hostility of the "more developed capitalist industrial countries." Once again, the failure was portrayed as a tragedy whose villains were somehow elsewhere. The SED appeared in this story as, at worst, a well-intentioned *Mitläufer,* and the PDS was conscientious enough for its members to "examine our political and intellectual tradition, critically and conscious of our own responsibility for the distortion of the socialist idea."[49]

The *description* of what the failure ("mistakes, errors, . . . and even crimes") looked like in the DDR, however, while rather discreet in its depiction of the crimes, contained an affirmation of liberal democratic institutional arrangements. This disjunction between description and causal attribution was fundamentally characteristic of the PDS's view of the past; it produced the alibi, and at the same time suggested the recognition of the "mistakes, errors, . . . and even crimes," responsibility for which the alibi was intended to allow people to avoid:

> The absolute opposition between plan and market led to the lack of self-regulating mechanisms in the economy and to total planning. Bureaucratic nationalization controlled social life . . . The traditional division of power was refused, the meaning of democratic elections was scorned; co-determination and the right to participate in decision making were proclaimed but too rarely realized. The result was a misguided security policy, informed in large part by distrust for our own population. To this was added the political domination of the judiciary, the violation of academic and creative freedom, the abuse of the media.[50]

Is it fair to draw this distinction between ideology and alibi? Which one was, in fact, the real life of the party? The PDS's ideological heterogeneity was expressed in the plethora of "platforms" and "forums" organized within its ranks. The presence of such groups itself indicated a break with the party's Leninist past, since fractional activity was always banned by Leninist parties. The most problematic elements of the party included the "Communist Platform" and the "Marxist Forum." The democratic qualifications of both groups were at best debatable. Organized on December 30, 1989, the Communist Platform became increasingly visible and vocal as the party leadership became more insistent on the fundamental nature of the PDS's break with the SED's ideological heritage. In 1995 the Communist Platform claimed some 4,000 members (out of a total party membership of 130,000).[51] As the intraparty debate over its SED heritage sharpened in the months following the 1994 Bundestag elections, Gregor Gysi announced that he would refuse to serve on the party's executive committee if Sahra Wagenknecht, the principal spokesperson for the Platform, were also elected; at the party conference in January 1995, Wagenknecht was defeated by a vote of 262 to 129 (33 percent of the voting delegates voted for her). Wagenknecht had conventionally negative communist views of parliamentary democracy as a means for achieving political ends, and of political freedom as an end in itself. "I believe," the twenty-five-year-old philosophy student said in an interview in January 1995, "that parliaments can limit damages and must struggle to do so, but that fundamental social change cannot be realized through votes in parliamentary chambers. For that, strong extraparliamentary movements are necessary." The purpose of the PDS, Wagenknecht argued, was to pursue an "anticapitalist policy." She defined socialism as "a society no longer subordinated to the profit mechanism," and when asked if unification had not brought east Germans democratic rights, she countered with a list of lingering social ills. Her overall judgment of the Federal Republic was depressingly predictable: "This state is neither social nor democratic, and in light of the banning of the KPD, the *Radikalenerlaß* [1972 decree excluding people suspected of extremist sympathies—in practice, leftists—from the civil service], and the political trials of DDR officials, one can hardly speak of a *Rechtsstaat*."[52]

Similar positions were represented in the PDS's parliamentary delegation by Uwe-Jens Heuer. In May 1995, Heuer was among the signers of an appeal titled "In großer Sorge" (With Great Concern) who then organized the Marxist Forum. The appeal denounced what it termed the "ghostlike battle in our own ranks . . . started under the absurd label 'Reformers vs. Stalinists.'"[53]

Wagenknecht and Heuer spoke for only a minority even of the party's elites, among whom SED holdovers were more important than among the party's voters. The positions the two represented were sharply rejected by the party leadership. But the positions remained part of the party's political baggage, in many ways licensed by the deliberate ambiguities of official party documents and required by the drive to produce alibis.

The sociological heterogeneity of the party—and especially of its electorate—made the party's chances for survival hard to predict. Both the membership and the electorate of the party were located overwhelmingly in the new Länder and in the formerly eastern sector of Berlin: of the 123,751 members reported in 1994, only 2,781 came from the old Länder and the formerly western sector of Berlin. In the 1994 Bundestag elections, the party won only 1.0 percent of the second-ballot vote in the west, but 19.8 percent in the east.[54] The party leadership emphasized that a mere fraction (approximately 5 percent) of former SED members joined the successor party; critical observers retorted that a crushing majority of PDS members were once members of the SED. Unlike traditional Western communist parties, the PDS did not draw its support primarily from the objectively disadvantaged elements of east German society. In the fall of 1994, they provided a nearly perfect reflection of income groups in the new Länder; at the same time, PDS supporters reported themselves subjectively as "losers" in the unification process. Among the party's membership, older age cohorts were overrepresented (70 percent over age fifty-four, as compared with 41 percent in the CDU/CSU and 35 percent in the SPD).[55] Among east Germans voting for the first time, however, nearly one third chose the PDS.[56]

The ability of the PDS to attract younger voters, the continuing organizational and electoral weakness of west German parties in the new Länder (in comparison to the approximately 121,000 PDS members in 1994, the CDU claimed 78,000 members in the new Länder, the SPD 28,000, the FDP 25,000, and Bündnis 90/Greens a mere 3,200),[57] the dedication of PDS militants, the presence of party activists in social organizations, and the difficulties of socioeconomic and cultural adjustment in unified Germany all suggested that the PDS might remain a feature of the German political landscape for the foreseeable future—regardless of whether or not the SPD considered it a potential partner.

The official positions of the party—easily accessible through party documents and campaign literature—provide one window on its character. Public statements made by its leaders, especially Gregor Gysi and Lothar Bisky, provide another. A platform cannot be interviewed; it cannot be challenged on its inconsistencies or asked about its past. Individuals, of course, can. Gysi and Bisky were particularly interesting figures because they consciously mediated between the party's many actual and potential audiences, and because they staked their continued services on the party's rejection of its Stalinist past. At the leadership level they were the best the PDS could offer—and both were compromising figures, in both senses of the word.

Gregor Gysi served as chair from December 1989 to January 1993. He remained head of the PDS parliamentary group in the Bundestag thereafter, and was the party's most articulate and visible spokesman, particularly in the old Länder. Gysi's effectiveness made him a frequent target for criticism, especially from political actors who saw the party's success as dependent on his presence, and who hoped by undermining him to undermine the party as a whole. Gysi was succeeded as party leader by Lothar Bisky, the chair of the Brandenburg state party and the former chair of the Brandenburg parliamentary investigatory commission that examined the Stolpe case.

Gysi exemplified many of his party's complexities. His father, Klaus, was already a communist during his student days in Berlin in the years spanning Hitler's seizure of power; "as a communist," his son recalled, "he [played] down his Jewish background." Klaus's father was a social democrat and a physician; his Jewish wife (Gysi's paternal grandmother) fled to France during the Nazi period and thereafter, as her grandson noted, divided the world into Jews and non-Jews. Gysi's mother's family had been prosperous entrepreneurs in St. Petersburg; they resettled in Berlin as the First World War began. Gysi's maternal grandfather was Jewish. When Germany attacked Poland in 1939, Gysi's parents were in Paris. The party sent Klaus Gysi back to Nazi Germany, where the pair survived the war. Other family members were less fortunate. When Gregor Gysi traveled to Israel in March 1991, he visited the Yad Vashem memorial to Holocaust victims, where he identified the names of his own relatives among the dead—"as a Jerusalem newspaper noted, a first among visiting German politicians."[58] Charlotte Wiedemann's description of André Brie, Gysi's former deputy, former PDS leader in Berlin, member of the party's executive committee—and former IM—was also indicative of Gysi's biography: "As the son of a Jewish communist . . . , he was socialized from childhood on into the framework of DDR thinking—not in a naive petit bourgeois submission to power, but in the complicated, self-made chains of an idealistically motivated incapacity to engage in critical thinking."[59]

Gysi was repeatedly—and persuasively—accused in the press of knowingly having acted as an IM, usually under the code name "Notar." In the course of one such controversy, Wolf Biermann called Gysi "a criminal" ("100 percent," Biermann added, "and not just a lousy 99.9 percent") and the PDS a "shit society."[60] As a defense lawyer, Gysi had defended a long list of prominent DDR dissidents, from Rudolf Bahro (who stood by him) and Robert Havemann (whose widow accused him of betraying her late husband's interests) to Bärbel Bohley (who defied a court decision enjoining her from calling Gysi an informant). The evidence produced by the Gauck-Behörde for the Bundestag's credentials committee was, at the very least, disquieting.[61] Whereas Stolpe admitted his contacts with the Stasi and conceded many of the points made against him, Gysi denied the accusations of his critics, using expressions such as "official character assassination" to describe the "campaign" waged against him. In contrast to Stolpe, Gysi was accused of more than reckless endangerment: the documents suggest that Gysi may have put Stasi interests before those of his clients. The facts of the case were relevant to Gysi's viability as a political leader because of PDS party statutes that require officeholders to state whether or not they worked as IMs, because of Gysi's own critical statements about the particular kind of betrayal that IMs committed, and because proof that he served as an IM would establish him—given both the content of the accusations and the nature of his denials—as a cynical and systematic liar. The accusations that he worked as an IM, however, may only have strengthened the bonds between Gysi and east Germans who felt aggrieved by the process of unification. In response to the accusations, a party poster portrayed an uncharacteristically serious Gysi, with the caption "This is not about me. This is about everyone who wants a different Germany."

The party's position on—and Gysi's perception of—the postwar development of the two German states recalled Christa Wolf's dismissal of "the West Germany of Adenauer and Globke" as an alternative to the DDR (see Chapter 3). Wolf was proceeding from a bad conscience about her own youthful commitments and those of her family; Gysi was proceeding from a good conscience about the commitments made by his family and the price that had been paid. The result was in significant ways similar. Gysi, born in 1948, took his loyalty to the DDR and his ties to the Communist Party for granted: "Of course I noticed that not everything in the DDR was in order, and of course I always knew that human rights were violated," Gysi admitted in 1991. "Nonetheless, my basic feeling was that we were on the right side of history."[62]

For Gysi as for Wolf, the DDR represented the "better" German state because of the goals it had set itself—and Gysi continued to describe the DDR this way, even as he argued that the goals had been perverted beyond recognition by the practices of the SED and the regime. In essence, he was using two arguments to defend the DDR. First, he contended that in the aftermath of the Third Reich, a failed cultural strategy was morally superior to a successful institutional strategy: the DDR deserved his loyalty because it had *tried* wholly to transform its part of Germany into an antifascist, socialist state, whereas the Federal Republic had not. Second, and even more important, Gysi was suggesting that the relevant categories of choice were capitalism versus socialism, rather than political freedom versus unfreedom. At the December 1989 party conference Gysi declared, "We need a complete break with the failed Stalinist, that is, administrative-centralist socialism in our country." Through 1990, however, Gysi argued for a "third way," unobjectionably "characterized by radical democracy and constitutional rule, humanism, social justice, the protection of the environment, the implementation of a real equality for women," but also described in terms that suggested a misunderstanding of the essential political choice between political freedom and authoritarianism. The third way, Gysi argued, was to be found "beyond Stalinist socialism and the domination of transnational monopolies."[63] This insistence on the primacy of social and economic organization led to an assessment of the DDR's record that indicated—at the very least—a certain lack of distance vis-à-vis past modes of thought and analysis.

As Gysi's audience changed, his language also changed, and as the context and constraints around him changed, he responded to the new incentives. Whether he would have been able to execute the reverse maneuver with equal ease and the same apparent conviction was of importance only if one thought that the Federal Republic was not simply a flawed democracy but a fundamentally unstable one. In reality, it is possible that Gysi's public discourse promoted the legitimacy of democratic politics during a critical phase of the transition process, and that its ambiguities, however unattractive they may have been to audiences who already took democratic norms for granted, have helped ensure that *his* audience, which was socialized with different assumptions, listened. Who still remembers—and what difference does it make—that Santiago Carrillo, after facilitating the transition to democracy in Spain by adopting "Eurocommunist" positions, later reverted to a hard-line interpretation of communism? Very quickly, Gysi found ways to talk about politics that did not include the word "superstructure." By the mid-1990s and even earlier, Gysi described the DDR as a dictatorship—"In the last analysis, we had a kind of absolutism, but more thoroughgoing than most kings would have dreamed of"—and he consistently maintained that unification, whatever its disappointments, had brought East Germans a net gain because it had given them freedom. "Real existing socialism failed," Gysi conceded in a conversation with Wolfgang Thierse. "In the end, it made no essential contribution to human progress." The Federal Republic, therefore, had been the "more progressive society," for "this society offers more in terms of democracy, freedom, efficiency, and ecology."[64]

In 1989, Gysi had hoped for a democratic, socialist, independent DDR—something better, as he frequently put it, than the Federal Republic. In the years that followed he continued to use the pejorative word *Anschluß* (as in "ein kolonialistisch[er] Anschluß," a colonial annexation)[65] to describe the process that led to German unification: the opportunities opened up in 1989, he wrote in *Das war's*, had ended "in a blind annexation at any price." And he added: "It was an attempt to keep the BRD unchanged."[66] His position remained substantially similar to the one he had articulated during the Unification Treaty debate in the Volkskammer in 1990: "This [the "Anschluß" of the DDR through Article 23] is regrettable, because there was an opportunity at least to try to install a Germany that would have been politically, militarily, socially, and economically much better than the DDR, but also much better than the BRD. That opportunity was wasted. We ended up with nothing but a bigger BRD."[67]

In its 1994 Bundestag campaign, the PDS used a poster that read, "Change begins with opposition." The slogan no doubt appealed to the many protest voters who cast their ballot for the PDS, but it can also be seen as part of the ongoing intraparty tug-of-war between those who believed that meaningful progress could be achieved through parliamentary politics and those who, like Wagenknecht, argued that only extraparliamentary opposition could promote "socialism." In 1996, Wagenknecht called the idea of governmental responsibility under capitalism "suicidal for a left-wing party."[68] After 1989, Gysi often argued that parliamentary and extraparliamentary action complement and complete each other; he repeated this argument at the party conference in January 1996.[69] But Gysi never flirted with violence, and in comparison to the Greens (especially the early Greens), the PDS's proclivities toward extraparliamentary activism have been very tame. Gysi argued openly that incremental change is preferable to "revolution." "In our century, heroes no longer conquer; they reverse false starts and dismantle faulty constructions," Gysi wrote in *Neues Deutschland* in October 1990, and in June 1991 he told the party conference, "In my opinion, the attempt to institutionalize countervailing powers and to create free space for emancipation is much more revolutionary than were perhaps the old Revolutions [the French and Russsian]."[70] This perception did not prevent Gysi from reverting to the usual communist expressions of contempt for social democratic incrementalism. "The SPD—as history proves," Gysi claimed during the 1990 Volkskammer campaign, "is always leftist and socially minded only when it feels pressure from its left," and in *Das war's* he criticized what he called "social democratic conformism."[71] Irritating though these remarks may have been to the SPD, they seemed to represent a residual emotional dislike for social democrats rather than an ideological rejection of incrementalism. Shortly before the 1994 Bundestag elections, Gysi argued in *Neues Deutschland* for a reformist rather than a protest strategy, and he accepted the risks the former entailed: getting involved, Gysi asserted, "is our only chance. And it always involves the risk of conformism and of becoming part of the establishment."[72]

The position was summarized in the penultimate paragraph of the "10 Theses on the PDS's Future Course" prepared for the Fourth Party Conference (January 1995), suggesting that Gysi's earlier remarks had not been intended merely to capture votes in the 1994 elections: "The emancipation of society can be achieved only through the winning of majorities and on the foundations of democracy and humanity. The PDS opposes the smashing of social and parliamentary-democratic institutions. It knows from experience that freedom, democracy, and political autonomy enrich people."[73]

Lothar Bisky, in his speech to the 1995 party conference, summarized the PDS's official view of the means-ends problem refracted through the experience of the DDR: "We won't justify the violations of human rights in the DDR with any argument or by citing any goal, no matter how lofty."[74] Four months later, in a sharply worded response to the "In großer Sorge" appeal, Gysi and twenty-one other PDS deputies defended the majority positions that had been accepted by the prior party conferences and promised, "We won't be part of a return to the SED."[75]

This survey of the PDS's ideological diversity suggests, at the very least, that without having to shift very far, large sectors of the party could move toward democratic normality. (Democratic normality, it is worth remembering, always has less attractive sides. It includes Franz Josef Strauß as well as Richard von Weizsäcker, and within its framework, Eberhard Diepgen won elections by maintaining a good cop–bad cop relationship with Klaus Landowsky, whom Klaus Böger, parliamentary leader of the Berlin SPD, pointedly and pertinently called "the PDS on the right").[76] Why, then, was the PDS as a whole so reluctant to call a dictatorship—and the acts committed by the dictatorship—by their right names? Although the party leadership became increasingly explicit in its denunciation of the East German regime, it continued to resist the term *Unrechtsstaat* as a label for the type of regime the DDR had.[77] The aversion to this term seemed to be shared by broad sections of the population of the former DDR. Many resented the ill-advised "Rückgabe vor Entschädigung" (return before compensation) property settlement adopted in the rushed months around unification; many (according to one poll 72 percent) feel unprotected by the law in the Federal Republic.[78] Many simply could not square their memories of normal life with a term whose negative connotations are so dramatic. Reinhard Höppner (b. 1948), a pastor's son who never worked for the Stasi, never joined the party, and never became the brilliant mathetician his teachers saw in him because he refused to show the necessary political conformism, remembered a life which a politically less sophisticated person might well have found at emotional odds with the term *Unrechtsstaat*:

> It makes me sad when people talk about forty lost years. For me, it was a full and happy life. I know that this statement may seem a provocation to people who were held back, tormented, imprisoned, or wounded by the DDR. But I can't be part of the hypocrisy that claims that we waited forty years expectantly for reunification in order to be released from the prison DDR.
>
> The DDR was our living space. We were happy and we celebrated. We accepted responsibilities and made mistakes. We were free to say yes or no. We had meaningful goals and broad hopes. I am thankful for this life. I won't let anyone take those forty full years from me.[79]

Other ex–East Germans rejected the *Unrechtsstaat* reference because they suspected a specifically conservative political agenda behind the term.[80] Gysi was representative of this group. To him the term seemed intended to assert an equivalence between the Third Reich and the DDR that was both emotionally and intellectually unacceptable: "Of course, there are always certain similarities of form between dictatorships," Gysi conceded in 1991, but there were also differences of considerable moral and political significance. "We have to stand up personally and see to it," he argued, "that the DDR and its institutions don't get globally condemned as an *Unrechtsregime* and criminal." The communist system had been *intended* to deliver on the dreams common to the democratic West:

liberty, equality, fraternity. But it had failed, producing instead unfreedom. Therefore, Gysi admitted, "no one should mourn this system. One can only mourn the fact that it was unable to introduce in a timely way the reforms that would have made possible a democratic socialism."[81] Gysi excluded nostalgic mourning but at the same time refused blunt condemnation.

The party as a whole—its leadership included—was equally adamant in its refusal to call the April 1946 unification of the KPD and the SPD in the Soviet zone a *Zwangsvereinigung* (forced merger). For the PDS, the *Zwangsvereinigung* remained a *Zusammenschluß* (merger). The facts of the case are reasonably clear.[82] In the period following the German capitulation, the SPD enjoyed far greater popular support than did the KPD. Among both parties' supporters, a deeply felt longing for working-class unity was widespread. Within the SPD, a minority—led by Otto Grotewohl (1894–1964), the self-appointed leader of the Berlin party organization, the *Zentralausschuß*—favored not only working-class unity but also organizational unity with the KPD. By December 1945, the Soviets had opted for organizational unity. Social democrats opposing unity were subjected to a full palette of coercive measures, up to and including long terms of imprisonment under conditions that sometimes caused death. The level of opposition is suggested by the results of the referendum called in Berlin on March 31, 1946, which put two questions to SPD members in the city: "Do you favor the immediate merger of the two workers' parties? Do you favor an alliance between the two parties that would guarantee common effort and exclude fraternal fights?" The Soviet occupation authorities prevented voting in the eastern zone of the city. In the western zone, 82.2 percent voted no on the first question (yes: 12.3 percent); 62.1 percent voted yes on the second question (no: 23.0 percent).

Zwangsvereinigung was, as the PDS alleged, a politically loaded term; it was also, however, a good summary description of what happened in 1946—and in the years immediately following 1946 the *Zwang*, the element of force, only increased. In the mid-1990s, the SPD made the term's acceptance a condition for any move toward cooperative relations between the two parties: to do otherwise, it was argued, would be to betray the courage and convictions of social democrats who stood fast in the face of communist persecution. The term first became a major issue after the October 1994 elections, when the Mecklenburg–West Pomeranian

SPD, caught in a choice between a grand coalition and some kind of arrangement with the PDS, made the latter solution conditional on the PDS's view of the *Zwangsvereinigung*. In the winter of 1995–96 the term moved again into the news, in part because of the approach of the fiftieth anniversary of the original event, and in part because the SPD under Lafontaine's leadership seemed more ready to consider a new relationship with the PDS. More than loyalty to persecuted comrades was at stake, however, in the SPD's intransigence. As the reporter Peter Merseburger argued: "Reopening at this moment the question of the origins of the SED aims at resolving the issue of responsibility for the origins of the failed experiment we know as the DDR. Without the SED, the DDR would not be thinkable; next to the Soviets and as their accomplice, the SED, the DDR's state party, bears the responsibility for the construction of the second dictatorship on German soil."[83]

It was the attribution of primary responsibility that the PDS consistently resisted, and that explained what Wolfgang Thierse called the party's "daily careful manuevering between the will to change and the satisfaction of nostalgia for the SED."[84] The party did not deny that coercion was used or that social democrats were persecuted, but it sought to diffuse responsibility—in part by making social democrats complicitous in the process that led to their subjugation (a narrative goal shared by the CDU/CSU, eager for other reasons to make the SPD co-responsible in the creation of the DDR). In this account, no one could have foreseen in 1945–46 the outcome of the story, and social democrats and communists together worked for unity. If the project went sour, it was because of Soviet initiatives and—especially—because of the the Cold War. The term *Zwangsvereinigung* was unacceptable to the PDS because it clearly distinguished between a subject (communists) and an object (social democrats), and the PDS adamantly refused to make this distinction. We did it, but we were not free agents, we did not intend the results that occurred, our actions were not decisive, and those who blame us for what happened share in the responsibility for the outcome: this was the PDS argument about the *Zwangsvereinigung,* and indeed more broadly about the DDR. It was no accident that it closely resembled Egon Krenz's trial defense.[85]

The inability or unwillingness to perceive oneself as a responsible agent—responsible irrespective of whether one's actions were in fact the effective cause of a given outcome—is a common legacy of dictatorship, not just because dictatorships implicate people in actions they later wish to deny (either because they themselves come to perceive the actions as blameworthy or because, in an environment dominated by different values, they do not wish to be perceived by others as blameworthy), but also because dictatorships seek systematically to strip individuals of their subjecthood. In his prison, Arthur Koestler's Rubashov slowly, hesitantly learns to use the first-person singular. Democracy assumes free moral agents. Ideally, its institutions allow individuals to make choices, demand that individuals stand by choices they have made, and require them to respect the choices made by other individuals. Democratic political culture is a culture of responsibility, and of respect based on responsibility.

Responsibility is a difficult subject in Germany, and not just among ex–East Germans. In the Federal Republic, on plaque after plaque and in speech after speech, the crimes committed between 1933 and 1945 "in the name of Germany" by an unnamed subject are deplored, as though the language offered only the passive voice. When President Herzog went to Poland in 1994 to commemorate the Warsaw Uprising and specified that Germans had committed the crimes, he was breaking the usual rhetorical pattern.[86] In its individual and collective refusal to see itself as a subject, the PDS was expressing the most pervasive cultural reality of a dictatorship. Within the party, members abdicated their responsibility to the party; outside the party, people were robbed of their right to be responsible. Now, suddenly, ex–East Germans found themselves defined as subjects: the politically active were held responsible for their past actions, and ordinary citizens were made responsible for their present lives. Both groups found the transition hard to negotiate.

A cultural strategy tends to view the psychological disposition to deny responsibility as politically disqualifying in itself. This in effect was the SPD's position, not because it deliberately adopted a cultural approach, but because it found no way to differentiate between a psychological disposition and an ideological position, and so took a refusal to acknowledge responsibility for an act to signify ideological approval of the act. An institutional strategy would argue that the sense of responsibility is best learned through inclusion in institutions that assume responsible actors. It would therefore make allowances for the psychological disposition to duck responsibility, and look elsewhere for indicators of ideological positions. We have looked elsewhere: party documents and leaders sent a mixed message. The dilemma posed for democratic actors recalls the situation John Kennedy faced in the critical hours of the October 1962 Cuban missile crisis. The American government had received two messages from the Kremlin: one was belligerent, the other left the door to accommodation open. After due deliberations, President Kennedy ignored the message that did not serve American interests (which included the survival of both freedom and the planet) and answered the other. The rest, as they say, is history. Politics is always a cacophonous place. Leaders are people who, amidst the cacophony of voices, know which messages to answer.

Democracy in the Driver's Seat

In Hungary, the communist successor party emerged victorious in the elections of May 1994; the party's leader, Gyula Horn, became prime minister. In the Polish presidential elections of November 19, 1995, Lech Walesa was defeated by the ex-communist Aleksander Kwasniewski; in the first round of balloting, held on November 5, the human rights activist and Solidarity veteran Jacek Kuron (Freedom Union) had won a mere 8.9 percent. These electoral results remind us of the manifold tensions and disappointments that attend democratization processes, but in neither case did electoral developments jeopardize the democratization process itself. However, the Polish and Hungarian successor parties, although they operate in fragmented party systems, do not have to compete with a strong social democratic party. Since the parties are clearly interested in winning elections, the system provides centripetal incentives.

My analysis of the PDS suggests that the party is a morally and politically plausible, if not terribly attractive, political partner. Any alliance between the SPD and the PDS in the years following unification would have been electorally very costly for the SPD in the short term. Since the party's prospects in this period were in any event gloomy at best, however, this cost should be assessed in other terms. In the longer run, cooperative arrangements with the PDS (and presumably with Bündnis 90/Greens) could make the SPD more competitive in national politics, not just because a broad coalition on the left might muster more votes, but because a tense and contentious relationship would force the SPD into a programmatic debate in which it might once again find a distinctive profile. The SPD would not be required to describe the *Zwangsvereinigung* as anything other than a *Zwangsvereinigung*. On the contrary, the democratic value of the new arrangements would be reduced if the SPD used any other term. But it would no longer turn its back when the PDS replied "Zusammnenschluß." Institutional inclusion of the PDS might then promote cultural change, slowly easing not just the PDS itself but (even more important) its voters and its broader pool of east German sympathizers into the culture of responsibility they find so difficult to adopt. German democracy would gain all down the line: from the renewed competitiveness of the party system, from the public rethinking of programmatic possibilities and priorities, and from the political resocialization of east Germans.

Such, at any rate, is the argument for an institutional strategy. How persuasive is it? We have very little experience in Western democracies with successor parties. The Polish and Hungarian experiences are of limited comparative value, in part because of the absence of a social democratic party. But if we know little about successor parties, we know more about extremist parties and the diverse conditions under which they prosper or decline, and under which they threaten or do not threaten the democratic order. In the 1970s, the newly reorganized French Socialist Party (PS) entered into an alliance with the organizationally and electorally superior French Communist Party (PCF).[87] The alliance was concluded in the wake of a failed attempt to construct a center-left coalition; its chief attraction was that it enhanced the electoral chances of the left in the new, conservative-dominated system of the Fifth Republic. In the resulting embrace, it was the PCF that was smothered—not just because the PS squeezed, but in part because of the intimacy.[88] The PDS represents an equally unattractive but less risk-ridden coalition partner for the German social democrats than was the PCF when François Mitterrand rebuilt the French Socialist Party around the option of a united left. Even if it were motivated to do so, the PDS lacks the organizational capacity to undermine the democratic character of institutions in which it participates—partly because of its own weaknesses, and partly because of the strength of the competition.

The PS, it might be objected, smothered the PCF and then itself imploded. Many factors brought about the in any event temporary demise of the PS, but I do not mean to argue that the smothering of the PCF and the implosion of the PS were unrelated developments. The Union of the

Left helped reduce the relevance of the PCF in French politics; the end of the Cold War, and of the Soviet Union, helped complete the job. Communism and anticommunism—the opposing cultures of the Cold War— were central organizing forces in postwar West European political life. The end of the Cold War contributed to the de-organization of partisan politics analyzed earlier in this chapter. The Union of the Left accelerated this trend, confronting French elites on both the right and the left with the task of reinventing a party system to fit a new world: one without communists, without the assumption of limitless growth, and where national borders often seemed fictitious.[89] The implosion of the PS was one response; its surprisingly rapid reemergence as a political force was another. The accompanying ideological, programmatic, and organizational renewal, however disruptive and uncertain it may initially appear, is a positive and necessary development if parties are to remain (or again become) the main actors in democratic political life.

Once the ideological threat posed by an extremist or successor party has been assessed, the rules of access to power, the rules governing action in power, and the availability of politically relevant resources would seem the most useful indices for judging the likely impact of an alliance between an extremist and a non-extremist party on the two partners and on the political system as a whole. The rules of access include the type of institutional set-up in place (a parliamentary system versus a presidential one; a centralized political system versus a decentralized one) and the expected stability of the set-up. The rules of access include the electoral laws used to elect public officials (the chief executive, parliamentary representatives, local governments). Assessing the availability of resources involves evaluating the geographic distribution of support for the extremist or successor party, the permeability or impermeability of politically relevant subcultures, the penetrability of social institutions, interest groups, and economic institutions, the presence or absence of an external advocate that could tip the balance of power decisively in favor of one or another party, and the distribution of resources—money, leadership, activists, organizational competence—among the various partisan players.

Ideologically, the PCF was not an alibi party; through all its many incarnations, it remained a Marxist-Leninist party with strong proclivities toward Stalinism. On other indices, the most significant difference between the PDS and the PCF would appear to lie in the combination of geographically concentrated PDS strength and a decentralized political system. PCF strength, representing around 20 percent of the postwar French electorate through the 1970s (as opposed to the PDS's 4.4 percent in the 1994 Bundestag elections),[90] could also be geographically concentrated—for example, in the so-called Red Belt around Paris—but during the years of peak PCF strength, the French political system was still highly centralized. The political significance of controlling the municipalities around Paris was negligible in comparison to the political significance of possible participation in one or more Land governments in the new Länder. The PCF, however, could make its cooperation conditional on the assignment of cabinet ministries in Paris (even if it was excluded from leading central cabinet departments such as defense and the interior), whereas in Germany, the SPD could engage in alliances in the Länder and wait to see the results before proposing an alliance at the national level.

The geographic concentration of PDS support, combined with the high rates of activism among its members and sympathizers, their relatively strong educational backgrounds, and the head start enjoyed by a former elite, make the social institutions and economy in the new Länder appear quite penetrable. Whether this penetration gives the PDS more or less potential blackmail power in social conflicts and policy processes and more or less staying power in electorally lean years than control of (for example) the powerful trade union organization, the Confédération générale du travail (CGT), gave the PCF is unclear.

Finally, executive figures (the president, the chancellor, the minister presidents or equivalent thereof in the Länder) are indirectly elected in the Federal Republic, and parliamentary bodies are elected using a system that is essentially one of proportional representation: on both counts we would expect the leverage of the more moderate electoral partner to be reduced. Yet given the distribution of opinion in the new Länder, the maintenance of proportional representation may leave elites with no choice except that between continuous grand coalitions or the construction of coalitions on the left that would include the PDS.

Despite the qualifications, these considerations would seem to urge caution on the SPD. Other considerations would suggest the risks to be minimal. The institutions of the Federal Republic are at least as stable as were those of the Fifth Republic in the 1970s and 1980s. In both France and Germany, the external environment made or makes it highly unlikely that the political advantage would shift to an antidemocratic left-wing party. When the PS concluded an electoral alliance with the PCF, the Soviet Union was still a superpower and an important resource and reference point for the PCF. It is unlikely that NATO would have looked on passively had communists been given core cabinet ministries or headed the government. Now the Soviet Union is gone—both as an ideological reference point and as a source of material assistance—but its mere memory is a liability: it is probably enough to ensure that Gregor Gysi will never become minister of defense.

If both ideological and structural factors suggest that cooperative arrangements with the PDS would not pose unreasonable risks, the question of a possible alliance must turn on policy and programmatic compatibility. The areas of political disagreement between the PDS and the SPD are no less, but also no more, significant than were the areas of political disagreement between the PCF and the PS: they focus on defense and security issues and on the organization of democratic politics. The SPD is divided on both issues, with a minority defending positions on the Alliance and on direct democracy that are close to those of the PDS. The Greens are similarly divided, and it is less clear which positions command a majority. It is fair to argue that an alliance with the PDS (and an alliance at the national level with Bündnis 90/Greens) might tend—as would any alliance with any external group—to strengthen specific policy preferences within the SPD, and that SPD members who have reason to think their positions would lose should oppose such an alliance, not on the grounds of democratic principle but on the grounds of everyday politics. It would then be incumbent upon SPD members favoring an alliance to propose a substantive agreement satisfactory to all sides. The programmatic clarification, whatever its outcome, would represent a gain for democratic processes.

The economic policies of the first Mitterrand government reflected the programmatic influence of the alliance with the communists. The policies failed, both economically and politically, and were eventually jettisoned by the government. The PCF responded by withdrawing its ministers and moving into veiled opposition. Among socialists and their sympathizers, the experience of governance imposed a long-overdue learning process about economics and the limits of state action.[91] At the same time, the constraints of governmental responsibility exacerbated divisions within the PCF, and the party's response reduced its audience.[92]

The main challenge to democratic politics, in both established and new democracies, is the crisis of representation described at the beginning of this chapter. This is the proper context in which to assess the role(s) played by successor parties and to determine the appropriate response of democratic actors. In the German setting, an institutional approach that makes cooperative relations with the PDS possible seems a better response to the crisis of representation than a cultural strategy that discourages cooperative arrangements.

Identity and Trust—
The Human Relations of Democratic
Government

No trust, no democracy: this is the position of democratizing elites who prefer cultural strategies. Its complementary assertion is: no truth, no trust. Only if our relations are transparent can I know who you really are, judge you to be trustworthy, and therefore trust you, and only if I trust you can I consider you a reliable party to the multiple reciprocities that define everyday democracy. Trust depends on truth because I suppose your present identity to be defined in large part by your past acts and by your present relationship to your past acts.[1] In this account, the refusal to talk about betrayal is both a refusal to acknowledge the act and an effort to hide one's identity: on both counts, it is an ongoing obstacle to trust.

By the end of 1994, some 750,000 ex–East Germans had requested access to their Stasi files,[2] a figure that suggests a preoccupation with betrayal, truth, and trust which had little to do with partisan calculations or media-driven sensationalism. The men and women who applied for access to their files simply wanted to know what they thought the Stasi documents would tell them: the truth about their previous relationships.

Informing for the secret police was the form of betrayal that captured the imagination of the public in post-unification Germany. But the body politic was burdened by other forms of betrayal as well: the betrayal of even the most elementary norms of human decency and solidarity in the Third Reich, the refusal to acknowledge responsibility, and the failure to speak openly about the past, both after 1945 and after 1989–90. Men and women did resist Hitler's murderous project; only about 1 percent of the East German population (though a greater proportion of its elites) responded to the Stasi's overtures; and neither the denial of responsibility nor the refusal to talk about the past was constant or universal. The legacy of two dictatorships was nonetheless in part a legacy of betrayal, and the resulting distrust has left deep and grubby footprints across the many paths of German democracy, most notably perhaps in a general pessimism about dialogue and persuasion as a means of defining common problems and arriving at mutually acceptable solutions. The debates analyzed in Chapter 3 were not just shrill, aggressive, and exclusionary; because participants talked past one another, they regularly repeated themselves. In Chapter 6, we saw how the CDU's distrust of the PDS was matched by the SPD's distrust of both the PDS and itself.

In the spring of 1995, as Germany prepared in diverse ways to commemorate the fiftieth anniversary of the end of World War II, a curious story appeared in the newspapers. In April 1945 an SS officer took Hamlet's advice: he assumed a virtue that he did not have. Hans Ernst Schneider, born in 1909, had a doctoral degree in German literature, and during the Third Reich he had held a responsible position in Heinrich Himmler's ministry. Now Hans Schneider became Hans Schwerte. He remarried his own wife, re-earned his doctoral degree, and wrote a well-received *Habilitation,* "Faust und das Faustische—Ein Kapitel deutscher Ideologie." He became the rector of the Technical University in Aachen and served the institution well, resisting both authoritarian reflexes and radical demagogy in the difficult years of the student revolt, when so many others in the academic community lost their political and psychological compasses. He was an imposing and respected individual, "a man of character and stature," to all appearances a liberal in all the best senses of the word.[3] Whatever dubious complicities may have assisted him in his formal change of identity, a real change also seemed to have taken place. "You are not looking at a former Nazi," he told Ulrich Greiner in 1995; Schneider had *become* Schwerte. It was, Greiner reflected, "a German life." Officials who have interviewed civil servants accused of working for the Stasi repeatedly encounter the feelings Christa Wolf expressed in her 1993 letter to the individual on whom she had informed: "It now seems to me as if I were apologizing for a stranger."

Schneider/Schwerte's story is troubling for many reasons. For years, rumors had circulated in Aachen: why had it taken so long for Schwerte's past to become public? This question is perhaps not so hard to answer, however multiple the answers were. The more difficult question concerns the political and social implications of Schneider/Schwerte's strategy. Greiner compares Schwerte to the protoganist of Max Frisch's novel *Mein Name sei Gantenbein,* who imagines identities for himself, and then plays at the identity he has imagined.[4] But Schneider did not just happen on an alternative identity, or adopt it as a game. Like religious converts or former drug addicts who associate a new name with a new life, Schneider *chose* a new identity: he wanted, he explained, to help build a new Germany. Was Schwerte a liar, a cheat, and a fraud, or was he a new man? "The reversal was more radical than Schneider would ever have been able to achieve," Greiner observes. "The deceit was so true that he himself fell for it."[5] Schwerte *did* help build a new Germany. Is it enough, from a democratic point of view, to assume a virtue? In a democracy, how much and what kind of moral ugliness can the "decent drapery" whose necessity Edmund Burke urged cover?[6] What kind of trust can assumed virtue sustain?

The problem with Schneider/Schwerte is that we do not know who he "really" is, and even he may not know who he "really" is. An institutional strategy accepts this fact as an insurmountable feature of the human condition generally, and of the human condition during transitional situations in particular. Instead of insisting on the connection between identity and action, it insists on the connection between institutional structures and action. In this assertion, it is supported by the explicit reflections of classical liberal theory in both its contractarian and its utilitarian variants, which sets power against power, turns self-interest into a public sentinel, and asserts that "[a] nation of devils (so long as they possess understanding)" is all a republic requires.[7] For all its talk about trust, the classical liberal account of trust is relatively flat and impersonal, and focuses on the conditions and dynamics of vertical trust (between rulers and ruled) rather than on the conditions and dynamics of horizontal trust (among citizens). Locke does suggest that societies are drawn together by something more than individual calculations of fear and interest, and he assumes that "those, who liked one another so well as to joyn into Society, cannot but be supposed to have some Acquaintance and Friendship together, and some Trust one in another" (*Second Treatise,* §107). "Cannot but be supposed" is a rather elliptical formulation for such an important point. Other theorists (beginning with Aristotle) have had much more to say about friendship; it is characteristic of classical liberal theory that it neglects friendship, and so avoids exploring the relationship between private trustworthiness and public reliability.

There are at least two problems with the liberal/institutional account of trust. One is that it does not offer an accurate account of liberal political life—or of democratic transitions. The second is that a rigid insistence on its validity can provoke a destabilizing counterinsistence on authenticity, transparency, and trustworthiness.

We know that institutional strategies work. We also know that they disappoint, and that they are either complemented or compromised by the introduction of cultural elements. They work by crippling the reproductive capacities of fallen dictatorships, and they do this by focusing directly on power structures. New structures create new patterns of behavior. This is different from saying that successful institutional strategies successfully "delegitimize" fallen dictatorships. It would be more accurate to say that institutional strategies build working democracies on the more or less intact moral ruins of a dictatorship; they assume that the new buildings will be more attractive than the ruins, and that workers within the buildings will eventually come to feel at home there and to find the architecture beautiful. Legitimacy and delegitimation are hard to define, and given a definition, the presence or absence of the defined phenomenon is difficult to ascertain. The advocates of institutional strategies tend not to pause over the definitional complexities: if domestic factors durably cripple the reproductive capacities of a fallen dictatorship and replace the dictatorship's institutions with democratic ones, then the dictatorship is finished. Schneider/Schwerte's soul is his own problem—and friendship is always problematic.

Tocqueville's keen eye caught a different reality at work in America: it was important, he reminded his readers, not to mistake a society's self-image for its reality. Americans are not, he argues, in fact as single-mindedly motivated by self-interest as they claim, but the claim makes them reliable: "Self-interest well understood is not an exalted doctrine, but it is clear and certain. It does not set itself great goals, but it achieves without much effort all the goals to which it does aspire." The ideology's intellectual and psychological accessibility makes it uniquely suited to the job of policing an egalitarian, liberal community, but it does not exhaust the realities of American social life.[8]

In real life, Schneider/Schwerte's identity problem is not just his problem; it is also our problem. Liberalism's explicit account of trust as reliability is simultaneously its great political strength and its primary psychological weakness. In its assertion that institutions can compensate for the lack of virtue and good intention among citizens and rulers alike, liberalism invites a preoccupation with virtue and authenticity in any situation where institutions do not seem equal to the seemingly daunting task assigned them. Democratization, in which institutions are by definition untested and fragile, is one such situation; a crisis of representation similar to that currently unfolding in the established advanced industrial democracies is another. In a country where, within living memory, a predominantly institutional strategy built a democracy on the ruins of unexampled public criminality and where at the moment a crisis of representation is playing itself out, it is hardly surprising that cultural strategies have an audience, and that the impact of their appeal often complicates the process of democratic consolidation. Disappointment is a cost of democratization; the thirst for authenticity and transparency is a cost of disappointment; and disappointment is, at the moment, a very widespread political sentiment.

With regard to trust, as in other critical areas, liberalism seems to depend on dispositions it cannot itself generate.[9] Liberalism talks about trust-as-reliability but presupposes a measure of trust-as-trustworthiness; institutional strategies create trust-as-reliability, but democracies need trust-as-trustworthiness. The German cases I have analyzed suggest that liberalism is not as helpless as this claim implies. There are many ways to poison the wells of democratic politics. No matter how great the temptations they face, men and women are always free to choose what they will do as they stand at the well. When politicians play to the politics of identity or denigrate the state, they contribute to public distrust and encourage a politics of authenticity; the only contest is then whether the public loses before the politicians, or the other way around. If democratic politics is to be a politics of persuasion and not just of bargaining, it requires civility. Civility, the venerable old *Oxford English Dictionary* reminds us, is "behaviour proper to the intercourse of civilized people; ordinary courtesy or politeness, as opposed to rudeness of behaviour; decent respect, consideration." Respect, significantly, is defined without regard to the sincerity of the actor: "To treat or regard with deference, esteem, or honour; to feel or show respect for." Civility creates an atmosphere in which we can all talk, not just about our actions but about our identities. Germany, like other communities scarred by dictatorship, has a great deal to talk about.

Abbreviations

AfNS	Amt für Nationale Sicherheit
BEK	Bund der Evangelischen Kirchen
BRD	Bundesrepublik Deutschland
CDU	Christlich Demokratische Union
CNR	Conseil national de la Résistance
CSU	Christlich Soziale Union
DA	Demokratischer Aufbruch
DA	*Deutschland Archiv*
DDR	Deutsche demokratische Republik
DJ	Demokratie Jetzt
DSU	Deutsche Soziale Union
EKD	Evangelische Kirche in Deutschland
FAZ	*Frankfurter Allgemeine Zeitung*
FDP	Freie Demokratische Partei
GG	Grundgesetz
IFM	Initiative für Frieden und Menschenrechte
IM	Inoffizieller Mitarbeiter
IMT	International Military Tribunal
KPD	Kommunistische Partei Deutschlands
MdB	Mitglied des Bundestages
MEK	*Materialien der Enquete-Kommission "Aufarbeitung von Geschichte und Folgen der SED-Diktatur in Deutschland"*
MfS	Ministerium für Staatssicherheit ("Stasi")
MRP	Mouvement républicain populaire
NSDAP	Nationalsozialistische Deutsche Arbeiterpartei
PDS	Partei des Demokratischen Sozialismus
PS	Parti socialiste
SED	Sozialistische Einheitspartei Deutschlands
SFIO	Section française de l'internationale ouvrière
SPD	Sozialdemokratische Partei Deutschlands
Spg	*Der Spiegel*
StUG	Stasi-Unterlagen-Gesetz
Tsp	*Der Tagesspiegel*

UFV	Unabhängiger Frauen Verband
VDBT	*Verhandlungen des Deutschen Bundestages*
VL	Vereinte Linke
ZERV	Zentrale Ermittlungsstelle zur Bekämpfung der Regierungs- und Vereinigungskriminalität

Notes

Introduction

1. The literature on democratization is old, rich, and vast; even where it is not cited, it has directly or indirectly shaped the arguments elaborated in this book. It is usefully divided into four categories. One group would include works by political or social theorists who reflected on the foundations of liberal politics: e.g., Montesquieu and Tocqueville. A second group would include the older social science literature on the origins of liberal politics: e.g., Barrington Moore's *Social Origins of Dictatorship and Democracy: Lord and Peasant in the Making of the Modern World* (Boston: Beacon Press, 1966). A third group would include studies of twentieth-century German political development: e.g., Alexander Gerschenkron, *Bread and Democracy in Germany* (New York: Howard Fertig, 1966), Fritz Stern, *The Politics of Cultural Despair: A Study in the Rise of the Germanic Ideology* (1961; rpt. Berkeley: University of California Press, 1974) and *The Failure of Illiberalism: Essays on the Political Culture of Modern Germany* (Chicago: University of Chicago Press, 1971), and Ralf Dahrendorf, *Society and Democracy in Germany* (Garden City, N.Y.: Doubleday, 1967). Finally, the most recent group deals with democratization cases from the 1970s on: see Samuel Huntington, *The Third Wave: Democratization in the Late Twentieth Century* (Norman: University of Oklahoma Press, 1991); Richard Gunther, P. Nikiforos Diamandouros, and Hans-Jürgen Puhle, *The Politics of Democratic Consolidation: Southern Europe in Comparative Perspective* (Baltimore: Johns Hopkins University Press, 1995); and Juan Linz and Alfred Stepan, *Problems of Democratic Transition and Consolidation: Southern Europe, South America, and Post-Communist Europe* (Baltimore: Johns Hopkins University Press, 1996). The recent literature tends to adopt a minimalist definition of democracy and a short time horizon on consolidation.
2. Robert A. Dahl, *A Preface to Democratic Theory* (Chicago: University of Chicago Press, 1956), p. 143; cf. p. 137.
3. Before 1989, the terms *Aufarbeitung der Vergangenheit* (working through the past) and *Vergangenheitsbewältigung* (mastering or overcoming the

past) were used by West Germans to denote their efforts to come to terms with the legacy of the Nazi years. The expressions have now been extended to include or signify efforts to come to terms with the DDR past. For an early and influential discussion of the *Aufarbeitung* concept, see Theodor W. Adorno, "Was bedeutet: Aufarbeitung der Vergangenheit" (1963), in *Erziehung zur Mündigkeit* (Frankfurt am Main: Suhrkamp, 1970), pp. 10–28.

4. For statements of or about the "communitarian critique," see Michael J. Sandel, *Liberalism and the Limits of Justice* (Cambridge: Cambridge University Press, 1982); Michael Sandel, ed., *Liberalism and Its Critics* (New York: New York University Press, 1984); Charles Taylor, *Hegel and Modern Society* (Cambridge: Cambridge University Press, 1979), *Human Agency and Language: Philosophical Papers 1* (Cambridge: Cambridge University Press, 1985), and *Philosophy and the Human Sciences: Philosophical Papers 2* (Cambridge: Cambridge University Press, 1985); Nancy Rosenblum, *Another Liberalism: Romanticism and the Reconstruction of Liberal Thought* (Cambridge, Mass.: Harvard University Press, 1987); and Michael Walzer, "The Communitarian Critique of Liberalism," *Political Theory* 18, no. 1 (February 1990): 6–23.

5. Beyond the set of post-communist democratizing countries, trials have also been held in Greece and Argentina. In both cases, however, the dictatorship had been a military regime of relatively short duration; it had implicated relatively limited numbers of people, and had provoked and then lost an external military conflict. South Africa, where trials began in the mid-1990s, is a more interesting case since the apartheid regime lasted longer and enjoyed broader support in the white community. See Chapter 4.

1. The Disappointments of Democratization

1. Jörg Friedrich, *Die kalte Amnestie: NS-Täter in der Bundesrepublik,* rev. ed. (Munich: Piper, 1994), p. 346. See also Norbert Frei, *Vergangenheitspolitik: Die Anfänge der Bundesrepublik und die NS-Vergangenheit* (Munich: C. H. Beck, 1996).

2. Walter Dirks, "Der restaurative Charakter der Epoche" (September 1950), in *Gesammelte Schriften,* vol. 4, *Sozialismus oder Restauration: Politische Publizistik, 1945–1950* (Zurich: Ammann, 1987), p. 326. The quotation in the section heading is from Walter Dirks, "Über Konrad Adenauer nach seinem Tod" (June 1967), in *Gesammelte Schriften,* vol. 5, *Sagen was ist: Politische Publizistik, 1950–1968* (Zurich: Ammann, 1988), p. 339.

3. Jean-Louis Curtis, *Les Forêts de la nuit* (Paris: René Julliard, 1947), p. 451; hereafter cited parenthetically in the text.

4. Charles de Gaulle, May 6, 1953, in *Discours et messages,* vol. 2, *Dans l'attente: 1946–1958* (Paris: Plon, 1970), p. 609.

5. Dirks, "Der restaurative Charakter der Epoche," p. 330.

6. Wolfgang Koeppen, *Das Treibhaus* (1953), in *Tauben im Gras, Das Treibhaus, Der Tod in Rom: Drei Romane* (Frankfurt am Main: Suhrkamp, 1986), pp. 221–390, quote at p. 227; hereafter cited parenthetically in the text.

7. Dirks, "Über Konrad Adenauer," p. 336.

8. Dirks, "Der restaurative Charakter der Epoche," p. 331.

9. Ibid., p. 333.

10. Dirks, "Über Konrad Adenauer," pp. 337–338.

11. Dirks, "Der restaurative Charakter der Epoche," p. 348.

12. Ibid., p. 326.

13. For accounts that suggest the successful transformation of West German political culture, see for example David Conradt, "Changing German Political Culture," in *The Civic Culture Revisited,* ed. Gabriel Almond and Sidney Verba (Boston: Little, Brown, 1980), pp. 212–272; and esp. Kendall Baker et al., *Germany Transformed: Political Culture and the New Politics* (Cambridge, Mass.: Harvard University Press, 1981).

14. Ralph Giordano, *Die zweite Schuld oder Von der Last Deutscher zu sein* (Hamburg: Rasch und Röhring, 1987), p. 26.

15. Alexander and Margarete Mitscherlich, *Die Unfähigkeit zu trauern: Grundlagen kollektiven Verhaltens* (1967), 2d ed. (Munich: Piper, 1977).

16. Giordano, *Die zweite Schuld,* pp. 11–12.

17. Ibid., pp. 11–12, 94. See also Ralph Giordano, ed., *"Wie kann diese Generation eigentlich noch atmen?": Briefe zu dem Buch Die zweite Schuld oder Von der Last Deutscher zu sein* (Hamburg : Rasch und Röhring, 1990).

18. Giordano, *Die zweite Schuld,* p. 95.

19. Willy Brandt, October 28, 1969, in *Reden und Interviews* (Bonn: Presse- und Informationsamt der Bundesregierung, 1971), p. 30. Early in his speech, Brandt summarized the fundamental goal of his government by proclaiming, "We want to dare more democracy" (p. 13).

20. Willy Brandt, *". . . Wir sind nicht zu Helden geboren": Ein Gespräch über Deutschland mit Birgit Kraatz* (Zurich: Diogenes, 1986), pp. 113–114, 118.

21. See Robert McCluer Calhoon, *The Loyalists in Revolutionary America, 1760–1781* (New York: Harcourt Brace Jovanovich, 1973); Robert M. Calhoon et al., *The Loyalist Perception and Other Essays* (Columbia: University of South Carolina Press, 1989), esp. chap. 11; John Shy, *A People Numerous and Armed: Reflections on the Military Struggle for American Independence*

(London: Oxford University Press, 1976); Michael Kammen, "The American Revolution as a *Crise de Conscience:* The Case of New York," in *Society, Freedom, and Conscience: The American Revolution in Virginia, Massachusetts, and New York,* ed. Richard Jellison, (New York: Norton, 1976), pp. 125–189. Edward Countryman tracks revolutionary attitudes toward and treatment of Loyalists in *A People in Revolution: The American Revolution and Political Society in New York, 1760–1790* (Baltimore: Johns Hopkins University Press, 1981).

22. See Paul E. Smith, "The American Loyalists: Notes on Their Organization and Numerical Strength," *William and Mary Quarterly* (hereafter *WMQ*), 3d ser., 25 (1968): 259–277.

23. Cecilia M. Kenyon, "Men of Little Faith: The Anti-Federalists on the Nature of Representative Government," *WMQ*, 3d ser. 12 (January 1955): 3–43.

24. Patrick Henry, June 5, 1788, in *The Debates in the Several State Conventions on the Adoption of the Federal Constitution,* comp. Jonathan Elliot, vol. 3 (Philadelphia: J. B. Lippincott, 1863), p. 45.

25. Possibly a petition by inhabitants of Morris County, *New Jersey Journal,* reprinted in *New York Packet* (hereafter *NYP*), April 17, 1783, p. 2.

26. "Probus," "To the Whigs of New Jersey," *NYP,* April 17, 1783, p. 2. The decisive battle took place at Yorktown, where on October 19, 1781, Washington's forces defeated General Cornwallis. The North ministry fell on March 20, 1782. The provisional articles of peace were signed in Paris on November 30, 1782, and ratified on April 15, 1783. The definitive treaty was signed on September 3, 1783. The text arrived in Philadelphia aboard the *Lord Hyde Packet* on December 5, 1783 (see *Freeman's Journal,* December 8, 1783). It was ratified on January 14, 1784. Articles 4, 5, and 6 were intended to protect the material interests of Loyalists and to facilitate their reintegration into postwar American life. The articles appear in identical language in the Provisional and Definitive Treaties.

27. Broadside, Poughkeepsie, N.Y., August 8, 1783 (New York Historical Society Archives, New York City).

28. "A Planter," *South Carolina Gazette and General Advertiser* (hereafter *SCGGA*), August 9, 1783, p. 4. Unless otherwise noted, I have not modernized or corrected original texts; they appear here as they appear in the source from which they are quoted.

29. "Brutus," "To the Friends of Freedom and Independence in the State of New York" (dated April 12, 1783), *NYP,* May 8, 1783, pp. 2–3.

30. Petition from Northumberland, June 10, 1783; reprinted in *SCGGA*, September 16, 1783, p. 3.

31. "Brutus," "To the Friends of Freedom and Independence."

32. Aedanus Burke, "At a Court of General Sessions of the Peace held for the District of Ninety-Six, November 26, 1783," *SCGGA*, December 16, 1783, p. 3.

33. [Alexander Hamilton], "Second Letter from Phocian" (April 1784), in *The Papers of Alexander Hamilton*, vol. 3, *1782–1786* (New York: Columbia University Press, 1961), p. 553.

34. *NYP*, April 17, 1783, p. 2.

35. "Common Sense," "An Evacuation Anecdote, With some Occasional Observations," *NYP*, January 15, 1784, p. 3. Thomas Paine tended to be rather possessive about his preferred pseudonym, but I have been unable to ascertain whether he was in fact the author of this column.

36. Benjamin Rush, *Considerations upon the Present Test-Law of Pennsylvania, Addressed to the Legislature and Freemen of the State*, 2d ed. (Philadelphia: Hall and Sellers, 1785), pp. 6–7.

37. Aedanus Burke, *An Address to the Freemen of the State of South Carolina* (Philadelphia: Robert Bell, 1783). Burke is better known as the author of a subsequent pamphlet attacking the creation of the Society of the Cincinnati; see Cassius [Burke], *Considerations on the Society or Order of Cincinnati . . .* (Charleston, 1783). Burke became an Antifederalist, served in the First Congress, and died in 1802. In citing Burke's *Address*, I have adopted twentieth-century spelling. For a description of revolutionary politics in South Carolina, see Jerome J. Nadelhaft, *The Disorders of War: The Revolution in South Carolina* (Orono: University of Maine at Orono Press, 1981). On the immediate postwar period, see also Robert M. Weir, "'The Violent Spirit,' the Reestablishment of Order, and the Continuity of Leadership in Post-revolutionary South Carolina," in *An Uncivil War: The Southern Backcountry during the American Revolution*, ed. Ronald Hoffmann, Thad W. Tate, and Peter J. Albert (Charlottesville: University Press of Virginia, 1985), pp. 70–98.

38. On the complexity of political cleavages and the extraordinary level of violence unleashed in South Carolina by the Revolutionay War, see Nadelhaft, *The Disorders of War*, chap. 3.

39. Burke, *An Address*, pp. 7–8. Burke quotes Hobbes from *Leviathan*, chap. 21. Cf. Locke, *Second Treatise*, chap. 19.

40. Burke hesitates in his judgment only when he discusses bills of attainder, which he seems to think can legitimately serve "as the ultimate resource upon extraordinary occasions." Bills of attainder did not threaten ordinary citizens, and they did not deprive the accused of the right of self-defense. See Burke, *An Address*, p. 20.

41. Ibid., pp. 23–24, 29, 18.

42. Ibid., p. 24.

43. Ibid., pp. 8; 12.
44. [Hamilton], "Second Letter from Phocion," p. 534.
45. Aedanus Burke, "Charge to the Grand Jury," Charlestown, June 9, 1783, *SCGGA,* June 10, 1783, p. 3.
46. Burke, "At a Court of General Sessions of the Peace held for the District of Ninety-Six, November 26, 1783," pp. 3–4.
47. "A Patriot," *SCGGA,* July 15, 1783, pp. 3–4.
48. Rush, *Considerations upon the present Test-Law,* p. 18; idem, "Address to the People of the United States," January 1787, in John P. Kaminski and Gaspare J. Saladino, *The Documentary History of the Ratification of the Constitution,* vol. 13, *Commentaries on the Constitution,* pt. 1, *21 February to 7 November 1787* (Madison: State Historical Society of Wisconsin, 1981), p. 49; reprinted from *American Museum,* February 1, 1787.
49. For a description of the Committee in its heyday, see R. R. Palmer, *Twelve Who Ruled: The Year of the Terror in the French Revolution* (1941; rpt. New York: Atheneum, 1965).
50. Speech in *Réimpression de L'Ancien Moniteur,* 30 vols. (Paris: Au Bureau Central, 1863–1870), 22: 18–26; hereafter cited parenthetically in the text. For an excellent analysis of politics in the fifteen months after Thermidor, see Bronislaw Baczko, *Comment sortir de la Terreur: Thermidor et la Révolution* (Paris: Gallimard, 1989). Lindet's speech is discussed on pp. 164–179.
51. See Tallien's speech of 11 Fructidor, Year II (August 28, 1794), *Moniteur,* 21: 612–615. See also Baczko, *Comment sortir de la Terreur,* pp. 78–83.
52. Bukharin's words (from 1925) are quoted by Stephen Cohen, *Bukharin and the Bolshevik Revolution: A Political Biography, 1888–1938* (Oxford: Oxford University Press, 1980), p. 181.
53. Benjamin Constant, *De la force du gouvernement actuel de la France et de la nécessité de s'y rallier* (1796), p. 16. This pamphlet was written after the royalist uprising of Vendémiaire, Year IV (October 1795). In it, Constant addresses both the government's conservative critics and the government itself. In the passage cited, he is criticizing the stance adopted by conservative skeptics during the constitutional deliberations of the summer of 1795.
54. The best study of the post-Liberation purges remains Peter Novick, *The Resistance versus Vichy: The Purge of Collaborators in Liberated France* (New York: Columbia University Press, 1968). On the problem of political memory in postwar France, see esp. Henry Rousso, *Le Syndrôme de Vichy, 1944– 198 . . .* (Paris: Le Seuil, 1987); and Eric Conan and Henry Rousso, *Vichy: un passé qui ne passe pas* (Paris: Fayard, 1994).
55. For the text of this speech, see Charles de Gaulle, *Discours et messages,* vol. 1, *Pendant la guerre, 1940–1946* (Paris: Plon, 1970), pp. 3–4.

56. Louis Aragon, "La Rose et le réséda" (summer 1942), in *L'Oeuvre poétique, 1943–1945* (Paris: Livre Club Diderot, 1979), pp. 305–307.

57. Charles de Gaulle, *Mémoires de guerre*, vol. 2, *L'Unité, 1942–1944* (Paris: Plon, 1956), p. 303.

58. De Gaulle, *Discours et messages*, 1: 466–467.

59. Henri Michel and Boris Mirkine-Guetzévitch, eds., *Les Idées politiques et sociales de la Résistance (documents clandestins—1940–1944)* (Paris: Presses universitaires de France, 1954), p. 216.

60. The exact figures are impossible to determine, and estimates vary widely. See discussions in Jean-Pierre Rioux, *La France de la IVᵉ République*, vol. 1, *L'Ardeur et la nécessité* (Paris: Le Seuil, 1980), pp. 49–67; and Novick, *The Resistance versus Vichy*, annex C.

61. Pétain died in detention in 1951.

62. De Gaulle, June 16, 1946, in *Discours et messages*, 2: 7; November 27, 1967, ibid., vol. 5, *Vers le terme: 1966–1969* (Paris: Plon, 1970), p. 268.

63. Albeit an advanced industrial democracy in which the deferred costs of an institutional strategy—the resurgence of memory, and the competition between different interpretations of the past—may play a dysfunctional political role; see Conan and Rousso, *Vichy: un passé qui ne passe pas.* "Normal" does not imply identical; see Stanley Hoffmann, "Look Back in Anger," *New York Review of Books*, July 17, 1997, pp. 45–50.

64. De Gaulle, April 2, 1945, in *Discours et messages*, 1: 570; October 14, 1944, ibid., 1: 482.

65. De Gaulle, August 29, 1944, ibid., 1: 467.

66. De Gaulle, *Mémoires de guerre*, 1: 79.

67. "St. François d'Assise" is a play on words, combining Saint Francis of Assisi ("Lord, make us instruments of your peace. Where there is hatred, let us sow love; where there is injury, pardon; where there is discord, union . . .") and the French word *assise*, a court hearing criminal cases. The debate between Camus and Mauriac began in the fall of 1944 and extended well into 1945. At the time, Camus was writing almost daily editorials for *Combat*; Mauriac was writing the editorial column for *Le Figaro* about three times a week.

68. Albert Camus, *Combat*, January 11, 1945, p. 1; reproduced in *Actuelles: Chroniques, 1944–1948* (Paris: Gallimard, 1950), pp. 70–74.

69. Camus, *Combat*, October 20, 1944, p. 2; discussed by Mauriac in "Réponse à *Combat*," *Le Figaro,* October 22/23, 1944, p. 1; reproduced in François Mauriac, *Le Bâillon dénoué* (Paris: Grasset, 1945), p. 72.

70. Camus, *Combat*, January 5, 1945, p. 2.

71. Camus, *Combat*, January 11, 1945, p. 1.

72. See Albert Camus and Arthur Koestler, *Réflexions sur la peine capitale*

(Paris: Calmann-Lévy, 1957). In 1948 Camus conceded the 1944–45 debate to Mauriac; see Camus, *Actuelles: Chroniques, 1944–1948,* pp. 212–213.

73. Camus, *Combat,* October 21, 1944, pp. 1–2; January 5, 1945, p. 1.

74. Collaborators were usually charged with treason under Article 75 of the existing penal code. The government did create a new noncriminal penalty, "l'indignité nationale," which entailed a loss of civic rights. Denmark, Holland, and Norway not only opted for retroactive laws (as did the Nuremberg Tribunal), but restored the death penalty as well. On the French choice, see Novick, *The Resistance versus Vichy,* esp. chap. 8.

75. Camus, *Combat,* January 5, 1945, p. 2.

76. Albert Camus, *Lettres à un ami allemand* (Paris: Gallimard, 1948). The "letters" were written in 1943–44.

77. Camus, *Combat,* January 11, 1945, p. 1.

78. François Mauriac, "Révolution et révolution," *Le Figaro,* October 13, 1944, p. 1; reproduced in *Le Bâillon dénoué,* pp. 63–66.

79. François Mauriac, "L'Année de la réconciliation" [January 1945], reproduced in *Mémoires politiques* (Paris: Grasset, 1967), pp. 220–221. The passage cited was presumably aimed primarily at communist militants.

80. François Mauriac, "Le Mépris de la charité," reproduced in *Le Bâillon dénoué,* p. 162; and idem, "La vraie justice," *Le Figaro,* September 8, 1944, p. 1, reproduced in *Mémoires politiques,* pp. 153–155.

81. It could be argued that Camus's allegorical novel *La Peste* (Paris: Gallimard, 1947) proposes a secular version of Mauriac's general argument.

2. No Trust, No Democracy

1. Eberhard Diepgen, Berlin, January 26, 1993, twenty-fifth hearing of the Bundestag Enquete-Kommission, "Aufarbeitung von Geschichte und Folgen der SED-Diktatur in Deutschland," protocol in *Materialien der Enquete-Kommission "Aufarbeitung von Geschichte und Folgen der SED-Diktatur in Deutschland,"* ed. Deutscher Bundestag (Frankfurt am Main: Suhrkamp, and Baden-Baden: Nomos, 1995), vol. 2, pt. 1, p. 420; hereafter cited as *MEK,* followed by volume and part number. The mission of the Enquete-Kommission is discussed in Chapter 4.

2. See esp. Václav Havel, *Summer Meditations* (New York: Knopf, 1992), pp. 1–20 and passim. For a set of critical reflections on the new emphasis on civil society, see Bob Edwards and Michael W. Foley, eds., Special Issue, "Social Capital, Civil Society, and Contemporary Democracy," *American Behavioral Scientist* 40, no. 5 (March/April 1997).

3. From unpublished interview with a DJ activist, cited by Jan Wielgohs and Helmut Müller-Enbergs, "Die Bürgerbewegung Demokratie Jetzt: Vom in-

nerkirchlichen Arbeitskreis zur politischen Opposition," in *Von der Illegalität ins Parlament: Werdegang und Konzepte der neuen Bürgerbewegungen,* 2d ed., ed. Helmut Müller-Enbergs et al. (Berlin: Ch. Links, 1992), p. 121.

4. Jürgen Fuchs, "Der Abschied von der Diktatur," in *Aktenkundig* ed. Hans Joachim Schädlich (Berlin: Rowohlt, 1992), p. 20.

5. Christa Wolf, "Das haben wir nicht gelernt," *Wochenpost,* 43/1989 (October 21), reprinted together with letters received in response to the original article and with a subsequent article by Wolf ("Es tut weh zu wissen," *Wochenpost,* 47/1989) in *Angepaßt oder mündig? Briefe an Christa Wolf im Herbst 1989,* ed. Petra Gruner (Frankfurt am Main: Luchterhand, 1990), p. 9.

6. Interview with Gerhard Rein, in *Die Opposition in der DDR: Entwürfe für einen anderen Sozialismus; Texte, Programme, Statuten von Neues Forum, Demokratischer Aufbruch, Demokratie Jetzt, SDP, Böhlener Plattform und Grüne Partei in der DDR,* ed. Gerhard Rein (Berlin: Wichern, 1989), p. 80.

7. Interview with Rupert Schröter and Peter Grimm, "Wir haben ein Defizit," in *Die Andere Zeitung,* 21/1990 (June 15), p. 4. For a documented description of Templin's political itinerary, see the special issue of *Der Spiegel* (hereafter *Spg*) (1/1993), "Stasi-Akte 'Verräter': Bürgerrechtler Templin: Dokumente einer Verfolgung." After unification, Templin joined the staff of the Haus am Checkpoint Charlie in Berlin.

8. Jens Reich, "Rechenschaftsbericht zur Gründungskonferenz des Neuen Forum," January 27–28, 1990, cited by Marianne Schulz, "Neues Forum: Von der illegalen Opposition zur legalen Marginalität," in Müller-Enbergs, et al., *Von der Illegalität ins Parlament,* p. 51.

9. New Forum, "Gründungsaufruf: Eine politische Plattform für die ganze DDR," in Rein, *Die Opposition,* p. 13.

10. Ibid., pp. 13–14.

11. New Forum, "Offener Problemkatalog: Vom vormundschaftlichen Staat zum Rechtsstaat," in Rein, *Die Opposition,* pp. 16–19.

12. "Zweiter Entwurf des Statuts des Neuen Forum," December 21, 1989, cited in Schulz, "Neues Forum," p. 40.

13. "Gegen eine Spaltung des Neuen Forum: Erklärung des Arbeitsausschusses des Landessprecherrates," pamphlet January 3, 1990, cited ibid., pp. 38–39.

14. Neues Forum, "Programmerklärung," published as insert in *Die Andere Zeitung,* 6/1990 (March 1), pp. 5, 6.

15. "Grundsatzpapier des Neuen Forum," December 16, 1989, cited in Schulz, "Neues Forum," p. 38.

16. Ibid.

17. See Ekkehard Schall, in *4. November '89: Der Protest, Die Menschen, Die*

Reden, ed. Annegret Hahn et al. (Frankfurt am Main: Propyläen, 1990), p. 155.

18. Bärbel Bohley, speech, September 9, 1990, *Die Andere Zeitung,* 35/1990 (September 19), p. 8.

19. Wolfgang Ullmann, "Demokratie braucht mündige Menschen" (1990), cited in Wielgohs and Müller-Enbergs, *"Die Bürgerbewegung Demokratie Jetz,"* p. 133. See esp. Wolfgang Ullmann, *Verfassung und Parlament: Ein Beitrag zur Verfassungsdiskussion* (Berlin: Dietz, 1992); and Bernd Guggenberger and Tine Stein, eds., *Die Verfassungsdiskussion im Jahr der deutschen Einheit* (Munich: Carl Hanser, 1991).

20. Joachim Gauck, *Die Stasi-Akten: Das unheimliche Erbe der DDR* (Reinbek bei Hamburg: Rowohlt, 1991), p. 98.

21. Bärbel Bohley, "Damit sich Geschichte nicht wiederholt: Keine Stasi-Mitarbeiter in die neue Volkskammer," *taz,* March 22, 1990, p. 10.

22. Ibid.

23. Werner Fischer in the conclusion of an interim report on the dismantling of the security apparatus; text in *Vom Runden Tisch zum Parlament,* ed. Helmut Herles and Ewald Rose (Bonn: Bouvier, 1990), p. 104.

24. Irena Kukutz and Katja Havemann, *Geschützte Quelle: Gespräche mit Monika H. alias Karin Lenz* (Berlin: BasisDruck, 1990); hereafter cited parenthetically in the text. See also Irena Kukutz, "Die Arbeit des Verzeihens," and Katja Havemann, "Zauberwort Rechtsstaatlichkeit," *Die Andere Zeitung,* 12/1991 (March 20), Beilage no. 3, pp. II and XVI, respectively. The quotation in the section heading is from Irena Kukutz, "Zu große Ergebenheit führt zur Verantwortungslosigkeit," *Die Andere Zeitung,* 16/1991 (April 17), Beilage, p. III. Robert Havemann pleaded throughout the 1960s and 1970s for a democratic socialism. He was excluded from the SED in 1964, fired from his post, and subjected to house arrest. Some three weeks after the opening of the Berlin Wall, he was rehabilitated.

25. See Vera Wollenberger, "Eine zweite Vergewaltigung," in Schädlich, *Aktenkundig,* pp. 154–165, and *Virus der Heuchler: Innenansicht aus Stasi-Akten* (Berlin: Elefanten Press, 1992). Wollenberger herself joined the SED in 1975, but was expelled in 1983 because of her involvement in the peace movement. She was arrested in January 1988 and expelled from the DDR in February; she returned in November 1989 and sat in the first all-German Bundestag as a Bündnis 90/Greens deputy.

26. Wolf Biermann, "'A la lanterne! à la lanterne!'" *Spg,* 81/1992 (September 29), p. 89.

27. Kukutz, "Zu große Ergebenheit führt zur Verantwortungslosigkeit," p. III.

28. Karl Jaspers, *Die Schuldfrage; Für Völkermord gibt es keine Verjährung* (Munich: Piper, 1979), p. 46.

29. Ibid., pp. 11, 14–15. I have used "lack of community" to translate Jaspers' term "Nichtgemeinsamkeit."

30. Ibid., p. 27. Jaspers develops the "liebender Kampf" (loving struggle) concept in *Philosophie,* vol. 2, *Existenzerhellung,* 4th ed. (Berlin: Springer-Verlag, 1973), esp. pp. 65–67. See also my discussion in Chapter 3.

31. Jaspers, *Die Schuldfrage,* p. 87; cf. p. 84.

32. Karl Jaspers, *Wohin treibt die Bundesrepublik: Tatsachen—Gefahren—Chancen* (1966; rpt. Munich: Piper, 1988), pp. 176–177.

33. [Werner Fischer], "Bericht der Arbeitsgruppe Sicherheit vor dem Zentralen Runden Tisch der DDR am 12. März 1990," text in David Gill and Ulrich Schröter, *Das Ministerium für Staatssicherheit: Anatomie des Mielke-Imperiums* (Berlin: Rowohlt, 1991), pp. 247, 246. On the possibility and desirability of organizing such conversations, see the debate in *Die Zeit* (Fall 1991). Several of the essays originally published in *Die Zeit,* as well as a number of other relevant contributions, are reprinted in *Ein Volk am Pranger? Die Deutschen auf der Suche nach einer neuen politischen Kultur,* ed. Albrecht Schönherr (Berlin: Aufbau, [1992]). The idea was again floated in January 1992 by Joachim Gauck, Friedrich Schorlemmer, Wolfgang Thierse, Wolfgang Ullmann, Gerd and Ulrike Poppe, Marianne Birthler, and three other former DDR activists; their January 23 statement is reprinted as "'Tribunal' als Forum der Aufklärung," *Deutschland Archiv* (hereafter *DA*) 2/1992 (February), pp. 222–224.

34. See accounts in photocopied irregular periodical *Zwie Gespräch: Beiträge zur Aufarbeitung der Stasi-Vergangenheit,* edited by Dieter Mechtel and Ulrich Schröter. The first issue appeared in February 1991.

35. Jens Reich, "Brave Bürger," *Die Andere Zeitung,* 13/1991 (March 27), Beilage no. 4, p. I; see also Klaus Wolfram, "Zivile Gesellschaft," ibid. In June 1990 the West German editorial staff of *taz* had published, as a separately sold supplement to their regular edition, a list of places used by the Stasi for meetings. The East German staff had objected to the publication. See short article in *Frankfurter Allgemeine Zeitung* (hereafter *FAZ*), "Stasi-Listen mit Wohnungen verteilt," April 19, 1990, p. 4.

36. Wolfram Kempe, "Versuch eines Gespräches," *Die Andere Zeitung,* 14/1991 (April 3), Beilage no. 5, p. I.

37. Die Redaktion, "Die Macht der Namen," *Die Andere Zeitung,* 14/1991 (April 3), Beilage no. 5, p. I.

38. Quoted in Kempe, "Versuch eines Gespräches," p. I; emphasis added.

39. Wolfram Kempe, "Wiederholungstäter in Sachen Widerstand: Innenansicht einer politischen Aktion," *Die Andere Zeitung,* 34/1990 (September 12), p. 3. This was the cover story, announced on p. 1 under the title "Tauziehen um die Akten."

40. Statement by group occupying MfS offices, ibid., p. 4.

41. Throughout the unification period, *Wende*, meaning "change" or "turn," was the word commonly used to denote the events of 1989–90; it was unusual to refer to those events as a "revolution," and such references usually had polemical intent. The term *Wende* had previously been used in West German politics as a label for the transition from Social Democratic to Christian Democratic rule after October 1982.

42. Wolfram Kempe, "Wem gehoren die Stasi-Akten: Innenansicht einer politischen Aktion, pt. 2, *Die Andere Zeitung*, 35/1990 (September 19), p. 9.

43. Bärbel Bohley, "Wiederholungszwang," *Die Andere Zeitung*, 12/1991 (March 20), Beilage n. 3, p. XVI.

44. Jürgen Fuchs, "Immer wußten sie unsere Namen," *Die Andere Zeitung*, 12/1991 (March 20), Beilage no. 3, p. I.

45. Bärbel Bohley, "Wer besieht mein Leben," *Die Andere Zeitung*, 14/1990 (April 27), p. 7.

46. Tina Krone, "Wer bläst da zur Hetzjagd?" *Die Andere Zeitung*, 13/1991 (March 27), Beilage no. 4, p. XVI.

47. Fuchs, "Immer wußten sie unsere Namen," p. 1.

48. For a particularly useful overview of the German transition, see Charles S. Maier, *Dissolution: The Crisis of Communism and the End of East Germany* (Princeton: Princeton University Press, 1997).

49. On the relationship between flight and protest, see esp. Albert O. Hirschman, "Exit, Voice, and the Fate of the German Democratic Republic: An Essay in Conceptual History," *World Politics* 45 (January 1993): 173–202.

50. Interview with Heinz Klunker, May 1, 1990; excerpts in *DA* 7 (1990): 1147.

51. See reports in *FAZ*: "Krenz bekundet Zorn und Scham," December 2, 1989, p. 3; and Peter Jochen Winters, "Einige SED-Abgeordnete weinen, andere schlagen die Hände vor das Gesicht," December 4, 1989, p. 5.

52. Term used by Walter Süß in an op-ed piece, "Belogen und betrogen: Das Ende der SED ist kaum mehr aufzuhalten," *taz*, December 5, 1989, p. 8.

53. For the January 1990 SED-PDS interrogation of and self-criticism by other leading SED figures, including Günter Schabowski, Kurt Hager, and Egon Krenz, see excerpted transcript, "'Ich hab' an den geglaubt,'" in *Spg*, 38/1992 (September 14), pp. 86–104.

54. Sebastian Pflugbeil, October 26, 1989, in Rein, *Die Opposition*, p. 26.

55. See "Aufruf zur Einmischung in eigener Sache," September 12, 1989, ibid., pp. 59–60.

56. "Aufruf zum 'Demokratischen Aufbruch'—sozial, ökologisch" [October 2,

1989], p. 34. DA later split, with the more conservative elements joining the CDU.

57. New Forum, "Erklärung zum 40. Jahrestag der DDR," October 6, 1989, ibid., pp. 14–15.

58. See Dietmar Halbhuber ("Für die ANDEREn"), "Nach-Ruf," *Die Andere Zeitung,* 3/1990 (February 8), p. 2.

59. Both in Hahn et al., *4. November '89,* pp. 164, 195.

60. Text and list of sponsors in Christa Wolf, *Im Dialog: Aktuelle Texte* (Frankfurt am Main: Luchterhand, 1990), pp. 169–170.

61. Text and list of sponsors, ibid., pp. 170–171; see also *FAZ,* November 29, 1989, p. 3.

62. The parliamentary elections had originally been scheduled for May; on January 28, Hans Modrow and the Round Table decided to go with the earlier date. In May 1993, Bündnis 90 merged with the Greens. See Chapter 5.

63. Gregor Gysi, December 8–9, 1989, in *Einspruch! Gespräche, Briefe, Reden* (Berlin: Alexander Verlag, 1992), pp. 24–26. For an assessment of Gysi's efforts to reform the PDS, see Chapter 6.

64. Wolfgang Templin, "Die SPD und der demokratische Sozialismus," *Die Andere Zeitung,* 4/90 (February 15), p. 7.

65. Interview with Rupert Schröter and Peter Grimm, "Wir haben ein Defizit," in *Die Andere Zeitung,* 21/1990 (June 15), p. 4. Cf. debate opened by Reinhard Schult, "Können wir uns gemeinsam wehren? Die PDS—Prügelknabe der Nation?" and Dieter Segert, interview with Uschi Goldenbaum, "'Wollt auch ihr den Sozialismus schlecht machen?'" *Die Andere Zeitung,* 22/1990 (June 22), p. 13; debate continues in subsequent issues.

66. Gregor Gysi, ed., *Wir brauchen einen dritten Weg* (Hamburg: Konkret-Literaturverlag, 1990); excerpted in Gysi, *Einspruch!* pp. 220–221.

67. See text of preamble to the coalition agreement, reprinted in the *FAZ,* "'Einheit auf der Grundlage des Artikels 23,'" April 14, 1990, p. 3. Article 23 of the Basic Law provided for the automatic extension of the Basic Law to areas acceding to the Federal Republic: "For the time being, this Basic Law shall apply in the territory of the Länder of Baden, Bavaria, Bremen, Greater Berlin, Hamburg, Hesse, Lower Saxony, North Rhine–Westphalia, Rhineland-Palatinate, Schleswig-Holstein, Württemberg-Baden, and Württemberg-Hohenzollern. In other parts of Germany it shall be put into force on their accession." Article 146, the last article of the Basic Law, reflected the anticipated provisional character of the original text: "This Basic Law shall cease to be in force on the day on which a constitution adopted by a free decision of the German people comes into force" (official translation).

68. Wolfgang Thierse, April 18, 1990, in *Mit eigener Stimme sprechen* (Munich: Piper, 1992), pp. 38, 39.

69. Reich began his commentary by noting, "We had grand coalitions for forty years." Jens Reich, "Große Koalition, hohle Worte," *Die Andere Zeitung,* 14/1990 (April 27), p. 2.

70. Jens Reich, "Bürgerbewegungen als politischer Faktor der Zukunft?" in *Die Andere Zeitung,* 50/1990 (December 12), p. 7.

71. See Chapters 5 and 6. See also Müller-Enbergs et al., *Von der Illegalität ins Parlament,* pp. 307–341, 366–375, and 376–391.

72. Weiß (DJ) was the first name on the Bündnis 90 list in Brandenburg for the December 1990 Bundestag elections. "'Macht ist nichts Schlechtes an sich,'" interview, *Die Andere Zeitung,* supp., 43/1990 (November 14), p. 14.

73. See figures in "Die Vereinigungen der Bürgerrechts-, Ökologie- und Frauenbewegungen im Wahljahr 1990," in Müller-Enbergs et al., *Von der Illegalität ins Parlament,* pp. 376–391.

74. Bärbel Bohley, speech, September 9, 1990, *Die Andere Zeitung,* 35/1990 (September 19), p. 8.

75. Werner Fischer, "Teppiche, Besen und Schleier: Anmerkungen zum Umgang mit der Vergangenheit," *Die Andere Zeitung,* 13/1991 (March 27), Beilage no. 4, p. II.

76. Klaus Wolfram, "Ost und West—Stasi und Verfassungsschutz," *Die Andere Zeitung,* 12/1991 (March 20), Beilage no. 3, p. I.

77. For an attempt to make sense out of Böhme's life, see Birgit Lahann, *Genosse Judas: Die zwei Leben des Ibrahim Böhme* (Berlin: Rowohlt, 1992).

78. For the report of one such committee, see Justus Werdin, ed., *Unter uns: die Stasi. Berichte der Bürgerkomitees zur Auflösung der Staatssicherheit im Bezirk Frankfurt (Oder)* (Berlin: Basis Druck, 1990).

79. See "Beschlüsse der 1. Sitzung des Rundtischgespräches am 07./08.12.89," in Herles and Rose, *Vom Runden Tisch zum Parlament,* p. 26.

80. In addition to documents cited throughtout this discussion, see for example Herles and Rose, *Vom Runden Tisch zum Parlament,* pp. 69–70, 84–86, and 187–188. See also Gill and Schröter, *Das Ministerium für Staatssicherheit,* pt. 2, and Uwe Thaysen, *Der Runde Tisch* (Opladen: Westdeutscher Verlag, 1990), pp. 55–70 and 73–76.

81. Herles and Rose, *Vom Runden Tisch zum Parlament,* p. 104. Declarations by New Forum, the CDU, and the Round Table in response to the demonstration are reprinted ibid., pp. 60–62.

82. Ibid., p. 301; Gill and Schröter, *Das Ministerium für Staatssicherheit,* p. 189.

83. See, for example, "Diestel bleibt politisch für die Stasi-Auflösung verantwortlich," *FAZ,* September 17, 1990, pp. 1, 2. In June 1990, Diestel left

the DSU; he joined the CDU in August. After unification, Diestel sat as head of the CDU parliamentary group in the Brandenburg Landtag, where his defense of Manfred Stolpe further alienated many veterans of the citizens' movements (see Chapter 5).

84. Text of bill quoted by Gauck, Volkskammer session 32, August 24, 1990, in *Volkskammer der Deutschen Demokratischen Republik*, vol. 29, p. 1453. The law was approved with two dissenting votes and a few abstentions. Volkskammer debates cited hereafter as *VK/DDR*, followed by volume and session numbers.

85. Gauck, August 24, 1990, *VK/DDR*, 29/32, p. 1453.

86. Marianne Birthler, August 24, 1990, *VK/DDR*, 29/32, p. 1540.

87. Jürgen Haschke, August 24, 1990, *VK/DDR*, 29/32, pp. 1456–57.

88. Tina Krone, "Akten her!" *Die Andere Zeitung*, 33/1990 (September 5), p. 2.

89. Text of the agreement in *Die Verträge zur Einheit Deutschlands*, 2d ed. (Munich: Beck/dtv, n.d.), pp. 73–75.

90. September 28, 1990, *VK/DDR*, 29/37, text of report on pp. 1811–13; debate follows.

91. The recommendations were reported out by Rolf Schwanitz (SPD), September 28, 1990, *VK/DDR*, 29/37, pp. 1814–15, with debate following.

92. Motion read by Wolfgang Ullmann (Bündnis 90/Greens), September 28, 1990, *VK/DDR*, 29/37, pp. 1817–18. Ullmann maintained his support for the motion when the Volkskammer's president, Sabine Bergmann-Pohl (CDU), withdrew hers; see p. 1819.

93. For the initial motion, moved on behalf of twenty deputies by CDU/DA deputy Buck, see September 28, 1990, *VK/DDR*, 29/37, p. 1807. The Rechtsausschuß, to which the motion had been referred, recommended against stripping Modrow of his parliamentary immunity, and its recommendations were accepted; see p. 1854.

94. Marianne Birthler, September 28, 1990, *VK/DDR*, 29/37, p. 1817.

95. Christine Grabe, September 28, 1990, *VK/DDR*, 29/37, p. 1824. The committee eventually voted (12–6–2) that the measure was "constitutional;" see p. 1827.

96. Werner Schulz, September 28, 1990, *VK/DDR*, 29/37, p. 1825.

97. Konrad Weiß, September 28, 1990, *VK/DDR*, 29/37, p. 1825.

98. See *VK/DDR*, 29/37, p. 1842. There was a total of four hundred deputies in the Volkskammer. It is unclear how many deputies were present when the vote was taken.

99. See speeches by Krause (CDU/DA), Gysi (PDS), Ortleb (FDP), Höppner (SPD), Schwarz (DSU), and Reich (Bündnis 90/Greens), as well as the closing remarks of Bergmann-Pohl, October 2, 1990, *VK/DDR*, 29/38, pp. 1863–69.

100. Jens Reich, "Adieu, Volkskammer," *Die Andere Zeitung,* 38/1990 (October 10), p. 2.

101. For the text of the Bundestag debate (first reading, June 13, 1991), the text of the bill, and the transcript of the bill's discussion at the German Historians' Association meetings in September 1992, see Klaus-Dietmar Henke, ed., *Wann bricht schon mal ein Staat zusammen! Die Debatte über die Stasi-Akten auf dem 39. Historikertag 1992* (Munich: dtv, 1993). The second and third readings of the bill occurred on November 14, 1991; debate in *Verhandlungen des Deutschen Bundestages* (hereafter *VDBT*), 12. Wahlperiode, vol. 159, pp. 4677–4725.

102. Ingrid Köppe, November 14, 1991, in *VDBT,* 12. Wahlperiode, vol. 159, pp. 4687D, 4686D. Köppe was the main spokesman for the Bündnis 90/Greens parliamentary group during the StUG debates, but the group was not entirely homogeneous: cf. Gerd Poppe's more temperate, and also more personal, contribution to the debate on November 14, ibid., pp. 4698C–4700A. In the final vote Poppe abstained "and not because I am undecided, but in order to make clear that I think that this law still requires a lot of work." (p. 4700A).

103. Ingrid Köppe, Bundestag, June 13, 1991, in Henke, *Wann bricht schon mal ein Staat zusammen!* pp. 145, 146.

104. For this exchange, see November 14, 1991, in *VDBT,* 12. Wahlperiode, vol. 159, p. 4688B. Büttner, a west German who had been elected in 1990 from an east German constituency, reported the bill out of committee for the CDU at the second reading in November; see pp. 4678A–4680B.

105. See *VDBT,* 12. Wahlperiode, vol. 159, p. 4682D (Schwanitz) and pp. 4704A, 4703B, 4702D (Barbe). Barbe attributed the last expression to *taz* editor Klaus Hartung.

106. Interview with Tina Krone and Peter Grimm, "'Man muß erst öffentlich beschuldigt werden,'" *Die Andere Zeitung,* 17/1990 (May 17), p. 6. Hirsch concluded: "And the only way to work through this are these documents. And they must be preserved." A co-founder of IMF, Hirsch had been imprisoned in 1988 and then expelled from the DDR. He was working as an assistant to Walter Momper, then SPD mayor of West Berlin, when the accusations against him surfaced. *Taz* covered the story in detail.

107. Cited by Schulz in Müller-Enbergs et al., *Von der Illegalität ins Parlament,* p. 49.

108. Willy Brandt, " . . . *was zusammengehört": Reden zu Deutschland* (Bonn: Dietz, 1990), pp. 39, 41.

109. Wilfried Geißler, "Was uns bleibt," *Sonntag,* 26/1990 (July 1), p. 2.

110. Cited in Rein, *Die Opposition,* p. 82.

3. After the Lie

1. For suggestive analyses of the tensions between liberalism and German political culture in the twentieth century, see esp. Fritz Stern, *The Politics of Cultural Despair: A Study in the Rise of the Germanic Ideology* (1961; rpt. Berkeley: University of California Press, 1974), and *The Failure of Illiberalism: Essays on the Political Culture of Modern Germany* (Chicago: University of Chicago Press, 1971); Peter Gay, *Weimar Culture* (New York: Harper & Row, 1968); and Gordon A. Craig, *The Germans* (New York: G. P. Putnam's Sons, 1982).

2. See in particular Hannah Arendt, *The Origins of Totalitarianism* (New York: Harcourt Brace Jovanovich, 1951); Carl J. Friedrich and Zbigniew K. Brzezinski, *Totalitarian Dictatorship and Autocracy* (New York: Praeger, 1956); Karl Dietrich Bracher, *Die deutsche Diktatur* (1969), in English, *The German Dictatorship: The Origins, Structure, and Effects of National Socialism*, trans. Jean Steinberg. (New York: Praeger, 1970), and *Zeitgeschichtliche Kontroversen: Um Faschismus, Totalitarismus, Demokratie*, 5th ed. (Munich: Piper, 1976). See also Raymond Aron, *Démocratie et totalitarisme* (Paris: Gallimard, 1965). For relatively early critical reflections on the concept, see Carl J. Friedrich, Michael Curtis, and Benjamin R. Barber, *Totalitarianism in Perspective: Three Views* (New York: Praeger, 1969); Herbert J. Spiro, "Totalitarianism," in *International Encyclopedia of the the Social Sciences* (New York: Cromwell Collier and Macmillan, 1968), 16: 106–113; and Robert Burrowes, "Totalitarianism: The Revised Standard Edition," in *World Politics* 17, no. 4 (1969):272–289. For alternative ways of conceptualizing communist regimes, see, e.g., Andrew C. Janos, "Systemic Models and the Theory of Change in the Comparative Study of Communist Politics," and T. H. Rigby, "Politics in the Mono-Organizational Society," both in *Authoritarian Politics in Communist Europe: Uniformity and Diversity in One-Party States*, ed. Andrew C. Janos (Berkeley: Institute of International Studies, 1976), pp. 1–30 and 31–80, respectively. The classic literary treatments of totalitarianism remain George Orwell, *1984* (New York: Harcourt Brace Jovanovich, 1949), and Arthur Koestler, *Darkness at Noon* (New York: Macmillan, 1941).

3. Ian Kershaw provides a very useful historiographic overview in *The Nazi Dictatorship: Problems and Perspectives of Interpretation*, 2d ed. (London: Edward Arnold, 1989).

4. Heiner Müller (1929–1995) was perhaps, after Bertolt Brecht, East Germany's best-known playright. Müller's father, a social democrat who had been imprisoned by the Nazis and threatened by the Russian authorities,

resettled in the Federal Republic in 1951. Like Christa Wolf, Müller had complicated relations with the East German regime; like Wolf, he was accused of having served as a Stasi informant. Heiner Müller, *Krieg ohne Schlacht: Leben in zwei Diktaturen* (Cologne: Kiepenheuer & Witsch, 1992), offers a relatively unvarnished picture of the author's personal, political, and artistic life.

5. Gustav Just, *Zeuge in eigener Sache: Die fünfziger Jahre in der DDR* (Frankfurt/am Main: Luchterhand, 1990), p. 18. Just, born in 1921, was deputy editor of *Sonntag* in the mid-1950s before his arrest. After unification, he sat as an SPD deputy in the Brandenburg state parliament, where he chaired the constitutional commission. He resigned in March 1992, when charges surfaced that he had participated in the execution of Jewish civilians during his wartime military service in the Ukraine; see Hanno Kühnert, "Die Schüsse im Leben des Gustav Just," *Die Zeit*, 15/1993 (April 9), p. 40. Just was cleared of the charges in early 1996.

6. Anna Seghers, *Das siebte Kreuz: Ein Roman aus Hitlerdeutschland* (1942; rpt. Berlin: Aufbau, 1991).

7. Merker was later purged and imprisoned as a "zionist agent" during the anti-Semitic wave of the early 1950s, then partially rehabilitated. He played an important role in Janka's trial as an apparently coerced witness for the prosecution.

8. See Just, *Zeuge*, p. 72.

9. The main elements of the surviving documentary record of Janka's trial may be read in *Der Prozeß gegen Walter Janka und andere: Eine Dokumentation* (Reinbek bei Hamburg: Rowohlt, 1990); see also Walter Janka, *Die Unterwerfung: Eine Kriminalgeschichte aus der Nachkriegszeit* (Munich: Carl Hanser, 1994). In addition to the account of the trial that Janka provides, see the perhaps more sophisticated analysis in Just, *Zeuge*.

10. Christa Wolf, "Erklärung zu Walter Janka, 28.10.1989," reprinted in Walter Janka, *Schwierigkeiten mit der Wahrheit* (Reinbek bei Hamburg: Rowohlt, 1989), p. 123.

11. See account in Walter Janka, *Spuren eines Lebens* (Reinbek bei Hamburg: Rowohlt, 1991), pp. 91–92.

12. Janka, *Schwierigkeiten*, pp. 37–38.

13. See Anna Seghers, *Der gerechte Richter* (Berlin: Aufbau, 1990). Seghers's novella, originally written in 1957–58, was published in *Sinn und Form*, no. 3 (May–June 1990): 479–501.

14. Arno Widmann, "Unfreundliche Bemerkungen zum Aufruf 'Für unser Land,'" *taz*, April 7, 1990, p. 40.

15. Heinrich Olschowski, "Vom Aufbruch und der Würde: Bemerkungen zur jüngsten Vergangenheit," *Sonntag*, 20/1990 (May 20), p. 3.

16. Erich Loest, "Plädoyer für eine Tote," *Sonntag,* 28/1990 (July 15), p. 2.

17. Christoph Hein, ". . . und andere," *Sonntag,* 1/1990, pp. 3 and 6; reprinted in Just, *Zeuge,* p. 12.

18. Interview with Detlev Lücke and Stefan Reinecke, "Der Waschzwang ist da, also muß gewaschen werden: Gespräch mit Christoph Hein über Christa Wolf und die Wirkung von Stasiakten," *Freitag,* January 29, 1993, reprinted in *Akteneinsicht Christa Wolf: Zerrspiegel und Dialog,* ed. Hermann Vinke (Hamburg: Luchterhand, 1993), p. 189.

19. Hein, ". . .und andere," in Just, *Zeuge,* p. 9.

20. Wolf Biermann, "Nur wer sich ändert, bleibt sich treu," *Die Zeit,* August 24, 1990, reprinted in *"Es geht nicht um Christa Wolf": Der Literaturstreit im vereinten Deutschland,* ed. Thomas Anz (Munich: Spangenberg, 1991), p. 149.

21. Christa Wolf, *Kindheitsmuster* (Berlin: Aufbau, 1976).

22. Christa Wolf, *Was bleibt* (1990; rpt Hamburg: Luchterhand, 1992), p. 7; hereafter cited parenthetically in the text.

23. Václav Havel, "The Power of the Powerless," in *Open Letters: Selected Writings, 1965–1990* (New York: Vintage, 1992), p. 189.

24. For a brief overview and assessment of Reich-Ranicki's career written before the controversy about the critic's own political past (discussed later in this chapter), see cover story, "Der Verreißer: Der Herr der Bücher," *Spg,* 40/1993 (October 4), pp. 268–279, and the interview immediately following, pp. 279–287. In 1991 Reich-Ranicki published a collection of his reviews of books published by East German authors under the title *Ohne Rabatt: Über Literatur aus der DDR* (Munich: dtv, 1993).

25. Christa Wolf, February 16, 1993, in Vinke, *Akteneinsicht,* p. 222.

26. Christa Wolf, "Eine Auskunft," *Berliner Zeitung,* January 21, 1993, p. 2, reprinted in Vinke, *Akteneinsicht,* p. 145.

27. Interview with Fritz-Jochen Kopka, "Margarete in Santa Monika: Wie fremd kann die Vergangenheit sein?" *Wochenpost,* January 28, 1993, pp. 4–5, reprinted in Vinke, *Akteneinsicht,* p. 165.

28. To Walter Kaufmann, the only person about whom she had filed a written report, Wolf wrote on January 28, 1993, "It now seems to me as if I were apologizing for a stranger"; text in Vinke, *Akteneinsicht,* p. 158.

29. "Margarete in Santa Monika," p. 165.

30. "Unerledigte Widersprüche: Gespräch mit Therese Hörnigk," June 1987–October 1988, reprinted in Christa Wolf, *Im Dialog: Aktuelle Texte* (Frankfurt am Main: Luchterhand, 1990), pp. 54–55.

31. Hans Globke served as Adenauer's state secretary from 1953 to 1963, and was, both then and later, a frequent target of those who deplored the way the Federal Republic had dealt with the legacies of Nazism. Ludwig Erhard

served as Adenauer's economics minister and is identified with the development of West Germany's social market economy. He was chancellor from 1963 to 1966.

32. "Schreiben im Zeitbezug: Gespräch mit Aafke Steenhuis," December 11, 1989, reprinted in Wolf, *Im Dialog,* p. 148.

33. See Frank Schirrmacher, "Literatur und Staatssicherheit," *FAZ,* January 28, 1993, reprinted in Vinke, *Akteneinsicht,* pp. 161–162.

34. I do not mean to imply that this was a uniquely West German phenomenon; I am arguing that in West Germany it had unique significance. In the postwar United States and elsewhere, "anti-totalitarianism" often meant anticommunism, and anticommunism often comforted illiberal tendencies, as the McCarthy episode richly illustrates. It would, however, be quite a reach to claim that anticommunism, let alone anti-totalitarianism, defined America's constitutional consensus or political identity at any time.

35. In the Berlin elections of January 1989, the extreme right Republikaner won 7.5 percent of the vote. They then went on to win 7.7 percent in the Bremen elections of September 1991, 8.2 percent in Schleswig-Holstein in April 1992, and 10.9 percent in Baden-Württemberg in April 1992.

36. See Günter Grass, *Die Plebejer proben den Aufstand: Ein deutsches Trauerspiel* (Neuwied: Luchterhand, 1966), reprinted in *Werkausgabe in zehn Bänden* (Darmstadt: Luchterhand, 1987), 8: 397–477, in which "Der Chef" is a thinly disguised representation of Brecht. The play is set in East Berlin during the June 1953 uprising. See also Grass's commentary in *Werkausgabe in zehn Bänden,* 9: 49–75.

37. Günter Grass, "Und was können die Schriftsteller tun?" *Die Zeit,* August 18, 1961, reprinted in *Werkausgabe in zehn Bänden,* 9: 33–34.

38. Günter Grass, "Wer schweigt, wird schuldig," *Die Welt,* August 18, 1961, reprinted in *Werkausgabe in zehn Bänden,* 9: 35–36.

39. See Günter Grass, *Gegen die verstreichende Zeit: Reden, Aufsätze und Gespräche, 1981–1991* (Hamburg: Luchterhand, 1991); *Rede vom Verlust: Über den Niedergang der politischen Kultur im geeinten Deutschland* (Göttingen: Steidl, 1992); and *Angestiftet, Partei zu ergreifen* (Munich: dtv, 1994). Grass's more differentiated effort to understand Germany during the unification period came in August 1995, with the appearance of his monumental novel *Ein weites Feld* (Göttingen: Steidl, 1995). The book—and its author—were subjected to slashing attacks in the press, with Marcel Reich-Ranicki again leading the charge. See Georg Oberhammer and Georg Ostermann, eds., *Zerreißprobe. Der neue Roman von Günter Grass 'Ein weites Feld' und die Literaturkritik. Eine Dokumentation* (Innsbruck: Innsbrucker Zeitungsarchiv, 1995).

40. "Nötige Kritik oder Hinrichtung? Spiegel-Gespräch mit Günter Grass über

die Debatte um Christa Wolf und die DDR-Literatur," *Spg*, July 16, 1990, reprinted in Anz, ed., *"Es geht nicht um Christa Wolf"*, p. 125 and passim.

41. Habermas's major works include *Legitimationsprobleme im Spätkapitalismus* (Frankfurt am Main: Suhrkamp, 1973); *Zwei Reden: aus Anlaß der Verleihung des Hegel-Preises* (Frankfurt am Main: Suhrkamp, 1974); *Theorie des kommunikativen Handelns* (Frankfurt am Main: Suhrkamp, 1981); *Moralbewußtsein und kommunikatives Handeln* (Frankfurt am Main: Suhrkamp, 1983); *Der philosophische Diskurs der Moderne: Zwölf Vorlesungen* (Frankfurt am Main: Suhrkamp, 1985); and *Erläuterungen zur Diskursethik* (Frankfurt am Main: Suhrkamp, 1991). See discussion of his positions during the *Historikerstreit* in Charles Maier, *The Unmasterable Past: History, Holocaust, and German National Identity* (Cambridge, Mass.: Harvard University Press, 1988), esp. pp. 34–65.

42. Jürgen Habermas, "Was bedeutet 'Aufarbeitung der Vergangenheit' heute? Bemerkungen zur 'doppelten Vergangenheit,'" in *Die Moderne—ein unvollendetes Projekt* (Leipzig: Reclam, 1992), p. 250.

43. Jürgen Habermas, testimony at the final hearings of the Enquete-Kommission, May 3–4, 1994, *MEK* 9:688. Habermas's testimony largely parelleled the earlier essay "Was bedeutet 'Aufarbeitung der Vergangenheit' heute?"

44. Habermas, "Was bedeutet 'Aufarbeitung der Vergangenheit' heute?" p. 254.

45. See Habermas, testimony at the final hearings of the Enquete-Kommission, *DA*, 7/1994, p. 773; cf. slightly different version in *MEK* 9:687.

46. *MEK* 9:690.

47. Habermas, "Was bedeutet 'Aufarbeitung der Vergangenheit' heute?" p. 258.

48. *MEK* 9:690. In an apparent printing or transcription error, the book replaces the verb *entbehren* with "eintreten"; cf. version printed in *DA*, 7/1994, p. 774.

49. Habermas, "Was bedeutet 'Aufarbeitung der Vergangenheit' heute?" p. 260.

50. See Jürgen Habermas, *Vergangenheit als Zukunft: Das alte Deutschland im neuen Europa? Ein Gespräch mit Michael Haller* (Munich: Piper, 1993), pp. 86–87.

51. Martin Ahrends, "Ach, ihr süßen Wessis," *Sonntag,* July 1, 1990, reprinted in Anz, *"Es geht nicht um Christa Wolf,"* p. 136. Cf. Martin Ahrends, "Betrachtung," *Die Andere,* 3/1990 (February 8), p. 12, and "Von Ost nach West: Ein deutscher Fall," *Die Andere,* 6/1990 (March 1), pp. 8–9; see also Martin Ahrends, *Mein Leben Teil Zwei: Ehemalige DDR-Bürger in der Bundesrepublik* (Cologne: Kiepenheuer & Witsch, 1989). For a very interesting West German attempt to get at "what life inside the DDR was like," undertaken just before unification, see Lutz Niethammer et al., *Die volkseigene Erfahrung: Eine Archäologie des Lebens in der Industrieprovinz der DDR* (Berlin: Rowohlt, 1991).

52. Ahrends, "Ach, ihr süßen Wessis," p. 137.

53. Erich Loest, "Wer zu spät kommt, den bestraft das Mißtrauen," *Die Welt*, January 22, 1993, reprinted in Vinke, *Akteneinsicht*, p. 151.

54. Uwe Kolbe, "Offener Brief an Sacha Anderson" November 14, 1991, in *MachtSpiele: Literatur und Staatssicherheit im Fokus Prenzlauer Berg*, ed. Peter Böthig and Klaus Michael (Leipzig: Reklam, 1993), p. 319.

55. Fritz J. Raddatz, "Von der Beschädigung der Literatur durch ihre Urheber: Bemerkungen zu Heiner Müller und Christa Wolf," *Die Zeit*, January 28, 1993, reprinted in Vinke, *Akteneinsicht*, p. 171.

56. Ibid., p. 170.

57. Fuchs intervened in the discussion that followed presentations by Karl Dietrich Bracher and Habermas. The text of his remarks is reproduced in *DA*, 7/1994, pp. 778–780, and in *MEK* 9:695–701 (with a shorter intervention at pp. 741–744). As with Habermas's testimony, I have checked the version printed in *MEK* against the version printed in *DA*.

58. *MEK* 9:698–699.

59. Ulrich Greiner, "Plädoyer für Schluß der Stasi-Debatte," *Die Zeit*, 6/1993 (February 5), p. 60.

60. Iris Radisch, "Krieg der Köpfe," *Die Zeit*, 4/1993 (January 22), p. 47.

61. Frank Schirrmacher, "Literatur und Staatssicherheit," *FAZ*, January 28, 1993, reprinted in Vinke, *Akteneinsicht*, p. 161.

62. Frank Schirrmacher, "Fälle: Wolf und Müller," *FAZ*, January 22, 1993, reprinted in Vinke, *Akteneinsicht*, p. 149.

63. Heinrich Böll had denounced a 1970s version of this game in *Die verlorene Ehre der Katherina Blum* (Berlin: Kiepenheuer & Witsch, 1974).

64. Marcel Reich-Ranicki, "Tante Christa, Mutter Wolfchen," *Spg*, 14/1994 (April 4), pp. 194–197; last quote at p. 195. In the article, *Staatsdichterin* (state poet) was erroneously set as "Staatsdienerin" (state servant), providing Reich-Ranicki with a further opportunity for commentary in a subsequent issue; see Reich-Ranicki, "Nicht jeder Hund ist ein Pudel," *Spg*, April 18, 1994, p. 10. The book Reich-Ranicki was reviewing is Christa Wolf, *Auf dem Weg nach Tabou: Texte, 1990–1994* (Cologne: Kiepenheuer & Witsch, 1994).

65. Marcel Reich-Ranicki, interview with Ulrich Greiner, "Ja, ich habe daran geglaubt," *Die Zeit*, 24/1994 (June 10), p. 53. On the Reich-Ranicki case, see "Nur das Beste: War der Kritiker Marcel Reich-Ranicki ein Mitarbeiter der polnischen Stasi? Im Fernsehen wurde es behauptet, aber nicht bewiesen," *Spg*, 23/1994 (June 6), pp. 202–204; "'Es waren harmlose Berichte': Interview mit dem Literaturkritiker Marcel Reich-Ranicki über seine Geheimdienst-Vergangenheit," *Spg*, 25/1994 (June 20), pp. 178–183; "Heikle

Post: Nach der Akte von 'Reich Marceli' kommen immer mehr Geheimdienst-Details aus der Vergangenheit Reich-Ranickis ans Licht," *Spg,* 26/1994 (June 27), pp. 174–175; "Treu und kämpferisch: Aktenfunde in Warschau belegen: Marcel Reich-Ranicki wurde 1957 wieder Partei-Kommunist—Ende einer Legende?" *Spg,* 29/1994 (July 18), pp. 142–143. See also Wolf Biermann, "Faule Tomaten: Wolf Biermann über den Fall Marcel Reich-Ranicki," *Spg,* 24/1994 (June 13), pp. 186–189; idem, "'In die Falle getappt: Offener Brief von Wolf Biermann an Jürgen Fuchs—in Sachen Reich-Ranicki," *Spg,* 27/1994 (July 4), pp. 134–138; and Hellmuth Karasek, "Des Bänkelsängers Fluch: SPIEGEL-Redakteur Hellmuth Karasek zu Tilman Jens, Marcel Reich-Ranicki und Wolf Biermann," *Spg,* 28/1994 (July 11), pp. 171–172. In *Die Zeit,* see esp., in addition to the interview already cited, Ulrich Greiner, "Der Kommissar: Nachdenken über Marcel R.-R.: Die Wahrheit der Intellektuellen,"*Spg,* 26/1994 (June 24), p. 45; and Janusz Tycner, "Die Akte Ranicki," *Spg,* 29/1994 (July 15), pp. 39–40.

66. Greiner, "Plädoyer für Schluß der Stasi-Debatte," p. 60.

67. For a stimulating analysis of the legitimacy problem as it was posed in and by the DDR, see Sigrid Meuschel, *Legitimation und Parteiherrschaft in der DDR: Zum Paradox von Stabilität und Revolution in der DDR, 1945–1989* (Frankfurt am Main: Suhrkamp, 1992).

68. Václav Havel, "The Power of the Powerless," in *Open Letters,* pp. 125–214; hereafter cited parenthetically in the text. The imaginary greengrocer first appears on p. 132, and then reappears frequently throughout the essay.

69. In "The Power of the Powerless" and elsewhere, Havel calls these systems "post-totalitarian," a term he admits is confusing: "I do not wish to imply by the prefix 'post-' that the system is no longer totalitarian; on the contrary" (131). Havel seems to want to distinguish not only between authoritarian ("classical") dictatorships and totalitarian systems, but also between developing totalitarian systems (of the right or the left) that rely on terror and mature totalitarian systems that no longer require terror; his discussion focuses on the latter, of which he thought Czechoslovakia was a prime example. His distinctions are not meant to create a moral hierarchy (à la Jean Kirkpatrick) between authoritarian and totalitarian states, and they are not polemical. Rather, Havel associates authoritarianism empirically with less modern societies and "post-totalitarianism" with more modern societies. To minimize confusion, I have substituted the term "totalitarian," with or without qualifiers (post-terrorist, mature) for Havel's term "post-totalitarian."

70. Cf. ibid., p. 136: "[People] need not accept the lie. It is enough for them to have accepted their life with it and in it. For by this very fact, individu-

als confirm the system, fulfill the system, make the system, *are* the system."

71. Havel explicitly includes Alexander Dubček, the leader who presided over the "Prague Spring" of 1968, in this indictment.

72. In a later essay, Havel developed the link between totalitarianism and modernity; see Václav Havel, "Politics and Conscience," February 1984, in *Open Letters*, pp. 249–271.

73. For Havel's "dream" of what a postcommunist Czechoslovakia might look like, see Václav Havel, *Summer Meditations* (New York: Knopf, 1992), esp. pp. 102–128.

74. Cf. ibid., pp. 53–59.

75. Václav Havel, *Letters to Olga: June 1979–September 1982* (New York: Henry Holt and Co., 1989), pp. 347–348.

76. Ibid., pp. 348, 354, 355. For Havel's understanding of conscience, see pp. 344–347.

77. See Karl Jaspers, *Philosophie*, vol. 2, *Existenzerhellung* (1932; rpt. Berlin: Springer-Verlag, 1973), pp. 65–67.

78. Karl Jaspers, *Die Schuldfrage: Für Völkermord gibt es keine Verjährung* (Munich: Piper, 1979), p. 87; hereafter cited parenthetically in the text.

79. Hermann Lübbe, "Der Nationalsozialismus im politischen Bewußtsein der Gegenwart," in *Deutschlands Weg in die Diktatur: Internationale Konferenz zur nationalsozialistischen Machtübernahme im Reichstagsgebäude zu Berlin. Referate und Diskussionen: Ein Protokoll*, ed. Martin Broszat et al. (Berlin: Siedler, 1983), p. 330; hereafter cited parenthetically in the text.

80. Lübbe in Broszat et al., *Deutschlands Weg in die Diktatur*, p. 376.

81. Manfred Kittel, in *Die Legende von der "Zweiten Schuld": Vergangenheitsbewältigung in der Ära Adenauer* (Berlin: Ullstein, 1993), pushes Lübbe's argument a step further, arguing not only that West Germans did not repress their past but that they had in fact confronted and worked through it.

82. For a very different, but not intellectually uncritical, assessment of the fascism school, see Tim Mason, "Whatever Happened to 'Fascism'?" in *Nazism, Fascism, and the Working Class* (Cambridge: Cambridge University Press, 1995), pp. 323–331.

83. Lübbe in Broszat et al., *Deutschlands Weg in die Diktatur*, p. 377.

84. Hans-Ulrich Wehler, a historian, and Hermann Rudolph, then with *Die Zeit* and subsequently editor of the Berlin daily *Tagesspiegel*, raised the issues of costs in the discussion; see Broszat et al., *Deutschlands Weg in die Diktatur*, pp. 358–360 (Wehler) and 360–362 (Rudolph).

85. See Hans Maier in Broszat et al., *Deutschlands Weg in die Diktatur*, pp. 364–365. Maier, a historian, was Bavarian minister of education and culture.

86. Lübbe, ibid., pp. 375–376. Lübbe was at the time a liberal, and lest his nearly blinding anger at the "'68ers" seem incomprehensible to a non-German or younger audience, it is perhaps worth recalling that in Germany the confrontations of the late 1960s were especially bitter, and that the terrorist sequels of "1968" extended into the 1970s and beyond: in the fall of 1977, Hanns Martin Schleyer was kidnapped and killed by the RAF (Rote-Armee-Fraktion, Red Army Fraction), a Lufthansa flight was hijacked, and three of the original RAF group committed suicide in Stammheim prison.

87. Lübbe, ibid., p. 376.

88. "Left" and "right" are clumsy terms in this context, and allies in one debate were not necessarily allies in all; but, to cite two examples whom no one would place on the "right," neither Jürgen Habermas nor Saul Friedländer was above using political criteria to disqualify arguments or approaches that could have been met on intellectual grounds.

89. Mason, "Whatever Happened to Fascism," p. 328.

90. Jürgen Habermas, "Geschichtsbewußtsein und posttraditionale Identität: Die Westorientierung der Bundesrepublik" (1987), in *Die Moderne—ein unvollendetes Projekt*, p. 160.

91. See Ernst Nolte, "Zwischen Geschichtslegende und Revisionismus? Das Dritte Reich im Blickwinkel des Jahres 1980" (July 1980), and "Vergangenheit, die nicht vergehen will: Eine Rede, die geschrieben, aber nicht gehalten werden konnte" (June 1986), both reprinted in *"Historikerstreit": Die Dokumentation der Kontroverse um die Einzigartigkeit der nationalsozialistischen Judenvernichtung*, ed. Rudolf Augstein et al. (Munich: Piper, 1987), pp. 13–35 and 39–47, respectively; Nolte, interview with Rudolf Augstein, "'Ein historisches Recht Hitlers'?" *Spg*, 40/1994 (October 3), pp. 83–103; and Nolte's contribution, "Sur la théorie du totalitarisme," pp. 139–146 in the March–April 1996 (no. 89) issue of *Le Débat*, devoted to a discussion of François Furet's 1995 book *Le Passé d'une illusion: essai sur l'idée communiste au XXᵉ siècle* (Paris: Calmann-Lévy).

92. Ralph Giordano, "'Wann ist Schluß mit der Traditionslüge, Herr Generalinspekteur?'" open letter to General Klaus Naumann, *Die Woche*, July 14, 1994.

93. Alfred Dregger, "Der Pflicht gehorcht," *Die Woche*, July 21, 1994.

94. Jens Jessen, "Als hätten die Enkel der Blockwarte gesiegt," *FAZ*, July 23, 1994, p. 25.

95. Richard von Weizsäcker, "Der 8. Mai 1945: Ansprache bei einer Gedenkstunde im Plenarsaal des Deutschen Bundestages," May 8, 1985, *Reden und Interviews*, vol. 1, *1.Juli 1984–30.Juni 1985* (Bonn: Presse- und Informationsamt der Bundesregierung, 1986), p. 290.

4. Successor Justice

1. C. S. Lewis, *The Problem of Pain* (1940; rpt. New York: Macmillan, 1973), p. 83. Lewis, of course, was speaking of retribution in a Christian context of sin and redemption, but the passage is instructive:

> Pain insists upon being attended to. God whispers to us in our pleasures, speaks in our conscience, but shouts in our pains: it is His megaphone to rouse a deaf world . . . (p. 81)
>
> When our ancestors referred to pains and sorrows as God's "vengeance" upon sin they were not necessarily attributing evil passions to God; they may have been recognising the good element in the idea of retribution. Until the evil man finds evil unmistakably present in his existence, in the form of pain, he is enclosed in illusion. Once pain has roused him, he knows that he is in some way or other "up against" the real universe: he either rebels (with the possibility of a clearer issue and deeper repentance at some later stage) or else makes some attempt at an adjustment, which, if pursued, will lead him to religion . . . No doubt Pain as God's megaphone is a terrible instrument; it may lead to final and unrepented rebellion. But it gives the only opportunity the bad man can have for amendment. It removes the veil; it plants the flag of truth within the fortress of a rebel soul. (pp. 81, 83)

   In Lewis's view, it too offers people a second chance.

2. The locus classicus of the retributionist argument is Kant's position in the *Metaphysische Anfangsgründe der Rechtslehre,* pp. 331–337 in the standard Königliche Preussische Akademie der Wissenschaft edition (Berlin, 1902–1938), vol. 6.

3. Joel Feinberg, "The Expressive Function of Punishment," *The Monist* 49, no. 3 (July 1965): p. 400, 403. The proper place of retribution in criminal justice has generated renewed debate in recent decades. See in particular H. L. A. Hart, *Punishment and Responsibility: Essays in the Philosophy of Law* (New York: Oxford University Press, 1968), esp. chap. 1 and 9; Jeffrie G. Murphy and Jean Hampton, *Forgiveness and Mercy* (Cambridge: Cambridge University Press, 1988); Joshua Dressler, "Hating Criminals: How Can Something That Feels So Good Be Wrong?" *Michigan Law Review* 88 (May 1990): 1448–73; and the essays in Wesley Cragg, ed., *Retributivism and Its Critics* (Stuttgart: Franz Steiner, 1992), esp. Jean Hampton, "An Expressive Theory of Retribution," pp. 1–25.

4. For a more optimistic account than I offer here, see Mark Osiel, *Mass Atrocity, Collective Memory, and the Law* (New Brunswick, N. J.: Transaction, 1997).

5. Jean Hampton, "Correcting Harms versus Righting Wrongs: The Goal of Retribution," *UCLA Law Review* 39 (1992): pp. 1686–87. Hampton's work is especially relevant to the discussion here, for her main concern is with wrongdoing that represents "an affront to the victim's value or dignity" (p. 1666). In addition to works already cited, see Hampton, "Liberalism, Retribution, and Criminality," in *In Harm's Way: Essays in Honor of Joel Feinberg,* ed. Jules L. Coleman and Allen Buchanan (Cambridge: Cambridge University Press, 1994), pp. 159–181.

6. *Die Zeit,* 14/1992, p. 44.

7. Albert Camus, *Combat,* January 5, 1945, p. 1.

8. See art. 3, paragraph 2 of the Basic Law and § 1 of the Strafgesetzbuch (Penal Code, hereafter StGB): "An act can be punished only if it was legally actionable before it was committed." Thus, the law makes the crime: "Crimes are unlawful [*rechtswidrige*] acts punishable by at least one year in prison" (§ 12 StGB).

9. Egon Krenz, February 19, 1996, to 27. Strafkammer, Berlin, excerpted in *Der Tagesspiegel* (hereafter *Tsp*), February 29, 1996, p. 5.

10. Judith N. Shklar, *Legalism: Law, Morals, and Political Trials* (1964; rpt. Cambridge, Mass.: Harvard University Press, 1986), pp. 149, 145 (emphasis added).

11. See trial transcript, Pierre Laval, *Le Procès Laval* (Paris: A. Michel, 1946).

12. The differences crystallized in discussions about whether prewar Nazi crimes committed against German nationals could be considered actionable, and about the use of conspiracy charges and organizational indictments.

13. Lord Shawcross, "Robert H. Jackson's Contributions during the Nuremberg Trial," in *Mr. Justice Jackson,* ed. Charles S. Desmond et al. (New York: Columbia University Press, 1969), p. 106, citing Robert Jackson's response to Soviet proposals.

14. Henry L. Stimson, responding to the Morgenthau Plan in a memo to President Franklin D. Roosevelt, September 9, 1944, excerpted in Bradley F. Smith, *The American Road to Nuremberg: The Documentary Record, 1944–1945* (Stanford: Hoover Institution Press, 1982), p. 20.

15. Cited in Telford Taylor, *The Anatomy of the Nuremberg Trials: A Personal Memoir* (New York: Knopf, 1992), p. 45.

16. Shklar, *Legalism,* p. 151.

17. Ibid.

18. Herbert Wechsler, "The Issues of the Nuremberg Trial," December 30, 1946, reprinted in *Principles, Politics, and Fundamental Law* (Cambridge, Mass.: Harvard University Press, 1961), pp. 143–144, 145 (emphasis added).

19. Cf. Steffen Heitmann, "Die Revolution in der Spur des Rechts: Verdienst und Schwäche des Umbruchs in der früheren DDR," *FAZ*, December 30, 1994, p. 6.

20. Most scholars who have written on the purges have avoided the empirically—and especially methodologically—difficult question of what impact the purges might have had. See, however, Peter Novick, *The Resistance versus Vichy: The Purge of Collaborators in Liberated France* (New York-Columbia University Press, 1968); François Rouquet, *L'Épuration dans l'administration française* (Paris: CNRS, 1993); and Henry Rousso, *Le syndrôme de Vichy, 1944–198 . . .* (Paris: Le Seuil, 1987).

21. Judith N. Shklar, *The Faces of Injustice* (New Haven: Yale University Press, 1990), p. 105.

22. *The Trial of the Major War Criminals before the International Military Tribunal*, vol. 2, *Proceedings 14 November 1945–30 November 1945* (Nuremberg: IMT, 1947), p. 102; hereafter cited as *TMWC*. The American occupation authorities tried to track public opinion in the months following the German capitulation. For an indication of how the Nuremberg Trial was viewed and what Germans claimed to have learned from the proceedings, see Anna Merritt and Richard L. Merritt, eds., *Public Opinion in Occupied Germany: The OMGUS Surveys, 1945–1949* (Urbana: University of Illinois Press, 1970), pp. 34–35, 93–94, 121–123, and 161–162. By October 1950, only 38 percent of a sample in the American Zone thought that the Nuremberg Trial had been just—down from 78 percent in 1946; see Ulrich Brochhagen, *Nach Nürnberg: Vergangenheitsbewältigung und Westintegration in der Ära Adenauer* (Hamburg: Junius, 1994), p. 35.

23. *TMWC* 2:102–103; 104–105; 130 (the verbs "annihilate" and "intimidate" are Jackson's); 99.

24. Ibid., pp. 99, 145, 147.

25. Ibid., pp. 155.

26. Erik Reger, *Tsp*, December 18, 1945, p. 3.

27. Ibid.

28. *TMWC* 2:104.

29. Ibid., pp. 151, 31.

30. Ibid., pp. 32, 72–73.

31. Cited in Shawcross, "Robert H. Jackson's Contributions during the Nuremberg Trial," p. 108.

32. Taylor, *Nuremberg Trials*, p. 387. For Taylor's account of the "very bad show" that led to the indictment of Gustav Krupp—who had suffered a debilitating stroke in 1941 and who by 1945 was "in an advanced state of senile decay, inarticulate, incontinent, and wholly incapable of standing trial"—in the place of his son Alfried, see esp. pp. 90–94 (quotes at p. 93).

33. *TMWC*, vol. 19, *Proceedings 19 July 1946–29 July 1946* (Nuremberg: IMT, 1948), p. 428.
34. Taylor, *Nuremberg Trials*, p. 35.
35. See Taylor, *Nuremberg Trials*, p. 516 (SS), p. 507 (Leadership Corps).
36. *TMWC*, vol. 22, *Proceedings 27 August 1946–1 October 1946* (Nuremberg: IMT, 1948), pp. 269–270.
37. The Smith Act made it a crime to advocate the overthrow of the government (or to "advise" the "desirability" of such a move), "to organize or help to organize any society, group, or assembly of persons who teach, advocate, or encourage the overthrow or destruction of any government in the United States . . . ; or to be or become a member of, or affiliate with, any such society, group, or assembly of persons, knowing the purposes thereof." The act was later used during the McCarthy era to prosecute alleged communists. The Supreme Court upheld its constitutionality in *Dennis v. United States*, 341 U.S. 494 (1951), but restricted its reach in 1957 in *Yates v. United States*, 353 U.S. 298.
38. Taylor, *Nuremberg Trials*, pp. 502–503.
39. Ibid., pp. 555–559, 556, 278, 287 (cf. p. 637).
40. Ibid., pp. 278, 279.
41. The expression of this disappointment was often (but by no means always) paired with sympathy for the communist enterprise in the Soviet zone (SBZ) or DDR; cf. Friedrich Wolf, speech to Berlin Kulturbund, November 25, 1945, approving the proceedings at Nuremberg: "It is a deeply tragic fact that through our own fault, our people lost the right to sit in judgment over these terrible criminals in our midst." Excerpts in Klaus Wagenbach et al., eds., *Vaterland, Muttersprache: Deutsche Schriftsteller und ihr Staat seit 1945* (Berlin: Klaus Wagenbach, 1994), p. 32.
42. Telford Taylor, *Guilt, Responsibility, and the Third Reich*, Churchill College Overseas Fellowship Lectures no. 6 (Cambridge: W. Heffer & Sons, 1970), p. 14.
43. See Lutz Niethammer, *Die Mitläuferfabrik: Die Entnazifizierung am Beispiel Bayerns* (1972; rpt. Berlin: Dietz, 1982). Niethammer's study remains, despite the sometimes questionable explanatory references to American capitalism, the most thorough and stimulating examination of denazification. Clemens Vollnhals provides a very useful documentary introduction, including documents regarding contemporary reactions to and assessments of denazification, in Clemens Vollnhals, ed., *Entnazifizierung* (Munich: dtv, 1991).
44. Justice Hans Hofmeyer, quoted in Gerhard Werle and Thomas Wandres, *Auschwitz vor Gericht: Völkermord und bundesdeutsche Strafjustiz* (Munich: Beck, 1995), p. 83.

45. For Lutz Niethammer's nuanced and suggestive assessment of the impact of denazification, see *Die Mitläuferfabrik,* pp. 21–27 and 653–666. For survey data on later German views of denazification, see Vollnhals, *Entnazifizierung,* pp. 335–338; and Elisabeth Noelle-Neumann, ed., *The Germans: Public Opinion Polls, 1947–1966* (Westport, Conn.: Greenwood Press, 1967), pp. 156, 219, 229. For an influential novel that itself exemplifies a response to denazification, see Ernst von Salomon, *Der Fragebogen* (Reinbek bei Hamburg: Rowohlt, 1951).

46. This assessment appears in a number of contemporary and more recent titles, for example, John Herz, "The Fiasco of Denazification in Germany," *Political Science Quarterly* 63 (1948): 569–594; and Tom Bower, *The Pledge Betrayed: America and Britain and the Denazification of Postwar Germany* (Garden City, N.Y.: Doubleday, 1982).

47. For an important exception, see Jörg Friedrich, *Die kalte Amnestie: NS-Täter in der Bundesrepublik* (Munich: Piper, 1994).

48. The three books, along with Christoph Meckel's *Suchbild: Über meinen Vater* (1980: rpt. Frankfurt am Main: Fischer, 1983), are discussed in Werner Schwan, *"Ich bin doch kein Unmensch": Kriegs- und Nachkriegszeit im deutschen Roman* (Freiburg: Rombach, 1990). Heinrich Böll, *Gruppenbild mit Dame* (1971; rpt. Cologne: Kiepenheuer & Witsch, 1994); Günter Grass, *Die Blechtrommel* (1959; rpt. Darmstadt: Luchterhand, 1984); Siegfried Lenz, *Deutschstunde* (1968; rpt. Munich: dtv, 1973).

49. Böll, *Gruppenbild mit Dame,* p. 186; hereafter cited parenthetically in the text.

50. Böll tells one story about Pelzer, but it would be possible to tell other stories about a man like Pelzer, and to tell them in a different tone from the one Böll uses. Our judgments too might then be more confused. This perceptual problem is suggested in Inge Deutschkron's two memoirs, *Ich trug den gelben Stern* (1978; rpt. Munich: dtv, 1985), and *Mein Leben nach dem Überleben* (1992; rpt. Munich: dtv, 1995). Deutschkron was born in 1918 and grew up in a social democratic household in Berlin. Her father was a World War I veteran and an *Oberstudienrat* (school administrator); he fled to England in 1939. Deutschkron and her mother were stranded in Berlin, where they were helped and hidden throughout the war by old and new friends. In the midst of terror and humiliation, Deutschkron describes occasional acts of courage and daring—and countless small acts of solidarity. Thus, the Deutschkrons' grocer continued to supply them, though it was illegal to do so: "The song of praise to these fine people who, disregarding the danger of denunciation by Nazi fellow citizens, at least in this way stood by their Jewish clients, will never be written, because those who could write it are no longer alive" (*Ich trug den gelben Stern,* p. 60). In *Mein*

Leben nach dem Überleben, Deutschkron recounts her life after 1945, and the anger and alienation she felt as she saw how well former perpetrators did and how poorly former victims fared in the new German democracy. "It may sound strange," she writes, "but only in Bonn, years after the end of the Third Reich, did I meet dyed-in-the-wool Nazis . . . They were every-where—in the bureaucracy, in the Bundestag, in the parties" (p. 129). The people of whom Deutschkron was most critical were not greengrocers but men who (like Hans Globke) had once been in positions of responsibility and now were again. But the Deutschkrons' grocer might have had a life the Deutschkrons did not see. What sentiment would then have ruled Deutschkron's memory?

51. Cf. analysis in Rudolf Wassermann, *Recht, Gewalt, Widerstand: Vorträge und Aufsätze* (Berlin: Arno Spitz, 1985), esp. Chaps. 1 and 2. The survey data on such questions is disappointing. Indicative data are available, however, on how West Germans characterized the political regime of the Third Reich, how they assessed the responsibilities of various groups (including themselves), and whether or not they felt that prosecutions should continue. See Noelle-Neumann, *The Germans: Public Opinion Polls, 1947–1966;* idem., ed., *The Germans: Public Opinion Polls, 1967–1980* (Westport, Conn.: Greenwood Press, 1981); and the Institut für Demoskopie Allensbach serial *Allensbacher Jahrbuch der Demoskopie.* One of the most interesting—and perhaps least noticed—polls reported in *The Germans: Public Opinion Polls, 1947–1966* (p. 313) asked, in the context of other questions about capital punishment (*not* about the war or the Third Reich), whether the respondent had ever witnessed an execution. Capital punishment had been banned by the Basic Law. In January 1958, 11 percent of male respondents (and 1 percent of the females) said that they had witnessed an execution. It is hard to imagine where so many men might have witnessed an execution if not during their wartime military service. According to survey data from the early 1960s (p. 7), 51 percent of the male population had performed military service during the war; 75 percent of this number had served in the army, and 54 percent had served in Russia. An August 1953 question asked: "Do you think that the German soldiers of the last war can be reproached for their conduct in the occupied countries?" (p. 202). Of the respondents, 55 percent (60 percent of the men) replied "no"; 21 percent (24 percent) answered "in some cases"; 6 percent (7 percent) replied "yes"; and 18 percent (9 percent) did not know. Another question repeated in August 1958, October 1963, and January 1965 (p. 315) asked respondents to imagine two men "discussing whether persons who committed crimes before or during the war should still be tried today." In the three polls, 54 percent, 54 percent, and 52 percent (gender differences are not

reported) agreed with the following position: "I feel we should cease trying people now for crimes they committed many years ago. It would be a good thing to draw a line under the past once and for all." Respectively, 34 percent, 34 percent, and 38 percent agreed with the following: "I feel that if it comes to light that a person committed a crime long ago he should still be punished for it today. I don't see why someone who has tortured or killed others should go scot-free." The polls reported 12 percent, 12 percent, and 10 percent of the samples undecided between the two positions. See also Bernd Hay, "Die NS-Prozesse—Versuch einer juristischen Vergangenheitsbewältigung," *Geschichte in Wissenschaft und Unterricht* 6 (1981); 331–362.

52. Lenz, *Deutschstunde;* hereafter cited parenthetically in the text.

53. From the Auschwitz Trial verdict; see Fritz Bauer et al., eds., *Justiz und NS-Verbrechen: Sammlung deutscher Strafurteile wegen nationalsozialistischer Tötungsverbrechen, 1945–1966,* vol. 21 (Amsterdam: University Press Amsterdam, 1968–1981), 595 a-70, p. 450.

The three most important printed sources of primary source material on the Auschwitz Trial are Hermann Langbein, ed., *Der Auschwitz-Prozeß: Eine Dokumentation,* 2 vols. (Frankfurt am Main: Verlag Neue Kritik, 1995), esp. for the testimony of witnesses and defendants, and esp. as that testimony relates to the task of reconstructing what happened in the camp; Bernd Naumann, *Auschwitz: Bericht über die Strafsache gegen Mulka und andere vor dem Schwurgericht Frankfurt* (Frankfurt am Main: Athenäum, 1965); and Fritz Bauer et al., eds. *Justiz und NS-Verbrechen,* 21:362–837 for the text of the court's verdict; appeals decisions follow, pp. 838–887. Werle and Wandres, *Auschwitz vor Gericht,* provides a useful introduction and set of documents aimed at the general public. The dialogue in Peter Weiss's play *Die Ermittlung* (Frankfurt am Main: Suhrkamp, 1965) is taken exclusively from trial testimony. For the sake of brevity, I have cited the Langbein and Bauer compilations by editor, volume, and page number.

54. Richard Baer, the last Auschwitz commandant, died on June 17, 1963, five months before the trial began; two cases were separated from the trial after it got under way.

55. Brochhagen, *Nach Nürnberg,* pp. 76, 78. On the creation of the Zentrale Stelle, see Adalbert Rückerl, *NS-Verbrechen vor Gericht* (Heidelberg: Müller, 1984), pp. 139–151.

56. Quoted in Werle and Wandres, *Auschwitz vor Gericht,* p. 43.

57. Bauer, vol. 21, 595 a-67, p. 447; a-68, p. 448.

58. Langbein 2:687.

59. Ibid. 1:199–202.

60. SS-Obersturmführer (Lieutenant Colonel) Rudolf Höß was commandant

in Auschwitz from 1940 through 1943. See Martin Broszat, ed., *Rudolph Höß: Kommandant in Auschwitz: Autobiographische Aufzeichnungen* (Munich: dtv, 1994).

61. Langbein 1:209, 186, 187, 206, 166, 206–207.
62. Ibid. 1:181, 165.
63. Ibid. 2:827–835; Hans Buchheim, "Befehl und Gehorsam" (expert testimony prepared for the trial), reprinted in Hans Buchheim et al., *Anatomie des SS-Staats* (1967; rpt. Munich: dtv, 1994), pp. 215–320; Herbert Jäger, *Verbrechen unter totalitärer Herrschaft* (Frankfurt am Main: Suhrkamp, 1982) esp. pt. 2; Adalbert Rückerl, *NS-Verbrechen vor Gericht: Versuch einer Vergangenheitsbewältigung* (Heidelberg: Müller, 1984), pp. 281–288; Christopher R. Browning, *Ordinary Men: Reserve Police Battalion 101 and the Final Solution in Poland* (New York: HarperCollins, 1992).
64. Werle and Wandres, *Auschwitz vor Gericht*, p. 84.
65. Langbein 2:711.
66. Hans Laternser, *Die andere Seite im Auschwitz-Prozeß 1963/1965: Reden eines Verteidigers* (Stuttgart: Seewald Verlag, 1966), pp. 208, 129, 386, and passim. Laternser had represented the General Staff–High Command in the Nuremberg Trial, replacing Franz Exner as defense counsel on January 27, 1946. In his closing argument at the Auschwitz Trial, Laternser made the usual references to the aerial bombardment of cities, especially Dresden, by Allied warplanes, and to the occupation of eastern Germany by the Soviet Union; see, e.g., p. 134.
67. Bauer, vol. 21, 595 a-75, p. 455.
68. Günther Diehl, April 23, 1969, quoted in Deutschkron, *Mein Leben nach dem Überleben*, p. 187. Diehl had been a member of the NSDAP and had worked during the war for the Foreign Ministry.
69. See, e.g., the testimony of Wilhelm Boger: "Intensive interrogations were, as ordered, carried out by me. I was not, however, active in the extermination of Jews, but in the fight against the Polish resistance and bolshevism" (Langbein 1:433). Boger, who had been a particularly brutal interrogator in the political unit in Auschwitz, had remained within the realm of Nazi common sense in other ways. When Justice Hummerich reminded him that statements made under torture were unlikely to be true, Boger replied: "I am of a different opinion, and especially as concerns Auschwitz. I am also of the view that in many cases today, beating would be appropriate, for example, in juvenile punishment. I didn't beat people to death, I carried out orders" (p. 382). Mulka uses the term "Terrorangriffe" (terror attack, e.g., p. 200), and explains why he immediately swung into action: "It was certainly not without danger, but as a German man, I felt myself obligated to help my fellows, to help anyone" (p. 210). For Weizsäcker's critically

important speech, delivered to the Bundestag on May 8, 1985, see Richard von Weizsäcker, *Reden und Interviews,* vol. 1, *1. Juli 1984–30. Juni 1985* (Bonn: Presse- und informationsamt der Bundesregierung, 1986), pp. 279–295.

In discussing this issue, I hope I have avoided both oversimplifying a complicated problem and complicating a simple one. Perpetrators are of course not immune from suffering (as, for example, when their neighborhood is bombed or their friends are killed in combat); their suffering, however, does not make them "victims" in the moral and political sense of the word. And victims did (and do) commit acts we associate with perpetrators (for example, administering lethal injections in camp "hospitals"). For case studies and a discussion of these problems, see Wolfgang Benz and Barbara Distel, eds., *Täter und Opfer,* Dachauer Hefte no. 10 (November 1994).

70. Bauer, vol. 21, 595 a-64, p. 444.

71. Ibid., a-66f, pp. 446–447.

72. Ibid., a-66f, p. 448. The StGB differentiates between *Täterschaft* (criminal responsibility, §25) and *Beihilfe* (aiding and abetting, §27) as follows: "A person who commits the crime himself or causes it to be committed by another is to be punished as criminally responsible." However, "A person who intentionally helps another person intentionally commit an unlawful act is to be punished as an accessory to the crime."

73. Bauer, vol. 21, 595 a-74, p. 454.

74. Stefan Baretzki, testimony in Langbein 1:317.

75. Laternser, closing argument, June 10, 1965, in *Die andere Seite,* pp. 208, 209.

76. Letter quoted by Primo Levi in *The Drowned and the Saved,* trans. Raymond Rosenthal (New York; Summit Books, 1988), pp. 176–177. Cf. Levi's reflections on the guilt felt by camp survivors, esp. pp. 70–87.

77. Langbein 1:232, 233. SS Hauptsturmführer (Captain) Hans Aumeier was an officer in Auschwitz in 1942–43; he was executed in Poland in December 1947. SS Hauptsturmführer Heinrich Schwarz was responsible for the work crews in Auschwitz. He was executed in France in 1947.

78. See the debate in the press around Hannes Heer and Klaus Naumann, eds., *Vernichtungskrieg: Verbrechen der Wehrmacht, 1941–1944* (Hamburg: Hamburger Edition, 1995), and the related public exhibition, organized by the Hamburg Institut für Sozialforschung. The debate was renewed by the approach of the fiftieth anniversary of V-E Day in May 1995 and resumed in 1996–97.

79. Naumann, *Auschwitz,* reproduces many of Naumann's reports from the courtroom. On press coverage of the trial, see Jürgen Wilke et al., *Holocaust*

und *NS-Prozesse: Die Presseberichterstattung in Israel und Deutschland zwischen Aneignung und Abwehr* (Cologne: Böhlau, 1995).

80. Taylor, *Guilt, Responsibility, and the Third Reich,* p. 14.

81. Johann Georg Reißmüller, "Die Sühne für Auschwitz," *FAZ,* August 20, 1965, p. 1. Twenty-five years later, when the DDR past was the object of prosecutorial attention, *FAZ* would defend a more expansive conception of the political capacities of democratic courts.

82. Deutschkron, *Mein Leben nach dem Überleben,* pp. 152–153.

83. Bernhard Schlink, *Der Vorleser* (Zurich: Diogenes, 1995); hereafter cited parenthetically in the text.

84. Antrag der Freien und Hansestadt Hamburg, March 3, 1969, Bundesrat, Begründigung, in Deutscher Bundestag, *Zur Verjährung nationalsozialistischer Verbrechen: Dokumentation der parlamentarischen Bewältigung des Problems, 1960–1979,* in *Zur Sache: Themen Parlamentarischer Beratung,* 4/1980, p. 357.

85. *FAZ,* February 24, 1996, p. 1. For a negative assessment of this record that both intentionally and unintentionally makes clear the legal obstacles that hamper prosecutions, see Günther Schwarberg, "Die Mörderwaschmaschine. Wie die bundesdeutsche Justiz die Verbrechen der Faschisten mit Hilfe von Einstellungsbeschlüssen bewältigte oder: Von den Massenerschießungen abgesehen, war die Sterblichkeit gering," in *Gegen Barbarei: Essays Robert M. W. Kempner zu Ehren,* ed. Rainer Eisfeld and Ingo Müller (Frankfurt am Main: Athenäum, 1989), pp. 324–345. See also Deutschkron, *Mein Leben nach dem Überleben,* esp. pp. 129–189.

86. The quotation in the section heading is from Steffen Heitmann (CDU justice minister in Saxony), Anhörung der SPD-Bundestagsfraktion zur justitiellen Aufarbeitung von DDR-Unrecht und zum Umgang mit den Stasi-Akten, Berlin, March 2, 1995, Documentation, p. 32. Heitmann's reluctance to respect in practice the insight of his own statement is significant.

87. "'Ein Strafprozeß gegen Mulka und andere': Aus der mündlichen Begründung des Urteils im Auschwitz-Verfahren," *FAZ,* August 20, 1965, p. 6.

88. These calls have come from different quarters and have been differently motivated. For a sense of the debate, which was particularly sharp in the winter of 1994–95, see interview with Egon Bahr, "'Ich will unser Blut zurück,'" *Spg,* 43/1994 (October 24), pp. 41–47; interview with Richard Schröder, "'Alle im Zwielicht,'" *Spg,* 1/1995 (January 1–2), p. 30; Uwe Wesel, "Plädoyer für ein Schlußgesetz," *Die Zeit,* 1/1995 (January 6), p. 3; interview with Wolfgang Thierse and Lothar de Maizière, "Ein Volk unter Verdacht," *Die Woche,* January 12, 1995, pp. 6–7; Marion Gräfin Dönhoff, "Gerechtigkeit ist nicht Vergeltung," *Die Zeit,* 2/1995 (January 13), p. 1; in-

terview with Richard von Weizsäcker, "'Das Strafen muß ein Ende finden,'" *Spg,* 4/1995 (January 23), pp. 22–25; Joachim Gauck, "Wut und Schmerz der Opfer," *Die Zeit,* 3/1995 (January 20), p. 5; interview with Wolfgang Schäuble, "'Keine Generation ist ohne Schuld,'" *Die Woche,* February 17, 1995, pp. 6–7.

89. On the creation of the Berlin Arbeitsgruppe and of the Zentrale Ermittlungsstelle zur Bekämpfung der Regierungs- und Vereinigungskriminalität (ZERV), see parliamentary debates in *Verhandlungen des Deutschen Bundestages,* 12. Wahlperiode, December 12, 1991, pp. 5782–92 and October 29, 1992, pp. 9793–99.

90. The absence of coherence is apparent not just in the indictments served but in the account of the effort given by Schaefgen; see Christoph Schaefgen, "Die Strafverfolgung von Regierungskriminalität der DDR: Probleme, Ergebnisse, Perspektiven," in *Eine Diktatur von Gericht: Aufarbeitung von SED-Unrecht durch die Justiz,* ed. Jürgen Weber and Michael Piazolo (Munich: Günter Olzog, 1995), pp. 49–87. Other essays in the book offer a useful overview of the problems German justice has faced since unification. See also Herwig Roggemann, *Fragen und Wege zur Rechtseinheit in Deutschland* (Berlin: Berlin Verlag A. Spitz, 1995); idem, *Systemunrecht und Strafrecht am Beispiel der Mauerschützen in der ehemaligen DDR* (Berlin: Berlin Verlag A. Spitz, 1993); and Ernst-Joachim Lampe, ed., *Deutsche Wiedervereinigung: Die Rechtseinheit,* vol. 2, *Die Verfolgung von Regierungskriminalität der DDR nach der Wiedervereinigung* (Cologne: Carl Heymann, 1993).

91. See Peter Jochen Winters, "Das Urteil gegen Krenz und andere," *DA* 5/1997, p. 696, and "Die Rechtsordnung der DDR schützt Staats-Straftäter nicht," *FAZ,* November 13, 1996, p. 2.

92. Bundesverfassungsgericht, November 12, 1996, opinion in *DA* 1/1997, p. 167.

93. Friedrich-Karl Föhrig, September 10, 1996, opinion in *DA* 6/1996, p. 868.

94. Peter Jochen Winters, "Der Mielke Prozeß," in Weber and Piazolo, *Eine Diktatur vor Gericht,* p. 101. Winters, a journalist, reported on related topics for *FAZ.*

95. Erardo Cristoforo Rautenberg, the district attorney in Neuruppin, was also the Brandenburg state prosecutor responsible for prosecuting crimes related to the DDR. He describes the Brandenburg approach in Erardo Cristoforo Rautenberg, "Plädoyer für ein begrenztes Straffreiheitsgesetz im Bereich des SED-Unrechts," *Neue Justiz* 49, no. 12 (1995): 617–625.

96. Along with Krenz, five other former Politburo members were accused of manslaughter *(Totschlag)* and attempted manslaughter. The accused included Krenz, Erich Mückenberger, Kurt Hager, Horst Dohlus, Günther

Kleiber, and Günter Schabowski. Excerpts of the indictment were reproduced in "'Grenzverletzer werden als Gegner gestellt und, wenn nötig, vernichtet,'" *FAZ*, February 20, 1996, p. 7. An estimated 248 citizens of the DDR were killed while trying to cross the border. On the Politiburo trial, see Dietmar Jochum, ed., *Die Beweisaufnahme im Politbüro-Prozeß* (I) (Berlin: Magnus, [1996]).

97. Günter Schabowski, February 22, 1996 to 27. Strafkammer, Berlin, excerpted in *Tsp*, Febrary 29, 1996, p. 5. For an idea of the itinerary Schabowski followed after 1989, see his books *Das Politbüro: Ende eines Mythos: Eine Befragung* (Berlin: Reinbek bei Hamburg, 1990); *Der Absturz* (Berlin: Rowohlt, 1991); and *Abschied von der Utopie: Die DDR—das deutsche Fiasko des Marxismus* (Stuttgart: Franz Steiner, 1994). See also Schabowski's commentary on Honecker after the latter's death, "Galionsfigur der Unbelehrbaren," *Spg*, 23/1994 (June 6, 1994), p. 33.

98. Erich Honecker, "Politische Erklärung vor der 27.Großen Strafkammer des Berliner Landgerichtes am 3.Dezember 1992," pamphlet containing complete text of statement (Hamburg: W. Runge, 1992), pp. 3, 14–15, 11.

99. Egon Krenz, February 19, 1996 to 27. Strafkammer, Berlin, excerpted in *Tsp*, Febrary 29, 1996, p. 5.

100. Manuela Thieme, "Noch ist die DDR nicht zu Ende," *Wochenpost,* 12/1996 (March 14), p. 10.

101. Krenz to 27. Strafkammer p. 5; statement to court, August 18, 1997, *DA* 5/1997, p. 698.

102. Only the statements by Krenz and Schabowski produced front-page news. By mid-March 1996, "at most twenty journalists" were attending the proceedings (along with fifty spectators, almost unanimously sympathetic to the defense); see Manuela Thieme, "Noch ist die DDR nicht zu Ende," *Wochenpost,* 12/1996 (March 14), p. 8. In the same article, Thieme reported on the trial then also in progress in Frankfurt an der Oder of seven of the judges and lawyers who had railroaded Robert Havemann: "There is hardly an audience, and for the most part only the local media are still reporting" (p. 10).

103. For the Latin American cases in which the exposure strategy was pioneered, see esp. *Nunca Más: The Report of the Argentine National Commission on the Disappeared* (New York: Farrar, Strauss, 1986); Servicio Paz y Justicia (SERPAJ), *Uruguay Nunca Más: Human Rights Violations, 1972–1985,* trans. Elizabeth Hampsten (Philadelphia: Temple University Press, 1989); and Lawrence Weschler, *A Miracle, A Universe: Settling Accounts with Torturers* (Harmondsworth: Penguin Books, 1990). See also Henry J. Steiner, ed., *Truth Commissions: A Comparative Assessment* (Cambridge, Mass.: Harvard Law School Human Rights Program, 1997). On the whole complex of

issues under discussion in this chapter, see the articles in *Law and Social Inquiry* 20, no. 1 (Winter 1995), devoted to "Law and Lustration: Righting the Wrongs of the Past."

104. Resolution adopted May 20, 1992, *MEK* 1:155, 154.

105. Speech to Bundestag, *MEK* 1:27.

106. *MEK* 1:740. See esp. the concluding section of the commission's final report, 1:178–778 (includes dissenting opinions). A new Enquete-Kommission, "Überwindung der Folgen der SED-Diktatur im Prozeß der deutschen Einheit" (Overcoming the Consequences of the SED Dictatorship in the Progress of German Unification), was created on June 22, 1995. This time the SPD voted against the commission, suspecting partisan motives among its supporters. See *DA*, 8/1995, pp. 878–880.

107. In practice, this list is an approximate description of how the Gauck-Behörde understood its mission in Germany. The Gauck-Behörde was not, however, in the business of publishing lists of who did what to whom where and when.

108. Weschler, introduction to SERPAJ, *Uruguay Nunca Más,* esp. pp. xvi–xviii.

109. Jürgen Fuchs, "Immer wußten sie unsere Namen," *Die Andere [Zeitung]*, Supplement no. 3, March 20, 1991, p. 1.

5. Compromising Compromises

1. See Manfred Stolpe, "'Man bekam dann einen Anruf . . . ,'" *Spg,* 4/1992 (January 20), pp. 22–27 and *Schwieriger Aufbruch* (Berlin: Siedler, 1992).

2. Manfred Stolpe, June 1990, in *Den Menschen Hoffnung geben: Reden, Aufsätze, Interviews aus zwölf Jahren* (Berlin: Wichern, 1991), p. 254.

3. This conviction was later confirmed by the crushing of the Prague Spring; see Stolpe, *Schwieriger Aufbruch,* p. 176.

4. Stolpe, January 1991, in *Den Menschen Hoffnung geben,* p. 12.

5. Stolpe uses the term "Lernprozeß"; see, e.g., text from June 1979 in *Den Menschen Hoffnung geben,* pp. 35 and 36.

6. Stolpe, "'Man bekam dann einen Anruf,'" p. 23. For a concise analysis of the BEK's position and role in the DDR, with useful bibliographical information, see Reinhard Henkys, "Thesen zum Wandel der gesellschaftlichen und politischen Rolle der Kirchen in der DDR in den siebziger und achtziger Jahren," in *Die DDR in der Ära Honecker: Politik—Kultur—Gesellschaft,* ed. Gert-Joachim Glaeßner (Opladen: Westdeutscher Verlag, 1988), pp. 332–353. See also BEK, *Kirche als Lerngemeinschaft: Dokumente aus der Arbeit des Bundes der Evangelischen Kirchen in der DDR* (Berlin: Evangelische Verlagsanstalt, 1981), and *Gemeinsam unterwegs: Dokumente aus der Arbeit des Bundes der Evangelischen Kirchen in der DDR 1980–1987* (Berlin:

Evangelische Verlagsanstalt, 1989). For the complicated role played by the church and church-affiliated or protected groups during the Wende, see Gerhard Rein, ed., *Die protestantische Revolution, 1987–1990: Ein deutsches Lesebuch* (Berlin: Wichern, 1990); Detlef Pollack, ed., *Die Legitimität der Freiheit: Politisch alternative Gruppen in der DDR unter dem Dach der Kirche* (Frankfurt am Main: Peter Lang, 1990); and Wolf-Jürgen Grabner et al., eds., *Leipzig im Oktober: Kirchen und alternative Gruppen im Umbruch der DDR; Analysen zur Wende* (Berlin: Wichern, 1990). The Bundestag Enquete-Kommission considered the role played by the churches in the DDR in several sessions; see *MEK* 6/1 and 2.

7. Stolpe, *Den Menschen Hoffnung geben,* p. 12; cf. p. 133.

8. For a standard introduction to West German foreign policy in the 1960s and 1970s, see Helga Haftendorn, *Sicherheit und Entspannung: Zur Außenpolitik der Bundesrepublik Deutschland, 1955–1982* (Baden-Baden: Nomos, 1983). On the domestic politics of Ostpolitik, see Christian Hacke, *Die Ostpolitik der CDU/CSU: Wege und Irrwege der Opposition seit 1969* (Cologne: Wissenschaft und Politik, 1975), and Karlheinz Niclauß, *Kontroverse Deutschlandpolitik: Die politische Auseinandersetzung in der Bundesrepublik Deutschland über den Grundlagenvertrag mit der DDR* (Frankfurt am Main: Metzner, 1977), as well as the memoirs of the leading protagonists. A. James McAdams covers both interstate and domestic aspects in *Germany Divided: From the Wall to Reunification* (Princeton: Princeton University Press, 1993). Relevant documentary material is available in the multivolume work published by the Bundesministerium für Innerdeutsche Beziehungen, *Dokumente zur Deutschlandpolitik,* and its sequel, *Texte zur Deutschlandpolitik* (Frankfurt am Main: Alfred Metzner).

9. Willy Brandt, June 17, 1970, in *Reden und Interviews* (Hamburg: Hoffmann und Campe, 1971), p. 190.

10. Egon Bahr, July 15, 1963, in *Dokumente zur Deutschlandpolitik,* 4/9 (1963), p. 572.

11. Brandt, June 17, 1970, in *Reden und Interviews,* p. 190.

12. Text of speech reprinted in *Dokumente zur Deutschlandpolitik,* 4/9:572–575; see esp. p. 575. On the development of Bahr's foreign policy ideas, see Andreas Vogtmeier, *Egon Bahr und die deutsche Frage* (Bonn: Dietz, 1996). In German, it is customary to differentiate between *Ostpolitik* (which concerned Soviet bloc countries exclusive of the DDR), *Deutschlandpolitik* (which concerned the DDR), and *détente.* I have used *Ostpolitik* here to denote both post-1969 Ostpolitik properly speaking and the accompanying *Deutschlandpolitik.*

13. *MEK* 5/1:756.

14. Cf. Brandt to the Bundestag, February 25, 1970, "Even if we can, we will

not play others off against one another, because we need trust and not new mistrust between ourselves and the states and peoples of eastern Europe," in *Reden und Interviews,* p. 83.

15. Brandt, June 17, 1970, ibid., p. 191.
16. Brandt, October 12, 1972, in *Texte zur Deutschlandpolitik,* 11:217, 216.
17. See *MEK* 5/1:758. Cf. Timothy Garton Ash, esp. *The Uses of Adversity: Essays on the Fate of Central Europe* (New York: Random House, 1989), and *In Europe's Name: Germany and the Divided Continent* (New York: Random House, 1993).
18. *MEK* 5/1:757.
19. Stolpe, June 1979, in *Den Menschen Hoffnung geben,* p. 33.
20. Ibid., p. 30.
21. Ibid., p. 141.
22. Manfred Punge, "Zum Gebrauch des Begriffes 'Kirche im Sozialismus'" (1988), partially reprinted in the documentary appendix to the paper Richard Schröder prepared (with Johannes Zachhuber, Karsten Laudien, and Christian Raschke) for the Enquete-Kommission, "Der Versuch einer eigenständigen Standortbestimmung der evangelischen Kirchen in der DDR am Beispiel der 'Kirche im Sozialismus,'" *MEK* 6/2:1386.
23. On the tensions within the church, see Pollack, *Die Legitimität der Freiheit.*
24. Manfred Stolpe, April 17, 1992, in *Demokratie wagen: Aufbruch in Brandenburg* (Berlin: Schüren, 1994), p. 62.
25. Punge, "Zum Gebrauch des Begriffes 'Kirche im Sozialismus,'" p. 1387.
26. The Berlin delegation could not formally participate in the vote; 12 deputies were for the treaty, 10 abstained.
27. The constitutionality of the treaty was upheld by the court on July 31, 1973 (2 BvF 1/73).
28. Franz Josef Strauß, May 9, 1973, *Texte zur Deutschlandpolitik,* 12:322. For a short summary of the Bavarian CSU government's position on the Basic Treaty's unconstitutionality, see under A, II, 1 of the opinion rendered by the Bundesverfassungsgericht; a summary of the federal government's position follows under point 2.
29. Egon Bahr, July 15, 1963, in *Dokumente zur Deutschlandpolitik,* 4/9:575.
30. "Der Streit der Ideologien und die gemeinsame Sicherheit," released on August 27, 1987, in *Texte zur Deutschlandpolitik,* 3/5 (1987), pp. 171–181.
31. See Gesine Schwan, "Die SPD und die westliche Freiheit," in *Wohin treibt die SPD? Wende oder Kontinuität sozialdemokratischer Sicherheitspolitik,* ed. Jürgen Maruhn and Manfred Wilke (Munich: Günter Olzog, 1984), pp. 38–52.
32. "Der Streit der Ideologien," pp. 176, 179, 178.
33. *MEK* 5/1:952.

34. See Vogel's testimony to the Enquete-Kommission, in *MEK* 4/1:944–956, esp. pp. 947–952. See also discussion in Hans-Jochen Vogel, *Nachsichten: Meine Bonner und Berliner Jahre* (Munich: Piper, 1996), esp. pp. 247–249 and 351–358. Vogel was chair of the SPD when the common paper was adopted. He had formerly been identified with the so-called Seeheimer Circle, a caucus of "right" social democrats, and had been justice minister from 1974 to 1981. During the controversy surrounding the two-track decision, however, he had sought to play a conciliatory role within the party.

35. *MEK* 5/1:949.

36. Rainer Eppelmann, *Fremd im eigenen Haus* (Cologne: Kiepenheuer & Witsch, 1993), quoted in *MEK* 5/1:950. After months of hesitation, Eppelmann called for Stolpe's resignation in an open letter published in *Bildzeitung:* "I wanted to overcome the SED dictatorship. You, in contrast, wanted to ensure a recognized place for the Protestant Church in the DDR. You were the church diplomat, prepared to submit to authority, prepared even to serve the public authorities secretly, in order to help the church." In what became an increasingly bitter exchange, Eppelmann testified before the Brandenburg Landtag investigatory commission that Stolpe had spoken out of both sides of his mouth and "trusted the state secutirity service more than us." *Tsp,* October 23, 1992, p. 6.

37. See, e.g., speeches of Helmut Kohl, Peter Hintze, and Wolfgang Schäuble to the CDU party congress, October 26, 1992, in *Protokoll, 3: Parteitag der CDU Deutschlands* (Düsseldorf, October 26–28, 1992), pp. 19–20, 41, 49.

38. The files were opened on January 1, 1992 (see Chapter 2).

39. Stolpe, "'Man bekam dann einen Anruf,'" pp. 22–27. The article contains no evidence of editing, but see "'Von Stolpe autorisierte Fassung,'" *FAZ,* April 28, 1992, p. 5, and Stolpe's comments in interview, "'Revolutionär? Sicher nicht,'" *Spg,* 21/1992 (18 May), esp. p. 34. The book from which the excerpts were taken, *Aufbruch: Vom Vorgestern ins Übermorgen,* was to have appeared in March 1992; it was published by Siedler (Berlin) in June 1992 under the title *Schwieriger Aufbruch.* The *Spiegel* excerpt is preceded by an article discussing the general issues Stolpe raises: "'Der erste Schritt zum Fall,'" pp. 18–22.

40. Stolpe, "'Man bekam dann einen Anruf,'" pp. 23, 24. (See also lengthier account in *Schwieriger Aufbruch,* Chapter 4.)

41. For statements of EKD (Evangelische Kirche in Deutschland) positions during the debate, see the lengthy statement issued by former chairs of the BEK in *FAZ,* April 27, 1992, p. 2. In mid-October 1992, the EKD responded to the growing controversy over the role played by the church in

the DDR by changing the title of the synod held in Suhl on November 1–6, 1992, from "Medien und Kirche" to "Kirche im geteilten Deutschland." Richard Schröder, a member of the EKD council, delivered the introductory remarks, reprinted as "Kirche im geteilten Deutschland," in Richard Schröder, *Vom Gebrauch der Freiheit: Gedanken über Deutschland nach der Vereinigung* (Stuttgart: Deutsche Verlags-Anstalt, 1996), pp. 153–173.

42. Synode der Evangelischen Kirche in Berlin-Brandenburg, "Schuld und Vergebung," April 10, 1994, included as an annex to the Bündnis minority report of the Brandenburg Landtag's investigatory commission, Drucksache D/3009, Annex 3.

43. EKD and Berlin-Brandenburg Church documents cited in "Keine Disziplinarmaßnahmen gegen Manfred Stolpe," *Tsp*, April 1, 1995, p. 1. The Berlin-Brandenburg Church report was released on March 31, 1995.

44. Klaus Gysi (Gregor's father) was state secretary for church affairs from 1979 to 1988.

45. Neubert's report was later submitted under the title "Untersuchung zu den Vorwürfen gegen den Ministerpräsident des Landes Brandenburg Dr. Manfred Stolpe" as an appendix to Günter Nooke's minority report and is accessible in the parliamentary records under Drucksache D/3009; the passage quoted here is at p. 38. See also Neubert's December 14, 1993 testimony to the Enquete-Kommission; "Die Kirchen und der Staatssicherheitsdienst" (where Richard Schröder was among the discussants), *MEK* 6/1:104–116; and "Die Rolle des MfS bei der Durchsetzung der Kirchenpolitik der SED und die Durchdringung der Kirchen mit geheimdienstlichen Mitteln," *MEK* 6/2:1026–47.

46. Cited in "In Zentrum der Auseinandersetzung steht die Frage, ob es unwissentlich geführte Inoffizielle Mitarbeiter gab," *FAZ*, April 18, 1992, p. 4.

47. *Spg*, 21/1992 (May 18), p. 35. See also Stolpe's personal statement to the Brandenburg Landtag, reported in *FAZ*, September 5, 1992, p. 4.

48. For differing assessments, see "Bericht des Untersuchungsauschusses 1/3," April 29, 1994, Brandenburg Landtag (LTBr), Drucksache 1/3009, pp. 208–237; and Neubert, "Untersuchung zu den Vorwürfen gegen . . . Stolpe," pp. 47–76.

49. Cited in Michael Mara, "Altbundeskanzler in Potsdam," *Tsp*, February 19, 1992, p. 8; both Schmidt and Hans-Dietrich Genscher later testified before the investigatory commission. Gesine Schwan links the Stolpe controversy to the Ostpolitik debate in "Vom schwierigen Handeln in der Grauzone," *Die Zeit*, May 2, 1992, p. 3; see also reporting in *Spg*, "Die geheimen Kontakte zwischen SED und SPD: Eine klammheimliche Kungelei," *Spg*, 35/1992 (August 24), pp. 44–63.

50. Christoph Stier, interview in *Spg*, 33/1992 (August 10), p. 32.

51. *Spg*, 33/1992 (August 10), pp. 32–33. The church guidelines regarding contacts with the MfS were in fact most clearly defined in Mecklenburg.

52. For another, later defense, see Friedrich Schorlemmer, "Zur Topographie der Kirche im Stasi-Staat," *Tsp*, May 9, 1992, p. 15.

53. Klaus von Dohnanyi, "Pakt mit dem Teufel," *Spg*, 5/1992 (January 27), pp. 36–38.

54. For a more complete idea of Schröder's ethical and political positions before and during the transition, see "Politik von Anfang an: Gespräch mit Richard Schröder am 4. Mai 1990," in Rein, *Die protestantische Revolution*, pp. 385–394, Richard Schröder, "Erblast der Gespensterfurcht: Notizen zum stürmischen Ende der DDR," *FAZ*, September 20, 1990; and esp. idem, *Denken im Zwielicht: Vorträge und Aufsätze aus der alten DDR* (Thübingen: Mohr, 1990), in which Schröder comments on the "Kirche im Sozialismus" formula (to which he would have preferred "Kirche in der DDR") in particular on pp. 49–54 and esp. 149–159. For later statements of his position, see Richard Schröder, "Die DDR einst—und jetzt?" supplement to *Das Parlament* (B41/92), October 2, 1992, pp. 3–12; and the paper Schröder prepared (with Johannes Zachhuber, Karsten Laudien, and Christian Raschke) for the Enquete-Kommission, "Der Versuch einer eigenständigen Standortbestimmung der evangelischen Kirchen in der DDR am Beispiel der 'Kirche im Sozialismus,'" *MEK* 6/2:1164–1231 and the accompanying documentary annexes (pp. 1231–1429).

55. Richard Schröder, "'Die Faust im Gesicht," *Spg*, 9/1992 (February 24), p. 32. Schröder used the hostage analogy again several months later in his speech to the EKD synod in Suhl; see Schröder, *Vom Gebrauch der Freiheit*, p. 160.

56. Schröder, "'Die Faust im Gesicht," p. 33.

57. Ibid.

58. Schröder, *Vom Gebrauch der Freiheit*, p. 160.

59. Friedrich Schorlemmer, "Zur Topographie der Kirche im Stasi-Staat," *Tsp*, May 9, 1992, p. 15.

60. Joachim Gauck, "Über die Würde der Unterdrückten," *FAZ*, June 27, 1992, p. 29.

61. Günter Nooke, LTBr, April 13, 1994, Plenarprotokoll 1/91, p. 7449.

62. Peter Wagner, LTBr, June 16, 1994, Plenarprotokoll 1/96, p. 7882.

63. Manfred Stolpe, LTBr, June 16, 1994, Plenarprotokoll 1/96, p. 7845; see also p. 7846.

64. Cited in Dohnanyi, "Pakt mit dem Teufel," p. 38.

65. Stolpe, LTBr, June 16, 1994, p. 7849.

66. *FAZ*, October 30, 1992, p. 2.

67. See "Unterschriftenliste gegen Stolpe," *Tsp*, October 31, 1992, p. 1.

68. See Ralf Georg Reuth, *IM-Sekretär: Die "Gauck-Recherche" und die Dokumente zum "Fall Stolpe"* (Frankfurt am Main: Ullstein, 1992), esp. pp. 39–52 and pp. 129–173. Reuth is consistently hostile to Stolpe.

69. See "Stolpe bekam Verdienstmedaille auf Befehl Mielkes," *FAZ*, September 8, 1992, pp. 1 and 2.

70. See Michael Mara, "Ein Übervater, nicht frei von Schwächen," *Tsp*, October 17, 1993, p. 3; cf. similar description in Andrea Beyerlein, "Stolpes Augen bleiben undurchdringlich," *Berliner Zeitung*, May 7, 1996, p. 3.

71. Quoted in "Der Vormann zeigt Nerven," *Spg*, 24/1993 (June 14), p. 72.

72. Quoted in Michael Mara, "Ein Übervater," *Tsp*, October 17, 1993, p. 3; cf. similar remarks made in interview with Michael Mara and Thorsten Metzner, "'Das Parlament muß das Affentheater schnell beenden,'" *Tsp*, April 2–4, 1994, p. 4. A draft of the commission's final report was circulated to members and their staff in late August 1993.

73. "Ein Übervater," p. 3.

74. Charges summarized in the commission's final report, "Bericht des Untersuchungsauschusses 1/3," April 29, 1994, LTBr, Drucksache 1/3009, p. 5.

75. See the positive assessment of Bisky by Peter Jochen Winters in *FAZ*, a newspaper not otherwise known for its PDS sympathies: "Hat einen guten Ruf," September 13, 1994, p. 16. Cf. the more ironic but still not hostile portrait by Konrad Schuller printed after the defeat of the Berlin-Brandenburg merger referendum, "Das Es der Partei," *FAZ*, May 7, 1996, p. 16.

76. For an early assessment of the report, see "Neue Diskussionen über Stolpes Stasi-Kontakte," *Tsp*, September 26, 1993, p. 7. See also "Stolpes Verrat an der Kirche," *Spg*, 35/1993 (August 30), pp. 33–36.

77. For an early account, see Helmut Müller-Enbergs, "Schwierigkeiten mit der Vergangenheit," *FAZ*, July 24, 1992, p. 8. Müller-Enbergs, co-editor and author of *Von der Illegalität ins Parlament*, was a Bündnis 90 staffer working with the commission.

78. Unlike Stolpe, Biedenkopf, the CDU minister president of Saxony, was an import from the West. The CDU won 58.1 percent of the vote in the Saxon Landtag elections of September 11, 1994.

79. PDS, Pressedienst, no. 11/95, p. 6; quoted in Jürgen P. Lang, Patrick Moreau, and Viola Neu, *Auferstanden aus Ruinen . . . ? Die PDS nach dem Super-Wahljahr 1994* (Sankt Augustin: Konrad-Adenauer-Stiftung, Interne Studien no. 111, December 1995), p. 25.

80. See "Im Schatten des Übervaters" [about Steffen Reiche], *Tsp*, February 10, 1993, p. 4. In April 1996, *Spg* cited the Brandenburg SPD's membership at 6,700; see interview with Stolpe, "'Explosives Gemisch im Osten,'" *Spg*, 15/1996 (April 8), p. 35.

81. See "Beim Bündnis 90 wächst Furcht vor Teilung," *Tsp*, February 10, 1993,

p. 8. Two years later the count was down to 460; see "Bündnisgrüne haben Schlappe kaum verdaut," *Tsp*, January 14, 1995, p. 12. The Bündnisgrünen reported the following membership figures for the new Länder for October 1995: Brandenburg, 492; Mecklenburg–Western Pomerania, 375; Saxony, 1,007; Saxony-Anhalt, 478; Thuringia, 470. See Frauke Stamer, "Die Bündnisgrünen suchen ihren Standort im Osten," *Tsp*, April 15, 1996, p. 3.

82. See Andrea Beyerlein, "Nach der Entscheidung fühlt sich niemand als Sieger," *Tsp*, April 17, 1993, p. 3.

83. The new party claimed about 800 members: 532 ex–Bündnis 90 and about 275 ex-Greens. Some 160 ex-Bündnis members left the party. See "Grüne und Bündnis 90 nunmehr vereint," *Tsp*, June 20, 1993, p. 9.

84. Diestel left politics in 1994 to practice law and become president of the Hansa Rostock soccer team.

85. The initial response of the CDU's national leadership was also hesitant; the party seemed reluctant to attack a man Helmut Kohl had once hoped would lead the Allianz für Deutschland in the March 1990 Volkskammer campaign and whose later defiance of his own party's leadership had enabled Kohl to secure passage in the Bundesrat of a bill raising the value-added tax. Kohl remained publicly silent on the Stolpe case until August 1992, when he declared: "If Stolpe were a member of the CDU, things would long since have turned out differently" (*FAZ*, August 17, 1992, p. 10).

86. The vote was widely portrayed as a referendum on Stolpe as well as the constitution, and the results were considered inconclusive. Turnout—47.9 percent (down from 67.1 percent in the Landtag elections of 1990)—was lower than the SPD had hoped. Of those who voted, 94.0 percent voted to approve the constitutional draft, while 6.0 percent voted to reject it. For background, analysis, and results, see relevant articles in *Tsp*, June 15 and 16, 1992; see also "Weder Brandenburgs SPD noch die CDU haben ihr Ziel erreicht," *FAZ*, June 16, 1992, p. 4.

87. See background article by Michael Mara, "Verlierer auf beiden Seiten der Front," *Tsp*, April 14, 1994, p. 3. The April 13 debate can be read in LTBr, Plenarprotokoll 1/91, pp. 7439–74.

88. The PDS abstained. The votes are given in LTBr, Plenarprotokoll 1/91, pp. 7475–76. See also "Potsdamer Landtag lehnt vorgezogene Neuwahlen ab," *Tsp*, April 14, 1994, p. 1.

89. Günter Nooke, LTBr, June 16, 1994, Plenarprotokoll 1/96, p. 7872; Hans-Otto Bräutigam, LTBr, June 16, 1994, Plenarprotokoll 1/96, p. 7893. To Bräutigam, Nooke's manner of argument recalled Carl Schmitt's "Freund-Feind-Verhältnis," and Bräutigam reminded Nooke, "Hate makes for blindness" (p. 7893).

90. Quoted in "BürgerBündnis lehnt Länderfusion strikt ab," *Tsp*, May 14, 1994, p. 6; see also "Bürgerbündnis Freier Wähler," *Tsp*, May 29, 1994, p. 6.

91. Quoted in Andrea Beyerlein and Michael Mara, "Ein Solo für den Chef," *Tsp*, September 12, 1994, p. 3.

92. Allied Control Council Directive no. 24, in *Official Gazette of the Control Council for Germany*, no. 5 (March 31, 1946): 98.

93. On the efforts made between 1945 and 1953 to open up civil service recruitment, to rid the service of its authoritarian reflexes, and to depoliticize it, see Curt Garner, "Schlußfolgerungen aus der Vergangenheit? Die Auseinandersetzungen um die Zukunft des deutschen Berufsbeamtentums nach dem Ende des Zweiten Weltkrieges," in *Ende des Dritten Reiches—Ende des Zweiten Weltkrieges,* ed. Hans-Erich Volkmann (Munich: Piper, 1995), pp. 607–674; Wolfgang Benz, "Reform des öffentlichen Dienstes? Deutsche Opposition gegen alliierte Initiativen," in *Zwischen Hitler und Adenauer: Studien zur deutschen Nachkriegsgesellschaft* (Frankfurt am Main: Fischer, 1991), pp. 155–183; and Udo Wengst, *Beamtentum zwischen Reform und Tradition: Beamtengesetzgebung in der Gründungsphase der Bundesrepublik Deutschland 1948–1953* (Düsseldorf: Droste, 1988). For an analysis of how the combined results of incomplete denazification and unsuccessful reform affected a key ministry, see Hans-Jürgen Döscher, *Verschworene Gesellschaft: Das Auswärtige Amt unter Adenauer zwischen Neubeginn und Kontinuität* (Berlin: Akademie Verlag, 1995). Benz describes the impact on the judiciary in "Die Entnazifizierung der Richter," in *Zwischen Hitler und Adenauer,* pp. 109–127.

94. For information about the act and its consequences, see Jeri Laber, "Witch Hunt in Prague," *New York Review of Books,* April 23, 1992, pp. 5–8. Comparable legislation has also been at the center of continuing debate in Hungary and in Poland, whose constitutional court struck down a controversial bill opening police files.

95. See the interesting exchange of views between German and other former East European political actors at a conference sponsored by the CDU, reported by Jörg Bischoff, "Wider die Jagd nach der Utopie der Gerechtigkeit," *Tsp*, June 13, 1992, p. 2.

96. For a post-1989 German example, see the sermon Friedrich Schorlemmer delivered in Wittenberg on October 31, 1989, "Laßt euch aufrichten," in *Räumt die Steine hinweg: DDR Herbst 1989; Geistliche Reden im politischen Aufbruch,* ed. Andreas Ebert et al. (Munich: Claudius, 1989), pp. 35–40. Schorlemmer consistently defended a "soft" line on reconciliation: see Friedrich Schorlemmer, *Versöhnung in der Wahrheit: Nachschläge und Vor-*

schläge eines Ostdeutschen (Munich: Knaur, 1992), and *Worte öffnen Fäuste: Die Rückkehr in ein schwieriges Vaterland* (Munich: Kindler, 1992).

97. Schröder, "'Die Faust im Gesicht,'" p. 35.

98. Unification Treaty, app. 1, chap. 19, Sachgebiet A, Abschnitt 3, Art. 1, no. 1.

99. For an analysis of how the *Abwicklung* process in universities and research institutes played out, see Charles S. Maier, *Dissolution: The Crisis of Communism and the End of East Germany* (Princeton: Princeton University Press, 1997), chap. 6; and Wolfgang Schluchter, *Neubeginn durch Anpassung? Studien zum ostdeutschen Übergang* (Frankfurt am Main: Suhrkamp, 1996).

100. Unification Treaty, app. 1, chap. 19, Sachgebiet A, Abschnitt 3, Art. 1, no. 1.

101. Beamtengesetz für den Freistaat Sachsen (Saxony Civil Service Code), Zweiter Teil, 1, Abschnitt §6, Abs. 3. The codes in Mecklenburg–Western Pomerania and Thuringia contained similar exclusions.

102. For a brief description of the diversity that existed, see "Durcheinander bei der Stasi-Überprüfung," *Tsp*, May 16, 1994, p. 6. For reports on how teachers were vetted in Thuringia and East Berlin, see Claus Peter Müller, "Die Überprüfung von Lehrern in Thüringen ist schwierig, langwierig und teuer," *FAZ*, June 30, 1993, p. 4; and Regina Mönch, "Ihre Kündigung empfinden Stasi-Lehrer als ein Berufsverbot," *Tsp*, September 29, 1994, p. 14.

103. LTBr, Drucksache 1/3098, June 16, 1994.

104. The seventh and final point of the motion urged the adoption of the articulated criteria by public authorities throughout Brandenburg. The voting on the motion is recorded in LTBr, June 16, 1994, Plenarprotokoll 1/96, pp. 7895–96.

105. Ibid., April 26, 1995, Plenarprotokoll 2/12, pp. 963–967.

106. Landesregierung Brandenburg, "Grundsätze der Landesregierung für die Überprüfung von Dienstkräften des Landes Brandenburg hinsichtlich einer Tätigkeit für das ehemalige Ministerium für Staatssicherheit/Amt für Nationale Sicherheit (MfS/AfNS)," *Amtsblatt für Brandenburg: Gemeinsames Ministerialblatt für das Land Brandenburg*, October 30, 1995, pp. 914–915. For the preceding Landtag debate, see "Stasi-Überprüfung bleibt umstritten," *FAZ*, September 9, 1995, p. 4.

107. Minister of the Interior Alwin Ziel reported to the Landtag on the continuing process in his response to Kleine Anfrage no. 785, May 22, 1996 (text communicated to author by Ziel's office).

108. Cf. Reuth, *IM Sekretär*, pp. 36–37, 65–67.

109. Open letter to Richard von Weizsäcker from Bärbel Bohley, Ralf Hirsch, Eckart Hübener, Freya Klier, Lutz Rathenow, Ev and Frank Rub, and

Wolfgang and Regine Templin; text published under the title "Spiel ohne Große," *Spg,* 12/1993 (March 22), p. 27.

110. Bärbel Bohley, March 2, 1993, in personal statement explaining refusal to testify before the investigatory commission; text attached as Annex 124 to the majority report (Anlagen zur Drucksache 1/3009, pt. A, Anlage 124), p. 4. After her arrest in connection with the Luxemburg-Liebknecht demonstration of January 17, 1988, Bohley left the DDR for England under circumstances that were later differently understood by different actors. She later helped found Neues Forum. For Stolpe's account of the Luxemburg-Liebknecht incident and its sequel, see *Schwieriger Aufbruch,* pp. 152–167.

111. Günter Nooke, LTBr, June 16, 1996, Plenarprotokoll 1/96, p. 7868.

112. Inge Deutschkron, *Ich trug den gelben Stern* (Cologne: Verlag Wissenschaft und Politik, 1978), p. 197.

113. On August 23, 1995, Nooke, Freya Klier, Wolfgang Templin, Konrad Weiß, and Katja Havemann met in Bohley's Berlin apartment with Helmut Kohl. See Wolfgang Templin, "Ein Gespräch an historischem Ort," *FAZ,* August 29, 1995, p. 8. For a bitter critique of the meeting by another former dissident and editor of *Die Andere,* see Wolfram Kempe's column in *taz,* "Tante Bärbels Sprechstunde," September 2–3, 1995, p. 10. See also Johannes Leithäuser, "Der Vorwurf heißt Verrat," *FAZ,* September 16, 1995, p. 12.

114. See Ehrhart Neubert, "Aussitzen, Abwiegeln," *Spg,* 24/1995 (June 12), p. 70; on the proposed Bürgerbüro, see Michael Cramer's commentary in *taz,* May 18–19, 1996, p. 10. The Bürgerbüro (Das Bürgerbüro—Verein zur Aufarbeitung von Folgeschäden der SED-Diktatur) was formally launched on June 17, 1996. Its precise mission remained unclear, as did its partisan implications. See Holger Kulick, "Keine Wauwaus von Helmut Kohl," *taz,* May 28, 1996, p. 4; Holger Kulick, "Große Koalition gegen Schlußpunktmentalität," *taz,* June 17, 1996, p. 4.

115. Cited in Holger Kulick, "Keine Wauwaus von Helmut Kohl," *taz,* May 28, 1996, p. 4. Other co-sponsors included Katja Havemann, Freya Klier, Neubert, Nooke, Wolfgang Templin, and Konrad Weiß.

116. Institut für Demoskopie Allensbach monthly poll in *FAZ,* November 13, 1991, p. 5. Thirty-two percent disagreed, and 21 percent expressed no opinion. The corresponding figures for the west Germans in the sample were 18 percent (agreed), 66 percent (disagreed), and 16 percent (no opinion).

117. Emnid survey of east German attitudes, conducted between mid-April and mid-June 1995, extensively reported in "Stolz aufs eigene Leben," *Spg,* 27/1995 (July 3), pp. 49, 46. See also Lothar Fritze, "Identifikation mit

dem gelebten Leben: Gibt es DDR-Nostalgie in den neuen Bundesländern?" in *Das wiedervereinigte Deutschland: Zwischenbilanz und Perspektiven*, ed. Ralf Altenhof and Eckhard Jesse (Düsseldorf: Droste, 1995), pp. 275–292.

118. "Explosives Gemisch im Osten,'" p. 35.

119. Fred Klinger, "Der Transformationsschock: Wirtschaftliche und soziale Entwicklungen nach der 'Wende,' in Altenhof and Jesse, *Das wiedervereinigte Deutschland*, p. 182. Schluchter, *Neubeginn durch Anpassung?*, esp. chap. 1; and Gerlinde Sinn and Hans-Werner Sinn, *Kaltstart: Volkswirtschaftliche Aspekte der deutschen Vereinigung*, 3d ed. (Munich: dtv, 1993).

120. See "Die Zahl der Arbeitslosen sinkt unter 4 Millionen" and "Lage bei den Lehrstellen weiter schwierig," *FAZ*, May 7, 1996, p. 17.

121. See "Besserung überwiegend in Brandenburg" (a reference to the previous month's unemployment figure of 16.4 percent), *Tsp*, May 7, 1996, p. 13.

122. See "Die Arbeitslosenquoten in den Bundesländern," *Süddeutsche Zeitung*, May 7, 1996, p. 19.

123. See "Stolz aufs eigene Leben," *Spg*, 27/1995 (July 3), p. 46.

124. "Explosives Gemisch im Osten,'" p. 35.

125. "The question: 'Do you find that conditions in the Federal Republic give one reason to be anxious, or not?' shows . . . a high level of anxiety. Sixty-seven percent in the old Länder, 76 percent in the new Länder see grounds for anxiety [*Beunruhigung*]. Only 23 percent in the west, 18 percent in the east are not anxious. Such a degree of nervosity has not been registered in Germany since the question was introduced at the beginning of the 1980s." See "Das Meinungsklima im August: Keine Ferienstimmung," *FAZ*, August 13, 1992, p. 5. See also Chapter 6.

126. See Christoph Seils, "Die Genossen sprechen sich Mut zu," *taz*, June 10, 1996, p. 5. The Forum convened its first session in Leipzig on June 8, 1996; the theme was "Netzwerk Zukunft: Für Ostdeutschland eine zweite Chance!" See Albert Funk, "Forum Ostdeutschland tagt in Leipzig," *FAZ*, June 10, 1996, p. 8.

127. Cf. Stolpe's self-assessment, both in the original excerpt from his book, *Spg*, 4/1992 (January 20), pp. 22–27, and in the interview "'Revolutionär? Sicher nicht,'" *Spg*, 21/1992 (May 18), pp. 32–36.

128. Stolpe, July 1990, in *Den Menschen Hoffnung geben*, p. 267.

129. Stolpe, *Demokratie wagen*.

130. Stolpe, July 1990, in *Den Menschen Hoffnung geben*, p. 272.

131. LTBr, Plenarprotokoll 1/5, December 6, 1990, p. 83.

132. Stolpe, September 1990, in *Den Menschen Hoffnung geben*, p. 276.

133. Stolpe, June 1990, ibid., p. 253.

134. Stolpe, LTBr, November 1, 1990 (immediately following his swearing in as

minister president), esp. p. 35. For Stolpe's more general assessment of Prussian history, see *Demokratie wagen,* pp. 71–74.

135. Interview, "Stolpe: Ich werfe nicht das Handtuch," *Berliner Morgenpost,* May 6, 1996, p. 3.

136. Interview, "'Ich will unser Blut zurück,'" *Spg,* 43/1994, (October 24), p. 44.

137. "Stolz aufs eigene Leben," pp. 49, 52. Responses to "I can be proud of my life" were recorded on a scale from 1 ("is totally the case") to 6 ("is not at all the case"): 1 (36 percent), 2 (17 percent), 3 (22 percent), 4 (10 percent), 5 (7 percent), 6 (6 percent). To the statement about applicability to others, 18 percent said that it applied "only to a small part of the population," and only 1 percent said that it applied to "almost no one."

138. "Stolz aufs eigene Leben," p. 49. In both 1990 and 1995, only a plurality (39 percent and 36 percent) favored making or keeping the Stasi records available to victims; a further 41 percent and 36 percent favored making or keeping the records available only for use in criminal investigations. In 1990, 14 percent favored destroying the records; in 1995, the figure stood at 25 percent.

139. See, for example, Michael Mara, "Für Stolpe ist der Wahlkampf ein Heimspiel ohne Gegner," *Tsp,* September 9, 1994, p. 14; cf. Nana Brink and Matthias Schlegel, "Sieg eines Optimisten [Biedenkopf]," *Tsp,* September 12, 1994, p. 3. For Biedenkopf's own account of his experiences, see Kurt Biedenkopf, *Einheit und Erneuerung: Deutschland nach dem Umbruch in Europa* (Stuttgart: Deutsche Verlags-Anstalt, 1996).

140. Gordon Craig, *The Germans* (New York: G. P. Putnam's Sons, 1982), p. 44.

141. Mara, "Ein Übervater," p. 3.

142. Cf. Art. 29 of the Basic Law. By agreement between the two parties, adoption of the merger required the adoption of the referendum proposal with the assent of at least 25 percent of those entitled to vote.

143. "SPD-Fraktionschef Birthler kritisiert Fusions-Kampagne," *Tsp,* May 2, 1996, p. 1; text of interview on p. 21. On the same day, Walther Stützle's first-page editorial column was a plea for the treaty, "Fusion—was sonst!"

144. "Mehrheit der Berliner ist für schnelle Fusion mit Brandenburg," *Tsp,* April 20, 1995, p. 1 and esp. several articles and graphics on p. 6.

145. Quoted in Michael Mara, "'Wir haben zu viele rosarote Wolken gemalt,'" *Tsp,* May 6, 1996, p. 14.

146. "Fusion von Berlin und Brandenburg immer unwahrscheinlicher," *Tsp,* April 27, 1996, pp. 1 and 10.

147. Michael Mara, "Die Stimmungslage lange verkannt," *Tsp,* April 25, 1996, p. 8.

148. Interview, "'. . . redlich sagen, daß nichts direkt rausklingelt,'" *taz,* April 29, 1996, p. 12.

149. Reported in Michael Mara, "'Hätten wir noch drei Wochen Zeit,'" *Tsp,* May 5, 1996, p. 16.

150. Interview, "'Es gibt in puncto Fusion jetzt keine Ausreden mehr,'" *Tsp,* March 24, 1996, p. 4; cf. "Stolpe sieht durch Berlins Finanznot Vorurteile gegen die Fusion wachsen," ibid., p. 1.

151. See, e.g., "Nicht jede Stimme gegen die Fusion eine für die PDS," *FAZ,* May 7, 1996, p. 4; and "Viele junge Leute stimmten gegen Fusion," *Tsp,* May 8, 1996, p. 13. The margin in favor of a merger was especially narrow in Kreuzberg, Neukölln, and Wedding.

152. *Berliner Zeitung,* May 7, 1996, p. 2; cf. *taz,* May 7, 1996, p. 1 and esp. Dirk Wildt, "Jugend vereint gegen Vereinigung," p. 3. The *Tsp* poll of April 20, 1995, had already suggested that the treaty was encountering particularly strong opposition among younger voters; see "Zwei-Drittel-Mehrheit befürwortet die geplante Länderfusion," *Tsp,* April 20, 1995, p. 6.

153. Interview, "Rücktritt ausgeschlossen," *Süddeutsche Zeitung,* May 7, 1996, p. 6.

154. Bremen's mayor, Henning Scherf (SPD), was openly relieved by the referendum results; see interview, "'Behutsam umgehen mit regionaler Identität,'" *Berliner Zeitung,* May 7, 1996, p. 5.

155. Quoted in "Diepgen und Stolpe: Weglaufen gilt nicht," *Tsp,* April 30–May 1, 1996, p. 2.

156. Walther Stützle, "Fusion—was sonst!" *Tsp,* May 2, 1996, p. 1. Cf. Frank Jansen and Axel Bahr, "Für die meisten Experten macht diese Landesgrenze keinen Sinn," *Tsp,* April 30–May 1, 1996, p. 13; and Peter Jochen Winters's retrospective editorial "Nur Verlierer," *FAZ,* May 7, 1995, p. 1.

157. "'Kein Konzept für den Fall der Vereinigung,'" *Tsp,* April 30–May 1, 1996, p. 14.

158. See "Fusion Berlin-Brandenburg gescheitert," *Die Welt,* May 6, 1996, p. 1. Before and after the referendum, Stolpe repeatedly used another, equally graphic image: he was not one, he said, to commit "Fahnenflucht" (deserting the flag); cited in *FAZ,* May 6, 1996, p. 1; cf. "Stolpe setzt uneingeschränkt auf Fusion," *FAZ,* May 3, 1996, p. 6.

159. Quoted in Michael Mara, "'Damit bringt Birthler das Ding zum Kippen,'" *Tsp,* May 3, 1995, p. 15.

160. Quoted in Andrea Beyerlein, "Stolpes Augen bleiben undurchdringlich," *Berliner Zeitung,* May 7, 1996, p. 3.

161. Interview with Theo Sommer, *Die Zeit,* April 24, 1992, p. 3.

162. Interview, "'Auch ich habe Fehler gemacht,'" *Publik-Forum,* August 25, 1995, p. 8.

163. Joachim Gauck, "Über die Würde der Unterdrückten," *FAZ,* June 27, 1992, p. 29.

6. The Crisis of Democracy

1. Hans-Jochen Vogel, *Nachsichten: Meine Bonner und Berliner Jahre* (Munich: Piper, 1996), p. 337. For Vogel's discussion of intraparty debates and inter-party relations in 1989–90, see esp. pp. 306–351.
2. Richard von Weizsäcker, with Gunter Hofmann and Werner A. Perger, *Richard von Weizsäcker im Gespräch* (Frankfurt am Main: Eichborn, 1992), p. 164; cf. p. 178. See also Gunter Hofmann and Werner A. Perger, eds., *Die Kontroverse: Weizsäckers Parteienkritik in der Diskussion* (Frankfurt am Main: Eichborn, 1992); and Hans Wallow, ed., *Richard von Weizsäcker in der Diskussion: Die verdrossene Gesellschaft* (Düsseldorf: ECON, 1993).
3. Weizsäcker, *Richard von Weizsäcker im Gespräch,* p. 162; see also p. 155 and passim.
4. Klaus J. Schwehn, "Rat an die SPD-Führung: 'Die Alteren müssen Raum geben,'" *Tsp,* November 9, 1995, p. 2.
5. See table in Wilhelm Bürklin and Dieter Roth, eds., *Das Superwahljahr: Deutschland vor unkalkulierbaren Regierungsmehrheiten?* (Cologne: Bund-Verlag, 1994), p. 13.
6. "Die häßlichen Enkel: Warum die Bürger ihre Politiker verachten—und wie sie künftig regiert werden wollen," *Spg,* 5/1994 (January 31), pp. 44, 45.
7. Wolfgang Schäuble, *Und der Zukunft zugewandt* (Berlin: Siedler, 1994), p. 160.
8. See esp. Michel Crozier et al., *The Crisis of Democracy* (New York: New York University Press, 1975); and Samuel Beer, *Britain against Itself: The Political Contradictions of Collectivism* (New York: Norton, 1982).
9. *New York Times,* January 24, 1996, p. A14.
10. Schäuble, *Und der Zukunft zugewandt,* pp. 164–165.
11. Readers familiar with the rhetoric and policies of the Republican right in the United States may question how particular even these traits are to Germany. Insofar as the traits have American counterparts, they also have, in at least one important respect, a common effect: that of calling into question the integration of minorities as a desirable goal and of making the goal at any rate harder to achieve.
12. Steffen Heitmann, "Vergeltung und Ausgrenzung, Amnestie und Versöhnung," *FAZ,* October 12, 1993, p. 10.
13. Steffen Heitmann, "Die Revolution verkommt zur 'Wende': Über die Mängel des Gemeinwesens muß gesprochen, der Kommunismus muß delegitimiert werden," *FAZ,* September 2, 1994, p. 13.
14. Robert Leicht, "So nicht—und den nicht," *Die Zeit,* 39/1993 (September 24), p. 1.

15. Heimo Schwilk and Ulrich Schacht, eds., *Die selbstbewusste Nation* (Frankfurt am Main: Ullstein, 1994).

16. Interview with *Süddeutsche Zeitung,* quoted in "Scharfe Kritik aus der FDP an Steffen Heitmann," *Tsp,* September 18, 1993, p. 2.

17. Quoted in Gunter Hofmann, "Das höchste Amt geht alle an," *Die Zeit,* 27/1993 (July 2), p. 3.

18. See "Rechter Mann, rechte Zeit," *Spg,* 36/1993 (September 6), p. 21.

19. Quoted in "Scharfe Kritik aus der FDP an Steffen Heitmann," *Tsp,* September 18, 1993, p. 2.

20. Quoted in "Nun auch Widerstand in der Union gegen Steffen Heitmann," *Tsp,* October 7, 1993, p. 2. In May 1996 Heitmann stewarded the appointment of Siegmar Faust as the *Land* official responsible for the regional branch of the Stasi archives. Faust was a former DDR dissident who had previously been relieved of his job at the Berlin Gauck-Behörde after it became known that he had helped a former concentration camp guard win reparations as a victim of Stalinism and had also taken a cut of the money; see "Erst gefeuert—jetzt befördert," *taz,* May 23, 1996, p. 4.

21. For election results, see *FAZ,* June 28, 1994, p. 7. The participation rate was 54.9 percent, down from 65.1 percent in October 1990.

22. See Klaus Wallbaum, "Magere Bilanz nach hundert Tagen Minderheitsregierung," *Tsp,* October 21, 1994, p. 5.

23. Interview in *Bild-Zeitung,* quoted in "Industrie will PDS-regierten Kommunen den Rücken kehren; Bayern fordert bundesweites Verbot der SED-Nachfolgerpartei," *Tsp,* December 12, 1993, p. 2.

24. Interview, "'Wie im Westen, so auf Erden,'" *Tsp,* December 27, 1993, p. 6.

25. The phrase was originally Kurt Schumacher's angry reply to the KPD's labeling of social democrats as "social fascists."

26. Interview in *Die Woche,* cited in "Höppner: PDS kommt als Partner nicht in Frage," *Tsp,* June 16, 1994, p. 5.

27. "Schäuble warnt vor der 'Heimsuchung' eines Linksbündnisses," *FAZ,* July 29, 1994, p. 1.

28. Quoted in "SPD-Parteitag billigt rot-grüne Koalition," *Tsp,* July 17, 1994, p. 4.

29. "Schäuble warnt vor der 'Heimsuchung' eines Linksbündnisses," p. 2.

30. CDU-Bundesgeschäftsstelle, "Zukunft statt Linksfront: PDS-Gefahr von links!" [Bonn, 1994], p. 3.

31. Poster reproduced and discussed in Rolf Linkenheil, "Die plötzliche Liebe der CSU zur ältesten der roten Socken," *Tsp,* August 3, 1994, p. 3. The CDU state party in Mecklenburg-Vorpommern declined to use the "Rote Socken" (red socks) poster produced by the national party, but narrowly approved a poster that showed the picture of Otto Grotewohl and Wilhelm

Pieck shaking hands in 1946, with the caption "Nein"; see "Schweriner CDU mit 'Händedruck'-Plakat," *Tsp*, August 3, 1994, p. 2. Other CDU state parties in the new Länder also declined to use the "Rote Socken" poster; see "CDU-Zentrale hält an der 'roten Socke' fest," *Tsp*, July 26, 1994, p. 4.

32. The *Tagesspiegel* reproduced a sample of campaign posters on October 14, 1995, p. 12.

33. See "'Nun gehet und mehret die Stimmen,'" *Tsp*, October 21, 1995, p. 9.

34. "Große Koalition als großer Verlierer," *Tsp*, October 23, 1995, p. 1.

35. M. Rainer Lepsius, "Zur Entwicklung der Bundesrepublik Deutschland 1972–1977," in *Demokratie in Deutschland: Soziologisch-historische Konstellationsanalysen, Ausgewählte Aufsätze* (Göttingen: Vandenhoeck & Ruprecht, 1993), p. 191.

36. Interview, "'Das kann doch nicht reiner Zufall sein,'" *Tsp*, November 5, 1995, p. 4. Inside the Berlin CDU there were also critical voices: see "Wohnzimmergespräche kontra Polemik," *Berliner Zeitung*, October 25, 1995, p. 16; see also commentary by Monika Zimmermann, "Berliner Verhältnisse: Wahlkampfwunden, strategische Mißverständnisse und der Auftrag der Wähler," *Tsp*, October 24, 1995, p. 8.

37. See "Kohl: Lafontaine will Magdeburger Verhältnisse," *FAZ*, November 25, 1995, pp. 1 and 2.

38. See "'Jawohl, wir sind eine Linkspartei,'" *taz*, November 18/19, 1995, p. 1.

39. *Das Parlament*, 48/1995 (November 24), p. 17.

40. Interview with Christoph Seils, "'Wir zittern nicht mehr, wenn die CDU 'PDS' schreit,'" in *Freitag*, 48/1995 (November 24), p. 4.

41. Interview in "'Die SPD will an unsere Wähler ran.' Von seinem Gespräch mit Oskar Lafontaine verspricht sich PDS-Chef Gregor Gysi vor allem eines: mehr eigenes Profil," *Neues Deutschland* (hereafter *ND*), November 22, 1995, p. 5.

42. Cited in Christoph Seils, "PDS fürchtet Erstickungstod," *taz*, December 5, 1995, p. 1.

43. Cited in "Gysi: Kein Grund, hasenfüßig zu sein," *Tsp*, December 5, 1995, p. 1.

44. See relevant discussion in Harry Eckstein, "A Culturalist Theory of Political Change," *American Political Science Review* 82, no. 3 (September 1988): 789–804.

45. "Programm der Partei des Demokratischen Sozialismus" (adopted by the Third Party Congress, January 29–31, 1993), in *Programm und Statut* (party brochure), pp. 27, 1.

46. "Statut der Partei des Demokratischen Sozialismus" (adopted by the Second Party Congress and confirmed by a membership referendum in August–September 1991), ibid., p. 29; cf "Programm," pp. 9–10.

47. "Programm," p. 17; see also pp. 14–15, 17–18, 24–26.

48. Ibid., pp. 5, 12.

49. Ibid., pp. 6, 7, 1–2.

50. Ibid., p. 7.

51. See "Berliner Landesamt für Verfassungsschutz erstellt umfangreichen Bericht über die PDS," *FAZ*, January 21, 1995. The Marxist Forum was not created until the spring of 1995, in connection with the "In großer Sorge" appeal discussed later in this chapter.

52. Interview with Wolfgang Hübner, "Wenn man alles Sozialismus nennt, verschwimmt der Begriff," *ND*, January 24, 1995, p. 11.

53. "In großer Sorge," *ND*, May 18, 1995, p. 3. A reply signed by twenty-two members of the PDS's parliamentary group appeared in *ND*, May 20–21, 1995, p. 3.

54. Jürgen P. Lang, Patrick Moreau, and Viola Neu, *Auferstanden aus Ruinen . . . ? Die PDS nach dem Super-Wahljahr 1994* (Sankt Augustin: Konrad-Adenauer-Stiftung, Interne Studien no. 111, December 1995), pp. 25, 170.

55. Ibid., pp. 187, 188, 27.

56. Joachim Nawrocki, "Genosse Rentner: Die PDS ist eine Partei der Alten und der alten Zeit. Die Jungen wählen sie trotzdem," *Die Zeit*, 49/1995 (December 1), p. 2. The statistic is not chronologically qualified and does appear to represent a pattern.

57. Ibid.

58. Gregor Gysi, *Das war's: Noch lange nicht!* (Düsseldorf: ECON, 1995), pp. 11, 234.

59. Charlotte Wiedemann, "Vordenker im Hintergrund. André Brie gilt als graue Eminenz der PDS, die am Wochenende ihre Zukunft diskutiert," *Die Woche*, January 26, 1996, p. 8.

60. Quoted in "Biermann nennt Gysi einen Verbrecher," *FAZ*, November 22, 1994, p. 4. For the context, see the cover story "Gregor Gysi und die Stasi: neue Dokumente," *Die Wochenpost*, 40/1994 (September 29), esp. article by Jürgen Fuchs, "Der IM 'Notar' wird eingesetzt . . .," pp. 4–5; and reply by Gysi, "Mit besonderer Beachtung des 16. Oktober," *Die Wochenpost*, 41/1994 (October 6), pp. 6, 8. The controversy continued through and after the Bundestag elections: Jürgen Fuchs, Vera Wollenberger, Angelika Barbe, Katja Havemann, Gerd Poppe, and Bärbel Bohley expressed their views of Gysi in "Nicht beantwortete Fragen," *taz*, November 11, 1994, p. 13. One week earlier, *taz* had published a two-page self-defense by Gysi.

61. See "Gauck: Gregor Gysi war eindeutig IM," *Tsp*, June 8, 1995, p. 2. The Bundestag's committee on qualifications and immunity had requested the report, which was then leaked to *Spg;* see "Beweise aus der Kladde," *Spg*, 22/1995 (May 29), pp. 20–24.

62. Gregor Gysi, *Einspruch! Gespräche, Briefe, Reden* (Berlin: Alexander, 1992), p. 286.

63. Ibid., p. 23, 25, 24.

64. Ibid., pp. 137 (cf. p. 312, where Gysi uses the term "Gewaltherrschaft," tyranny); 152–153; 158.

65. Ibid., p. 272; in the "10 Theses" prepared in December 1994 for the party conference in January 1995, the expression employed under point 8 is "ein bloßer Anschluß" (a pure annexation); see *ND*, December 6, 1994, p. 14.

66. Gysi, *Das war's*, p. 252.

67. Gysi, *Einspruch*, p. 165.

68. Quoted in "Bisky: Wechsel nur mit der PDS," *Tsp*, January 28, 1996, p. 2.

69. "Die PDS schließt eine Beteiligung an Regierungsbündnissen nicht mehr aus," *FAZ*, January 29, 1996, p. 4. Cf. statement by Petra Sitte, the PDS parliamentary leader in Saxony-Anhalt: the PDS, Sitte told the party conference, had "no principle about staying in opposition or participating in government, but only the principle of pursuing a reasonable political course." Cited in Stefan Dietrich, "Kein Wort über den Strick im Haus des Henkers," *FAZ*, January 29, 1996, p. 4.

70. Gysi, *Einspruch*, pp. 195, 263.

71. Ibid., p. 71; Gysi, *Das war's*, p. 251.

72. *ND*, October 13, 1994, p. 7.

73. *ND*, December 6, 1994, p. 14.

74. *ND*, January 28–29, 1995, p. 6.

75. *ND*, May 20–21, 1995, p. 3.

76. Klaus Böger, quoted in Dirk Wildt, "CDU-Landowsky löst Koalitionskrise aus," *taz*, May 13, 1996, p. 21.

77. Cf. Gysi, *Das war's*, p. 205.

78. See Elisabeth Noelle-Neumann, "Kein Schutz, keine Gleichheit, keine Gerechtigkeit," *FAZ*, March 8, 1995, p. 5. The corresponding figure in west Germany was 33 percent; 54 percent of west Germans, but only 16 percent of east Germans, felt protected.

79. Reinhard Höppner, *Segeln gegen den Wind* (Stuttgart: Radius, 1996), p. 33.

80. In 1996 a state prosecutor from west Germany posted in one of the new Länder suggested resolving the terminological dispute by replacing the term *Unrechtsstaat* with the term *Scheißstaat*. The latter term has the advantage of being both descriptively evocative and politically uncontaminated. The proposal, made only half in jest, expressed a frustration widely felt among west and east Germans equally fed up with the polemics analyzed in Chapter 3 and with the reluctance of so many east Germans to call a dictatorship a dictatorship.

81. Gysi, *Einspruch*, pp. 295, 278, 192.

82. For an account of SPD politics in the period surrounding the *Zwangsvere-inigung*, see Peter Merseburger, *Der schwierige Deutsche: Kurt Schumacher, Eine Biographie* (Stuttgart: Deutsche Verlags-Anstalt, 1995), pp. 240–317. For documentation, see Andreas Malycha, ed., *Auf dem Weg zur SED: Die Sozialdemokratie und die Bildung einer Einheitspartei in den Ländern der SBZ* (Bonn: J. H. W. Dietz Nachfolger, 1995).

83. Peter Merseburger, "Es war eine Zwangsvereinigung," *FAZ*, February 22, 1996, p. 10.

84. Wolfgang Thierse, "Eiertanz zwischen Erneuerungswillen und Be-friedigung der SED-Nostalgie," excerpts from speech to "Forum der His-torischen Kommission der SPD" on the *Zwangsvereinigung*, reproduced in the party weekly *vorwärts*, 5/1996, p. 20.

85. The official PDS position on the *Zwangsvereinigung* is expounded in a lengthy, convoluted, evasive document, "Zum 50.Jahrestag des Zusammen-schlusses von KPD und SPD," produced by the party's Historical Commis-sion and released on December 11, 1995 (PDS, Pressedienst no. 50/95). The document was drafted by Günter Benser.

86. Herzog concluded his August 1, 1994 speech in Warsaw with the words: "I ask forgiveness for what was done to them [the fighters of the Warsaw Uprising and all Polish victims of World War II] by Germans." *FAZ*, August 2, 1994, p. 3.

87. On the PCF, see esp. Annie Kriegel, *Les communistes français* (Paris: Le Seuil, 1968); Georges Lavau, "Le Parti Communiste français dans le système politique français," in *Le Communisme en France,* ed. Georges Lavau [Paris: Armand Colin (Cahiers de la Fondation nationale des sci-ences politiques no. 175), 1969], pp. 7–81; idem, *A quoi sert le parti com-muniste français* (Paris: Fayard, 1981); and Martin Schain, "The French Communist Party: The Seeds of its Own Decline," in *Comparative Theory and Political Experience,* ed. Peter Katzenstein et al. (Ithaca, N.Y.: Cornell University Press, 1990), pp. 119–143.

88. In the 1980s, the Front National (FN), an extreme right party, managed to carve out an apparently durable place for itself in the French electoral landscape. The parliamentary right made numerous rhetorical and policy concessions to the FN, but generally refused to enter into electoral alli-ances with it. I have not used the FN as a comparative example because in the view of democratic actors in France (and in mine), the party, with its xenophobia and its appeals to hatred, failed to meet the elementary re-quirements of democratic respectability. Furthermore, unlike the PDS (but rather like the PCF), it was a product of the political system, rather than an external element requiring integration.

On the FN, see esp. Nonna Mayer and Pascal Perrineau, eds., *Le Front national à découvert* (Paris: Presses de la Fondation nationale des sciences politiques, 1989); and Pascal Perrineau, "Le Front national: 1972–1992," in *Histoire de l'extrême droite en France,* ed. Michel Winock (Paris: Le Seuil, 1993), pp. 243–298; as well as the relevant chapters of Pascal Perrineau and Colette Ysmal, eds., *Le Vote de crise: l'élection présidentielle de 1995* (Paris: Département d'études politiques du *Figaro* and Presses de la Fondation nationale des sciences politiques, 1995); and two volumes edited by Philippe Habert, Pascal Perrineau, and Colette Ysmal: *Le Vote sanction: les élections législatives des 21 et 28 mars 1993* (Paris: Département d'études politiques du *Figaro* and Presses de la Fondation nationale des sciences politiques, 1993); and *Le Vote éclaté: les élections régionales et cantonales des 22 et 29 mars 1992* (Paris: Département d'études politiques du *Figaro* and Presses de la Fondation nationale des sciences politiques, 1992).

89. For a self-conscious contribution to this effort at reinvention, see Lionel Jospin, *L'Invention du possible* (Paris: Flammarion, 1991).

90. PCF strength dipped early in the Fifth Republic, and again in the wake of the events of May 1968.

91. See Alain Fonteneau and Pierre-Alain Muet, *La Gauche face à la crise* (Paris: Presses de la Fondation nationale des sciences politiques, 1985).

92. For a suggestive analysis of what happens to Western communist parties that enter into governmental coalitions, see Sidney Tarrow, "Transforming Enemies into Allies: Non-Ruling Communist Parties in Multiparty Coalitions," *Journal of Politics* 44, no. 4 (November 1982): 924–954.

Conclusion

1. For a discussion of these issues that focuses on the problem of guilt, see Gesine Schwan, *Politik und Schuld: Die zerstörerishe Macht des Schweigens* (Frankfurt am Main: Fischer, 1997).

2. Wolfgang Stock, "Versöhnung ohne Aufarbeitung?" *Das Parlament,* 45–46/1994 (November 11–18), p. 16.

3. See Ulrich Greiner, "Mein Name sei Schwerte," *Die Zeit,* 20/1995 (May 12), p. 41. See also Karl-Siegbert Rehberg, "Eine deutsche Karriere. Oder: Gelegenheit macht Demokraten," *Merkur* 562, no. 1 (January 1996): 73–80. The full facts of the Schneider/Schwerte case were not clear at the time of this writing; Schneider was quickly advised by counsel not to make statements.

4. Max Frisch, *Mein Name sei Gantenbein* (Frankfurt am Main: Suhrkamp, 1964). Identity problems play a central role in Frisch's works; see also Max Frisch, *Stiller* (Frankfurt am Main: Suhrkamp, 1954).

5. Greiner, "Mein Name sei Schwerte," p. 41.

6. Edmund Burke, *Reflections on the Revolution in France* (Harmondsworth: England: Penguin, 1969), p. 171. On the general problem of authenticity and political life, see Marshall Bermann, *The Politics of Authenticity: Radical Individualism and the Emergence of Modern Society* (New York: Atheneum, 1972); Sissela Bok, *Lying: Moral Choice in Public and Private Life* (New York: Pantheon Books, 1978); and Judith Shklar, *Ordinary Vices* (Cambridge, Mass.: Harvard University Press, 1984).

7. Immanuel Kant, "Perpetual Peace: A Philosophical Sketch" ("Zum ewigen Frieden: Ein philosophischer Entwurf," 1795), in *Kant's Political Writings,* ed. Hans Reiss (Cambridge: Cambridge University Press, 1970), p. 112.

8. Alexis de Tocqueville, *De la démocratie en Amérique,* vol. 2, pt. 2, chap. 8, in *Oeuvres complètes,* ed. J. P. Mayer (Paris: Gallimard, 1961); see also vol. 1, pt. 2, pp. 128–129: "The doctrine of interest rightly understood does not produce great acts [*grands dévouements*], but every day it suggests small sacrifices; alone, it could not make a virtuous man, but it makes for a multitude of disciplined, temperate, moderate, foresighted, and self-restrained citizens; and if it does not lead directly to virtue through the will, it gets there discreetly by the habits it engenders."

9. Cf. Michael Walzer, *The Revolution of the Saints: A Study in the Origins of Radical Politics* (1965; rpt. New York: Atheneum, 1971), p. 18. Discussing the relationship between Puritanism and liberalism, Walzer argues that liberalism "did not create the self-control it required."

Index